William Roscoe Thayer

The dawn of Italian independence

Italy from the Congress of Vienna, 1814, to the fall of Venice, 1849. Vol. 2

William Roscoe Thayer

The dawn of Italian independence
Italy from the Congress of Vienna, 1814, to the fall of Venice, 1849. Vol. 2

ISBN/EAN: 9783337231835

Printed in Europe, USA, Canada, Australia, Japan

Cover: Foto ©ninafisch / pixelio.de

More available books at **www.hansebooks.com**

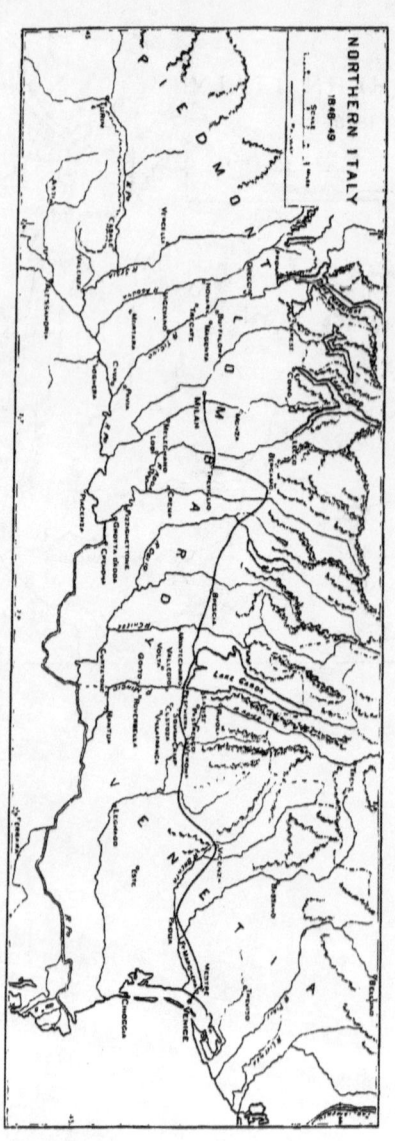

THE DAWN OF ITALIAN INDEPENDENCE

ITALY FROM THE CONGRESS OF VIENNA, 1814
TO THE FALL OF VENICE, 1849

BY

WILLIAM ROSCOE THAYER

> *S' io al vero son timido amico,*
> *Temo di perder vita tra coloro*
> *Che questo tempo chiameranno antico.*
>   DANTE: Paradiso, xvii, 118-120.

IN TWO VOLUMES
VOLUME II

BOSTON AND NEW YORK
HOUGHTON, MIFFLIN AND COMPANY
The Riverside Press, Cambridge
1893

Copyright, 1892,
BY WILLIAM ROSCOE THAYER.

All rights reserved.

The *Riverside Press*, *Cambridge*, *Mass.*, *U. S. A.*
Electrotyped and Printed by H. O. Houghton & Company.

CONTENTS OF VOLUME II.

BOOK FOURTH.
REVOLUTION TRIUMPHANT.

CHAP.		PAGE
I.	THE WONDER OF THE WORLD, A LIBERAL POPE	1
II.	GIOBERTI'S POPE AT HOME AND ABROAD	22
III.	IN THE RAPIDS, 1847	42
IV.	THE SHOWER OF CONSTITUTIONS, JAN.–MARCH, 1848	77
V.	EXIT METTERNICH; MILAN AND VENICE FREE	100
VI.	THE WAR OF INDEPENDENCE DECLARED	127
VII.	FROM GOITO TO PASTRENGO	142
VIII.	THE FIRST MASKS FALL	165

BOOK FIFTH.
DISINTEGRATION: DEMOCRACY: DISASTER.

I.	FUSION VERSUS CONFUSION	185
II.	DEMOCRACY INVADING	225
III.	REPUBLICS AT ROME AND FLORENCE	266
IV.	NOVARA	294
V.	THE QUENCHING OF FLORENCE AND ROME	330
VI.	VENICE ALONE	384

INDEX		417

BOOK FOURTH.

REVOLUTION TRIUMPHANT.

Virtù contra furore
Prenderà l' arme ; e fia 'l combatter corto,
Che l' antico valore
Negl' italici cor non è ancor morto.
      PETRARCA, *Canzone a' Grandi d' Italia.*

CHAPTER I.

THE WONDER OF THE WORLD, — A LIBERAL POPE.

THE death of a pope should be, we conceive, the solemnest event that could overshadow the Catholic world; for he, of all earthly sovereigns, should be the most venerated, the most beloved. By whose fault, then, has it come about that the deathbed of a pope is more cheerless, more pitiful, than that of many a pauper in the almshouse? Why is it that his last hours, if watched at all, are watched by the eyes of men eager to see him die, — of men who, while they count the throbs of the failing pulse, calculate how they can profit by his death?

From the deathbed of Gregory XVI even such reluctant watchers as these held aloof. During the spring of 1846 his infirmities had increased so rapidly that his friends and his enemies looked for his speedy dissolution. Friends? he had no friends; the cardinals and courtiers and servants paid perfunctory respect to his office; to him they were bound neither by gratitude nor common humanity. Like persons who buy tickets in a lottery, they were intent on the day of the next drawing, — the day when he should die. As he grew more and more sick, in the last week of May, loneliness widened round him. Prelates were busy elsewhere intriguing over his successor, and trying to secure other prizes for themselves; the members of his household were busy packing their boxes and taking whatever they could purloin without too great risk. Even Moroni, the barber-favorite, abandoned the master who had enriched him. Gregory himself had not at first felt alarmed; then, when his condition grew more serious, he asked to see his physician. By whose negligence or wickedness did it happen that the physician was sent to him neither that afternoon nor the next day, and came at last only when the patient was surely dying? The story was told, and believed, that an old gardener to whom Gregory had once given a piece of silver, hearing of the Holy Father's dangerous condition, wished to receive a last blessing from him. Without difficulty he made his way through the halls and corridors of the palace, — for they were deserted, — until he came to the papal bedchamber. That, too, had been quitted by the attendants. The gardener approached the bed, and, kneeling down noiselessly, for fear of rousing the sleeping Pope, he kissed the hand that hung heavily on the edge of the bed. The hand was cold. The gardener started up, looked into Gregory's face — the eyes were glassy, the features rigid; the Pope was dead. In grief and astonishment, the gardener cried out. Presently members of the household came, and bade him under threats of severe punishment not to babble of what he had seen.[1] But at Rome nothing, whether sacred or profane, could long be kept secret; the Romans soon knew how Gregory had

[1] M. D'Azeglio: *Ricordi*, ii, 222-4.

been left to die in solitude, whilst those who should have comforted him were collecting booty against their departure.[1]

The pomp to which the corpse of a pope is subjected contrasts strangely with the neglect and friendlessness of his last days. The Cardinal Camerlengo formally visits the death-chamber, and tapping thrice with a little mallet on the cold forehead, he thrice calls out the name of the defunct. There coming no answer, the Cardinal announces that the Pope is dead, and breaks the Ring of the Fisherman from the stiff forefinger. Then the body is left to embalmers and attirers, who prepare it for lying in state at St. Peter's. The churches are draped in black, the bells toll out a dismal knell, masses are celebrated, requiems chanted, and Rome puts on during the Novendiale, or nine days' obsequies, all the habiliments of woe. But real grief is nowhere visible. The faces in the streets wear the aspect of mingled relief, merriment, and curiosity. Ecclesiastics hurry to and fro with the anxious expression of men who, seeing a great prize almost within grasp, would lose no time in seizing it. In the palaces of prelates and diplomats there are secret conferences, bargains, and promises; in the drawing-rooms and coffee-houses every one is sounding his neighbor's views on the great question, "Who will succeed?" In boudoirs not less than in cloisters, webs of intrigue are hourly spun. Meanwhile the carpenters and drapers make ready the catafalque at St. Peter's, and above the noise of their hammers you can hear their bursts of laughter as they regale each other with salacious gossip about the dead pontiff, and with the scandals of the living Cardinals, from among whom his successor will be chosen.[2]

---

[1] The autopsy showed that the Pope had been long without nourishment, only a few lemon seeds being found in his stomach. Gualterio, iv, 336.

[2] Cf. Mendelssohn's *Letters from Italy*, 73-4.

The Novendiale is a period when every politician in the Holy City strives, with a zeal and cunning rarely equaled by worldly politicians, to secure either his own election or that of some patron who will be a ladder to mount by.

Gregory XVI died on June 1, and though the public was at first surprised, having had no intimation that his end was so near, it speedily rejoiced. The news flew over the Peninsula, bringing a sense of relief to all the inhabitants of the Papal States, and awakening elsewhere the liveliest hopes. If any persons grieved, they grieved because they feared that the offices they had held under Gregory would be taken from them, and not because they loved him. The Liberals of every shade, who had declared that the rule of the Turks would be less abominable than that which they had endured, now thanked God that their taskmaster was dead. For years the belief had been growing that Gregory's death would not only be a turning-point in their misery, but also the dawn of a new era for Italy: and now, as they mingled their mutual congratulations, they speculated as to the strength of the parties in the Sacred College, and as to the policy which each of the favorite candidates would probably pursue were he given the tiara.

At Rome, meanwhile, the government was provisionally carried on by three Cardinals. The customary medal of the vacant See, with the legend *Non relinquam vos orphanos*, was struck, and the Quirinal was put in readiness for the Conclave. The recollection of the tumults which had followed close on the death of Pius VIII increased the anxiety of the Cardinals, but even a common alarm could not frighten them into harmony. At their very first meeting, when they discussed the appointment of provisional governors for the provinces, discord broke out, and showed the cliques into which the College was divided. Ordinarily, the Secretary of State and his friends form one party, and all the other Cardinals, who,

from jealousy or grievance oppose him, form the other;
but in the present case special motives existed for intensifying partisan hatred. Lambruschini, the Secretary
of State, not only represented his own ambition, but also
the policy of the extreme Reactionists, who insisted upon
perpetuating the mediæval system which had made Gregory's reign detestable. It is a proverb at Rome that "no
man can be pope twice;" by which it is meant that the
Secretary of State, who is often the real head of the
Church, — the Pope being merely a tool in his hands, —
must not expect to have both the reality and the symbol
of power; and it invariably happens that his enemies pay
off their old scores against him by defeating his election
to the pontifical throne. In spite of precedents, however,
Lambruschini determined to make the fight, supposing
that he could count on the loyalty of many cardinals who
owed their elevation to his good-will; and being fully
conscious that he outranked all the other members of his
party in ability and force. The majority of his opponents was composed of men who had either a personal
grudge against him, or who, reading the signs of the
times, believed that the Papal administration must be
reformed if it would not burst asunder of its own rottenness. Besides these two principal parties of Gregorians
and Liberals, there was the so-called "Flying Squadron,"
— half a score of trimmers, whose only anxiety it was to
lean at the profitable moment to the winning side. Independent of all these stood Micara, Dean of the Sacred
College, and the most picturesque if not the most remarkable cardinal of the century. His tall and commanding stature, his white hair, his long white beard
reaching almost to his girdle, his pale, thin, mobile features, his flashing eyes, gave him a presence in which the
venerableness of age was strangely mingled with the intellectual energy and strength of manhood's prime. He
had been for many years General of the Order of Capu-

chins, a downright, blunt, austere man, who tolerated no laxness among his inferiors, and who could not blink the amazing discrepancy between the professions and the practices of the Church. He had the strange belief that men who called themselves the disciples of Jesus Christ should be humble and frugal, instead of being haughty and luxurious; that men who had taken the vow of chastity should not outdo worldlings in libertinism; that servants engaged in the work of the Lord should not spend their days in idleness and their nights in vice. But while he was a Puritan in morals,[1] Micara would not see the authority of the Roman Pontiff curtailed by one jot; rather would he restore it to its pristine supremacy by infusing vigor and justice and honesty into its administration. He was a belated survivor of that race of fighting ecclesiastics who were as much at home in a coat-of-mail as in a chasuble — real soldiers of the Church Militant, who went into battle as gladly as they went to mass. Looking at him you thought instinctively of Hildebrand and the great Innocent, or of Julius II, who bade Michael Angelo represent him with a brandished sword.

At the first meeting of the Cardinals, therefore, Micara led the attack on Lambruschini and the Gregorians. He charged the Secretary of State with having unwarrantably kept secret from him, — the Dean of the Sacred College, — and from the Grand Penitencer, the imminent death of the late Pope, when it was their right to be informed. He hinted that the fact had been withheld from them not so much in order to guard against an insurrection as to afford to the Cardinal Secretary time to drill his forces against the opening of the Conclave. And then the dauntless Capuchin went on to arraign the administration of the Cardinal Secretary, which by its wayward severity had made the Pope's subjects discontented, and had increased the public debt and caused religion to be hated

[1] Report, however, charged Micara with avarice.

through its ministers. Instead of piety, there was infidelity; instead of prosperity, there was pauperism; instead of loyalty, rebellion threatened to lift up its head. Micara's frankness may well have amazed that assemblage of men trained in the arts of giving polite names to ugly facts, and of dissembling their personal feelings towards each other. Openly to assail a colleague who might by a stroke of Fortune become pope was an act of rashness which few of the politic Cardinals ever indulged in. But Micara despised policy; he was both brave and sincere, and the truth that he told, even had it not been edged with sarcasm, would have wounded Lambruschini and his minions as only the truth can wound. It was evident that the battle, then informally begun, would be waged without mercy in the Conclave.

At Rome order prevailed in spite of the general foreboding that the malecontents would rebel. Popular enthusiasm made idols of Micara and Gizzi. The fierce Trasteverines especially favored the Capuchin Cardinal, whom they knew to be honest and whose condemnation of clerical abuses led them to hope that, should he be elected, the government would be decent and just. But Micara was as blunt to his friends as to his enemies. "Take care," he said, to a multitude that cheered him; "under me you would lack neither bread — nor gallows." Both at Rome and throughout Italy the majority of the Liberals set their hearts on Gizzi, who had recently been praised by Massimo d'Azeglio for his conciliatory treatment of political offenders at Forlì where he was legate. Except for the assassination of Allegrini, a detested police officer at Ancona, the provinces remained quiet; all the elements of insurrection were prepared, but they were held in check by the wise efforts of the Moderate leaders, who warned their vehement comrades that a disturbance would only exasperate the Sacred College and lessen the chance of its electing a pope desirous of reforms. At Bologna, the nobles and professional men drew up a petition, — a veritable Bill of Wrongs, — in which they calmly stated the burdens under which they groaned, and the remedies which ought speedily to be applied. Other cities — Ravenna, Forlì, Ferrara — did likewise, although the Papal governors objected to even this pacific expression of public opinion. In their eyes it was impudent for subjects to dare to address their sovereign concerning the administration he saw fit to bestow upon them. Some of the petitions were confiscated by the police; but the petitioners forwarded copies of them by trusty messengers to the foreign ambassadors at Rome, and at least one escaped through the post-office by being superscribed "for most grave cases of conscience." The citizens of Osimo placed their address in the hands of their Bishop, Cardinal Soglia, when he set out to attend the Conclave.

At length the Novendiale came to an end. The obsequies, which really served as an arming-time for the factions, were concluded by the deposition of Gregory's body into the pontifical receiving-tomb. The last perfunctory prayer had been said, and the Cardinals could turn without interruption to the great business which, as official mourners, they had been obliged to defer. On June 13 they assembled at the Quirinal. On their way thither the populace showed plainly what hopes it cherished by applauding Gizzi most of all. "Neither a monk nor a foreigner," was a phrase oft repeated; but among the monks they excepted Micara, the patriarchal, honest Capuchin.

In the Quirinal each Cardinal had a cell to himself, and was allowed a secretary, or "conclavist." The doors and windows were closed up with plaster, to prevent communication with the outer world, but sharp eyes might detect that little holes had been bored in more than one place through the plaster. According to custom, the

Diplomatic Corps gathered in the anteroom adjoining the Cardinals' apartments, and heard Count Rossi, the French ambassador, address the Conclave. He spoke through a little slide in the door, beyond which the Cardinals heard as best they could. He spoke seriously, earnestly, — referring in general terms to the needs of the times, and dilating upon the supreme importance at this crisis of choosing a pope who should not only look zealously after the souls of the Catholic flocks scattered throughout Christendom, but who should also promote the temporal welfare of the subjects intrusted to his immediate care. Seventeen years before, on a similar occasion, Chateaubriand had given similar warning and advice, — with what results we know; would Rossi's words bear better fruit? When he ceased speaking, Micara, as Dean, brusquely replied, that "the Sacred College knew its duty, and would perform it." Then the diplomats withdrew, the slide was closed, and the rival factions were left face to face.

By a logical assumption the Holy Ghost is supposed to preside over the Conclave which elects a pope; and, indeed, if it be admitted that the Pope is infallible, that his word is the word of God, it is impossible to think that God, if He have any interest in the salvation of mankind, would neglect to designate in unmistakable manner the candidate whom He deemed most fit to represent Him on earth. In practice, both the Cardinals and the Great Powers show that they have little confidence in the intelligence, and little respect for the judgment, of the Holy Ghost: for the latter presume to dictate their wishes to Him, and they presume, when He is not compliant, to thwart His decision; while the former, instead of seeking spiritual guidance only, communicate with the outside world in ways that would seem ridiculous were not so solemn a matter as God's Vicarship involved. In spite of the formal precautions, the secrecy of every

Conclave has been violated: billets of tissue paper have slipped through the little holes in the plaster; hollow coins, with important news, have dropped at night on the pavement in front of the palace, where trusty eyes have seen, and nimble hands have gathered them. Every day the Cardinals' lackeys bring their food to the anteroom, where it is closely inspected by a bishop before it is passed in through the slide; but, in spite of the bishop's vigilance, missives have been successfully secreted in unsuspected places, and reached their destination. More than once has the belly of a capon or the heart of an orange served as post-bag for letters which affected the decision of the Conclave.

Still more indicative of their hypocrisy and irreligion, and of their lack of confidence in the wisdom of the Divine President, was the assertion by several of the Catholic Powers of the right to exclude candidates whom they disliked. Each cabinet intrusted some cardinal with the name of the candidate who was to be excluded in case his election seemed imminent. Thus in the Conclave of 1823, when the necessary majority of votes had actually been secured for Cardinal Severoli, Cardinal Albani, as agent of Prince Metternich, announced that Austria would not accept Severoli; and so he was rejected, and the Holy Ghost had to designate a pope whom Metternich would recognize. In the present case, the Austrian chancellor was strangely negligent. Gregory had died, and the Conclave had assembled, and still no instructions had come from Vienna. Cardinal Gaysrück, who was to be Austria's spokesman, still lingered at Milan for orders. Perhaps Metternich, who had already dictated the action of three Conclaves, felt that the Holy Ghost must by that time know his wishes, and would not try to traverse them; perhaps he shared the common belief that this Conclave would be long protracted, not only because of the warring parties, but because, as Gaysrück remarked, most of the

Cardinals were inexperienced. The fact that fifty-three of the Cardinals had been created by Gregory XVI afforded the best ground for hoping that Gregorian ideas, which Metternich thoroughly approved, would prevail.

The Sacred College, when complete, has seventy members, of whom a majority are always Italian, to insure the control of the Papacy to Italian hands. At Gregory's death there were eight vacancies, and of the actual sixty-two Cardinals, only fifty-one entered the Conclave. Gaysrück still tarried, and it was not expected that some of those who lived at a great distance would arrive in time, if at all. After performing mass and chanting the *Veni Creator Spiritus*, the College proceeded to ballot. Lambruschini led with eighteen votes. Falconieri, Soglia, and Mastai, each had a few supporters, and the remaining votes were scattered by ones and twos among half a dozen candidates. Lambruschini, evidently encouraged, and believing his party to be compact, determined to force the fighting without delay. He therefore insisted that, as the edge of one of the ballots was unsealed, the voting was illegal and must be repeated. After long debate he carried his point; but at the second count he lost four votes. "Ah," exclaimed Bernetti, "the first time the Holy Ghost was absent!" The crowds that gathered in front of the Quirinal that evening saw the smoke curl out from the little chimney of the chapel, and knew that, as the ballots had been burnt, no pope had been elected. Lambruschini, having failed to carry the election at the first onset, now changed his tactics, and strove to hold his adversaries in check until the arrival of reinforcements. Seven of the Cardinals yet to come would, he believed, assist him, among them being Gaysrück, formidable as the bearer of Metternich's instructions and as a most adept wire-puller. He contrived to inform Lützow, the Austrian minister in Rome, of his strait, and he received a reply, concealed, it is said, under the label of a champagne-bottle, bidding him to persevere, as Gaysrück had already started from Milan, and would arrive in a few days. On June 14 the customary two ballots were taken, but without showing any significant changes, except that Fieschi and Piccolomini, two of Lambruschini's henchmen, deserted him. His opponents now realized that not a moment was to be lost; their forces were divided, and might gravitate, as is the nature of small bodies, to the larger body of Gregorians; or, if Lambruschini, convinced that his own prospect was hopeless, withdrew, he might effect a compromise with the waverers and name the Gregorian who should be chosen in his stead. Above all, the knowledge that Gaysrück and six other Reactionists were on their way, and that their arrival, like that of the Prussians at Waterloo, would decide the contest, warned Lambruschini's antagonists to come to a speedy agreement.

As often happens in elections, we cannot discover who first turned the current towards the candidate who eventually won. The story goes that Piccolomini and Fieschi conferred with Micara, and asked him which of the three anti-Gregorians who had thus far received the largest number of votes they should coalesce upon. Micara, confined to his bed since the opening of the Conclave, replied, with his habitual sarcasm, that they should choose the least known and most colorless candidate, — him, in a word, against whom the fewest objections to his past opinions or deeds could be raised. Soglia, Falconieri, and Mastai were the three, and of the three Mastai best fulfilled the condition of being uncompromised by any record of decisive character. Accordingly he became the favorite of Lambruschini's opponents. That night there was no sleep in the Quirinal. To and fro through the dim corridors flitted the Cardinals, passing from cell to cell in their quest for votes. What entreaties, what promises, what inducements of a golden hue, what appeals to passion or policy, those walls witnessed between vespers and matins, we can only surmise. Falconieri and Soglia, Mastai's chief rivals, had to be persuaded to withdraw in his favor, — a stretch of renunciation to be measured only by realizing what that prize is which a "popeable" candidate gives up. Bernetti, too, leader of the Flying Squadron, must be enticed to Mastai's perch, — a task which Fieschi successfully achieved: for Bernetti had never forgotten how unceremoniously he had been deprived of the Secretaryship of State, and had never forgiven Lambruschini for superseding him. His main purpose, therefore, was to block Lambruschini's way to the Papal throne. He also had information — conveyed in the hollow handle of a table-knife — of Gaysrück's approach, and that made him all the more willing to listen to Mastai's advocate. So the coalition gained strength. Nor must we imagine that the Gregorians, on their side, calmly shut their doors and tried to sleep: their canvassers were likewise busy all through the night, trying to fix doubtful voters, and to coax back those who had already gone over to the enemy. The ears of waverers on that night heard many conflicting arguments and many strange appeals.

At length morning put an end to the intrigues, and the Conclave reassembled in the chapel. The faces of those old men were haggard from sleeplessness and suspense. Both parties felt that a crisis, perhaps the final decision, was at hand, but neither felt sure of the result. Again the solemn notes of the *Veni Creator Spiritus* swelled through the hall. Then Cardinal Micara, who, on account of his feebleness, had had to be carried into the Conclave, spoke vehemently. Instead of agreeing with Lambruschini that they ought in propriety to await the arrival of their foreign colleagues, he "declared that the time was now come when the government must no longer be subjected to foreign influences, but be conducted in a manner more in harmony with the progress of the age."[1] Then the ballots were written and sealed and placed in the urn on the altar, and Mastai, Fieschi, and Vannicelli were appointed to count them. With what pleasure Vannicelli, one of Lambruschini's lieutenants, broke seal after seal and saw the name *Mastai*, may easily be guessed; and as the number grew, Mastai himself became more and more agitated. The count reached twenty almost without a break; then twenty-five, then thirty, at which point Mastai begged Cardinal Fieschi, who was reading the ballots, to be silent. At the thirty-third he fainted; but the count was soon finished, — Mastai had thirty-six votes, more than the required two thirds majority, and was therefore elected. His partisans, bursting into a tumult of exultation, bore him unconscious to the altar. "After monks, girls," remarked the caustic Micara; "long live St. Peter!" "Well, well!" exclaimed Bernetti, "the Papacy is done for: Gregory covered it with blood; this one will prostitute it." Meanwhile, by the aid of Cardinal Oppizzoni's snuff-box, Mastai had been revived sufficiently to protest that his youth and inexperience made him unfit for the supreme honor to which he had been chosen, but that with God's help he would endeavor to do his duty. Pontifical robes were brought out and put upon him; and then the Cardinals performed the act of adoration, — an act, it has been remarked, in which more reverence is shown for God's Vicar than Catholics ever show to God himself, — and received from the Pontiff's lips the Kiss of Peace.

That evening the crowds outside the Quirinal, seeing no smoke rise from the chimney, knew that they had another sovereign. It was rumored that the smallest pontifical robes had been called for, — three sizes, adapted to large, medium, or small stature, are kept in readiness

---

[1] *Correspondence respecting the Affairs of Italy*, 1846-9 (Parliamentary Blue-Book), i, 18.

during a Conclave, — and from this the Romans inferred that Gizzi, their favorite, a little man, had been elected. Popular joy ran high. The glad news spread through the city, and Gizzi's servants celebrated their master's supposed triumph in unseemly carousals. On the morrow, June 16, the Square of the Quirinal was packed with eager multitudes, — windows, walls, and roofs were thronged, — the "horses of Phidias" seemed to be galloping over a pavement of human heads. Presently there was the sound of hammers as the masons demolished the plaster screen before one of the balconies of the palace, and then, when the space was clear, a hush fell over the vast concourse, and all eyes turned to behold the new Pope, borne to the balcony on his portable throne. All eyes turned to see him, and those ears which were nearest could hear a cardinal announce in sonorous tones that the Conclave had elected Giovanni Maria Mastai Ferretti, Bishop of Imola, who took the title of Pius the Ninth. The new Pontiff bestowed his blessing upon the spectators, who broke out into applause, and then was carried back into the palace. The crowds dispersed, not without disappointment over the defeat of the favorite Gizzi, — Gizzi, who had never received one vote in the Conclave, so little did the Cardinals care for the wishes of the people, — but relieved that neither Lambruschini nor any other Gregorian had snatched the prize. "Who is this Mastai Ferretti? What will he do?" were the questions that all were asking, as they returned homewards from this Old World pageant to the accompaniment of salvos from the cannon of Castle St. Angelo, and of the boisterous jangling of innumerable bells.[1]

[1] I draw my account of this Conclave from Bianchi, v, 8-9; Farini, i, 149-53; Gabussi: *Memorie* (Genoa. 1851). i, 31-5; La Farina, iii, 5-15; *Correspondence*, etc., i. 2, 15-18; Petruccelli de la Gattina: *Storia Arcana del Pontificato di Leone XII. Gregorio XVI, e Pio IX* (Milan. 1861), chaps. 20-24; E. Cipoletta: *Memorie Politiche sui Conclavi da Pio VII a Pio IX* (Milan 1863), 223-40.

That the new Pope should be comparatively unknown rather illustrated how much chance ruled the decision of the Conclave, than furnished any evidence that he was unfit. At the present juncture it was most desirable that a man uncompromised and unclogged by his past should ascend the throne: a Puritan like Micara, might, indeed, with indomitable will, have purged the morals of the hierarchy and established a better system of justice, but he would not have yielded an inch before the political demands of the reformers; a Lambruschini, bound to the Gregorian policy, would surely have hastened a revolution. It was better, therefore, both for the Papacy and the people, that a new-comer like Mastai, unembarrassed by any record, should be lifted suddenly from obscurity to the highest position in the Church. Five-and-twenty years earlier, Mastai was not unknown to the fashionable society at Rome. His handsome face and agreeable manners made him then — what he remained to the last — a favorite among women, and secured for him, in spite of a painful infirmity, the good-will of patrons by whom his preferment was cared for. He was born at Sinigaglia, May 13, 1792, of a family of provincial counts. At the age of ten he was sent to Volterra to the school of the Scolopists, — unflagging opponents of the Jesuits, — and there he stayed until 1809, when he had to be taken home on account of the epileptic attacks to which he was subject. For a long time it seemed as if his career would be blasted by this malady. He went to Rome in 1815, and enrolled himself in the Papal Guard, but being soon obliged to resign, and being involved in an unfortunate love-affair, he determined to take orders, — the only ladder of promotion for a Roman subject, whatever were his tastes or his religious qualifications. He was ordained priest in 1819, but with the provision that he should never read mass without an assistant, and then he served for a time in the hospital of Tata Giovanni, an institution for poor boys. In 1823, Leo XII, who, as Cardinal della Genga, had been Mastai's stanch patron, sent him with Monsignor Muzio on a mission to Chile, and on his return raised him, in 1827, to the archbishopric of Spoleto. Five years later he was transferred to the see of Imola: he received the red hat in 1840, and was still leading an uneventful life, when he was summoned to the Conclave in 1846.

These were the chief stages in the new Pope's advance: but Gossip, the Clio of Papal Rome, furnished details after her fashion that gave lifelikeness to this meagre sketch. She recalled how in early days the young count used to win the money of old Princess Chigi at faro, and how he affected the smartness of a dandy; she whispered tales of gallant adventures, naming names and citing times; but in fact she proved no more than that Mastai, whether as Noble Guardsman or as prelate, had not been free from the vices common to his caste. But in a society which concerned itself but little with the private morals of ecclesiastics, except to gossip about them, men sought far more eagerly for information respecting the new Pope's political opinions; and on this head Gossip reported not unfavorably. During the revolution of 1831, Mastai had dissuaded Sercognani and his band of Liberals from marching on Rome; and though he was said to have accomplished this by buying off the leader, yet it was certain that he had listened graciously to the grievances of the insurgents, and that he had protected some of the Liberals when the day of retaliation came. It was also certain that his own brothers had been forced to flee into exile because of their complicity in the insurrection. As Bishop of Imola he had shown sympathy for the common people, bestowing alms upon them; and he had closed his ears, so far as it was prudent, to the political whisperings of the milder reformers. Gregory's centurions and spies and instigators had found no encouragement with him.

All this, and more to the same effect, Gossip babbled to the Romans as they returned from witnessing the elevation of their new ruler; and now they awaited in suspense his first official acts, to see whether their favorable impression would be confirmed, or whether, as had so often happened, the change of rulers would mean only a change in the shape of the yoke under which they groaned. Rumors sped abroad that Pius greatly admired Gioberti, and that he had been deeply moved by D'Azeglio's book. Hints came from the Quirinal that he was intent upon decreeing an amnesty to political offenders, and that he would come to a decision after he should receive a report on the affairs of the realm that a Committee of Cardinals was preparing for him.[1] Then it was insinuated that the Reactionists in the Sacred College had the upper hand, and that the Pope, in spite of his preferences, had yielded to them. The contradiction in these rumors only reflected the contradictions in Pius's character: but to this the Romans had as yet no clue. They wondered, indeed, that he should even temporarily consult Lambruschini, but they were more surprised by Pius's kindly manners. He appointed a day — Thursday — in each week, upon which any of his subjects could have an audience; he went abroad without a pompous retinue; he was known to visit convents, and to bestow alms on the poor; he quashed the military commissions in Romagna, spoke encouragingly of railways and took the ban off of scientific congresses; and he had a good word for those who wished to reform education. Even towards the Jews, who had from time immemorial been treated at the capital of Christendom like reptiles, Pius showed a merciful disposition.[2] But finally, on July 16, all doubts were dispelled by the publication of an amnesty. This instrument had so im-

[1] *Correspondence*, etc., i, 18.
[2] Gabussi, i, 36-7; Bersezio: *Trent' Anni di Vita Italiana* (Turin, 1878), ii, 115.

portant an influence on the destiny of the Italians that we must quote the most significant passages in it, as follows:—

"Pius the Ninth to his faithful subjects, Peace and Apostolical Benediction.

"On the days in which we deeply felt the public joy at our exaltation to the Pontificate, we could not suppress the painful sensation we felt that so many families of our subjects were prevented from participating in the general joy, because they were deprived of domestic happiness by the absence of those who had offended against society, public order, and the sacred rights of the Sovereign. We looked with compassion on the inexperience of youth drawn into fallacious hope in the midst of public tumult, and, as appeared to us, seduced and not seducers. From that moment we meditated extending our hand, and from our heart offering peace to those unfortunate youths, provided they showed themselves sincerely penitent. Now as the affection our good people have shown to us, and as their veneration to Holy Church and to our person has been demonstrated, we are persuaded that we may pardon without danger to the public. The commencement of our pontificate is, therefore, to be solemnized by the following act of grace.

"1. All our subjects who are in prison for political crimes are to be pardoned, provided they make a solemn declaration in writing that on their word of honor they will not in any way or at any time abuse this, our act of grace, but faithfully fulfil the duties of a good subject.

"2. The same condition applies to all political refugees, provided they testify to the Apostolical Nuncios, or other representatives of the Holy See, within one year from the date of the present, their wish to avail themselves of this act of clemency.

"3. We also absolve all those who have participated in plots against the State, and who are under surveillance of the police or declared incapable of holding situations in municipalities.

"5. It is understood, however, that in the dispositions given in the preceding articles, the very few ecclesiastics, military officers, and government employees are not comprised, *i. e.*, those who have received their sentence and those who are still under prosecution. For these we reserve to ourselves future determination when their cases come to our cognizance.

"We feel sure that those who may avail themselves of our clemency will henceforward always respect our rights and their own honor; and we further trust that, touched by our forgiveness, they will lay aside those civil animosities which are always the cause and effect of political passions, and so may be restored that bond of peace in which it is the will of God that all the children of one Father should be united. If, however, we are disappointed in our hopes, painful as it may be to us, we shall always bear in mind that if clemency is the sweetest attribute of a sovereign, justice is the first of his duties."[1]

Viewed closely, this proclamation concedes no rights to the subjects of the Holy See; it allows no question to be raised as to whether the political prisoners and refugees were condemned justly or unjustly; it implies sarcastically that the men who had been for thirty years sacrificing their lives for the amelioration of their country were but youths easily seduced; it assumes that for citizens to dare to object to any measures their governors see fit to order is impious and incendiary. Pius, in the benevolence of his heart, forgives his erring children, but they must not infer that they have any right to his clemency; nay, whoever avails himself of the amnesty thereby confesses that he has done wrong and pledges himself to submission in future. Such, read literally, is the purport of Pius's famous act.

[1] Translation in *Correspondence*, etc., i, 21, 22; text in Farini, i, 157.

But the Romans, and the Italians, and the world gave it another interpretation, according to their wishes. They regarded it as a sign that the new Pope had broken with tradition, — broken with the system of Gregory and Leo, — and that he had set up kindness instead of cruelty as the beacon of his policy. *Amnesty!* the very word, when uttered by pontifical lips, seemed a miracle, an earnest of the largest reforms. The Head of Catholicism had tacitly discredited the Treaty of Vienna, by which Europe had been oppressed since 1815, and surely what he did no man could gainsay. The prisons were unlocked, exiles returned from Tuscany and Piedmont and foreign lands, all hearts beat with gratitude for the peerless benefactor from whom all good gifts were possible. Upon the publication of the amnesty, the Romans flocked in a body to the Quirinal, and there shouted, "Long live Pius!" until he came to a balcony, and in the sound of that rejoicing multitude and in the sight of their waving handkerchiefs and tossing caps, he felt the seduction of popularity. Again and again he blessed them, and again and again they cheered, until, overcome by emotion, tears rolling down his cheeks, and faintness from excess of joy seizing upon him, he had to retire. And in the provinces, although more than one legate attempted to delay the operation of the act, the populace gave themselves up to similar rejoicings, and lifted the name of their benefactor to the skies.

CHAPTER II.

GIOBERTI'S POPE AT HOME AND ABROAD.

FROM the day of the amnesty, Pius and his subjects, mutually deceived and mutually deceiving, lived in an Enchanted World. What are those quaint tales of philters which caused deadly enemies to forget their wrath in an ecstasy of love? No witch nor beldam ever brewed potion so magic-strong as that which now fluttered the hearts and exalted the heads of the Romans; and from them the contagion spread over all Italy. Liberals were everywhere willing to see in Pius the Messiah whose coming had been foretold by the prophet Gioberti; and when they shouted their *Viva Pio Nono!* they meant to express not only their admiration for the Ninth Pius himself, but also their hope that he would fulfil the great mission set down for Gioberti's Pope.

In Rome popular enthusiasm swelled week by week. The appointment of Gizzi — the beloved Cardinal Gizzi — as Secretary of State (August 8) seemed to leave no room for doubting Pius's Liberalism. If he stayed in his palace, the crowds assembled under the windows and cheered, and would not be satisfied till he showed himself to them; if he went abroad on foot, a body-guard of admirers respectfully accompanied him; if he drove in his coach, they unhitched the horses and drew the vehicle as proudly as college youths do like duty for a *prima donna*. By night, long processions of enthusiasts, with torches in their hands and hosannas on their lips, wound up the slope of the Quirinal; by day, on occasions of State ceremony, there were triumphal arches, and streets festooned with bunting, and balconies gorgeous with rich cloths and carpets, as in Carnival time: and when the Pope passed and heard the acclamations of his subjects and saw these signs of their affection, he smiled benignantly and nodded approval, and often those who were nearest to him could see tears of joy in his eyes. He was intoxicated with popularity, and proud to be the cause of such general gladness. If ever a great revolution could be accomplished by hand-clapping and huzzas, then was the time and Rome was the place. But wind can only destroy, it cannot build.

Nevertheless, the tactics adopted without preconcert by the Romans would have done credit to politicians of far greater experience than theirs. Many sincerely believed that Pius was a genuine Liberal, whom the Reactionists were hindering from carrying out reforms as rapidly as he wished; therefore, the exasperating delays and the acts which could not be reconciled with this theory of his Liberalism must be charged to his agents and advisers. The cardinals were blamed and abused, and the populace, in cheering "Pius alone," showed plainly enough that they regarded him as a benevolent father who yearned to bestow upon them all that they asked, but who was thwarted by men whom he could not yet shake off. To testify their gratitude for favors already received, to attribute all benefits to himself, to make him feel that he had his subjects with him, and could trust them, to persuade him that the voice of the people *was* the voice of God, — such was the purpose embodied in the jubilations which the Romans showered upon Pius. Their tact was as remarkable as their moderation; for it must be remembered that behind all their demands for local reforms there brooded a desire constantly growing stronger, — the desire to be rid of foreign oppressors, and to have a national existence. And so they refrained from deeds which might have forced the Pope's hand. although to refrain required a degree of self-control little to be expected from masses so impulsive. As time wore on the cry *Viva Pio Nono!* was coupled with *Viva l'Italia!* and the belief did not diminish that Gioberti's Pope would redeem Italy.

That Pius the Ninth ever dreamt of becoming the leader of Constitutional Liberalism, or that he would have admitted that any of his acts justified the assumption that he wished to have done with the Past, I do not believe. Those who at first blessed him as the Messiah, and afterwards cursed him as the Judas, of the Italian Revolution misjudged both his character as a man and his character as a pope. His nature was not profound, but it was tenacious. On the surface he seemed often as wayward as a coquette, now all smiles, and now pouting or snappish; but the sudden fit of petulance was quickly succeeded by serene and winsome affability. His emotions were easily stirred, — epilepsy doubtless made his nervous system unusually sensitive, — and persons who did not know him well mistook the mood of the moment for a permanent quality; whereas these moods were but as ripples the wind raises on a stream, and nowise affected the direction of the current. His good-heartedness was very genuine, but it was of a sort akin to selfishness; the gratification of the giver being of more importance than the betterment of the receiver. He enjoyed seeing his subjects happy, but they must be content with the means of happiness that he accorded to them. The very graciousness of manner with which he received petitioners they mistook for acquiescence in their designs. He took an almost boyish delight in beholding himself the idol of his people, and there was in him a strong vein of superstition that seems to have made him magnify himself to himself, as a providential man who ought to be idolized. Except in outbursts of temper, which the public rarely saw, he seemed the incarnation of kindliness; his benignant smile, the bright, interested expression of his eyes, his soothing voice, encouraged confidences and seemed to bespeak compliance. And yet, beneath this surface, so conciliating and genial, self-will ruled as the dominant trait in his character. Had he never been thwarted, had his subjects been content to limit their desires within the little circle he prescribed, the world would have believed to the end that Pius was the mildest, the most bountiful of autocrats. But when opposition came against him, he resisted it with all the force of a self-will rooted in instinct and not in reason.

Intellectually, Pius was not a deep scholar, even when judged by the standard of the shallow scholarship of the Romish clergy of the time. He got impressions easily, rather than knowledge, and, being a facile talker, who had always an opinion ready, he produced upon his hearers an effect out of proportion to his learning. He had that cleverness and vivacity of speech, flavored with a drop of sarcasm, peculiar to all classes of Italians, — qualities which enliven conversation, but which usually evaporate in print. He accepted without question the dogmas of the Church; he believed in miracles and omens, and was a rigid formalist. He felt the responsibility of his position as head of Catholicism, and the duty placed upon him, but he had not the slightest intention of bringing the Roman theology into harmony with modern thought; on the contrary, as if the great heap of irrational dogmas bequeathed by the Middle Age were not already a heavy burden to stagger under, he loaded the Church with two others, — that of the Immaculate Conception and of Papal Infallibility, — and he fostered the worship of new saints and the propagation of latter-day miracles. The most that he aimed at, and this was in the beginning of his reign, was the substitution of ecclesiastics of decent life for those who had debauched the Papal States: but after he fell under the sway of Cardinal Antonelli, he abandoned even this attempt, and the corruptness of his later administration was as flagrant as that of Gregory had been.

But it was Pius's political views about which there was the greatest misunderstanding. As the Italians learned to their cost, he never was a Liberal: he differed from his predecessors in methods, not in principles. If he spoke of reforms, if he listened complaisantly to the advocates of Liberalism, it was because the words meant to him something different from what they meant to them. Count Pasolini relates how many times he and Cardinal Mastai discussed the political condition of Italy together; how the Cardinal's emotions were aroused by the pictures of the degradation and misery of the Papal subjects; how he was kindled into enthusiasm by Gioberti's glowing pages and convinced by D'Azeglio's temperate arguments: till Pasolini, the honest Liberal, believed that Mastai and himself agreed perfectly.[1] The truth is that they played at cross-purposes. The Cardinal, becoming Pope, had the same enthusiasm, the same sincere desire to work improvement: but he did not suspect that improvement meant revolution. His benevolent nature wished to relieve the distress of his people, but he did not suppose that by appointing good judges instead of bad, or by reforming the police, or even by removing unjust taxes, he was sanctioning the schemes of the real reformers. He believed in the inviolability of the Temporal Power, and in a paternal government: but he wished to be a kind rather than a severe autocrat, and he never imagined that his subjects would claim as their right favors which he, out of the goodness of his heart, deigned to bestow on them. As an Italian, he would have been glad to see Italy relieved from foreign oppression, and as Pope he wished to be master in the Papal States; but he never dreamt that driving out foreigners implied the establishment of constitutional governments, or that the cutting

[1] Costa de Beauregard: *Épilogue d'un Règne* (Paris, 1890), 16–21.

off of Austrian and French support from Rome must involve the loss of his own temporal sovereignty. His first benefactions won him immense popularity, which he enjoyed as a man enjoys hearing praise which he feels he has merited: but when he found that these acts of his were interpreted as signs of his sympathy in a great political revolution, he withheld his hand, and complained that the Liberals had wilfully misunderstood him. It was so easy to grant! so sweet to quaff the praise! and had he not always the absolute right to refuse? We shall see that no genuine reform ever came from him voluntarily; that all changes directed towards Liberalism were wrung from him in the hope that he could thereby save himself from being swept away by the stream on which he had unwarily embarked. Later, when the Revolution had collapsed and he had been restored to Rome, he showed how completely the Liberals had been deceived in thinking that he was one of them, and how consistent and inflexible was his belief in autocracy. He never fully understood the purport of the mighty drama in which he was cast for a leading part. To paint the outside of the building, to put new hinges on the door, that was his method of cleansing the Augean stables![1]

But had Pius been the ardent reformer that the Liberals pictured him, the task to be wrought far exceeded his strength. "They would make a Napoleon of me," he said, "whereas I am only a poor country curate."[2] Had he had the fierce energy of Sixtus V instead of his own easy-going nature, he could not have mastered the opposition inherent in every root and branch and twig of the Papal government. The men and methods could not be

[1] It is impossible to cite all the sources from which I have drawn hints for this estimate of Pius; his acts are, of course, the best guides. Gabussi, chap. iii; Döllinger: *Kleinere Schriften* (Stuttgart, 1890), pp. 558-602; Minghetti, Farini, Perreus, Bianchi, C. Maréchal: *Historie de Pie IX* (Paris, 1854), La Farina, Pasolini, and others have furnished evidence from different sides.

[2] Beauregard, *Épilogue*, 19.

reformed: they were what they were, corrupt or incompetent, the inevitable products of the system in which they grew: they must be cut down and consumed and new seeds must be planted: to talk of reforming them was as idle as to expect that briars could be converted to the uses of the oak. As there are men who exist for a long time under a complication of diseases, but die very quickly when an attempt is made to cure one of their diseases, so it was with the Papal system; the very life of the whole was endangered if any part were touched. Would you purge the tribunals? then you found that their rotting suckers were intertangled with the Police, and this perhaps with the Inquisition, and this again with the Treasury, and so on through every department of administration and up through the theologic departments to the Pope himself. Touch any civil abuse, and you set some dogma vibrating; mark any odious privileges for pruning, and your knife was blunted against the pontifical patent which long ago sanctioned them.

We have already seen something of the nature of the Papal government, and now we must look at it more closely, in order to know the magnitude of that Matterhorn of abuses that the too-fond Liberals expected Pius to demolish. The one dominant fact, the natural outcome of theocracy, was the omnipresence of ecclesiastics. The Papacy was a close corporation, or as we might say in modern parlance a "ring," which managed both the temporal and spiritual affairs of Rome for its own interests. In the course of centuries, almost every noble Roman family had had at least one pope, and that meant the permanent planting of that family within the narrow field of privilege. Thanks to nepotism, against which there was no safeguard, the pope's "nephews,"— frequently a euphemistic name for his illegitimate sons, — and his other relatives, were bestowed in comfortable places. As his reign was usually short, it being the custom to elect old men to Peter's throne in order that the chance of other aspirants might soon come round, he must use dispatch: the privileges he granted were hereditary, and it was easy for him to create new offices where no vacancy occurred in the old ones. The Pontifical Treasury came to be regarded as a hoard contributed by faithful Catholics in all parts of the world for the benefit of a few score patricians at Rome. This oligarchy, whose members were indifferently clerics and worldlings, had no scruples, no qualms of conscience: they believed that they had a divine right to enrich themselves for the glory of God and the honor of Mother Church. God, to their thinking, would have been a very vulgar Being had He intrusted His Church to lowly and devout men, rather than to those whose veins purpled with the blood of Orsini and Colonna. He ought, indeed, to be proud to be worshiped by aristocrats whose title in many cases antedated that of the most powerful monarchs.

Thus every few years the grand prize in the richest lottery on earth was drawn, and the successful ticket-holder made haste to turn the wealth and prestige it brought him to the aggrandizement of his family. All measures, all legislation, — if that may be called legislation which was the whim or scheme of an arbitrary ruler, — aimed at building up his family and at extending the prerogatives of the Papal oligarchy; and since places and favors went to ecclesiastics, every man who aspired to rise put on the clerical garb. Thus the offices of the Church were filled by many men who had nothing of religion about them except its livery, and the offices of the State were administered by men who, even when genuinely pious, had neither fitness nor training for secular affairs. By an inevitable process, theocracy promoted incompetence and dishonesty.

The absence of all responsibility left every door open to officials who knew that they were serving not the public, but themselves and their coterie. St. Peter himself, had he been pope during the fourth decade of the nineteenth century, would have found that, although he held the keys, he had little authority over the locksmith. For the Pope was hedged about by the Cardinals, who kept from him whatever they did not wish him to know. At best, he could infer from the character of any particular cardinal the probable nature of his stewardship: to scrutinize details was beyond the scope of pontifical vigor.

The Secretary of State was the practical head of the government, but he was master only in his own department. Without doubt he strove to hold his underlings accountable to him, yet without doubt each of them, from highest to lowest, imitated the example of his superiors and only reported to them what he could not conceal. Each adopted for his rule the motto, "Help thyself." In the department of finances, for instance, there was no methodical bookkeeping, no accuracy nor restraints; but a thousand leaks for extravagance, and as many taps for dishonesty. The Papal financial system was a labyrinth to which no contemporary had the clue, nor can posterity explore its dark and tangled mazes. The public never knew on what principle the fiscal estimate was made, never saw a sworn statement of receipts and expenditures, never had proof that they had been audited: only learned from time to time that the public debt had increased. The prelate who presided over the Treasury, and who, on laying down his office, became a cardinal, was responsible to the Pope alone, and we should show little respect for his skill if we imagined that he could not arrange his ledgers so as to mystify the Holy Father. Tosti, the Treasurer under Gregory XVI, is said to have remained poor himself, but many of his subordinates and associates enriched themselves by usury, by letting out contracts, and by frauds in the management of public works.[1] In 1814,

[1] Farini, i, 127.

when Pius VII returned to Rome, the French had wiped
out the public debt: thirty-two years later, when Gregory died, a new debt had risen to the sum of thirty-seven
million crowns,[1] and each year marked an increasing deficit. Taxes were laid without any regard for justice or
for economic effectiveness: ecclesiastical property being
exempt, the burden fell all the more heavily on civilians
and peasants. There was a grist-tax, and a tax on
almost every article of food. Added to all these was
the tax of a protective tariff, and of duties on various
exports. The Papal financiers at least carried the system
of protection to its logical ends, creating monopolies and
establishing a tariff for the benefit of anybody who had
influence with them: they indulged in no cant about their
affection for the horny-handed sons of toil. And as if
these evils were not enough, the collecting of the revenue
was farmed out to private bidders, thereby giving opportunity for extortion and cruelty. But what could a Cardinal Camerlengo, trained perhaps in a cloister, know of
economic laws? This was a pious government, and his
only text-book was the missal. Under these conditions
commerce and industry could not thrive: the volume of
trade of the States of the Church was relatively as one to
twenty compared with that of England, and Roman workmen's wages averaged about five twelfths of those of English workmen.[2] But smuggling throve mightily, and the
smugglers had "offices and administrative bureaux, with
insurers, bookkeepers, and dispatchers," besides a "militia with captains, guides, and escorts," and the customs
officers proved to be their allies rather than their enemies.[3]

[1] The Roman *scudo*, or crown, was worth approximately one dollar.
[2] Bowring's *Report* (Parliamentary Blue-Book), 1837. The disparity in wages was still larger ten years later, when England had secured commercial emancipation.
[3] Farini, i, 128. See also Monsignor Morichini's report on Papal finances, December, 1847; quoted by Farini, i, 285-309.

From its financial administration we can infer much concerning not only the material prosperity of a State, but also the honesty of its inhabitants. The inference we draw concerning the Papal fiscal officers is confirmed when we examine the Papal judiciary system. In that, too, there was hopeless confusion. The numbers and variety of courts, the exemptions granted to nobles and ecclesiastics, the different penalties attached to the same offense, the refusal to confront the accused with their accusers, the secrecy surrounding the trials of political prisoners, the allowing judges to conduct the prosecution as well as to pass sentence, the lack of *habeas corpus* and of bail, the long delays in cases of appeal, the great expenses, the uncertainty, the general belief that the result of a suit depended upon the prejudices or venality of the judges, — these things indicated that the Papal department of justice was mediæval and incompetent. The judges received so small a stipend that they might easily give way to the temptation of taking bribes. The upper courts at Rome — the Rota, the Segnatura, the Consulta — were all in charge of high ecclesiastics; but, since legal knowledge was not necessarily imbibed with theology, each cardinal or prelate had lay lawyers to prepare the cases for him. The tribunal of the Inquisition, although its jurisdiction was legally restricted to the examination and punishment of heretics, sometimes reached over and dealt with political suspects. Of the extraordinary tribunals, appointed to chastise alleged rebels, we need not speak; they did their work with the partisanship, and often with the cruelty, expected from them. Latin was the language of the courts: it was appropriate that churchmen who conducted God's worship in a tongue which the people did not understand, should also interpose a foreign language between the people and Justice.

Over the Police Department ruled the ubiquitous prelate. He had priests and laymen for his agents, and besides the regular constables he employed many spies and secret instigators. The so-called Congregation of Good Government, headed by a monsignore or cardinal, under the pretense of keeping order in the cities, pried into the affairs of every family, hired tell-tales and eavesdroppers, and made domiciliary searches and arrests on the vaguest suspicion. Public education, maintained to fit new swarms of priests, paid slight attention to culture. The Universities at Rome and Bologna were each governed by a cardinal; the smaller colleges by the local bishop or archbishop; the communal schools by the parish priest. In 1836 the State appropriated 372,000 crowns for prisons, and only 108,000 crowns for Public Instruction, Fine Arts, and Commerce.[1] It was estimated that about one child in fifty attended the public schools. No person was allowed to teach in private, or to lecture, without the license of the authorities. At the Universities no student received a degree unless he could certify to having attended mass and the confessional as often as the rules prescribed. Every literary work had to run the gauntlet of seven censors.

Surely if sacerdotal government were desirable, it would have proved itself so at Rome, where all affairs, clerical and secular, were alike intrusted to it. There was one member of the clergy for every six families, and the result was such that we might assert that a community is degraded in proportion to the number of priests, of whatever sect, who batten upon it. The States of the Church sank under Gregory's reign below the level of the other depraved countries of Christian Europe. Not even Naples harbored so many abominations; for at Naples the abuses were chiefly perpetrated by laymen, whereas at Rome churchmen, who should have been patterns of holiness and justice, were the great offenders. Let the

[1] Bowring, 74.

Papal code declare what it would, the crime of a priest was as much more reprehensible than that of a layman, as the former's responsibility was greater than the latter's. Private and domestic morals corresponded to the debased material and administrative conditions. Licentiousness permeated every class. The remark made by a cobbler revealed the method by which plebeians obtained favors or promotion from their priestly rulers: "If I had had a handsome wife," said he, "I should not now be mending shoes."[1] An occasional harrying of prostitutes, followed by the imprisonment of some and by the extortion of hush-money from others, seemed a joke in view of the undisturbed general profligacy. As at Rome nothing could be kept secret, so the scandalous lives of the ecclesiastics and grandees were, next to the prospect of the Pope's death, the favorite themes of gossip and pasquinade; nevertheless, says Farini, "there is almost no instance of a sentence for adultery."[2] The tradesman who, on returning home, found his wife's confessor's shoes outside the door, wisely decided to take another stroll, instead of interrupting their devotions. Roman husbands, except among the populace of Trastevere, thought too little of their wives' infidelity to make it an excuse for violence or for a duel, after the fashion of melodramatic Frenchmen. Idleness, born of laws which crushed commerce and industry, was fostered by the knowledge that prosperity came, not as the reward of honest labor, but as the gift of a patron. The large sums annually distributed for charity encouraged beggars, of whom no less than seventeen thousand appealed to Czar Nicholas for alms, when he visited Rome in 1845.[3] The lottery further encouraged thriftlessness, and the presence of two priests, one holding a crucifix in his hands, at the weekly drawing in Piazza Colonna, was not an edi-

---

[1] Stendhal: *Promenades dans Rome*, ii. 27.
[2] Farini, i. 142.   [3] Minghetti: *Miei Ricordi* (Turin, 1889), i, 170.

fying sight. The Eternal City astonished every traveler as much by the disparity between the pious professions and the corrupt practices of its rulers, as by the contrasted pomp of its ceremonials and the squalor of its multitudes. Well might Niebuhr say, in 1830, "I have never seen a more cheerless nation."[1] So Goethe, after witnessing the Roman Carnival more than forty years before, had declared, "the most unpleasant feeling about it is, that real internal joy is wanting."[2] As the picturesque but desert Campagna drew a girdle of miasma round the City of Rome, so the government of the Pope shed a moral pestilence over all his subjects. No one now can say how much of the evil should be charged to wicked intent and how much to incompetence; but the result was the same, for the theocratic system of necessity gave full play to the wicked and to the incompetent.

From this brief survey we shall understand why the obstacles confronting any pope who aspired to reign righteously were insuperable. There was but one cure possible, — the secularization of the government, which would inevitably lead to the extinction of the pope's temporal power. To expect that the privileged caste would voluntarily submit to this was to expect more than human nature could perform. No dominant class has ever given up its supremacy without a struggle; much less has it committed suicide at the request of a weaker class. Gioberti and the Neo-Guelfs had not foreseen this; they thought that the Pope would be able by simply correcting abuses to rule like a benevolent father, as one might put off a suit of soiled and worn-out garments for a new one. They did not realize that the Papacy, bone and sinew and blood, was diseased beyond remedy. Nor did Pius himself, at the outset, understand that all the minor changes

[1] Quoted by J. Whiteside: *Italy in the Nineteenth Century* (London, 1848), ii, 299.
[2] *Italienische Reise*, Feb. 27, 1787.

he proposed could affect only the surface, unless these culminated speedily in that great and final change which he had not the least intention of making.

But there were persons who, even amid the general illusions at the beginning of Pius's reign, saw clearly that reforms were incompatible with the existence of the temporal sovereignty at Rome. One of these persons was Metternich. "A Liberal pope is not a possible being,"[1] he said; and he was so firmly persuaded that the hierarchy recognized this truth, that he delayed to send instructions before the Conclave met. The Austrian minister at Rome had, indeed, intimated on his own responsibility that the election of Gizzi would be vetoed, and Cardinal Gaysrück was at length posting to Rome with orders to exclude any other Liberal candidate, including Mastai, when the Conclave suddenly finished its work. Gaysrück reached Rome just in time to adore the Pontiff he had been commissioned to defeat. But Metternich was not discouraged. He immediately set about winning the ascendency over Pius, in the hope of checking any acts that might excite the revolutionary party into open rebellion. It was Austria's policy to have a weak government at Rome, so that the Pope must rely upon her support; but the Papal government must not be so weak as to embolden the Liberals to act, because a disturbance in the Papal States would arouse Austria's Italian subjects and endanger the peace of the Peninsula. To keep things as they had been, and to prevent Pius from making his government either strong or popular, was therefore Metternich's plan. He advised the Pope to consent to the introduction of railways, and arranged with the Rothschilds to supply the funds, thereby hoping to take the matter out of the hands of sectaries, who would have used it as a political weapon.[2] He instructed Pius how to

---

[1] Metternich, vii. 440.
[2] *Ibid*, 155; but the project fell through.

organize his administration, and then urged him to grant no amnesty. "God accords no amnesty," wrote the Machiavellian Chancellor; "for the very idea of such an act, in so far as amnesty sets aside the existence of the crime, would be opposed to the idea of divine justice, which necessarily holds moral wrong in horror as long as it lasts. God's mercy only operates through pardon, and repentance is the condition indispensable to pardon."[1] Continuing his instruction, Metternich warned the Pope against making concessions. "Acts of justice, of prudence, in short the acts of a good government, are not concessions made by the throne to its subjects: they are matters of reason and duty. The government which makes concessions follows, on the contrary, a line of weakness, and behaves like a capitalist who lives on his capital instead of on the interest of his capital."[2]

That Pius approved of these views I have no doubt: but while he was flooded with such counsel from Vienna, and was constantly importuned by Lützow, the Austrian minister at Rome, he also listened gladly to Count Pellegrino Rossi, the French representative at the Papal Court. Rossi was an Italian who, exiled in his youth, had attained distinction in Switzerland as a professor of political economy, whence being called to a chair at the College of France, he had risen into favor with Guizot, the French Prime Minister, had been created a peer and dispatched to Rome, just at the end of Gregory's reign. Rossi, patriotic and Liberal, and a clear-sighted man, withal, — for he had predicted that the temporal power would fall without battle or efforts when foreign aid should be withdrawn from it,[3] — had a delicate part to play: as an Italian he wished to hasten the redemption of his native land; as the envoy of Louis Philippe he must try to undermine Austrian influence in the States of the Church. While Rossi, therefore, kept assuring Pius that the French

[1] Metternich, vii, 251. [2] Ibid, 252. [3] Bersezio, ii, 111.

government welcomed every sign of reform, Lützow kept painting the dangers that lurked in any change. Pius's superficial acts seemed to indicate that Rossi had the upper hand, but in his heart he agreed with the Austrian.

England, having no calico nor cutlery interests at stake, applauded Pius's new régime, and encouraged him to persevere in a course laid down in the Memorandum of 1831 and shamefully abandoned by Gregory. Among the populations of the smaller Italian States, the rejoicing at the first acts of Gioberti's Pope was almost as widespread as among the Romans themselves, although their fearful rulers strove to curb demonstrations which, they quickly detected, were not addressed solely to the spiritual head of the Church. In Naples, the Bourbon government relaxed nothing of its brutal tyranny; in Tuscany the tide of official reaction had not yet turned; in Piedmont, although Charles Albert stood resolute against Austria in the quarrel over wine and salt, he gave to Liberals no positive encouragement. Nevertheless, in private he did not hide his satisfaction. Gizzi's nomination, he wrote to a confidant, "proves that the Pope is determined to tread the path of progress and reforms, — blessings on him for it! It is a campaign which he undertakes against Austria, *evviva!* "[1] But the supporters of the Old Régime knew well the danger their cause would run should the King's wavering nature be suddenly fixed by the example of a Liberal pope, and honest Count Solaro not only redoubled his Absolutist counsels to Charles Albert, but also made a journey to Rome in order to see with his own eyes the strange Pontiff who was playing with Liberalism as unconcernedly as a child with fire. Pius received the Piedmontese minister graciously, and apparently calmed his fears by declaring that,

[1] L. Cibrario: *Charles Albert* (French translation by C. de la Varenne, Paris, 1862), 88.

beyond giving the remedies which the times demanded, he would not allow himself to be drawn into the whirlpool of revolution. But the Count, expert in reading the symptoms of the body politic, saw that, in spite of the Pope's reassurance, the outlook was bad. "Unless Austria and France interfere," he wrote, "a catastrophe is inevitable." [1]

Pius himself, in his Encyclical [2] of November 9, 1846, stood firmly by the mediævalism of the Church, declaring that to rely upon reason instead of faith was damnable, condemning Bible Societies for circulating the Scriptures in a language the people could understand, [3] condemning communism and the misguided champions of progress, fulminating threats against secret societies and against political conspiracies. He exhorted bishops everywhere to inculcate among the Christian people obedience and subjection to princes and governments, teaching them, after the precept of the Apostle, [4] that the powers that be are ordained of God, and that they that resist shall receive to themselves damnation. He further reminded princes that their power was given them in order that they might defend the Church, and he called upon them for support. The printing-press he regarded as Satan's machine for sowing falsehoods broadcast; to progress he applied the epithets seducing, lying, deceitful, perverting, seditions, malign, demented, destroyer of religious and civil society; and those persons who wished to introduce progress into the Church he called sacrilegious.

This instrument, consistently obscurantist and effete,

[1] Solaro della Margarita: *Memorandum Storico-Politico* (Turin, 1851), 381-2.
[2] The Encyclical is entitled *Qui pluribus*.
[3] Pius, like other popes, though fond of quoting Scripture, seems never to have pondered the notable remarks of St. Paul in *1 Corinthians* xiv, 9-17.
[4] Quoting *Romans* xiii, 1, 2.

might well have staggered the Liberals, were it not that few of them read the ten pages of turgid Latin through, and fewer still heeded it, for they regarded it merely as a conventional utterance which did not express Pius's real opinion. The fashion of attributing to him every hint of reform, and of crediting the cardinals with every backward stroke, was too deeply rooted to be shaken. So the Liberals forgave the Encyclical, as they had forgiven the honors heaped on Freddi and other odious agents of Gregory's persecution, and as they forgave the dilatoriness of the commissions appointed to direct the railways and to draw up new codes. And in spite of Pius's endeavors to check the frequent demonstrations of devotion to himself, — endeavors suggested by fear lest the multitude might suddenly flare into rebellion, — his steps were accompanied by enthusiastic crowds wherever he went, and his name was cheered in every gathering.

But the great body of the higher clergy, and all those grandees whose interests were bound up in the preservation of the iniquitous Gregorian system, took alarm at Pius's coquetting with Liberalism; and, not content with warning him of the danger he was inviting, not content with opposing the inertia of tradition to every suggestion of change, they set about organizing active but underhand resistance. They stirred up the Sanfedists to renew their wrangles with the Liberals; they hired agents to foment tumults; and when the failure of the wheat-crops caused distress and discontent, they strove to have it appear that the disorders sequent thereto were due to the Pope's imprudence in exciting the political hopes of the revolutionists. Everywhere the Gregorians or partisans of the Old Régime were bent on picking a quarrel with the Pians, as the party was called which looked to Pius to fulfil their expectations.[1] Some of the bishops went so far as to insinuate doubts of Pius's orthodoxy.[2]

[1] Farini, i, 162.   [2] Bersezio, ii, 119.

Among the Liberals themselves, the old divisions showed no signs of healing. The Republicans, and all the sects more or less influenced by Mazzini, were for immediate action; the Moderates, comprising Neo-Guelfs and Constitutional Monarchists, insisted upon waiting until public opinion should be educated; and to educate it they would employ only legal means.[1] Recognizing the value to their cause of the moral support of the Pope, they discouraged any act which might scare him to abandon them. Fortunately their temperate counsels prevailed, and the year 1846 closed without witnessing an untimely outbreak. Together with Pius's popularity, which grew openly day by day, there was crystallizing the belief that Charles Albert was predestined to be the Sword of the Italian cause. The time was past when no man might utter the words *Italy* and *Liberty*, when actors were required to substitute *Ausonia* for the former and *loyalty* for the latter.[2] The Scientific Congress, meeting at Novara, discussed many things not set down in the text-books of science, and not recorded in the minutes of the Congress; daring even to salute Charles Albert as the "liberator of Italy," and to strike a medal in his honor. On December 6, the Genoese celebrated, by permission, the centenary of the expulsion of the Austrians from Genoa, and not only all Piedmont, but Tuscany and the Papal States joined in the celebration. There were banquets and speeches, mutual congratulations and significant predictions, the beacon fires burned brightly on the Apennines, and above all could be heard the cry as ancient as the Sicilian Vespers, "Out with the barbarians!"

[1] La Farina, iii, 33.   [2] Minghetti, i, 48.

CHAPTER III.

IN THE RAPIDS, 1847.

AT the opening of the year 1847 Pius IX was the most conspicuous sovereign in the world. Tidings of his deeds and promises had sped in all directions. Italians blessed him as their long looked for redeemer: foreigners were kindled to enthusiasm for this benevolent and Liberal Pope. The single word *amnesty* had such magic in it, that Garibaldi, an exile in Montevideo, Republican and priest-hater though he was, wrote to offer his sword and life to the Pope who had taken up Italy's cause. The game of mutual deception went on, — the Romans bent on flattering Pius into reforms which should make independence inevitable, Pius dreaming only of surface improvements, and believing that whenever he chose he could allay the excitement he had aroused. Of actual material gains, except the amnesty, after half-a-year's waiting, there was little enough. Pius early discovered that the best way to get rid of importunate demands was to refer them to a commission, which quietly let them die from want of attention, like infants intrusted to a heartless nurse: so there were commissions innumerable, supposed to be busily engaged preparing reforms, but giving no signs of themselves whether they were asleep or awake. Reckless dilatoriness this proved to be, for the Romans were day by day nearing the conviction that they were strong enough to take without asking. Their romantic sentiment for Pius must not be strained too far; it sprang from their belief that he sincerely shared their aspirations; once let them learn their mistake, once let them suspect that he was deceiving them, and they would show how little they cared for him either as man or as pope.

Whether Pius's procrastination be charged to unwillingness or ineptitude, or to the resistance of cardinals and prelates, its effect was equally harmful. His subjects clamored and petitioned: he at first refused, then promised, then delayed, and finally, clamor and petitions becoming urgent, he conceded: never a reform granted spontaneously, never a forestalling of popular wishes, but always the concession doled out grudgingly, as a sop to Cerberus. The tact and moderation of the people certainly deserved much praise, although doubtless self-interest prompted them to refrain from violence so long as they could coax or flatter their sovereign to do, however tardily, their will. Agitations in the market-places, speechifying in cafés and taverns, parades in the streets, and demonstrations before the Quirinal, kept the populace in a fever, and offered numberless chances for disorder. Yet Rome had not been so free from grave disturbance since the time when the French ruled there. This tranquillity was largely due to the influence upon the masses of one of the most picturesque characters thrust into view during that epoch of upheaval. Angelo Brunetti was a plebeian who took pride in the belief that the blood of the old Romans flowed in his veins. A wine-carrier by trade and industrious by nature, he earned money enough to buy a hostelry near the Porta del Popolo, and he had always a penny or a paul to spare for a needy acquaintance. Of a powerful frame and ready tongue, and endowed with common-sense, he became a leader among his class, who appealed to him to settle their disputes, and took his counsel as gladly as they took his alms. From the day of Pius the Ninth's election, Ciceruacchio — that was the nickname by which first his fellows and later the world called Brunetti — was foremost in every popular demonstration: he led the cheers before the Palace, and when the Pope appeared on foot or in his coach in the streets, Ciceruacchio walked beside him, and prevented the crowd from pressing too near. He had an infatuation, half religious and half patriotic, for the Holy Father, and when the latter gave him a friendly smile or word, the people felt all the prouder of their honest chief. He did the most to spread, if indeed, he did not originate, the myth that Pius was a genuine reformer, only held back by the resistance of the Gregorians. He became a power whom the government took note of; he was consulted and flattered by important personages; he was even admitted, it appears, to the Quirinal. But neither the caresses of the great nor the enthusiasm of his own class turned his head. Over those multitudes which might at any moment become a mob his word was final: he bade them do nothing to displease the Holy Father, who, if they waited patiently and showed their loyalty, would grant them all they desired; and so effectual was his restraint, that the British consul wrote from Rome during the summer of 1847: "The influence of one individual of the lower class, Angelo Brunetti, hardly known but for his nickname of Ciceruacchio, has for the last month kept the peace of the city more than any power possessed by the authorities, from the command which he exerts over the populace!"[1] Nevertheless, that Rome should be at the mercy of her populace, that the Pope and hierarchy, Swiss Guards and Papal police, should be dependent on the honesty and commonsense of a poor wine-carrier, reveals the depth to which the Pontifical government had sunk.[2]

[1] *Correspondence*, i, 70.
[2] For Ciceruacchio see E. Martinengo Cesaresco: *Italian Characters* (London, 1890), 279-82; C. E. Maurice: *Revolutionary Movement of* 1848-9 (London, 1887), 142; Bersezio, ii, 122-6. Garibaldi praised Ciceruacchio "for his charity for the powerful: one of the rarest virtues of the weak when they are called upon to take the place of the strong."

The outward events of this year seem almost trivial in comparison with the great forces struggling to free themselves: mere spirts of steam and low rumblings, preceding a Vesuvian eruption. In March Cardinal Gizzi published a new press law. Hitherto, before a literary work, no matter how brief, could be published, it must submit to seven ordeals: it must receive the approval of the literary, ecclesiastical, political, and Holy Office censors, the *publicetur* of the bishop's court and of the police, and the final inspection of the Holy Office.[1] The new law established a council of four lay members and one ecclesiastic who should supervise the political press, and it allowed the publication of such opinions on current affairs as did not tend, directly or indirectly, to injure the government. A writer might appeal from the decision of one of the censors to all of them; but so much time was wasted in this procedure that, even where the full bench reversed the earlier decision, it was usually too late for the publication to be effective.[2] Nevertheless, the Moderates accepted the law as a sign of improvement, and for the first time the Papal States had newspapers of their own which were allowed to discuss, albeit with the greatest caution, topics of public concern. The old *Diario di Roma* had printed the official acts, and such important news as that "the Pope attended mass in the Sistine Chapel on Sunday," or "Cardinal So-and-So will perform mass at the Lateran on the Festival of St. John." Now sprang up at Rome the *Bilancia* with conservative principles, and the *Contemporaneo*, mildly progressive: at Bologna, which had long been both in politics and enlightenment the most advanced of the Papal cities, Minghetti, Montanari, and other Liberals founded the *Felsineo*, and Pichat edited the *Italiano*. From the clandestine press issued such journals as the *Amica Veritas* and the *Sentinella del Campidoglio*, full of a Radi-

---

[1] Minghetti, i, 223. [2] Farini, i, 183.

calism which insisted, truly enough, that the government was but whitewashing here and there the outside of the social edifice whose foundations had already crumbled and whose walls were about to collapse.

Still the Moderates preached patience, and dubbed the Radicals Exalted (*Esaltati*) or Hot-heads, whose impetuosity would ruin the common cause. In April the Secretary of State tossed another sop to them. In the previous autumn the Pope had intimated his willingness to summon a consultative body which should make suggestions to the government: now the Legates and Delegates were commanded to propose the names of three notables in each province, from among whom the government would chose one, and those so chosen were to form the much talked of Consulta. A body so constituted, without power or responsibility, and expected to speak only when it was spoken to, was of course but a phantom; nevertheless, the name itself had magnetism, and the fact that laymen might be called upon for advice was auspicious: might not the Pope who conceded an inch soon concede an ell? So the newspapers approved, and the customary processions marched up the Quirinal hill, and bombarded the Palace with cheers, until Pius appeared on the balcony and gave his benediction. And when, a little later, June 14, there came the announcement of the formation of a Council of Ministers, although all of them were ecclesiastics and some of them were Gregorians, there was the usual exercise of the lungs. To celebrate the anniversary of Pius's election and coronation kept throats and hands and legs busy for forty-eight hours; harangues and *vivas*, the singing of national hymns, the tossing of caps, the waving of torches by night, left the excited Romans no time for repose nor for work. Was it not a fit retribution that the government which had for generations fed the souls of its people on wind, should now be at the mercy of the people's shouts? Pius, who had long been anxious lest his Jericho should topple upon him, at the roars of his devoted subjects, issued an edict forbidding popular assemblages, on the ground that they distracted youths from their studies and artisans from their work. But the Romans assumed that this remonstrance came from Gizzi, and not from the Pope himself, and in determining not to heed it, they began to murmur against the Secretary of State.

Demands were now made with open throat that had only been whispered a few months back. The people, convinced that Pius was thwarted in his Liberal purposes by his ecclesiastical surroundings, clamored for the secularization of the government; but on this point, at least, Pius was resolved. "I cannot, I ought not, I will not," he replied laconically to any one who suggested this remedy to him. The regiments of Swiss mercenaries were a perpetual reminder to the Romans of their subjection to foreign influence: therefore, they clamored for the dismissal of the Swiss, and for the organization of a Civic Guard. At Bologna, the police being unable to hold the criminal classes in check, Pius at length permitted reputable citizens to enroll themselves in a sort of vigilance committee which patrolled the streets by night. But he still withheld his consent to the larger demand. His amnestied subjects showed want of tact in circulating a petition for the Civic Guard: they surely ought not to expect the Pope to grant so radical a reform at their request, and he intimated to the Moderates that such a petition would embarrass him. There was another interval of pause, during which the people had leisure to measure their gains with their desires; the former seemed slight in comparison with the latter. "Nothing has yet been done," Rossi wrote to Guizot; "thus far only promises, proposals, and Commissions that do not work: hence it is no wonder that the country begins to distrust and to be vexed. It does not accuse the Pope of double-dealing, but it suspects him of weakness."[1]

Political assassinations became frequent in the provinces. The Gregorians displayed a venomous activity, which indicated either desperation or a sudden access of hopes. Rumors flew about that Pius was secretly negotiating with Austria for the dispatch of troops into the Papal States, and the reinforcement of the Austrian army in Lombardy gave color to these suspicions. At length, on July 5, against the opposition of his Court, Pius decreed the institution of a Civic Guard at Rome, and he hinted that the institution might, if necessary, be extended to other cities. Two days later Cardinal Gizzi, who had opposed this innovation, resigned. A well-meaning, but feckless minister was Gizzi: raised by a sudden gust of popularity to a height he could not maintain, he vainly fluttered in mid-air for a while, and then, having neither pinions nor parachute, he inevitably dropped to earth, and was forgotten. In many traits he resembled Pius, but he had not Pius's affability. "If I remained in the ministry only twelve months," he said, "the cardinals who come after me will not remain six months, for it is impossible for a minister of sense and good intentions to work in harmony with a man like Pius IX."[2] Gizzi was succeeded by Cardinal Ferretti, one of the Pope's kinsmen, popular for his benevolence, estimable for the courage with which he tended the victims of the cholera during the great epidemic, but without experience in governing, and without that clear-sightedness and resolution which are indispensable to a statesman. He was a man who would follow bravely, but could not lead.

But if ever Providence seemed willing to give a ruler a fair test, it did so in the case of the Ninth Pius. Chance after chance came to him and he seized it not, yet still was a reprieve granted to him. Blunders and omissions

[1] Farini, i, 192.   [2] *Ibid*, 199.

were not imputed against him; the fiction held that he was all that his subjects and Italy and the world wished him to be. And now, just as the demand that he should give some substantial proof of his sincerity became troublesome, destiny, which the shallow call luck, brought about two events which made his popularity greater than before.

The first of these was the discovery of a plot engaged in by the Gregorians and by all the enemies of progress, to exterminate the Liberals and to imprison the Pope: having him in their power they would compel him either to abdicate or to abandon his Liberal views and associates. What grounds existed for believing that this melodramatic plot was to be carried out will never be known: but the Romans believed it, and in a trice Rome was in a ferment. On July 14 the walls of the city were covered with placards giving the names of the chief conspirators and calling on the citizens to take swift vengeance. The police could neither remove the posters nor keep order. Excitement grew throughout the night, and all the next day. At last the Civic Guard was called out. Many of the accused hid themselves or fled; others surrendered to the police, and asked to be allowed to prove their innocence in court. There were promiscuous arrests, and searchings of the houses of suspects. Grassellini, Governor of Rome, was called upon to resign and quit the city within six hours. Morandi, his successor, appealed to the citizens to calm themselves. The Secretary of State visited the quarters of the Civic Guard, praised its loyalty and moderation, and uttered a phrase which tickled the public and became famous. "Let us show Europe," he said, "that we suffice unto ourselves." A strange exhortation on the lips of the premier of a government which had for thirty years depended upon foreign troops to protect it from its own subjects! After a week the crisis passed, and the return of quiet made it evident that the Pope's enemies had succeeded only in increasing his popularity. The trial of those of the alleged conspirators who had been taken failed to pierce the mystery; at the most, it was shown that the Gregorians had a scheme of provoking tumults in order that the Austrians might be called in to interfere, and that Pius might be frightened out of his Liberalism. That Austria was a party to the conspiracy needed only to be suggested to be believed: that she would deny her complicity was as certain as that she would cover up her tracks. Metternich was too old a fox to leave incriminating chicken-bones at the door of his burrow.[1]

Another event, falling at the same time with this attempt to abduct the Pope, caused even greater indignation in Italy, and alarmed Europe with the prospect of immediate war. On July 17 a troop of eight hundred Croats and sixty Hungarians marched into Ferrara, their muskets and three cannon loaded, their matches lighted, and their demeanor that of conquerors taking possession of a hostile city. Cardinal Ciacchi, the Papal Legate, drew up a formal protest before a notary, and dispatched a messenger to Rome. The Secretary of State published the protest in the *Diario di Roma*, and instructed the Pope's representative at Vienna to call Austria to account for this act of invasion. Marshal Auersperg, the Austrian commander at Ferrara, replied to Cardinal Ciacchi's protest that he had simply carried out instructions given him by his superiors: the Ferrarese, he alleged, had become so insolent and unruly that the Papal police could not restrain them, and that a certain Captain Jankovich, returning to his quarters late at night, had been roughly handled in the streets; for the present, Austrian soldiers would patrol the city and mount guard at the gates. In Metternich's explanations, surprise was mingled with in-

---

[1] Farini, i, 202-7; La Farina, iii, 40-44; *Correspondence*, etc., i, 63-4, 70, 72-3.

jured innocence. He was shocked that the Legate should have made public his objections through the vulgar medium of a notary, instead of through the usual diplomatic channels, — an innovation which the Austrian Cabinet strongly censured;[1] he declared that in sending a reinforcement to Ferrara, Austria had only exercised the right conferred upon her by the Treaty of Vienna, and sanctioned by custom during more than thirty years;[2] finally, he shifted the responsibility from himself to Marshal Radetzky, the Military Governor of Lombardy and Venetia.[3] The Papal government, which had from the first grumbled at that article in the Treaty which permitted Austria to garrison Ferrara and Comacchio, insisted that the word "places" in that article referred only to the citadel of each town. Metternich rejoined that if citadel had been meant, the word "citadel" would have been used, but that "place" evidently included all the military positions and works connected with the citadel.[4]

We need not watch the shuttling to and fro through several months of this disputed question: the Austrians maintained their truculent attitude in Ferrara, and made no apology; the Papal government, refusing to recognize Austria's claim or to compromise on a joint-control, fired volleys of protests into the Cabinets of all the Powers. The effect of the invasion was out of all proportion to the interests involved, for it confirmed the suspicion that Austria had connived with the Gregorians to overwhelm Pius and his Liberal policy. The rumors circulated from Vienna that Pius was about to call upon the Emperor to intervene had been fruitless; the efforts of secret agents to stir up troubles which should give Austria a pretext for interfering had likewise failed; therefore, Metternich had devised a still more cunning trap which should be sprung simultaneously at Rome and Ferrara. But his

[1] Metternich, vii, 466.
[2] *Ibid*, 464-8.
[3] *Correspondence*, i, 230.
[4] Metternich, vii, 465.

craft overshot the mark. The Papal subjects, instead of allowing themselves to be goaded into tumults for him to repress, acted with rare self-control; and the Pope, instead of being frightened back into the obscurantist party, turned away from them to the Liberals. His popularity had now a solid base: for the first time a wide breach had been opened between Rome and Vienna, and not only the Romans, but also the other Italians were fired with enthusiasm for a pope who had been insulted by Austria and whose territory Austria threatened to invade. At Rome all classes united in showing their loyalty to the Pope and their mutual good-will. Ciceruacchio sat at a banquet beside Prince Borghese, and was complimented for his patriotism in dissuading the populace from violence during the crisis; the populace cheered Cardinal Ferretti, the Secretary of State, for his firmness in resisting Austria's insolence. Volunteers flocked to the Civic Guard, now reconstituted and amplified; there was talk of forming a military camp of fifteen thousand men at Forlì to repel any further encroachment of the Austrians. Priests blessed the banners; even the Liberals joined the Clericals in urging the Pope to excommunicate the impious Emperor. It was proposed to recall the legate at Vienna, Monsignor Viale, a Gregorian who had persistently intrigued against his government and engaged in unauthorized negotiations. From Tuscany and from Piedmont came messages of approval and encouragement. Charles Albert wrote to Pius, "Whatever may occur, I will never separate my cause from yours." The greatest happiness that the King desired was to take part in a war for national independence, with the Pope as its head.[1] England, though without an ambassador at the Holy See, took pains informally to express her sympathy with Pius in his assertion of his dignity and in his measures of reform. France, though Guizot now hung on Metternich's in-

[1] Beauregard: *Épilogue*, 41.

structions as a pilgrim on the utterances of the Delphic Oracle,[1] hinted that, should Austria interfere in the Papal States, she, too, would send an army thither; and Rossi, the French envoy, did not hide his personal satisfaction at the swelling of the stream of Independence. Evidently, Metternich, the omniscient and astute, had bungled: his trick had recoiled on himself! The wedge which he drove in to split the Pope and Liberalism asunder had struck a different line of cleavage and made a fissure, daily widening, between the Pope and Austria.[2]

And yet in all the course of his career Metternich never displayed more remarkable versatility nor greater energy than in this year 1847. He foresaw that a mighty storm was gathering, not only over Italy but over Europe, — "that the situation was the worst in sixty years,"[3] — and he spared no diligence to prepare for it. He won over Guizot and Louis Philippe all the more easily because they had broken with England in the question of the Spanish Marriages; but in Northern Germany, and especially in Prussia, dangerous reforms were springing up in spite of his warnings. In Lord Palmerston, the British Foreign Secretary, he saw a marplot and an enemy; for Palmerston had recently declared, when Austria strangled the little Republic of Cracow, that if the treaties were null on the Vistula they might also be torn

[1] See an effusive letter from Guizot to Metternich, in the latter's *Memoirs*, vii, 395–6.

[2] I ought not to omit to allude to the theory that this Ferrara business was concocted between the Papal government and Metternich; that the protests of the former were as perfunctory as the latter's explanation. Although there is no reason to believe that the Papal diplomats were above a trick of this kind, I prefer, in the absence of sufficient evidence, to give them the benefit of the doubt. Gabussi (i, 77–82) shows what grounds there are for accepting the theory of collusion. Bianchi (*Storia Documentata*, v, 24) also credits this theory. But it is an undoubted fact that at this very time Pius was debating the probable necessity of quitting Rome should the Austrians advance, and that Charles Albert offered him troops, and placed a man-of-war at his disposal, if he should decide to leave Rome.

[3] Metternich, vii, 420.

up on the Rhine and the Po; and Palmerston was instructing the British diplomatic agents everywhere to preach the doctrine, that only by granting concessions demanded by the times could the princes of Europe avert a catastrophe. Metternich, on the other hand, cautioned them that the first concession would start the avalanche of revolution; and he who had so frontlessly violated the Treaty of Vienna at Cracow insisted that every one else should strictly observe it. To the Grand Duke of Tuscany he wrote almost in the terms of a sovereign to a vassal, bidding him beware of making any changes. "The cry of Italian nationality," he said, "is but a blind; the cause into which the schemers would draw the rulers of Italy is the cause of the Republic; listen to them and you throw away your crown; between the so-called Liberals, between Gioberti, Balbo, and D' Azeglio and the real Radicals, — Mazzini and his crew, — there is no difference, — one and all of them aim at your destruction; remember that an expelled ruler never comes back."[1] Towards the Papal government the wily Chancellor adopted another tone, flavoring his advice with theological arguments to suit the palates of those whom he wished to take it. He reminded them that the Church rested on the principle of authority; take that away, admit the claims of Protestants and freethinkers to liberty of conscience, and what would remain to the Pope? The only possible government for the Papacy was a theocratic government. How dangerous, how insane it would be, therefore, to attempt to uphold the principle of authority in matters of the Church, and to relinquish it in matters of State![2] As a devout Catholic, Metternich could but contemplate with horror the peril by which the only true religion was assailed. He and religion were, to borrow a phrase from Burke, "a rare

---

[1] Metternich to Leopold, vii, 401–6.
[2] M. to Lützow, vii, 400–9.

and singular coalition." He warned the Pope that under the cover of mere political reforms the democratic element in the Church, urged on by such wicked fellows as Lamennais and Gioberti, would bring to pass an ecclesiastical revolution in comparison with which the social revolution would be trivial.[1] These warnings sank deeper than was supposed into Pius's heart.

The princelings at Lucca, Modena, and Parma gave Metternich no anxiety; they were but toy balloons of which he held the string, to pull in or let out when he chose; but Charles Albert, with his wavering and mysticism, his indiscreet words and inconsistent acts, kept the Chancellor in a state of mingled irritation and contempt. The man who never spoke until his mind was made up, and having made up his mind never faltered, had no patience for a king whose opinions seemed as variable as the temperature of an ague-stricken child. "That which this Prince cannot forget," wrote Metternich, "is that he has two shoulders; and where he makes his mistake is, that God has not given men shoulders to put *for* on one, and *against* on the other."[2] But Charles Albert's case was too grave to be treated by sarcasm only, and so Metternich's dispatches to Turin abounded in reproofs and warnings and ominous hints, nor were allusions to the King's compromising experience in 1821 omitted.

Thus did the Chancellor, now crying, like Cassandra, with a "scare-babe voice," now stating his views with the sententiousness of Nestor, now arguing calmly in a tone of specious frankness, — artfully appealing to reason or prejudice or fear, touching every string, political, dynastic, and religious, — thus did he endeavor, throughout the year 1847, to resist the torrent which he saw was rising, rising, and which, he knew, threatened to sweep away the dam. All the resources of his fifty years in statecraft he deployed against his adversaries; nor did

[1] Metternich to Lützow, vii, 424, 429. [2] *Ibid*, 430.

he content himself with words alone. He poured new battalions into Lombardy and Venetia, until the Austrian armies there numbered about 70,000 men;[1] he held constantly over Piedmont, Tuscany, and Rome the probability of an Austrian invasion; he showed openly by the occupation of Ferrara, and secretly by the instigation of his paid agents, that he wished to goad the Italians into a reckless tumult, which would justify him in interfering. "The Emperor is determined not to lose his Italian territories,"[2] was his oft-repeated declaration. On that purpose all his energy was centred. Radicalism seemed to him less formidable than Liberalism, — for it is better to know the worst than to be wracked in suspense, — and therefore he chafed at the days and months of a Liberal agitation which to him was worse than war. "Italy is a geographical expression,"[3] he wrote in a circular letter to the diplomats of Europe. This brutal phrase, coming from the man who had for thirty-three years exerted his influence to keep Italy a mere name and the Italians degraded and disunited, had a double sting, and would not be forgotten. That Metternich did not order the Austrian troops to cross the Papal frontier as early as the month of August, 1847, — that in fact, he allowed Liberalism throughout the year to grow swiftly strong, instead of sending an army to stamp it out, — I attribute chiefly to one fact: the presence of Lord Palmerston in the Foreign Office at London. For the first time since Canning died the voice of a British minister gave pause to the autocratic cabal of Europe, and brought cheer to the peoples struggling for freedom.

We have seen how Metternich's words and intrigues miscarried at Rome. Unquestionably he told the truth when he said that the Liberal agitators would not be ap-

---

[1] The average for ten years previous was about 36,000 men.
[2] *Correspondence*, i, 74.
[3] Circular dispatch to Apponyi, August 6, 1847 (*Memoirs*, vii, 410).

peased by mere administrative reforms; unquestionably, too, the Pope and his ministers knew this, and perhaps they wished that Austria, disregarding their official protests, would interfere; but they were all being borne on a current which would soon wash away Metternich's own dikes. When Pius sanctioned the creation and arming of the Civic Guard he put into the hands of the Revolution the control of the physical force of his kingdom. But he could not do otherwise, and for the present the Revolution did not abuse its power. No shouts resounded more lustily along Tiber's concave shores than the *vivas* to Pio Nono, and to these were now added huzzas for Italy, for National Independence, and for the Customs League, together with the ominous, "Down with the Jesuits," and "Death to the Austrians." Even Pius himself is reported to have exclaimed, when irritated at the indignity put upon him at Ferrara, "Out with the Barbarians."

On October 2 the Municipality of Rome was instituted by the Pope's *motuproprio*. This was the first practical reform granted after sixteen months of promising and delay. Imagine a city governed by the vestry of one of its churches for the sole benefit of the vestrymen, without regard to the citizens; imagine, further, that through many centuries of irresponsibility the methods of that vestry have become corrupt, — that peculation goes unpunished, that there is no redress from extortion or negligence, and that favoritism rules the tribunals, the civil service, and the assessment of taxes; imagine all this, and you have a faint picture of the government of Rome. The new law gave the Holy City an administration similar to that which the other Papal municipalities had enjoyed since 1831, not the best, not even up to the standard of the French and English cities, but still better than that of the irresponsible prelates. Two weeks later (October 15) another *motuproprio* announced the names of the members who were to form the Consulta of State, and summoned them to Rome to begin their labors in November. Twenty-two laymen and one monsignore, for the most part men of distinction in their respective provinces and Moderates in politics, composed this body, of which Cardinal Antonelli was President and Monsignor Amici Vice-President. They were denied all political action, but they might suggest to the Papal government any reforms they deemed necessary in civil and fiscal matters, and they might express their opinions on any other matter on which the Pope should deign to consult them. But some of the Consultors were determined that, although they had only a phantom influence, — being but as dolls to say *Yes* or *No* when they were pressed, — they would take means to inform the public that they had definite convictions, and what those convictions were. Accordingly, after overcoming Pius's objections, they presented to him an address in which they sketched the policy which they believed ought to be carried out, and they got permission for the publication by the official journal of the Consulta's proceedings. Then they set earnestly to work to explore the sink of Papal abuses, but before they had finished this stupendous task, the Revolution was upon them.[1] One other reform, to which the Liberals attached immense hopes, marked the close of the year 1847. The Pope announced that he had completed negotiations with Tuscany and Piedmont for the formation of a Customs League, but that the details of the agreement could be published and its provisions take effect only after the King of Naples and the Duke of Modena had consented to it. That a commercial union would foster political friendliness, and help the national spirit, was inevitable, — are not hostile tariffs still one of the chief causes of international strife? — but though the League existed on paper, it stuck there, like the projected railways and other promised blessings.

[1] Minghetti, i, 295-303.

These changes at Rome had a tremendous influence in the other Italian States. Pius's name became the watchword of the Liberals, who commended his example to their own princes. If he, the head of the most conservative institution on earth, and the supreme judge of right and wrong among men, deemed it prudent and just to listen to his people's wishes, surely no other ruler could refuse to do likewise. The moral effect of having the Pope — even apparently — on the side of reform could hardly be exaggerated; and the Liberals were most studious to extend it. But the Catholic princes showed that while they thought Pius a safe guide in religion, they did not trust to his infallibility in statecraft.

In Tuscany, since the death of Fossombroni, — the ninety-year-old prim little minister who invented the political maxim, "The world goes of itself,"[1] and who kept the grand duchy stationary for five-and-twenty years, — in Tuscany the government had been drifting astern. Baldasseroni, the most forcible of the Grand Duke's advisers, believed in a system of repression which should be firm and regular, and he did not disdain to employ detested agents. The police, both public and secret, swarmed everywhere. The Tuscans themselves were, on the average, the most intelligent and prosperous of the Italians, and as they had felt less than their brothers the iron hand of tyranny, so their patriotism was less passionate and less insistent. To avenge themselves on their oppressors by an epigram, to vent their discontent in a Parthian volley of ridicule, — these were the methods which their keen and agile intellect resorted to. They had a sense of humor which detected the extravagant and absurd in every cause, and withheld them from plunging with heart and soul into any cause: for zeal never thrives on humor or criticism alone. Nevertheless, forces were at work kindling earnestness and enthusiasm in the too critical

[1] "*Il mondo va da sè.*"

Tuscans. Among the nobility there was a leaven of able Liberals, of whom Gino Capponi was the venerated chief. In a constitutionally governed country, Capponi would have been a consistent but not dogged Conservative; in Tuscany, under the Grand Duke's paternalism, he was a Moderate. Second only to him in the general esteem, and superior to him in the management of practical affairs, was Baron Ricasoli, — a Puritan, strangely sprung from the worn-out soil of Catholicism, an aristocrat, who set the rights of citizenship above the privileges of his caste. Round these gathered Ridolfi, Serristori, and other nobles, and they were joined in friendship to the untitled men of letters and professional men who at that time gave lustre to Florentine society. But while moderation was the trait of the majority in this circle, and while most of them leaned towards the Neo-Guelfism which Gioberti had heralded, two of the most conspicuous Tuscan writers of the century held more radical views: Niccolini, the dramatist, believed that the Papacy was gangrened beyond hope of recovery, and that even the best of constitutional monarchies must, in the new age, yield to the republic; Giusti, the satirist, spared neither Pius nor Charles Albert, neither the Reactionists, who from their old-time queues were called *Codini*, nor the Hot-heads, who thought to usher in the millennium of independence and liberty by hurrahs and rant. Giusti's genius had first showed itself in light satires on social follies; but soon realizing that he had at his command a weapon of unexpected power, he consecrated it to the great cause of his country. Wit, pure wit, — keen and unerring, even when it seemed merely playful, — was never used more effectively; he did not slash the air, nor botch, nor wound; he always thrust straight to the heart, and his verses, passing in manuscript among his friends, — for the censor would not let thoughts with a Toledo edge slip through the press, — soon had a remarkable vogue. No other poet-satirist of the century, except Lowell, has had so deep an influence on a political movement. Giusti's poems, like Lowell's "Biglow Papers," are so saturated with the idiom of the soil as to be untranslatable; they excel in wit, as these excel in humor; but behind Lowell's stream of humor was a whole watershed of moral indignation; whereas Giusti's wit had sources less profound, but was as perfectly adapted to stir his countrymen, who had five centuries of intellectuality behind them, as Lowell's genius was to rouse his countrymen, just recoiling from straight-laced, unimaginative Puritanism.

This group, which constituted the *élite* of the Tuscan Liberals, and trusted in the slow education of public opinion rather than in the offensive warfare of the sects, would have given the Grand Duke little anxiety. It was from a different direction and by men of a bolder stripe that his repose was threatened. Montanelli perhaps better than any one else represented the patriotism of the middle classes. He was one of those men who are constant only in the zeal with which they adopt new opinions, and the frequency with which he changed his mind never made him doubt but that the latest change was final. In religion he had been a Voltairean, a St. Simonian, and now, fired by enthusiasm for Pius IX, he was a fervent Catholic. He had studied to be first a musician, and then a doctor; then he practiced law, and at the age of twenty-seven (1840) he was chosen to a professor's chair at the University of Pisa. His lectures on Commercial Law were inspired with patriotism; he exercised the widest influence over the students; he organized a secret society; he directed a clandestine press, which, despite the vigilance of the police, dropped its leaves even on the steps of the throne. Montanelli was averse from violence; he believed that by agitating persistently within legal lines, the government would be forced to concede.

In his newspaper he pleaded at first for only mild reforms, — such as the suppression of the lottery, — about which there was no dispute; then he set about replying to himself, urging that those matters were mere bagatelles compared with the great needs of Tuscany; and by this simple journalistic ruse he provoked discussion and disseminated more audacious views.

Still more advanced than Montanelli and his party was a democrat, Guerrazzi, — novelist, conspirator, disciple of Mazzini, self-willed and arbitrary, ruling men by sheer force of intellect, where Montanelli won them by his sympathetic personality and by a certain romantic charm. Guerrazzi, like Mazzini, despised the Moderates as being cowards and hypocrites and coolers of patriotic ardor; for himself, he advocated action, and as he had his headquarters at Leghorn, one of the most turbulent cities in Italy, he found a multitude ready to listen to him, and to carry out his teaching.

By petitions, by vociferation, by applause for Pius IX, by the sowing of clandestine tracts and newspapers, and by more than one street brawl at Leghorn, the various parties made the Grand Duke aware that his subjects had waked up and could be pacified only by reforms. But Leopold was a thorough paternalist, and he had, moreover, Metternich's reprimand constantly before his eyes. Nevertheless, on May 7 he deemed it wise to issue a press law in which the rigors of the censorship were somewhat slackened. The Florentines, taking their cue from the Romans, flocked that evening to the Pitti Palace, and testified their satisfaction by prolonged cheers, among which some were addressed to the Grand Duke's heir, expressing the hope that he might some day be King of *all* Italy.[1] At Leghorn there was a more disorderly celebration, accompanied by insults to the Austrian consul. Authorized newspapers at once sprang up, to instruct the

[1] *Correspondence*, i, 41.

public in the doctrines of the respective groups. The restrictions on the press "could not hinder us from saying everything, if the revolution triumphed," Montanelli remarked; "if, on the contrary, the government proved the stronger, we could say nothing, despite all the concessions. Our tactics were to take these reforms as an instalment, to praise them more than they deserved, to consider as virtually granted that which the government had no intention of granting, to strive to wring from it, in a word, all the liberty we could."[1] The scheme worked well; Leopold, having once yielded, yielded again and again. He appointed a Commission to revise the codes; he summoned the notables of Tuscany to meet at Florence in August; he meditated the creation of a Consulta. Each "instalment" was greeted with acclamations, and then the agitators cried for more until their cries sounded so much like threats that the Grand Duke, after delaying as long as he dared, heeded them. Austria's aggression at Ferrara set the Tuscans in a frenzy, — they must be prepared to defend themselves, they must have a Civic Guard. Leopold demurred, hesitated, and then consented; Metternich frowning, Palmerston approving, all Tuscany applauding.[2] From every village and commune came enthusiastic swarms to take part (September 12) in the celebration of that event, and never had Leopold been more popular than when, from the balcony of the Pitti Palace, he pointed to the Tuscan colors, and the dense multitudes below rent the air with their cheers. He had put off the Austrian uniform which he was accustomed to wear, and had put on the Tuscan, — a sign, as all believed, that he was resolved to be master instead of lackey in his own house.[3] There was a rush for enrolment in the Civic Guard; every one aspired to be a citizen soldier; the parade-grounds resounded with the commands of the

[1] Quoted by Perrens, 369.   [2] *Correspondence*, i, 145.
[3] *Ibid*, i, 135.

drill-sergeants, the streets were enlivened by the uniforms and the red-and-white cockades of the Grand Duke's volunteers. Even Giusti, poet and satirist, caught the patriotic fever and sent for four muskets with percussion caps: the old flint-lock blunderbusses would no longer do.[1] In general, the grand duchy behaved temperately with its newly-acquired privilege, — only at Leghorn did the excitement break through the bounds of order, — for all save the extreme Radicals realized the need of refraining from violent acts which might bring down upon them the white-coated regiments of Austria. The Grand Duke earned further applause by making changes in his Cabinet, where the presence of Serristori and Ridolfi seemed an indication that he would not turn back from the path of reforms.

Meanwhile the ferment had reached Lucca. Charles Louis of Bourbon, the ruler of that little duchy, was a vulgar and trifling fellow, whose character may be inferred from the fact that he took an English horse-jockey, Tom Ward, for his favorite, dubbing him baron, and appointing him chief minister. Charles Louis sneered at Pope Pius, and boastfully proclaimed that he would concede nothing to the demands of his own rabble subjects. But when, on July 7, some three thousand of these came, with resolution in their faces, to the villa where he was staying, he appeased them with promises of reform and a Civic Guard: and then he sneaked off to Modena to put his precious skin out of danger.[2] By the treaty of Vienna the Duchy of Lucca was to revert to Tuscany on the extinction of the Bourbon line or on its finding an establishment elsewhere. Maria Louisa, Duchess of Parma, was not expected to live long, and as Charles Louis had been designated to succeed her, and had no desire to return to his obstreperous Lucchese, he negotiated for the immediate transfer of Lucca to Tuscany. The bargain was

[1] Giusti: *Epistolario*, ii. 283, 298.   [2] La Farina, iii, 60-6.

made, and Leopold formally received the Lucchese under his government, to their great satisfaction. But by the terms of the same treaty, Tuscany was obliged to cede a little strip in the Lunigiana to Modena, and another patch to Parma.[1] The inhabitants of Fivizzano, the principal town in the former district, were enraged at the prospect of passing under the odious Modenese rule, which, although Francis IV, the "Butcher," had died in the previous year, was diligently perpetuated by his son, Francis V, and the Tuscans were alarmed to see their northwestern frontier left open for an Austrian invasion. There was talk of an armed resistance, there were offers of compensation in money, but the Duke of Modena, instigated by Metternich, insisted on the letter of the law, and his troops took possession of the Lunigiana. The irritation did not lessen for several months, nor was it Metternich's intention that it should lessen, his policy being to goad Italy to the point of frenzy, when he might step in with a straight-jacket.

In Piedmont half the year passed without bringing any substantial gain to the Liberals. Their disappointment was all the greater because they had convinced themselves, and were persuading their brother Italians, that Charles Albert was with them, and that destiny had at last brought to pass that happy conjunction of Liberal Pope and Liberal King under which Italy's redemption would be achieved. Pius the Banner, Charles Albert the Sword, of Italian Independence, — had not that been clearly set down in Gioberti's horoscope? And yet the perverse monarch would not move, though Fate was pointing the way, and Italy stretched out her hands to him. Words slipped from him that set patriotic heads a-throbbing, but no corresponding deeds followed; rather, deeds which seemed to reveal a heart either hopelessly wavering or profoundly insincere. Nevertheless, Charles

[1] Treaty of Vienna, §§ 101, 102.

Albert rejoiced in Pius's great popularity; his devout spirit gave thanks that the Pope, the leader of the Guelf party, had sanctioned the aspirations of those Italians who yearned for independence; but this did not deter him from prohibiting the introduction into Piedmont of newspapers which the Pope's censors authorized in Rome. Than Charles Albert no king was more honestly imbued with the doctrines of the divine right of kingship, and none felt more earnestly the responsibility laid upon him. The question of independence had, he thought, nothing to do with the question of liberty; he wished to see Italy free, but he wished also to preserve unclipped those autocratic rights with which, he believed, the welfare of the people was bound up. And behind all was that pledge, given by him nearly a quarter of a century ago, not to alter the organic institutions of his kingdom. Conscience and patriotism struggled for mastery in him, and the struggle was all the harder owing to his Hamlet nature.

He had held stanchly to his rights in the dispute with Austria over wine and salt; he had resented Metternich's attempt to lecture him concerning his attitude in Italian politics; and yet he had supplied arms and encouragement to the Sonderbund, the league of those Catholic cantons of Switzerland which, under the instigation of Metternich and the Jesuits, were endeavoring to disrupt the Swiss Confederation. The Piedmontese, less effusive than their southern neighbors, were beginning to show signs of impatience, and to adopt the noisy tactics which had proved so efficacious at Florence and Rome. The cheers for Pio Nono and Gioberti and Italy broke out in spite of the police; ladies wore white and yellow ribbons, — the Pope's colors; men wore cravats à la Mastai Ferretti, and a sprig of white and yellow flowers in their buttonholes;[1] busts of the Pope and of Gioberti were

[1] Brofferio, part iii. p. 6.

almost as common as in Tuscany and the Papal States. Tracts flew about, and among them was a satirical poem entitled "King See-Saw," which described only too faithfully Charles Albert's vacillation. It smote him with a pang of regret, for he felt that he had been misjudged, misunderstood.[1] But not till news came of the Austrian occupation of Ferrara did he flash forth the signal which the Liberals had grown weary of watching for. His offers of succor to the Pope could only be guessed at by the public; but it happened that an Agrarian Congress was in session at Casale, and that, as usual, other matters besides the cultivation of rice and the breeding of cattle engaged the gentlemen farmers. Suddenly, at one of the meetings, — suddenly and quite irrelevantly, Lanza, a physician, raised the cry, "Long live Italy!" All the delegates took up the cheer, and when their throats were tired, they indited an address to Charles Albert asking for large concessions. Thereupon Colobiano, who had presided at the meeting, sent off in alarm a report of it to the King; but Castagnetto, who was general president of the Congress, and the King's intimate friend, sent another report, in which he laid stress on the really Italian character of the demonstration. The following morning, Colobiano received a brief reply: "The promoters of disorder must be handcuffed and sent to Fenestrelle," — the nearest State prison. Castagnetto also had a letter from his sovereign, which he read before the astonished Congress. "Were I to write at length," wrote Charles Albert, "I could only repeat what I told you at Racconigi concerning the sentiments and views which must be expressed, for the present and the future. Add, only, that if ever God grant us the grace of allowing us to undertake a war of independence, it is I alone who will command the army, and that then I am resolved to do for

---

[1] This clever poem, at first attributed to Giusti, was by Domenico Carbone; it may be read in Bersezio, ii, 447.

the Guelf cause that which Schamyl is doing against the vast Russian Empire."[1]

This, the first official public utterance of Charles Albert's patriotic resolve, set the gentlemen farmers into an ecstasy of enthusiasm, and flew from town to town throughout the land. The Genoese were emboldened by it to send a deputation to Turin to petition the King for reforms, but he refused them an audience. His hot fit had been followed by the inevitable chill. To Balbo and Doria he explained that the "war of independence" which he had referred to meant a war for the preservation of Piedmont, — not for the liberation of Italy.[2] The country whose hopes were thus rebuffed became sullen, yet inclined to blame the King's ministers and courtiers rather than himself. On his birthday, crowds collected in front of the Palace and mingled their cheers for him with demands for the expulsion of the Jesuits and of the unpopular advisers. Though there was no disorder, the police rushed in and maltreated many of the shouters. Protests and appeals for redress thereupon rained on the King's table. Whether they really influenced him, or whether he had deliberately reached the conclusion that the moment had come for breaking loose from the Past, I know not; certainly he had a philosophic contempt for the favor of the populace, — "which to-day shouts *Viva*, and to-morrow *Death*," — and he saw no reason why his birthday, which had passed unacclaimed for seventeen years, should now be made a festival;[3] but the fact is that he at once removed Villamarina and Solaro della Margarita from his Cabinet. Villamarina had not been unpopular, but his reputation for Liberalism seems to have been due to the contrast between his very Moderate views and the very decided Conservatism of his colleagues, rather than to any more positive reason. With Della Marga-

[1] Beauregard: *Épilogue*, 43–4.   [2] Minghetti, i, 290.
[3] Beauregard: *Épilogue*, 50.

rita departed a typical exponent of the Old Régime, — a man made all of one piece, without streak or flaw or mortise, an honest, narrow man, and the loyalest of subjects, who looked up to his king as a divinely-appointed master, whom to serve was the first of duties, and the noblest of privileges. He no more doubted that the system he upheld was the only true one than the savage doubts that the sun rolls round the earth. To you, too, strenuous and faithful Della Margarita, latest specimen of an outworn type, we can at last do justice![1]

The dismissal of these two men, who had so long been rivals in controlling the King, gave boundless satisfaction. All Piedmont felt that it had shaken off an incubus. Soon afterward (October 30), the official journal announced that his Majesty had given his consent to a revision of the Criminal Code, to reforms in the administration of the police and fiscal departments, to improvements in the laws concerning municipalities and public meetings, and to a mitigation of the censorship, "compatible with the interests of religion, of morals, and of the regular conduct of public affairs."[2] Only promises these, but readily accepted by all the King's subjects as an earnest of performances soon to come. Turin celebrated the victory by a mighty concourse, and this time the police did not interfere with those who sang the "Hymn to Pius," or cheered for "the King of Italy," or hissed the Jesuits. Amid this multitude Charles Albert rode pensive from the Palace down the Via di Po to Valentino, his tall figure on horseback rising above the crowds on foot, who hurrahed and waved tricolor banners and tossed wreaths and flowers, while in every balcony and window were little groups of spectators, equally en-

---

[1] Della Margarita's autobiographical *Memorandum Storico-Politico* is an interesting presentation of the creed and methods of the politician of the Old Régime.

[2] L. Cappelletti: *Storia di Carlo Alberto* (Rome, 1891), 315–6.

thusiastic and equally desirous of showing their gratitude
to their king. Sober Turin had caught the hysterical
affection of the year, and Charles Albert, in spite of himself, was moved by that great spectacle of a whole people
expressing their devotion and their hopes. At Genoa,
whither he went, the demonstration was repeated. Never
before had that city, anciently republican, given a monarch so overwhelming a reception as it gave Charles Albert. Forty thousand citizens of all classes defiled before
the Palace, cheered the King and quietly dispersed; and
when, later, he rode out, unattended by police or guards,
there was the same orderliness, the same respect.[1] Yet
the thought that Genoa and Piedmont were thinking, the
desire that thrilled every heart, found utterance. "Sire,"
exclaimed a youth, who had made his way close to the
King's horse, "cross the Ticino, and we will all follow
you!"[2] A month later, when Charles Albert returned to
his capital, the Turinese had prepared to welcome him
with equal fervor; but the royal carriage was driven
through the streets at a gallop, and the disappointed people got not a nod of recognition from the King, who sat
taciturn behind the closed windows. Strange being! in-
explicable to others and a mystery to himself.

In Lombardy and Venetia, where the Italians yearned
not for reform but for freedom, there were few events to
mark the progress of the revolutionary spirit which was
manifesting itself by signs so salient elsewhere. Men
talked and plotted in secret, but the police and the reinforced army kept down any demonstrations. To cheer
for Pius IX, or to have in one's possession Tuscan or
Roman newspapers, was a criminal offense. Nevertheless, the Milanese lost no occasion, however slight, to
agitate within legal limits. They wished to celebrate
with decent honors the funeral of Cardinal Gaysrück, —

[1] *Correspondence*, i. 218.
[2] The youth was Nino Bixio; see Cesaresco: *Italian Characters*, 310.

who, though a foreigner, had been more just than most of his race to them, — but they were forbidden; and when the new Archbishop — Pius's appointee — came, they wished to welcome him, but again the government forbade. A crowd which persisted in singing the Pope's Hymn at Milan, on September 8, gave the government an excuse for violently interfering. The gendarmes laid about them with their swords; the troops were called out, and about a hundred persons were wounded, some fatally.[1] For two or three days the disorders were repeated, the authorities acting as if they were glad of the chance to show their subjects that Austria had no sentimental scruples against shedding blood, if she could not secure obedience by her ordinary methods of repression. The reputable citizens protested against this unwarranted ferocity, and called for justice: but the government, instead of punishing its bloodthirsty minions, merely released those of the populace who had been arrested and found innocent. Sullenness increased on both sides: the nobles abstained from social intercourse with their foreign masters; the middle and lower classes showed, by silence and angry looks, feelings which it would have been dangerous to utter. Great was the astonishment when Giambattista Nazzari, a lawyer and a member of the Central Congregation, — a body which was nominally authorized to suggest measures pertaining to local administration, but which had long been tongue-tied, — proposed that a committee be nominated to examine into the condition of the Lombard provinces and to report upon the prevailing discontent (December 9).[2] The Governor admonished Nazzari to withdraw his motion, but many citizens, emboldened by his courage, supported him, and Count Spaur, after having scolded Nazzari, announced that the committee would be appointed, but that it would not be allowed to discuss the cause of Lombardy's grievances.

[1] *Correspondence*, i. 140.   [2] *La Fariua*, iii, 120-1.

At Parma, where the ex-Duke of Lucca became the ruler on the death of Maria Louisa (December 18), the Austrians had full sway: even the chanting of the *Te Deum* at religious services was forbidden, lest it should have a seditious interpretation. To Modena, Austrian regiments came at Francis V's summons, and they were ready to pour into the Lunigiana.

The Venetians, who had been uniformly less demonstrative than the Milanese, saw the year go by without their giving any sign that the new sap was tingling their veins. Here and there a half-smothered cheer, or revolutionary mottoes daubed by night on the walls, afforded slight indication of the ferment below the surface. The Scientific Congress met at Venice, — as if Metternich wished to announce that he had no fears of vaporers who muddled science with politics, — and it gave the Venetian Liberals an opportunity to confer with their comrades from the West and South. Most conspicuous of the delegates was Charles Bonaparte, Prince of Canino, a clever-witted, round-bellied, theatrical member of the House of Bonaparte, whose untruthfulness had become proverbial at Rome, — where a particularly stiff lie was called a *caninata*, — and whose love of creating a sensation kept him constantly in the public eye.[1] To Venice he came, wearing the uniform of a plain soldier of the Roman Civic Guard, while his secretary appeared in a captain's regimentals; and not content with calling upon the Austrian governor in this guise, he mounted a table at one of the cafés and harangued an amused audience on the prospect of Italy's speedy regeneration. He succeeded in making a stir, but he had no chance to repeat it, as the Austrian police escorted him across the frontier within forty-eight hours. Only one other event, at the close of the year, deserves mention. Daniel Manin, a

---

[1] Minghetti, i, 203–4; T. A. Trollope: *Tuscany in 1849 and in 1859* (London, 1859), 71.

lawyer who had for some time endeavored to assail the
Austrian government by all lawful means, proposed that
the Venetian Congregation should imitate the Lombard,
and request the appointment of a committee to investigate the existing causes of complaint. Like Nazzari at
Milan, his purpose was to show the world that Austria
was deaf to reasonable petitions, and that she dared not
carry into effect the very laws which she spread upon her
statute-books.

While the Central and Northern Italians were thus
advancing, often boisterous, but for the most part not
violent in their methods, the people of the Two Sicilies,
exasperated beyond endurance by Ferdinand's brutal
regimen, broke out into active insurrection. The incendiary doctrines of Mazzini had greater power in the South
than elsewhere in Italy, and the chronic lawlessness of
the administration in the provinces, coupled with the
fiery character of both Neapolitans and Sicilians, made it
easy for the conspirators to find agents willing to obey
them. The advocates of legal agitation did, indeed,
strive to restrain the more turbulent from an untimely
uprising, and in the vigorous *Protest* by Settembrini,
they announced to Europe the nature of the abuses under
which they groaned and against which they appealed for
redress. But neither written protests nor moderate counsels prevailed over the party of action. On September 1
a dash was made to seize the officers of the garrison at
Messina while they were at dinner; the attempt failed,
but the insurgents captured the town and held it for
nearly a week. Then reinforcements arrived, and the
revolt was put down with swift and indiscriminate vengeance: the ringleaders who were captured were tortured
and executed; those who escaped had a price set upon
their heads, — 1,000 ducats apiece if taken alive, 300 ducats if killed. Simultaneously, another band seized Reggio across the Straits, only to be dispersed and punished

when the royal troops recovered from their surprise. Among the victims of this second enterprise was Giandomenico Romeo, one of a family which gave many martyrs to the Italian cause: his head was chopped off and displayed as a warning to the Calabrian peasantry.[1] At Naples, the police arrested many leading citizens on suspicion; in the congested districts, military assizes dispatched their bloody work without hesitation. Yet so strong was the feeling that the day of redemption from bondage was near at hand that the Moderates could not be discouraged by imprisonment, nor the Radicals frightened by violence. One and all, they remembered Romeo's last message: "If I die be not disheartened, but go straight ahead;" one and all, they redoubled their various forms of agitation.

King Ferdinand, whose attitude had been satirized by the Messinese when they stuffed tow into the ears of his statue and wrote, "He will not hear," on a placard beneath, fumed at his ministers for their incapacity. "It is your duty to suppress these disorders, now," he had said as long ago as midsummer to the Minister of Police. "If I have to interfere," he added, "I need only sign my name and 20,000 Austrian troops are at my disposal."[2] He cursed the "wretched little priest" (*pretarello*) who had stirred up the Italian wasps'-nest by the reforms at Rome: let not the Neapolitans flatter themselves that their king would "imitate any political dandy who happened to be in the fashion."[3] Jesuits circulated expressions abusive both of Pius's intelligence and of his orthodoxy. Cheers for the King were as rigidly prohibited as were cheers for the Pope or Italy or the Customs League. One demonstration of this kind before the Royal Palace was hushed by the bayonets of the Guard.[4] Ferdinand amused himself by watching, spy-glass in

[1] La Farina, iii, 73; Settembrini, i, 231-4.
[2] *Correspondence*, i, 76. [3] Settembrini, i, 226. [4] Perrens, 425.

hand, from his terrace, the blacksmiths riveting fetters on the ankles of political suspects at the Wet Dock on the shore, and as an attendant named the prisoners, the King would point them out to the Crown Prince at his side.[1] Nevertheless, Ferdinand, in spite of his police and troopers, in spite of his wolfish bravado, felt no security: he, too, knew that the day of reckoning was at hand, but Bourbon-like he persisted in those iniquities which were hastening that day's approach.

As 1847 closed, every patriotic heart in Italy had better reason to be hopeful than it had had for over thirty years. Public opinion become articulate — the campaign by acclamation — the tightened grip of Austria in the North, not less than the barbarities of the Bourbons in the South, the plots of Gregorians, not less than the plots of Mazzinians — the insinuations and intrigues of the Jesuits, as well as the open preaching of the Moderates, — all had contributed to make the issue plain and to hurry on the crisis. "Out with the Barbarians! Death to the Austrians!" In that battle-cry was summed up the one purpose on which Liberals of every color agreed; on all else they were confused, discordant. And from Vienna came Metternich's counter-cry, "The Emperor does not intend to lose his Italian possessions."

We have seen by what means, fair and foul, the Chancellor prepared first to divert the revolutionary current, and then, diversion being impossible, to raise bulwarks to resist its onset. Radetzky, the grim, eighty-year-old marshal, still hungry for war, posts his reinforcements in the strongholds and along the frontiers. Count Ficquelmont, a diplomatist trained by Metternich, makes a last trial, from Milan, of the weapons of craft. But, on the other hand, the forces of Liberalism are quick to discern rosy portents all along the horizon. Lord Minto, Palmerston's agent, passes from city to city bearing mes-

[1] La Farina, iii, 73.

sages of sympathy to the people, and warnings to the rulers who would disregard the handwriting on the wall. D'Azeglio is everywhere busy, urging the Liberals to be prudent, and telling the princes to be quick to grant what will otherwise soon be wrested from them. For the first time in modern history the name of a pope has become the watchword of the party of Progress, and the Catholics of Naples and of Lombardy are punished for pronouncing it. Is the world mad? Are these paradoxes realities, or but delusions as vivid and as fleeting as the phantasmagoria of a dream? Only yesterday, Metternichism and Papalism seemed as immovable as Teneriffe or Atlas; to-day they are visibly slipping, melting; by to-morrow they may have passed like an exhalation. To-morrow? If the very foundations of the Old Régime can thus crumble and dissolve, if flint and steel fade thus before an impalpable Spirit, will earth itself not vanish, a puffed-out bubble, into Infinity, ere to-morrow break? The visitor to Niagara should go first to the little wedge of rock whence he can see the Rapids — an avalanche of water, a mile-broad torrent — sweeping towards him. Here and there the stream chafes upon a resisting boulder, or foams and eddies round a half-sunken reef; but these are mere points, soon unobserved, as the eye, bewildered, scans the breadth and volume of that mighty flood. The myriad separate parts of that spectacle produce at last one impression, — the impression of Force, immeasurable, swift-rushing, and irresistible. And above the noise of the hurrying, desperate waters, there rises, awful, — like the voice of Doom, — the distant roar of the Falls. The year 1847 was for Italy and Europe as the Rapids of Niagara, — a year in which events served only to mark the swiftness with which the political stream was plunging headlong to the brink of an abyss.

CHAPTER IV.

THE SHOWER OF CONSTITUTIONS, — JANUARY–MARCH, 1848.

HITHERTO in this history, we have had to deal chiefly with symptoms; henceforth we shall follow the swift torrent of events. To the decades of clandestine plotting succeeded the years of acclamations and loud-voiced demands, which secured, at least on paper, many superficial reforms. But the passions of a whole people, kindled slowly during more than thirty years, and fixed at last on the attainment of a great object, were not to effervesce in mere noise: after the victory of tongues the Italians must win the victory of arms. For of what use is it to a man to be allowed to say what he chooses, if he be forbidden to do what he chooses? This latter right depends, as the world is constituted, not on the tongue's skill, but on the body's strength.

From Sicily, the land of immemorial participation in the mighty currents of ancient and modern history, came the first decisive deed of the revolutions of 1848. On January 9 the walls of Palermo were placarded with an address stating that the time for prayers and protests had gone by, and that at dawn on January 12 would begin the glorious epoch of universal regeneration, in which reforms adapted to the century and willed by Europe, by Italy, by Pius, would be established. Union and order, respect for property, — robbery to be declared treason to the patriotic cause, and punished as such, — these the simple admonitions of the manifesto; these, and a phrase worth pondering: "The uniting of the peoples is the downfall of the kings."[1] This declaration of war — the work, it seems, of a youth named Bagnasco, and not of any revolutionary committee, it not being the fashion for conspirators to give notice of their intentions — caused surprise among the Royal officials and curiosity among the citizens. When the 12th broke, except for the placing of extra guards in the quarters where disorders were feared, the city wore its usual holiday aspect, this being the King's birthday. Great crowds were in the streets, partly to celebrate the festival and partly to see what would come of the singular announcement. No band of liberators appearing, however, a young man named Buscemi drew from under his cloak a gun, and brandishing it in the air, shouted, "To arms! to arms!" The crowd applauded, and other armed men hurried to the spot, where Abbé Ragona and a priest, Venuti, were exhorting the people to rise in God's name. La Masa, a well-known Liberal, improvised a tricolor flag by tying red, white, and green handkerchiefs on a stick, and tricolor cockades sprouted as if by magic on the hats of the little company which was to carry out the purpose of the manifesto. Presently the bells of the Church of St. Ursula rang out a tocsin, and the bells of the Convent of Gangia replied. The excitement grew. Knots of insurgents collected and marched cheering through the streets, preceded by a vanguard of singing and frolicsome small boys, — the whirl of dust before the tempest, — while from windows and balconies women in holiday garb waved encouragement. The cannon of Castellamare were firing a royal salute and the troops were drawn up in the forts and barracks, but not a battalion moved to check the incipient rebellion. Perhaps the soldiers remembered the punishment their predecessors had received in the narrow streets of the city in 1820, or perhaps their commanders were stricken with that fit of indecision which

[1] Text in *Ruggiero Settimo e la Sicilia* (Palermo, 1848), 1.

so often palsied the Bourbons and their underlings at a critical moment. The vast majority of the citizens held aloof in suspense; tradesmen closed their shops to prevent robbery, and left the streets in possession of the most daring or the most inquisitive. There was a cry for leaders, a demand for arms, from those who were eager to begin the fray; but in the absence of the former, the most vigorous men who happened to be on the spot assumed the leadership, and each man took whatever weapon — pistol, musket, or dagger — he could find. The engagement that day was limited to encounters between the bands of insurgents and the squads which patrolled the streets, and resulted in the killing of only two of the revolutionists and ten Royalists. But the moral gain for the revolutionists was out of all proportion to their number: when night fell they had not been suppressed, — that was the crucial fact, — and during the night they were reinforced by crowds from the city and the surrounding country. In order to give their movement a head and organization, La Masa, who had hitherto been the most active in directing the spontaneous outburst, proposed that four committees be formed and that they be filled by citizens of approved patriotism and influence. Accordingly, on January 14, by which time the revolution had shown that it had vitality, a committee to superintend the public stores, with Marquis Spedalotto, the Prætor[1] of Palermo, at its head, was organized; a second, for war, had the Prince of Pantelleria for its president; a third, for finance, Marquis Rudinì; and a fourth, which supervised proclamations and announcements, Admiral Ruggiero Settimo.

From barely fifty insurgents provided with firearms on January 12, the number swelled to several thousands in a few days, and from the Old Market-place, where the little band had first intrenched itself, it soon got pos-

[1] The Palermitans called their mayor 'prætor.'

session of nearly all the interior of the city; but the Royalists still held the Royal Palace, many of the public buildings, and most of the gates, besides, of course, the fortifications. For two days General de Majo, the Lieutenant-Governor, bombarded the town from Castellamare, until the foreign consuls protested against this barbarity and obliged him to desist. Then the Count of Aquila, the King's brother, was dispatched from Naples with nine men-of-war and five thousand troops, commanded by General de Sauget, to restore order, but the citizens would not even listen to propositions for a truce. A few days later came four decrees, signed by the King on January 18, in which amnesty was promised, larger power was granted to the Sicilian Consulta, and the Count of Aquila was nominated Governor of the Island. But the insurgents, though hard pressed for munitions, replied, through their Prætor, "that they would not lay down arms nor suspend hostilities until Sicily, reunited in a general parliament at Palermo, should adapt, according to the needs of the time, the Constitution which she had possessed for many centuries, which under the influence of Great Britain was remodeled in 1812, and was implicitly confirmed by the royal decree of December 11, 1816."[1] The bombardment was renewed, but the Palermitans, goaded to desperation, made such a show of strength that De Majo lost heart, and having handed over his authority to General de Sauget, he sailed away to Naples. From that moment the King's cause was lost. The insurgents took and looted the Royal Palace, not so much for the sake of plunder as to wreak their hatred on objects belonging to the King; they captured the Bank, leaving its treasure in the hands of the Finance Committee; they carried the outposts, and laid siege to the garrison in Castellamare. De Sauget, though he had been secretly bidden by Fer-

[1] *Ruggiero Settimo*, 16.

dinand to raze Palermo to the ground, and plant a garden on its site, if he could not otherwise bring the rebels to submission, deemed it hopeless to prolong the conflict, and withdrawing his troops by night, he embarked with them at a little port several leagues up the coast (January 31). Before his departure he let loose the convicts from the prisons, — as a cuttlefish covers his retreat under a murk of sepia, — and destroyed what material of war, including many cavalry horses, he could not take with him.[1] For the second time Palermo was her own mistress. She had liberated herself after a gallant struggle, marked, on the whole, by admirable self-control. Excesses there were of course, but chiefly excesses against those of the police and officials whose previous cruelty had enraged the people beyond endurance. The Royalists, on the other hand, were charged with many atrocious acts, hard now to verify or believe, though they are attested by English witnesses as well as by the Sicilians. Especially would we discredit the story that one hundred and thirty prisoners — or convicts, it matters not which — were smothered in a pen, whether their death was due to the Black-Hole dimensions of that place or to the fumes of burning brimstone dropped on them from above. But as the Bourbons and their agents had, during half a century, shrunk from no atrocity, so the presumption is against them in the case of this crime too.[2]

While Palermo, and indeed all Sicily, — for the other towns followed the example of the capital, and revolted, — was winning her freedom, great was the consternation of the King. He sent transports loaded with troops and provisions, and generals armed with authority to exterminate the rebels. He received messages that Palermo

[1] La Farina: *Storia d' Italia*, iii. 126–38; also his *Rivoluzione Siciliana*, i, 25–54; for documents consult *Ruggiero Settimo*, and La Masa's *Rivoluzione Siciliana*.
[2] La Farina, iii, 139.

and Messina had been bombarded,— a practice which erelong earned for Ferdinand the nickname "King Bomba" by which he is best known in history, — and yet neither the telegraph nor messenger brought him word that the rebellion was put down. The news of the revolutionists' successes in Sicily gave the Neapolitans courage. The conspirators in Naples, who had been forestalled by their colleagues in Palermo, prepared for an immediate outbreak. Salerno and the district of the Cilento raised the tricolor flag and worsted the Royal troops. Ferdinand, thoroughly alarmed, turned to Austria, the last resort of sinking despots. The Austrian minister promised him as many regiments as he needed, but when Ludolf, Ferdinand's agent at Rome, asked the Secretary of State whether the Austrian troops might cross the Papal States, Ferretti replied that he would himself go to the frontier and resist their passage by all the means in his power.[1] Then Bomba issued the decrees of January 18, according concessions which, a few weeks before, might have appeased the greedy clamorers, but which were now received with murmurs and with demands for a constitution. He released the prominent Liberals who had been locked up on suspicion in December, but this only seemed to the party of revolution a sign of weakness, and restored to them leaders of prudence and sagacity. The Royal troops could not be depended upon; even the Commander of the Castle of St. Elmo informed the King that he would not bombard Naples though the worst befell. Bomba and his Cabinet and his Court realized that the day of bullying and bravado had set; but Delcaretto, the minister who had for nearly twenty years held the tiller of government and made himself hateful by his mercilessness, thought to save himself in the impending wreck by urging the King to grant a constitution of which he might claim the credit. His rivals in the Cab-

[1] Bianchi, v, 88.

inet, however, checkmated him, as he had checkmated his rival, Intonti, seventeen years before, and Bomba had no intention that his whilom favorite should reap whatever popularity the granting of a constitution might ripen. Delcarretto was summoned to the Palace, where, instead of the King, General Filangieri received him with pistol cocked, and told him that by the King's command he must embark immediately for foreign parts. A steamer was ready in the harbor, and the fallen minister, denied even time to bid his wife farewell, was soon hastening into exile. Neither at Leghorn nor Genoa could he land, as the inhabitants threatened to tear him in pieces, and when at length he was tossed ashore, like an infected thing at Marseilles, he was so hounded that he had to seek shelter in the obscurity of a little town in Provence. His old comrade in infamy, Monsignor Cocle, the King's confessor, was banished with similar dispatch.[1]

Bomba, having made scapegoats of the men who had best served his wishes, — Bomba, who had once declared that he had rather be a colonel in the Czar's army than rule constitutionally over his own kingdom, — now looked to the Constitution as his last hope. He was reduced to that state of fear in which he would promise anything; perhaps, too, he remembered how his grandfather found promises as easy to break as to make. He therefore signed a decree in which, after the usual make-believe that the project was most agreeable to the sovereign's will, it was announced that a constitution would be promulgated within ten days. "Don Pius IX and Charles Albert," he said to his ministers, as he laid down his pen, "have wished to throw a stick between my legs, and I throw them this beam."[2] Bomba could not forgive the rulers whose timidity or ambition had brought Italy to such a pass that the King of Naples, deprived of Aus-

[1] Nisco: *Ferdinando II* (Naples, 1890), 130-1.
[2] Settembrini, i, 251.

trian succor and surrounded by a realm in revolt, had to concede anything to the Liberals.

The decree, made public on January 29, aroused exaggerated enthusiasm. The populace, which but last week had cursed Bomba and was preparing to overthrow him, had not lungs enough to cheer him as they desired. Arches festooned with laurel and olive, the city illuminated by night, the Place of San Ferdinando in front of the Palace swarming with jubilant multitudes by day, the King himself bowing from his balcony — some thought they saw tears of joy in his eyes — or passing familiarly among his "beloved subjects" in the streets, — these were sights to cause a sober spectator to moralize on the fickleness and gullibility of the masses. Their eyes were as the eyes of those who suddenly experience religion: now they saw clearly that their gracious sovereign had all along been their best friend, that he had been yearning to grant them their wishes, and had been prevented through the opposition of wicked ministers, now happily pitchforked into space. So "Long live good King Ferdinand!" (bad King Bombarder no more), and again "Viva, Viva!" "We got out of that scrape in fine style,"[1] said this newly-revealed Trajan to his intimates, as he returned from acknowledging his people's transports. If the Neapolitans had been sufficiently calm to read the decree critically, they might have found in it inconsistencies to abate their enthusiasm. It declared, for instance, that the army and navy should be dependent, not on the ministers, who were responsible, but on the King, who was irresponsible. But they were not critical; they had the concession, — what mattered this or that phrase in it?

Ferdinand appointed a new ministry, among whom was Charles Poerio, the accepted leader of the Liberals, re-

[1] "*L'abbiamo scappata bella!*" Bomba's language was proverbially slangy.

leased from prison only ten days before, and Bozzelli, who had spent most of his manhood in exile on account of his patriotic principles. To Bozzelli was intrusted the framing of the new Constitution, which he had ready for promulgation on February 10. It was, in fact, merely a new model of the French Charter of 1830, providing for a House of Peers, chosen by the King, and a House of Commons, elected by citizens duly qualified as tax-payers. Freedom of the press, except on topics subversive to the State religion; complete amnesty for all political offenders; prohibition against hiring foreign mercenaries without the sanction of Parliament; any other form of worship than the Catholic forbidden, — these were the prominent outlines of Ferdinand's compact with his people. The King, not content with having a *Te Deum* sung in honor of his bounty, gave permission, a few days later, to tie tricolor ribbons above the red banner of Naples. The popular hysterics continued. Strangers embraced each other in the street, muttering the magic word "Constitution." Boys shouted, men shouted and chattered. Few of Naples's hundred thousand lazzaroni knew what this strange thing really was, whether it would raise the dead and heal the sick, or merely put coppers into empty pockets and dinner into empty stomachs; but it must be something good, since so many learned and noble signors had suffered death or the galleys for merely asking for it; and the King must now be blessed and cheered for granting it. Nor did Ferdinand himself shrink from repeating each scene in the drama of the Perfidious King as first played by his grandfather. On February 24, in the Church of St. Francis of Paul, he took oath[1] on the Holy Gospels to abide by and defend the Constitution, and though the multitude applauded, a remnant who had listened to a similar ceremony twenty-eight years before recalled Machiavelli's

---

[1] The oath is given by Nisco, 141.

maxim that a show of religion is the most necessary of all a tyrant's equipments, because the "plebs are always deceived by appearances."[1] Nevertheless, for the present all was hope and exuberance at Naples; the new ministry and their subordinates went to work vigorously, Parliament was convened for May 1, and Ferdinand enjoyed such popularity, that many discussed quite seriously the probability of his being after all the long-sought champion of Italian independence.

The news of the revolution at Palermo had hardly had time to astonish and delight the Central and Northern Italians before the still more astonishing announcement came that Bomba, the implacable and detested Bomba, had granted at one stroke a constitution to his people, and that they were idolizing him therefor. The impetus given by this news to the revolutionary movement cannot be described. Last month men clamored for reforms; now they demanded a constitution. In Tuscany, the more violent agitators had already forced a crisis. Guerrazzi, accusing the government of treachery in giving up Pontremoli to the Duke of Parma, goaded on the boisterous Livornese to arm and rise against an imminent invasion of the Austrians. Ridolfi, the Prime Minister, very properly had Guerrazzi arrested and sent for safekeeping to Porto Ferrajo. But the discontent grew. The Tuscans were too excited to recognize that it was the duty of a Liberal minister to preserve order by locking up a patriotic leader; they complained that Ridolfi and his colleagues were as slow as the Reactionists themselves. At Florence, they celebrated the news from the South by a service in the Cathedral; they congratulated the Sicilians, but not Bomba's ambassador; and they beset the Grand Duke, night and day, with demands for a constitution. On January 31 he announced his intention of introducing larger reforms in the administration; but it

[1] *Il Principe*, chap. 18.

was too late for half measures. The rumble of revolution waxed louder, and on February 11 he expressed the deep satisfaction he felt in being able at last to realize a thought he had long cherished. Tuscany should have a representative government, and have it immediately. Six days later (February 17) the Constitution was published, — an improvement over the Neapolitan in that it established religious toleration, and freedom in commerce and industry. So the Grand Duke swam in a flood of popularity.

The Romans soon discovered that, although they had a Consulta composed of able and willing men, and although these were endeavoring by every legal means to exert a greater influence than had formally been conferred upon them, the expected benefits did not come. In the provinces, political assassinations and disorders were frequent: at the capital, Mazzinians were inoculating the masses with the virus of rebellion, and the Reactionists were agitating the Pope. On New Year's day, the populace thought to make one of its customary demonstrations before the Quirinal, but it was surprised and angered to see the streets lined with extra forces of policemen, and to hear that extra regiments were drawn up at the Palace. A riot seemed inevitable. Prince Corsini, the Senator of Rome, hurried to the Quirinal and told Pius of the danger: the unwelcome forces were recalled, and the Prince, adjuring the multitude to be calm, explained that the appearance of the military had been a mistake and had no hostile significance. Pacified but still disappointed, the crowds sent up a cheer for "Pius IX *alone*."[1] Pius shifted the odium from himself, who had given the order, to two of his police officials, whom he dismissed. The following day, when the Pope drove through the Piazza del Popolo the masses greeted him with the old-time enthusiasm, and Ciceruacchio jumped

[1] *Correspondence*, ii, 30.

up behind the pontifical coach, and there, where the footmen usually stood and held on by straps, he brandished a banner on which was the motto, "Holy Father! Confide in the People." Pius, betwixt fear and exasperation, smiled the benignant smile, and after many exhortatory gestures he succeeded in inducing the crowd to make a channel for his vehicle, and, when he reached the Quirinal, to disperse. But evidently the town was now at the mercy of any spark. When news came that the Austrians had massacred some Lombards, the Romans held funeral ceremonies and listened to eulogies of the slain. Gavazzi, a Barnabite friar, inflamed one congregation by a fervent appeal for war. The Consulta urged upon the Pope and his ministers the need of organizing an army to repel the possible invasion of the Austrians, and, after delays, it was decided to request the King of Piedmont to send some officer fitted for this work. Ferretti, to whom the duties of Chief Secretary had become intolerable, resigned; Bofondi succeeded him. But still no progress was visible. And indeed, what progress was possible in such a confused administration? The Consulta, which alone had vigor and clear-sightedness, was irresponsible; the Cardinals were reluctant and numbed by the inertia of a tradition which paralyzed all movement; the ministers were but heads of departments, impotent to originate legislation without the sanction of the Pope; the Pope himself was vacillating and superstitious.

And now demands for arms mingled with demands for a secular ministry and — Sicily and Naples having given the word — for a constitution. A layman, Prince Gabrielli, became Minister of War, — an insignificant fact so far as the man himself was concerned, but significant historically, because he was the first layman admitted into the Pope's Cabinet. On February 8 a great demonstration nearly resulted in a riot, the populace having been maddened by the report that the ministers were opposing the Consulta's efforts at an armament. Again the aged Prince Corsini hurries to the Quirinal and informs the Pope of the threatened cloud-burst, and again he is instructed to return and soothe the mob with promises of a new ministry. Ciceruacchio stands beside the Prince on the balcony of the Corsini Palace and joins his exhortations for order.[1] The mob stays its hand, but insists that the ministers shall be laymen, and it cries, "Death to the Jesuits."

Two days later, Pius issued a proclamation in which, amid a mist of religious generalizations, he announced that he had decided to augment the lay party in the Cabinet. He extolled Faith as the most precious gift of the Italians, and prayed God to bless Italy. Indescribable the delirium of joy which these words provoked. All Rome poured into the Quirinal Square, acclaiming and praising their benefactor, until he appeared. Then complete silence fell over the vast concourse, and the Pope spoke. "Before the benediction of God descends upon you, upon the rest of my State, and, I repeat, upon all Italy, I pray that you may all be harmonious, that you may keep that faith which you have promised to the Pontiff." Suddenly a shout like thunder went up. "Yes, we swear!" "I warn you, however," Pius continued, "that certain cries, which are not of the people but of a few, must not be raised, and that there must not be made to me demands contrary to the sanctity of the Church, that I cannot, I ought not, I will not admit. On this condition, with all my soul I bless you. O great God, bless Italy!" Filled with awe by the earnestness of the Pope's words, the multitude slowly broke up. "The Pope has tried an heroic remedy," said Pellegrino Rossi to Minghetti, as they turned from this scene, "and this time it will not fail him; but woe to him if he should

[1] La Farina, iii, 171.

attempt to speak to the people again; all his prestige would be lost."[1]

On February 12 the new ministers were announced, — Pasolini, Sturbinetti, and Prince Gaetani being the lay members of it whose appointment gratified the people. At the same time a commission, composed wholly of ecclesiastics, was nominated to deliberate upon further reforms. But the demands for a constitution could not be silenced. Every post brought tidings that in Naples, in Tuscany, in Piedmont, the Absolutist rulers had given way, that the government was passing into the hands of the people, and that the National Spirit, aroused at last and allowed free expansion, was getting control. The news of the French Revolution of February 24 gave the final sanction to the Liberal movement, for France since 1789 had been looked up to in Europe as the great leader in revolutionary politics. The initiative belonged to her; she had again exercised it, and her example would shake the Continent. Those princes who had already made concessions could now congratulate themselves on their promptness; they might hope to ride out the gale under a lee shore, while those who had stubbornly disregarded the portents of the past year would be caught with all canvas spread, and swept into the open, merciless sea. Pius himself was too shallow a politician to sound the meaning of the revolt in Paris. He was not sorry to be rid of Louis Philippe and Guizot, who had bothered him by their half-concealed opposition: he expected that the Republic would be more docile in matters of religion; he wept when he heard that the Parisian populace had paused for a moment in its attack on the Tuileries, to kneel before a crucifix.[2] To his narrow, parish-priest mind, this seemed more important than the chasing out of the King and the shattering of the monarchy. But he delayed no longer in granting to his subjects the Constitutional gov-

[1] Minghetti, i, 327.   [2] Minghetti, i, 329.

ernment which they were prepared to seize by force. And in order, as he said, that this act might appear spontaneous on his part, the Constitution was framed entirely by ecclesiastics, no layman being consulted.

Even before the publication of the new Statute, Pius appointed (March 10) another ministry, of men who were kept in the dark as to the nature of the government they were to uphold. Of the new members, Marco Minghetti of Bologna, though the youngest, was the ablest; Recchi had the longest record of honorable service in the Liberal Cause; Cardinal Mezzofanti was renowned throughout the world as a linguist who spoke forty tongues, but his learning in no wise corresponded to his special gift, and he lacked both experience and energy in public affairs; Galletti was one of those cork-like politicians who float in tempestuous crises when men of more weight sink. On March 14 the Constitution was promulgated, accompanied by a warning from Pius that he reserved to himself the final decision in the concerns of the government, whether these were temporal or spiritual or mixed. The College of Cardinals formed the Senate; a High Council and a Council of Deputies composed the Parliament, the former being appointed for life by the sovereign, the latter being elected for four years, or until the dissolution of the Chamber; measures having been proposed and passed by the two Councils were referred to a secret Consistory of the Cardinals, at which the Pope gave or refused his sanction to them. These were the more noteworthy provisions of the Papal Constitution; but as if they did not sufficiently preserve the theocratic character of the government, the following prohibitions were added: "The Councils may never propose any law that (1) regards ecclesiastical or mixed affairs, or that (2) is contrary to the canons or discipline of the Church, or that (3) tends to vary or modify the present Statute;" and they were forbidden to discuss the diplomatic-religious relations of the Holy See with foreign countries.¹

No better criticism can be passed on this instrument, which Europe hailed as an indication of Pius's Liberalism, than was passed by La Farina. "In Rome," he said, "betrothals, marriage, testamentary acts, education, public charity, ecclesiastical tribunals, religious corporations, ecclesiastical property, and a hundred other matters are all either ecclesiastical or mixed, so that by splitting hairs a little, as the Roman lawyers are wont to do, there was possible no civil law which might not fall within the terms of the prohibition."² Nevertheless, Pius's subjects accepted the Constitution in good faith, and celebrated its promulgation in the usual fashion. They were as light-hearted as collegians at receiving their parchment diploma, which is really but a little piece of sheepskin engrossed with high-sounding words, and may or may not have a bearing on their future career. Was it merely by chance that Pius chose the day on which the Statute was made public for issuing another proclamation against those who had been molesting the Jesuits or calling for their expulsion? "We invite you all, and warn you," he said, "to respect and never to provoke the terrible anathema of an angry God, who would fulminate His holy vengeance against the assailants of His anointed."³ Surely it was not Pius's fault if his subjects failed to comprehend that the churchman in him lay deeper than the patriot or the reformer.

Meanwhile the Piedmontese were watching with intense interest the transformation going on to the south of them. The concessions they had secured on October 30, 1847, operated but slowly, and it was evident that their utmost benefit could not long slake the popular thirst. The modification of the censorship allowed public

---

¹ Text of the Statute in Farini, i, 347-62.
² La Farina, iii, 195.   ³ *Ibid*, 196.

THE SHOWER OF CONSTITUTIONS. 93

opinion to express itself through its natural organ, the newspapers, of which the *Risorgimento*, founded at Turin by Count Camillo Cavour, Cesare Balbo, D'Azeglio, and other Moderate Liberals, at once took the lead.[1] In the political clubs and in informal gatherings, the agitation was kept up. Public dinners, another modern institution for promoting any object, from a revolution to a lying-in hospital, had also come into fashion. Cobden, the English apostle of commercial emancipation, had been dined on his recent tour in Italy, by the prominent Liberals in each city; at Rome, Ciceruacchio and Prince Borghese had touched elbows at the same banquet. Leaders from different parts of the Peninsula were constantly interchanging ideas and hopes. To Piedmont all were looking, and yet Piedmont seemed, at the beginning of 1848, to have fallen into one of her periodic torpors.

Not to the country itself, however, but to the King was this apparent inertness due. Charles Albert was in the coils of one of those physical and moral crises to which he had been subject since his youth. His long régime of asceticism, his fasts and vigils, his hair shirt and habitual loss of sleep, had made him a prematurely old man. His tall and emaciated figure stooped in spite of his effort to stand with a soldier's erectness; his hair and moustache were white; his cheeks, haggard and pale, wore a melancholy deeper than any physical cause, deep as his soul itself. And while his confessor urged him to persevere in the ascetic practices, his physicians bled him to relieve the ills which inevitably ensued from his hermit life. Not unfounded was the suspicion that both the religious and the medical advisers were in league throughout

[1] Other influential journals were the *Messagiere Torinese*, edited by the fiery Democrat, Brofferio; the *Concordia*, in which Valerio set forth Giobertian doctrine; the *Monarcato* (subsequently called the *Costituzionale*) of James Durando.

Charles Albert's career to keep him in so morbid a physical state that he should be incapable of long-continued or of decisive action:[1] if ever a ruler were the victim of pathological torture, that ruler was Charles Albert. Yet now, above all times, strength of body and firmness of will were demanded of him.

The reports from Lombardy, where Radetzky's soldiers were cutting the Milanese to pieces, and the appearance of Austrian reinforcements along the Piedmontese frontiers, set Charles Albert's people in commotion. They were eager that their government should make reprisals; should show its sympathy for the outraged Lombards; should unsheathe the sword and lead Italy against her oppressors. But Charles Albert did not move, and so fixed was their trust in his honor that the Piedmontese attributed his immovableness not to lack of sympathy, but to a desire to save his capital from the possible disasters of a premature campaign. The grateful Turinese thereupon presented to the sovereign an address in which one and all, rich and poor, they begged him to use their fortunes and their lives for the honor of their country. The King, deeply touched by this evidence of loyalty and devotion, spoke freely to Robert d' Azeglio, who lay the popular message before him. Italy, he said, was still politically disunited. There was but one army, the Piedmontese, which though brave was too small to cope single-handed with Austria. The Liberals, so prompt to promise and so slow to perform, were actually the greatest danger to the Italian cause. "We need soldiers and not lawyers to conduct our great enterprise aright," said the solemn King. "Infinite, therefore, would be the danger of a constitution which, handing over the tribune to the deputies, would enfeeble the force of the government, diminish the discipline in the army, and by their indiscretion add to the difficul-

[1] Cappelletti, 317-9.

ties, already overwhelming, of the command. Remember, Marquis d'Azeglio," he said, with still greater earnestness, in concluding the interview, "that I, like you, desire the emancipation of Italy, and remember that on that account I will never give a constitution to my people."[1]

But the time had come when the constitutional agitation in Piedmont, though retarded for a few weeks by the King's resistance, could not permanently be checked. Especially in Genoa, where the doctrines of Mazzini on the one hand and those of Gioberti on the other had numerous and very active disciples, the popular clamor for reforms, and a Civic Guard, and against the Jesuits became ominous. The discovery, real or pretended, of a secret correspondence between the Jesuits and Austria aroused so much anger, that a deputation of citizens hurried to Turin to convince Charles Albert that, unless concessions were speedily made, grave trouble could not long be avoided. The Moderates at Turin, deeming the moment propitious for expressing their own wishes, received the Genoese deputation at a meeting in which, after many suggestions had been made, Count Cavour bluntly asked, "Why go on and on begging for provisions which conclude little or nothing? I propose that we implore from our magnanimous sovereign the greatest boon of a public discussion before the country, — a discussion in which shall be represented all the opinions, all the interests, all the needs, of the Nation. I propose that we demand the Constitution."[2] Cavour's proposition startled the meeting, which, after long debate that day (January 7) and the next, decided that it was too bold to adopt, and as a petition to have weight with the King must be unanimous, none was then framed. The Genoese envoys, denied an audience at the Palace, had to return unsatisfied

[1] Beauregard, *Épilogue*, 79.
[2] Chiala: *Lettere di Cavour* (Turin, 1883), i, introduction, p. cxx.

to their turbulent city. But the events of each day justified Cavour's boldness; the government felt that it had no solid backing of any kind, and so was timorous and ineffectual; the agitation gathered force as it went, threatening in Genoa, arguing in Turin. News of Austrian recrudescence in Lombardy, of the Sicilian revolution, of Bomba's consent to a statute, fell like the blows which knock away the last shoring from a ship about to be launched.

By the beginning of February, Charles Albert himself realized that he could no longer delay. Piedmont and Italy were waiting for his decision; the British minister, Mr. Abercromby, was warning him that his only chance of safety lay in joining the popular movement, which if longer thwarted would break into civil war; his own advisers were beginning to whisper the word Constitution which so displeased him. On February 5 the Municipal Council of Turin, a body of eminent and temperate citizens, resolved, by a vote of 36 to 12, to petition the King to grant immediately a constitution and to authorize the organization of a Civic Guard.[1] But already, on February 3, Charles Albert had summoned a secret session of the Council of State. For weeks past he had been wrestling with his conscience, which told him that if he granted a constitution he would both break the pledge signed by him twenty-four years before, and transmit to the future kings of Piedmont a diminished authority. He shrank from both, as from acts which would stain his honor. He had asked Balbo the mysterious question, "What account ought a Christian to make of an engagement which for him has the validity of an oath?" and Balbo, not knowing the nature of the problem which was tearing the King's soul, had nothing to reply. He even contemplated abdication, but this last resort, while it would technically absolve him from his pledge, would

[1] *Correspondence*, etc., ii, 58.

throw upon his successor, Victor Emanuel, the burden of a crisis for which he was not responsible. Perplexed and wearied by his inward conflict, Charles Albert therefore summoned his Council to allay his doubts. One by one the members pronounced their views in favor of a constitution. The Foreign Secretary declared that the Liberal movement in Piedmont could now be checked only by an appeal to foreign intervention; the Minister of War believed that though the army should remain loyal and should put down the present turmoil, a terrible reaction would thereupon ensue; Marquis Alfieri emphasized the need of confronting the extravagant schemes bred by the popular imagination by an exact statement of the interests of the country. But the King was not yet convinced: his counselors had justified the Constitution as a political necessity, they had not quieted his conscience.

The next day he sent for Monsignor d'Angennes, Archbishop of Vercelli, and unbosomed his scruples. Was it not plain, he asked, that Providence had brought to pass the day when, for the good of his people and the salvation of his honor, he ought to abdicate? Monsignor d'Angennes, at once a sensible and pious man, replied that, on the contrary, it was the King's duty to stand by the post where God had placed him, and to protect the faith of his subjects. But the pledge of 1824, the oath he had solemnly taken never to alter the organic system of government in Piedmont, — how could he disregard that without incurring the rebuke of his conscience and the scorn of the world? Again the Archbishop uttered the needed rational word. "Your first duty," said he, "is to provide for the tranquillity of your people; all other promises are subservient to that." But there is nothing in the world so persistently unreasonable as a morbid conscience. Charles Albert, though relieved by the sane decision of his spiritual adviser, when left alone, fell again into the eddy of doubt, and could not act without once more consulting his Council. On February 7, from nine in the morning till four in the afternoon, he listened to their opinions. "I ask but two things of you," he said as they assembled: "to maintain intact the authority of our holy Catholic religion, and to respect the dignity of the country." The discussion showed that every one now deemed the concession of a statute to be inevitable. Yet the King still hesitated, and the Council broke up, to meet again that evening at nine o'clock. In the interval, the Committee of the Municipality came to present the address agreed upon two days before, and an orderly crowd of less than a thousand persons had gathered in the square outside the Palace. The King received the address very coldly, saying to its bearers, "I will see," and adding that he would do nothing so long as the crowd beset his gate. Upon the reassembling of the Council, his hesitation ceased, and having once given his consent to a constitutional government, he neither wavered nor demanded restrictions, nor harbored afterthoughts. At noon the next day, February 8, the news got abroad that the State printers were setting up a proclamation in which the King announced that he had determined to grant the Constitution to Piedmont. Forthwith the city resounded with joyful acclamations, which were reëchoed across the Alps in Savoy, on the shores of Lake Maggiore, and by the waters of the Mediterranean at Genoa and Nice. On February 27 the whole realm sent delegations, in which every class and guild was represented, to take part in a grand celebration at Turin. A procession fifty thousand strong marched down Via di Po, whose long porticoes reverberated with cheers, to the Church of the Great Mother of God across the river, where the *Te Deum* was chanted, and then the concourse passed in review before Charles Albert. The excitement was heightened as the news spread that on the previous evening couriers had come hurrying into the city with the report that Louis Philippe had been chased from Paris, and that a Republic had been set up in France. On March 4 the Statute was published: its Liberal character can be inferred from the fact that it remains to-day, after more than forty years, with only such modifications as time has made necessary, the basis of government in Italy.[1]

Thus in two months' time Naples, Rome, Tuscany, and Piedmont had secured without bloodshed — except in Bomba's kingdom — the right of self-government. To understand the immense enthusiasm and the extravagant expectations which these mere paper covenants aroused, we must put ourselves back into the state of mind of those peoples who had never enjoyed civil rights, whose property and lives had been at the mercy of tyrannical and irresponsible masters, and who had come to look upon a constitution as the panacea for all the ills of the Past and as the guarantee of all future blessings. The Italians only gave themselves up to that tendency of our era, both in Europe and America, to overestimate the virtue of written laws; but to them, in 1848, the winning of a constitution was an indispensable preliminary to the winning of those social and political qualities without which constitutions are illusory, and with which they are almost superfluous.

[1] Beauregard: *Épilogue*, 81–101; Cibrario, 110–16; Brofferio, pt. III, chap. 2; Cappelletti, chap. 17.

CHAPTER V.

EXIT METTERNICH: MILAN AND VENICE FREE.

"THE Emperor does not intend to lose his Italian possessions," — that was Metternich's defiance to the rising tide of nationality in Italy. Any other resolve would have been unbusinesslike, because Lombardy and Venetia, though containing only one sixth of the inhabitants of the Austrian Empire, had paid for over thirty years about one third of the revenues of the Imperial treasury. But even had Austria been content to give up this rich tribute, she could not risk setting an example which would have been construed as weakness to the other races — to the Magyars, Bohemians, and Croats — which she held in grasp. Yet Metternich saw that the times were very evil. 1847 passed without offering the chance he desired of letting the cannon speak; courting as he did a hand-to-hand conflict with the Radicals, he feared the slow, undermining process of Liberalism. And while he was watching in compulsory inactivity, the revolution was sweeping up the Peninsula and manifesting itself in Lombardy and Venice. Then it was that Metternich, adopting the Cassandra rôle, which was one of his favorites, mingled with his warnings many an "I told you so." The government of those provinces was bad, inefficient, responsible for the present dangers; if he had been listened to, it would have been strong. The great mistake Austria had committed in her dealings with the Lombards and Venetians could be summed up, he said, in a few words. "We have bored them (*ennuyés*). A people which wants *panem et circenses* does not want to be bored. It wants to be governed with a strong hand — and amused."[1] He had as low an opinion of the Milanese, even though many of them had braved death or the Spielberg, as of any Italian, whether of Charles Albert, riding a "steeple-chase to win a false popularity," or of the weather-cock Pope. And yet, as I have hinted, he had tried upon those same Milanese all those forms of amusement which he had hoped would enervate them, — he had provided ballet dancers and actresses, he had encouraged dissipation, he had enticed them with honors and blandishments to the Viceregal Court, but in spite of all his lures and in spite of his intimidations the desire for independence was formidable among them.

If "governing" could keep down a people, surely the Lombards ought never to have lifted a finger against their masters, for Austrian tyranny at Milan was a seven-headed monster. There was the Viceroy, Archduke Raynier, the Emperor's uncle, a mediocre man; there was Count Ficquelmont, recently sent by Metternich to exercise a general supervision over the other officials and to apply another treatment of banquets and flattery to the aristocracy; there was Spaur, Governor of Milan, an obedient executor of the Metternichian policy; Torresani, the chief of police, was past-master of all the methods by which that most important branch of the Metternichian system kept the surface calm; his two adjutants, Bolza and Pachta, had shrunk from no work, however dirty or cruel, nor refrained from any injustice, during their long, abominable service; finally, there was Field Marshal Radetzky, commander-in-chief of the Austrian troops south of the Alps, a soldier without sentiment for suffering, a strict disciplinarian, merciless as a Turkish pasha towards mutiny or rebellion, a man whose favorite motto was "three days of bloodshed secure thirty years of peace." Nevertheless, these heptarchs, with their

[1] Metternich to Ficquelmont, 17 Feb., 1848 (vii. 583).

regiments and innumerable spies and underlings, were letting the revolutionary contagion leach through Lombardy, and were calling down upon them Metternich's contemptuous rebuke.

The first overt act of rebellion occurred at the beginning of the new year. A professor of physics, named Cantoni, wrote a manifesto calling upon the Milanese to abstain from tobacco in order to deprive the Austrian Treasury of the revenue it drew from that source. He cited the example of the fellow-citizens of Washington and Franklin, who had thrown overboard the taxed tea of "avaricious England," and he warned the Milanese not to regard so trifling a sacrifice as ridiculous or ineffective, but as a means of showing their patriotism.[1] The manifesto was widely circulated, and on New Year's day no smokers, except they were Austrian officials, or natives who had not been forewarned, were seen in the streets. The police made sport of so whimsical an expression of Lombard petulance. But on the following day, Sunday, a squad of policemen used unnecessary violence in breaking up a swarm of youths who had gathered to hiss any casual smoker, and when Count Casati, the Podestà (or mayor) of the city, remonstrated, one of the officers struck him a fist-blow in the face, and arrested him. Being quickly released, however, Casati applied for redress to Torresani, who, after some preliminary rudeness, promised to reprove his over-zealous subordinates. But an order[2] was secretly issued for the troops to be given cigars, and the next afternoon (January 3) knots of soldiers appeared smoking in the streets; some, to make the taunt more evident, stuck two cigars in their mouths; and it was not long before the irritation which, by their overbearing behavior, they caused the citizens, and which the citizens caused them by hooting and hissing, resulted in

---

[1] Ottolini: *Le 5 Giornate Milanesi* (Milan, 1889), gives the text, pp. 22-3.
[2] Suggested, it is said, by the Viceroy.

several collisions. Before order could be restored, five or six of the citizens had been killed and ten times that number wounded.

Immense indignation took possession of the Milanese. Deputations waited upon the Viceroy to protest against the turning over of the city to an irresponsible, ferocious soldiery. "I have seen the French, I have seen the Russians," said the aged archpriest, Monsignor Oppizzoni, to Raynier, "but deeds like these I have never seen. To kill citizens in the streets in this fashion is not to punish, but to murder."[1] The Viceroy issued a proclamation deploring the recent outbreak as the work of evil-minded brawlers, who, if unchecked, would dash his own "best-founded hopes" that the "progressive ameliorations" he was to bespeak from the Emperor would be granted. The Milanese Municipality likewise exhorted their fellow-citizens to coöperate with them in maintaining peace and in discouraging those who, arrogating to themselves the functions of public censors, had tried to enforce an old statute against smoking in the streets.[2] The Viceroy and Radetzky, perhaps satisfied that sufficient terror had been inspired for the present, kept the troops in their quarters after January 4, but though there was outward quiet, the public temper was so feverish that any petty event might precipitate another conflict. The Viceroy's "well-founded hopes" became a laughing-stock, when in a stern edict the Emperor announced that "he had granted all possible benefits to his Italian provinces and had no intention of granting more."[3] Stricter police ordinances were adopted. The Lions' Club, which had been for many years the fashionable club of the Milanese aristocracy, was closed.

---

[1] Ottolini, 32.
[2] Twice before, in 1751 and 1766, riots had occurred on account of the law against smoking in the streets; see Carlo Casati: *Nuove Rivelazioni sui Fatti di Milano nel 1847-8* (Milan, 1885), ii, 7.
[3] Ottolini, 41.

Of several prominent persons, some were arrested and sent across the Alps, others were summarily bidden to quit the country. And while the civil authorities thus harried the city, Radetzky held over it the threat of military chastisement. He boasted, in an order of the day, that "he still brandished with a firm hand his sword tried by sixty-five years and countless battles;" woe to Milan if "he were constrained to raise the standard of the Austrian eagle, whose wings were still unclipt!"[1]

And yet, in the face of threats and repression, Milan showed by clear signs her unalterable hatred of the Austrians. The ladies put on mourning for the victims of the recent massacre. They collected money for the bereaved families, they nursed the wounded. A strange harmony united all classes. The word was passed to attend the theatre, and the theatre was crowded; or to stay away from it, and the actors played to empty benches; but pry as they might, the police could discover neither him who gave the order nor those who circulated it. For some time past the Milanese had refused to buy dress stuffs not manufactured in Lombardy; now every woman who could afford it bought a velvet or silk garment to help the local weavers. When the news of the Sicilian rebellion came, the men put on Calabrese hats; when the Neapolitan Constitution was announced, nobles and bourgeois, as if spontaneously, attended the ordinary mass in the Cathedral. They deserted their favorite promenade, the Corso di Porta Orientale, calling it from the blood shed there "Corso Scellerato,"[2] and congregated instead on the Corso di Porta Romana, which they renamed "Corso Pio" after the beloved Pope. Many members resigned from the Noble Guard. Count Borromeo returned the insignia of the Golden Fleece with which he had been decorated. On one occasion the ladies appeared at the opera dressed in white and blue, the colors of the House

---

[1] Order of the day, Jan. 15, 1848.   [2] "The Wicked Way."

of Savoy, and the men wore white cravats and yellow
gloves, the colors of the Pope. The police were kept
busy erasing from the walls such incendiary mottoes as,
"Long live Italy," "Out with the Barbarians," "The
apple is ripe." On one dilapidated building was found
the inscription, "This is the House of Austria." Further
to impoverish the Austrian Treasury, playing in the lottery and the use of stamped paper were discouraged.[1] In
a word, the Milanese adopted every means, however insignificant, to manifest their resentment and their hopes.

The Austrians, baffled in their attempts to discover the
centre from which this passive rebellion was directed,
applied harsher measures. On February 22 martial law
was declared; it became a treasonable offense to wear
certain colors or badges, to sing *certain* songs or hymns,
to applaud or hiss *certain* passages in a drama or opera,
to collect subscriptions, or to do aught else that the
authorities deemed a "political demonstration." Fresh
regiments constantly arrived, till the army of occupation
in Lombardy and Venetia numbered about 100,000 men.
Benedek and Breindl, who had won an infamous notoriety by their bloody acts in Gallicia, were sent to keep
Brescia quiet. Radetzky strengthened the fortifications
of Milan. Yet throughout the provinces there were frequent disorders, punished with indiscriminate severity.
Cremona, Como, Mantua, Brescia, had each its baptism
of blood. At Pavia and Padua the students became
unruly and the universities were closed. The Austrians
spared no efforts to foment class-hatred, and so to weaken
the revolutionary spirit. They told the working classes
that the nobility, while pretending to be their friends,
were really their enemies; they warned the nobility that
an alliance with the working classes would, in case of a
revolution, give the latter the power to sweep the former

[1] The loss suffered by the Austrian Treasury through these various abstentions was estimated at fifteen million francs; Perrens, 225, note 1.

away; they played on the innate repugnance of the bourgeoisie to any disturbance which might interrupt the golden current of trade, and they insinuated that the agitators were really communists in disguise. Before Louis Philippe's downfall, Metternich had secured his consent to the passage of Austrian troops over the St. Gotthard;[1] and the Chancellor, besides approving the military preparations for holding Lombardy and Venetia, had drawn the Dukes of Modena and Parma into a compact by which Austrian troops occupied those duchies. He further advised the removal of the Viceroy from Milan to Verona, ostensibly on the ground that Verona was nearer the centre of the kingdom, but really in order to give Radetzky an open field for martial rule.[2] He recalled Ficquelmont to Vienna, — the time having passed when that gentleman could pacify the Milanese by dinner parties and diplomacy, — and at the same time he sent Count O'Donell, a man of supposed energy, to act as Vice-Governor while Count Spaur also went to Vienna.

The aged Chancellor knew that the crisis was at hand, but he did not shrink from it. "Two months from now," he wrote on February 19, "many things will be differently placed, — if we do not fall."[3] Falling was a possibility, but he did not seriously believe that it would come to pass; he believed, rather, that after a sharp encounter, when the smoke should have cleared away, the forces of Revolutionary Europe would be seen scattering in utter rout, with the armies of the Old Régime in full pursuit. "As I prefer light to darkness," he wrote a few weeks earlier, "I think that in a little while it will be easier to get our bearings than it is to-day."[4] Even the convulsion in Paris did not alarm, outwardly at least, the "old practitioner"[5] in diplomacy, but it set the incendiary element

---

[1] *Correspondence*, ii. 79.   [2] Metternich, vii, 588.
[3] *Ibid*, 587.   [4] *Ibid*, 573–4.
[5] An epithet he applied to himself (vii, 583).

at Vienna in a passion. Metternich would not temporize. The muttering against him deepened into growls; he would concede nothing. On March 13 the storm broke. The university students threatened a riot; their spokesman appeared in the Palace; the streets were filling with an angry multitude. "Reforms," and "Down with Metternich," summed up the popular demands. The half-imbecile, epileptic Emperor would grant anything, and Metternich was forced to resign. But this did not suffice: the people whom he had so long oppressed, finding him deserted by the Emperor, unprotected, unbefriended, cried out for his life.

A few hours, and what a change! The mainspring of European despotism had snapped. Late that night he succeeded in reaching his own dwelling, — he, but this morning the most conspicuous figure in Vienna, stole homewards like a thief. "As rats leave a sinking ship, so were we forsaken by many frightened friends," writes Princess Melanie bitterly in her diary. Forsaken by most, but not by all. Count Taaffe offered shelter in his palace; Princess Esterhazy took charge of the children; Hügel, a loyal servant, remained with the Chancellor and his wife. But Taaffe's protection would avail nothing if the Viennese, who had already sacked Metternich's own residence, should track him to this hiding-place. After dinner on the 14th, therefore, it was decided to set out at once for Feldsberg, a country-place of Prince Liechtenstein. Into a cab Metternich accordingly got, and, huddled between his wife Melanie and trusty Hügel, who blocked the windows as much as they could, he was driven to a suburb, where the Liechtensteins had another carriage in readiness. The road being clear, Hügel mounted the box, and the flight began. The old man — you saw now that he, who but yesterday had carried his seventy-five years so gallantly, was an old man — sat "quiet and composed." Princess Melanie, a mettlesome, haughty woman, strove also to seem calm, though anxiety for her children and wrath at the ingratitude of the world, sympathy for her husband's downfall, and bewilderment as to the future, "broke her heart in a thousand pieces." "What had we done? Had we deserved this?" These wild thoughts rioted in her head, but she uttered them not, out of pity for the broken companion beside her. And he? He, too, was silent, — doubtless revolving many things, striving above all to recover from astonishment. The cries of the angry Viennese still rang in his ears, and behind them he might have heard the exultant roar of Revolutionary Europe. Out into the bleak March night Hügel urged the horses; hour after hour the carriage rolled and jolted over the deep-rutted roads: we might almost imagine it a hearse speeding oblivion-wards with the dead incarnation of the Old Régime. From time to time, either the cold or a jolt brought a groan from Metternich's lips. At length, at two in the morning, Feldsberg loomed sepulchral out of the darkness. The shivering old man was helped into the castle, where neither food nor fire awaited him; but there were his children, and as he lay jaded and chilled on a sofa, they wrapped their shawls and cloaks about him, till a fire could be lighted and he could be removed to bed. So ended the first stage of his flight: to be continued as opportunity offered till he reached England, — hated, Liberal England, Palmerston's country, — and found refuge there. Later, the revolution being spent, he might safely crawl back to Austria, all his power and prestige gone, there to live into his eighty-sixth year, denouncing the Present, glorifying the Past, resolutely insisting that he alone had been right, and that the world, rejecting his counsel, was sweeping to perdition. That Europe for five-and-thirty years was controlled by a man whose fall had nothing of grandeur, nothing of dignity nor of valor about it, — is not that fact as damning against that Europe as against Metternich? What a contrast between his rabbit exit from the stage where he had ruled, and the dramatic downfall of his great adversary, the Promethean outlaw whom all Europe, after infinite toil, riveted to St. Helena's rock!"[1]

The news of the uprising in Vienna reached Milan by official telegraph late on March 17. That very day Archduke Raynier set out quietly for Verona, quitting the city over which he had been as a Persian satrap for more than thirty years, without leaving friend or any beneficent memory behind him. Inklings of the Viennese insurrection leaked out almost as soon as they were received by the officials, and during the night of the 17th knots of patriots met at some of the cafés[2] they were used to frequent, and agreed that the moment had come for a demonstration. On the morning of the 18th Count O'Donell, who, after the departure of the Viceroy and of Count Spaur, was at the head of the civil administration, issued a brief notice stating that a dispatch sent from Vienna on the 15th announced that the Emperor had "determined to abolish the censorship and to cause a press law to be published without delay, besides convoking the Estates and the Central Congregation of Lombardy and Venice for the 3d of July.[3] To the crowds already in the streets this concession seemed beggarly; they shouted for a Civic Guard and for the expulsion of the Austrians. Led by Cernuschi and Anfossi, two resolute men of the middle class, they marched to the Broletto, or Town Hall, and asked Count Gabrio Casati, the Podestà, to be their spokesman before Vice-Governor O'Donell. Casati was naturally a peacemaker, whom Fortune, in one of her sardonic moods, now called to com-

[1] The best account of Metternich's flight is given in Princess Melanie's diary (vii, 541-6).
[2] The Café Cervetto, in the former Via Rebecchino, and the Cecchino, in Piazza della Scala, were two favorite resorts of the patriots.
[3] Text in Ottolini, 54.

mand a violent crisis. Reluctantly he consented to do the mob's wishes. As they approached the Governor's palace a sentry fired upon them, whereat the citizens, losing all self-control, fell upon him, disarmed the rest of the Guard and poured into the palace. Amid indescribable confusion, they found O'Donell trembling for his life, his Councilors having deserted him. He begged Casati for protection, but when the errand on which the multitude had come was broached, he at first protested that he had no authority to grant the demands. Cernuschi, however, insisted, and leading the frightened official to a balcony, there in the presence of the crowd below him, O'Donell signed three orders, authorizing the immediate enrolment of a Civic Guard, abolishing the general direction of the police, — the safety of the city to be transferred to the Municipality, — and bidding the police to consign their arms to the Municipality.[1] Having gained their object, the multitude started to return to the Broletto, but on the way they encountered a body of troops which discharged a volley at them. There was a sudden stampede, every one seeking shelter in the nearest house or darting down the nearest lane: Casati, with O'Donell and several of the citizen leaders, took refuge in the house of the Vidiserti. A messenger was sent to Marshal Radetzky at the Citadel to inform him of the orders issued by O'Donell, but Radetzky refused to recognize them, on the ground that they had been given under compulsion. Torresani, also, the Director of Police, when bidden to hand over his authority, replied that he had received it from the Emperor and would submit to no one but the Emperor, and then he seized the first chance to escape, disguised as a gendarme, to the Citadel.

By this time the city was in a tumult in all directions.

[1] A facsimile of these orders is given in C. Casati's *Nuove Rivelazioni*, ii, 88.

There were scuffles between squads of soldiery and the ill-armed citizens, and it was evident that a serious conflict could not be prevented. But the insurgents lacked a head: Casati was cooped up in Casa Vidiserti; three of the Municipal Councilors — Greppi, Bellotti, and Belgiojoso — were at the Broletto; elsewhere, each group had its local chief. The three Councilors wrote to Radetzky, begging him, in view of the extraordinary danger, to restrain his troops from any act that might exasperate the already over-heated temper of the public. To this the Marshal replied that they should immediately cause the insurgents to lay down their arms; "but if," he added, "contrary to my just expectations, this most fatal struggle should be prolonged, I shall find it necessary not only to bombard the city, but also to use all the means which an armament of 100,000 men and 200 cannon places in my hands to lead back a rebellious city to obedience." The Councilors rejoined that, as it was already too late for them to act that evening, they hoped his Excellency would suspend his threatened severity until the next day, when they might have had time to deliberate. Nevertheless, they put forth an appeal to the Milanese to refrain from all defense, as it must lead to an inevitable slaughter.[1] Meanwhile, there was a rushing to and fro of zealous patriots, and a sowing of inflammatory manifestoes. Tricolor flags[2] began to wave from many windows, tricolor cockades and ribbons fledged every hat or fluttered in every buttonhole. Incessant the cheers for Italy, Independence, Pius IX; deepest of all the cry, "Out with the Barbarians." Hundreds of citizens flocked to the Broletto to be mustered into the Civic Guard, and they were still swarming there when they were startled by the approach of two of Radetzky's regi-

[1] Ottolini, 62-3.
[2] The Italian tricolor (red, white, and green) was first adopted by a legion of Lombard troops, by Bonaparte's order, in 1796; Ottolini, 55, note 1.

ments. The Broletto, situated on a little square between two streets, was easily surrounded. Finding their escape cut off, its inmates barred the great door and prepared for resistance, though they had not above fifty muskets, and a scanty supply of ammunition. From seven till nine in the evening they maintained a desperate defense, throwing tiles and furniture down upon their assailants when their powder was exhausted, and never slackening until the Austrians, having brought up a twelve-pounder, battered down the door. The half-savage Croats, whom Austria relied upon to do her butcher's work for her, rushed into the breach and could with difficulty be prevented by their officers from massacring the garrison. They did, indeed, dash some boys from the roof, where they had taken refuge, to the pavement below. The three Councilors and their comrades in the defense were led away to the Citadel, and Radetzky dispatched a courier to Vienna to announce that he had "cut the sinew of rebellion."

In 1848 Milan had 160,000 inhabitants. The Austrian garrison numbered about 15,000 troops; the police and gendarmes 900. The city had not yet been modernized: its streets, except a few avenues leading to the gates, were narrow and irregular, often mere alleys in which two carts could not pass abreast. The dwellings, built of stone, with lower windows heavily grated and street-doors strongly barred, could easily withstand an ordinary assault, and their spacious courtyards afforded shelter to a goodly squad of defenders. The city lay like a nearly circular shield on the Lombard plain, the spire of the Cathedral glistening boss-like in its centre. Like all Italian towns, it was surrounded by walls strong enough to repel an enemy unprovided with heavy guns. Between the circumference and the centre a canal, not more than a few yards broad, formed an almost complete ring inclosing the densely populated heart of the city. On the northwest, about half a mile from the Cathedral and still within the fortifications, was the massive Castello or Citadel, once the stronghold of the Visconti and the Sforza, beyond which stretched the drilling-ground, three sevenths of a mile long and of almost equal width. On the northeast lay the Public Garden, in area nearly equal to the drilling-ground, sloping upwards to the level of the bastion, which here was a favorite promenade. The belt between the canal and the walls, being less thickly built upon, had many open spaces and gardens. The city as a whole was admirably adapted to a prolonged resistance by the insurgents: its flatness gave the cannon at the Citadel no commanding point, mortars being needed to throw bombs into the centre; its streets were nearly all too narrow for a cavalry charge and too crooked to be effectively swept by artillery, and the few squares were too small for the massing of any considerable body of infantry.

When the 18th of March closed amid a heavy rain, the Austrians, as we saw, had captured the Broletto. They had seized the Archiepiscopal Palace and posted Tyrolese sharpshooters on the roof of the Cathedral, whence, protected by the myriad statues and pinnacles, they could pick off any insurgents in the square below or in the windows of the opposite buildings. Their troops were distributed among the public buildings in the heart of the city and in several outlying barracks, but the greater part of them garrisoned the Citadel or bivouacked on the adjacent drilling-ground. The insurgents had as yet no centre of operations, although Casa Vidiserti, in which Casati, with the remaining members of the Municipal Council and the prominent men who rallied round him, were assembled, may be regarded as the headquarters of the insurrection. But throughout the city, in the narrow streets and the fortress-like dwellings, the insurgents had already begun to intrench themselves, and during this night and the following day they worked with incessant energy at throwing up barricades. Never before was this species of defense used on so large a scale or with greater success. Every one — men, women, and children, priests and laymen, nobles and artisans — joined in the work, and everything served them for material. They tore up the pavement; they threw on benches and bedsteads, confessional-boxes and organ-pipes, clothes-presses, mattresses, troughs and hen-coops, — in some cases not stopping to let out the hens; they ransacked the Viceroy's stables, and doomed sixteen of his coaches to the patriotic cause; they seized many bales of stamped paper; they shattered the Imperial arms over the portals of the public buildings, and threw the broken escutcheons and two-headed eagles — fit emblems of rapacious Austria — on their miscellaneous breastworks: till across every street they had drawn one, two, three, or more lines of defense, against which dragoons dared not venture, and infantry shot their muskets in vain. Before the contest ended, the Milanese had covered their city with a network of 1,650 barricades.

But this was only a part of their work. The fighters must have arms, and few arms were to be had, for the Austrian government had made it a criminal offense to keep a gun. Now from closets and hiding-places old fowling-pieces and blunderbusses were brought to light. Some young men who, in spite of Austria's prohibition, had recently procured arms of modern pattern, were the envy of their ill-equipped fellows, who rushed to the gunsmiths' stores, and, when these were exhausted, rifled the collections of old armor and antique weapons. One took a halberd that may have last been used by one of Carmagnola's mercenaries; another swung a battle-axe that may have crushed through the helmet of one of Anjou's troopers. A cleaver snatched from the shambles, a bludgeon bristling with spikes, a blacksmith's hammer, a sharpened stake, anything that could edge a blow with death, served to equip these determined Milanese. As they had scant supplies of powder, chemists taught them how to manufacture more. Some of the women moulded bullets and rolled cartridges for the fighters; others picked lint and made bandages for the wounded. All day long the children carried stones and flower-pots and crockery up to the roofs to be hurled at the enemy; housewives heated water or oil to pour on the passing whitecoats. Astronomers stationed themselves in the towers and church spires to observe the enemy's movements, and from time to time sent messages attached to iron rings which slid down a wire to the combatants below. On the second day, or the third, the seminarists inflated balloons and let them loose, bearing brief reports of the conflict and appeals for assistance; some of these drifted westward into Piedmont, others northward into Switzerland, others came to earth in Piacenza. Nor were measures forgotten for distributing victuals and for preparing hospitals.

In the retrospect it seems well-nigh impossible that operations so various and on the whole so effective could have been carried on without previous organization: yet such was the case. As we can single out no one man as the originator of the insurrection, so we can point to none as its head during the Five Glorious Days. All classes staked their lives on its success, and each class obeyed the directions of a few of its members. Legally, Casati and the Municipal Council were responsible for the city's action, but they soon increased their number by calling in eight influential citizens. For greater security they removed their quarters to Casa Taverna, from which, in case they were attacked in front, they could escape through gardens in the rear. But Casati, and most of his colleagues, lacked aggressiveness; they had constantly in view the possibility that the revolt would fail, and if it failed they knew what Austria's vengeance would be. If they hesitated, therefore, or spoke with more moderation than was pleasing to the men fighting at the barricades, this was not because they were half-hearted, but because their immense responsibility weighed too heavily upon them. But the Milanese had entered upon one of those supreme moments in the life of a people when it snaps the rusty bands of the past, despises tradition, scorns to imitate, is filled with but one desire, one resolve, — to achieve its present purpose, in comparison with which all other objects, including mere existence, seem stale and unworthy. They had not time to compute risks and reckon costs, not time to consider whether the wages of their daring would be death or imprisonment; under the spell of an emergency which called for heroism and permitted neither calculation nor wavering, they were heroic, dreaming not of failure. To repel an assault on this barricade, to dislodge a company of Croats from yonder barracks, this was their present business, let nightfall or the morrow bring what it might. A people roused to this pitch of passion needed strong words and decisive counsel, and it got both. Cattaneo, Terzaghi, Cernuschi, and Clerici formed a Council of War, and issued from Casa Taverna bulletins full of courage and proclamations full of hope. Cattaneo was the most conspicuous Milanese who took an active part in these great events: eminent as a writer on economic subjects and a consistent advocate of republicanism, he had held aloof from conspiracies and from the more recent passive resistance, but after the 18th of March, when he found that the battle was at last joined and that, for weal or woe, it must be fought out, he came from his retirement, and was second to none in fiery exhortation and in prompt resolves. Cernuschi was a fighter, passing from the council chamber to the barricades and back again, with sleepless activity. Manara, Della Porta, Dandolo, Anfossi, they, too, were fighters, whose valorous example was more precious than many harangues. Nor should Corrienti be forgotten, wise in planning, quick to execute, nor Dr. Bertani, who organized an ambulance corps and tended the wounded on the battle-ground.

Of the details of the insurrection many hundred pages have been written, but so minutely as to leave but a confused impression; nor, indeed, could it be otherwise. As well try to track the course of every drop of blood through all the arteries and veins and vesicles of a fever-stricken patient, as to follow separately the operation of the Milanese and their antagonists during the Five Days' contest. But the general results from day to day are ascertainable. Radetzky, holding the entire circle of fortifications, prevented the insurgents from communicating with, or receiving reinforcements and provisions from, the outside. If, therefore, he could keep his lines intact, he must erelong reduce the citizens to starvation. But he also had detachments of troops in the public buildings within the inner circle, and in barracks in the outer circle. Many of his stores of ammunition and food lay near the heart of the city. The insurgents, on their side, by throwing up barricades both prevented the invasion of any large force into the inner circle and hindered the troops already there from getting out. So there was a siege within a siege. Recognizing, however, that their supplies would soon be exhausted, their hope lay in capturing one of the city gates in order to establish communication with the country. By the end of the second day, Radetzky saw the futility of hurling his men at the barricades, and he accordingly kept them in the outer zone. Then the garrisons in the public buildings one by one withdrew or surrendered. His situation grew hourly worse; the rebellion he had hoped to drive in and strangle gained on him street by street. On March 19th one of his officers, Major Hettinghausen, was taken prisoner,

— perhaps he purposely allowed himself to be taken, — and, as if on his own motion, he sounded the directors of the rebellion at Casa Taverna as to the terms on which they would agree to an armistice. Various the opinions. Litta thought that a few days' respite would allow time for the Piedmontese army, which was supposed to be on the march, to come to their assistance; Cattaneo insisted that they should agree to nothing less than the complete evacuation of Lombardy by Radetzky and all his non-Italian troops; others foresaw that any suspension of hostilities would be as profitable to him as to the Milanese. Finally, the Major was sent back to inform his chief that the citizens would fight on. At about the same time, the Cathedral having been abandoned by the Austrians, the tricolor flag waved from its spire, — a happy omen, seen far and wide throughout the Lombard plain. At night an eclipse was interpreted as a favorable portent by the Milanese, who had drawn similar encouragement from a rare display of the aurora borealis a few weeks before. On the 21st Radetzky made a second attempt to secure an armistice. The foreign consuls, who had already protested against his threatened bombardment, visited him at the Castle at seven in the morning, to inform him of the result of a conference they had had with the Municipal authorities. Radetzky thereupon told them that he was willing to grant a truce for three days, during which both belligerents should pass freely to and from the city, and replenish their stores. When the consuls announced these terms to the Council in Casa Taverna, there was another heated discussion. Durini argued in favor of accepting the proposition; it would give time to organize the defense more solidly and for the Piedmontese to arrive. Mauri, on the contrary, held that it would be fatal to check the present momentum; with the gates open, the timid would flee from the town, and by their example cool the enthusiasm of the combatants, while the Austrians would have leisure not only to send their emissaries among the people, but also to intimidate the peasants rising in the country. Borromeo warned them that they had food and ammunition for only another day. To this Cattaneo retorted with vigor. "The enemy," said he, "having furnished us with munitions thus far, will furnish them still. Twenty-four hours of victuals, and twenty-four of hunger, will be many more hours than we shall need. This evening, if the plans just now arranged succeed, the line of the bastions will be broken. At any rate, even though we should lack bread, better to die of hunger than of the gallows."[1] This resolution was approved by as many of the men at the barricades as could be consulted, and Radetzky's offer was rejected.[2] The old Marshal's comment was to renew the cannonade.

At the beginning of the insurrection Count Arese had hastened to Turin to urge Charles Albert to go to the rescue of the Milanese. On the 21st Count Martini, a Lombard exile in Piedmont, having succeeded in entering the beleaguered city, told the Council that he had the best of reasons for believing that Charles Albert was ready to cross the Ticino, but that some pretext must be invented to appease the diplomatic protests that would surely ensue. If the Austrians attempted any aggression on Piedmontese territory, that would be an excuse; or if the Lombards should formally appeal to the King, that, too, would give a color of legality to his interference. Here was planted a seed of discord whose fruit was to be as the apples of Sodom to Italy. The insurgents had hitherto fought without regard for the future, men of all parties merging their political preferences in a common cause, — the emancipation of their city from Austria. They had looked to the coming of the Piedmontese as

[1] A. and J. Mario: *Carlo Cattaneo* (Rome, 1884), 35.
[2] The documents of these negotiations are given in *Correspondence*, ii, 214-21.

sailors in distress look to a ship of rescue, without thought of salvage or compensation. Now the question was posed whether, Milan being free, she would establish an independent government or give herself to Piedmont. It cannot be doubted that a majority of the leaders of the insurrection favored a monarchy, but several of the ablest of them — chief among whom was Cattaneo — were uncompromising advocates of a Republic, and they insisted that no step should be taken which might prejudice the future. If Charles Albert came to succor the Lombards, he would merit the people's gratitude. If he won, who would deny him the crown? If he lost, what profit would there be in having offered it to him?[1] Thus they argued, and not content with speech, Cattaneo defined their position in the following terse note to Martini: "The city belongs to the combatants who have conquered. We cannot call them from the barricades to deliberate. Night and day we sound the tocsin to summon assistance. If Piedmont responds generously, she will have the gratitude of the generous of every opinion. The word *gratitude* is the only one that can silence the word *Republic*."[2] The line of division was thus clearly drawn, but for the moment the action of the Milanese could not influence Charles Albert, since Martini was unable to quit the city, and the citizens were absorbed in the last throes of their defense. The Council, which had hitherto acted "in the absence of the Imperial authorities," was now converted into a Provisional Government, — a change which marked the passage from mere insurrection to acknowledged revolution. It immediately issued a proclamation to estop the incipient discord. "While the struggle lasts," so ran the address, "it is not opportune to put in debate opinions on the future political destiny of our most dear fatherland. For the present we are called to reconquer its independence; and good citizens are bound to devote themselves

[1] La Farina, iii, 283.   [2] Mario, 37.

to nothing else except fighting. The cause won, our destiny will be discussed and fixed by the nation."[1] That phrase — "the cause won" (*a causa vinta*) — stuck in all minds, and all hands redoubled their activity to achieve the victory.

Most of the buildings within the inner circle had by nightfall on the 21st been captured. Radetzky's own palace was stormed, and that famous sword which he had "brandished for sixty-five years" was passed amid laughter from hand to hand. Brave Anfossi, leading a charge on the Engineers' Barracks, was struck dead by a bullet, but a fearless fellow named Sottocorni hobbled on crutches to the door of the building, set fire to it, and so hastened its surrender. Down at the Ticinese Gate, where for four days the inhabitants of that quarter had been fighting an isolated fight, the combat never slackened. In the east, Manara was massing his volunteers for a final assault on Porta Tosa. The capture of storehouses and prisoners had steadily improved the equipment of the insurgents, and though provisions were running low, hunger, as Cattaneo had remarked, would make desperation invincible.

On the morning of the 22d Radetzky realized that his situation was critical. The heart of the city was irrevocably lost to him; the probability that the rebels would break through his outer line was imminent. His victuals failed. The 1,200 bombs he had sent for had not yet come. He had no certain news from Vienna, and only the most alarming reports from Lombardy. The Austrian garrison at Monza had capitulated; bands of countrymen were flocking to relieve Milan, and threatened to hem him in. His soldiers were disheartened, too, at having to bivouac in the rain, which, with the exception of Sunday, had poured with but occasional interruptions. Above all, he expected at any moment to see the blue

[1] La Farina, iii, 284.

banners of Piedmont bear down on him from the west. Without bombs his cannonade of shot and Congreve rockets could do little damage to the interior of the city, and with his present force he would be no match for the Piedmontese. Nevertheless, he decided to hold out during the day. Towards evening he learned that the insurgents, after having five times assaulted and five times been driven back at Porta Tosa, had by the use of movable barricades at last stormed that position and opened the gate,[1] through which bodies of countrymen were now swarming to their aid. After night fell he gave orders for a general retreat, keeping up a heavy cannonade from the Citadel until it came time for the gunners themselves to withdraw.

Early on the 23d the Milanese were puzzled by the unwonted stillness at the Austrian headquarters; but they soon discovered the reason, and the city broke into a tumult of joy. The bells, which had hardly paused in their awful, maddening tocsin for more than a hundred hours, now pealed forth merrily. Milan was free; by her own indomitable valor redeemed from Austria, the supposed arbitress of Europe. But amid their rejoicing the Milanese, besides feeling natural sorrow for dead comrades, were horrified as they learned the full measure of the inhumanities which Radetzky's savage troops had wreaked upon many unfortunates who fell into their hands during the siege. Not only were women and old men and children slaughtered in cold blood; but the hands of living women were chopped off in order that some covetous soldier might the more quickly seize a ring or bracelet; infants were skewered on bayonets; unborn babes had been ripped from their mothers; prisoners were burned to death, — in one case a husband and wife were bound together and roasted; the bodies of men were

---

[1] Which they immediately rechristened "Porta Vittoria," the Gate of Victory.

mutilated, women's legs were cut from the body; a company of nine persons was buried alive. We read of the horrors of war; here were the horrors of war perpetrated by the soldiers of a monarch who bore the title "*Apostolic* Majesty." Austrian historians, from their long list of whipped generals, have singled out Radetzky as the paragon of Austria's military heroes, but as long as his name is remembered it will call up deeds of blood and brutality, not of glory.[1] The humaneness of the Milanese, both during the contest and after they had triumphed, was as praiseworthy as Radetzky's cruelty was fiendish. They treated the family of Torresani and of other Austrian officials with kindliness; they let the old Marshal's mistress go unharmed; they even spared Bolza and Pachta, those two agents of the police who, during their long regimen of wickedness, had never shown mercy. Bolza they discovered hiding half dead with fright in a haymow; infamous Pachta they dragged from a privy, — fit refuge, in sooth, for the caitiffs whom Austria had made the tools of her pitiless and vulgar despotism. But Milan resisted her first impulse to retaliate, and no ferocity stained the record of her triumph. The losses on each side cannot be accurately stated. The Milanese had about 430 killed in the streets, including 28 women, many of whom fought beside their brothers at the barricades; their wounded probably numbered at least a thousand. The Austrians, according to their own report, lost less than 600 killed, wounded, and prisoners,

[1] The evidence of the brutality of Radetzky's Croats is, as Perrens remarks (p. 237), too circumstantial to be rejected. Hübner, Metternich's special envoy, knew the habits of Austria's soldiers, and dreaded them. See his *Une Année de ma Vie*, 1848-9 (Paris, 1891), 75-6. He also bears witness to the humanity of the Italians, *ibid*, 82. See also I. Cantù: *Rivol. Lombarda*, 126-30; La Farina, iii, 256-7. For the insurrection consult also A. Casati: *Milano e i Principi di Savoja*; Ottolini: *Rivol. Lombarda*; Schneidawind; *Feld Marschall Graf Radetzky* (Augsburg, 1851); Rüstow: *Italienische Krieg von 1848-9* (Zürich, 1862); Dandolo: *Volontari Lombardi* (Turin, 1849); and the works cited above.

but the Italians claimed that 4,000 of Radetzky's troops were put out of fighting trim; and certainly the former figure seems suspiciously low, for the Austrians were exposed more than the insurgents, and it is hardly likely that so stubborn a fighter as Radetzky would have retreated when only one twenty-fifth of his force was disabled.

During the anxious days when Milan's redemption was still uncertain, the principal towns of Lombardy and Venetia were following her example, or rather, it is more precise to say that like her they rose spontaneously as soon as they had news of the revolt in Vienna. In most places, little blood was spilled, as the stupefied Austrians either granted the concessions asked for or withdrew after a brief skirmish. In Venice the arrival on the 16th of a courier from Vienna was the signal for the outbreak of long-gathering discontent. Manin and Tommaseo, two men who had fomented agitation for the acquisition of rights to which the Venetians were legally entitled according to the laws Austria made, but did not carry out, had been imprisoned a few weeks before. On the 17th, therefore, crowds collected before the Governor's palace and demanded that Manin and Tommaseo be set free. Palffy, the Governor, hesitated; the crowds became more threatening, and shouted, "We wish it, and at once." A party rushed to the adjacent prison, overpowered the jailers, and unlocked the cells of the patriots; but Manin refused to leave without a legal order duly signed. This soon came, and Manin and Tommaseo were borne on the shoulders of their deliverers into St. Mark's Place. Soldiers drawn up there had an encounter with the scuffling crowds: a few broken heads, one victim trampled to death, summed up the casualties for that day. The next morning, the masses, wearing tricolor badges, reassembled, and called loudly for a constitution. Palffy declared that he could not satisfy them until he received instructions from the Emperor. Then there was another tumult between the populace and the troops; those hurling stones, these using their muskets and bayonets, order not being restored till five Venetians had been killed and a score wounded. Carrer, the Podestà, and the Municipal Council, waited upon the Governor, and urged him to authorize the formation of a Civic Guard as the only means to check the growing tumult. Palffy consented: songs of joy rang through the city, which for two days thereafter busied itself with its new privilege. On the 21st the workmen at the Arsenal mutinied against their superintendent, Marinovich, — a man whose cruelty had made him odious, — and but for the interposition of the Civic Guard they would have torn him to pieces. But Marinovich would not be warned, and when, on the morning of the 22d, he persisted in returning to the Arsenal, he was forthwith slain. The Municipality hastened to admonish the Governor that unless the military positions of the city were handed over to the citizens, nothing could delay the imminent revolt. Under the windows of his palace, the populace, fresh from dispatching Marinovich, shouted ominously, "He is one," which led Palffy to reflect that himself might be Number Two, and he quickly resigned his authority to Count Zichy, the Military Commander, who in turn was quickly forced to capitulate. He agreed to evacuate the city and forts, with all the Austrian regiments, — except those composed of Italians, who had already showed signs of deserting to their countrymen, — and to leave all munitions and the public treasure behind him. That afternoon, in St. Mark's Place, Manin proclaimed the Venetian Republic: tricolor banners were hoisted on the three tall masts from which the yellow and black ensigns of Austria had hung for thirty-three years; the winged lion of St. Mark's drove out the two-headed eagle of Hapsburg; a Provisional Government, with Manin as its President, took the place of Metternich's frightened servants. Thus, by March 23, the very day when Milan celebrated her victory over Radetzky, Venice, after an almost bloodless struggle, was free.

She let the garrison of her late oppressors embark and depart unmolested, and whether she looked southward to Malamocco and Chioggia, or whether she looked westward to Marghera and Mestre, she saw the flag of the Republic waving over those outposts. The Consul of the United States immediately recognized her independence. Her Patriarch blessed her standards; her people assembled in St. Mark's Church, where their fathers had assembled to give thanks for their victories over Byzantines and Turks, and gave thanks to God and their patron saint for their recovered freedom. If the Venetian emancipation seemed less dramatic than the Milanese, it was because there had been no Radetzky to call forth their valor: from them, also, heroic deeds should flash, as we shall see.[1]

[1] P. Contarini: *Memoriale Veneto* (Capolago, 1850), 5–15.

CHAPTER VI.

THE WAR OF INDEPENDENCE DECLARED.

WHEN Piedmont learned that Milan was in revolt, the greatest excitement prevailed. Bands of Genoese volunteers hurried towards Lombardy, only to be stopped at the frontier by the Royal authorities. At Turin the masses bellowed for war; the Radical newspapers encouraged them, the Moderate newspapers encouraged them. Even the cool-headed Cavour wrote bluntly in the *Risorgimento:* "The supreme hour of the dynasty has struck: there are circumstances where audacity is prudence, where temerity is wiser than calculation."[1] Day followed day, but brought only scanty news from the beleaguered city: a balloon came with its little message of hope and its appeal for succor; a messenger, fresh from the outskirts, reported that the contest was still raging,— he had heard the clanging of the tocsin above the rumble of Radetzky's guns, he had seen the tricolor flag waving from the Cathedral spire. Turin, Piedmont were in so high a fever that the government despaired of preserving order. Crowds, establishing themselves permanently in the market-place, clamored for war, cheered their Lombard brothers, denounced the inactivity of the ministers. "Every one has lost his head," wrote Marchioness d' Azeglio to her son.[2] The Piedmontese felt that they would be guilty of fratricide if they left the Lombards in the lurch.[3]

[1] Beauregard: *Épilogue,* 131.
[2] *Souvenirs de Constance d'Azeglio* (Turin, 1884), 217.
[3] Brofferio, iv, 69.

With what emotions Charles Albert saw the freshet of patriotism rising in his own kingdom, and knew that the moment had come when he must swim with it, or sink, we can better imagine than describe. He had conferences with the Milanese envoys, he had frequent sessions with his Cabinet: his heart was for war, but he knew the danger of war, and he hesitated to take the irrevocable step. Besides, what reason could he give that diplomacy would accept for opening hostilities? Austria had in no wise menaced him; not one of her soldiers had violated his territory, she had made no move on Alessandria. Only last week he had expressed to her his determination to abide by the treaties. What right had he to interfere in behalf of her rebellious subjects? Had he not strenuously insisted on the principle of non-intervention in the internal affairs of a neighboring State? If he drew his sword, Europe would be justified in regarding him as a military adventurer who, impelled by dynastic ambition, only respected international agreements when it suited him to respect them. The English minister, who had been most urgent in pressing reforms upon him, now warned him that, if he made an unprovoked attack on Austria, he would not only forfeit the moral support of England and endanger the peace of Europe, but also seriously compromise the interests and welfare of Piedmont and the House of Savoy.[1] But the pressure became too strong. On March 22 the Minister of War issued orders calling out the remaining contingents of the active army, and bidding the reserves to be ready to march at a moment's notice.[2] A little later, Count Martini reached Turin with the news that Radetzky had evacuated Milan. The King, having summoned a Cabinet meeting, and having learned that the Republican agitators were on the eve of exploding a revolt in his own kingdom, gave his consent to war. Coming out from the

[1] *Correspondence*, ii, 204.   [2] *Ibid*, 184-7.

Council, he said to Martini, Adda, and Arese, the Lombard suppliants: "Announce to the Milanese my armed intervention in Lombardy: but at the same time tell them that I will enter Milan only after having beaten the Austrians. I will not appear before so valiant a people until I have proved to the world that I am worthy of such a people."[1] It was the evening of March 22. Multitudes, made angry by long suspense, swarmed sullenly in the streets, at the mercy of any violent suggestion; but when the Lombard envoys, from the windows of their hotel, said to them, "We have achieved a great revolution. You are going to fight a great war," the sullenness changed to a delirium of joy. They surged towards the Royal Palace, where all was silent and sombre. Hour after hour they waited for a sign; they grew impatient; they began to suspect that the King had repented of his resolve. At length, just after midnight, the casements of the balcony of Pilate, at the corner of the palace looking out on the great square, were opened. Two valets bearing torches appeared; then Charles Albert, pale, solemn, followed, with his two sons, Victor Emanuel, Duke of Savoy, and Ferdinand, Duke of Genoa; behind them, the three Lombard Counts. A hush fell upon the myriad-faced multitude, which stretched far out into the darkness, beyond the reach of the flickering lights. Charles Albert strove to speak, but a whirlwind of cheers swept his words away; he could only wave a tricolor scarf, and listen to the enthusiasm of his people.[2]

But it was one thing to declare war amid the feverish applause of his subjects, and quite another thing to make that declaration valid in the eyes of jealous Diplomacy. Marquis Pareto, Minister of Foreign Affairs, addressed to the representatives of the Great Powers a circular note, in which he stated the reasons for Piedmont's course. The certainty that the Republican faction in

[1] Beauregard, 137. [2] Ibid, 138.

Lombardy would, if left to itself, set up a Republic which might involve a civil war there and would jeopard the peace of the neighboring States, had made it imperative, he said, for the King to interfere. His own people could no longer be restrained. France, on the west, was a Republic; a Republic was threatened in Lombardy, on the east; the monarchical cause in Italy could be upheld only by the King's assuming control over the revolutionary movement. Moreover, he had reversionary rights over Parma, Piacenza, and Modena, and as those duchies were in revolt, it was his duty to guard his interests in them, especially since Austria, in violation of the Treaty of Vienna, had, on December 24, 1847, entered into a compact with the Dukes of Modena and Parma by which she had virtually become mistress of their territories.[1] When passion runs high, a pretext is easily found for giving it a semblance of reason, and Pareto's pretext was neither better nor worse than many another which has been invented for diplomacy to toy with when nations have gone to war. The real reason was that which Metternich gave for his own downfall. "The most invincible of forces, that of things," swept Charles Albert and Piedmont and Italy into the vortex.

Simultaneously with Marquis Pareto's circular note Charles Albert published the following manifesto to the peoples of Lombardy and Venice: "The destiny of Italy is ripening: a happier lot smiles on the intrepid defenders of down-trodden rights. From love of our common race, from the intelligence of the times, from community of desires, we were the first to join in that unanimous admiration which Italy pays to you. Peoples of Lombardy and Venice! Our arms, which were already concentrating on your frontier when you anticipated the liberation of glorious Milan, come now to offer to you in the later trials that aid which brother expects from bro-

[1] Text in *Correspondence*, ii, 185.

ther, friend from friend. We will support your just desires, trusting in the aid of that God who is visibly with us, of that God who has given Pius IX to Italy, of that God who, with such marvelous impulses, enables Italy to work out her own salvation.[1] And in order still better to show by outward signs the sentiment of Italian union, it is our will that our troops entering the territory of Lombardy and Venice bear the shield of Savoy superimposed on the tricolor Italian flag."[2] This proclamation, vague and a little grandiloquent, was the first official utterance by an Italian prince of his determination to redeem Italy from bondage to Austria. Charles Albert's motives have been variously judged. Some of his critics concede to him no impulse higher than dynastic ambition; they would have it that he merely put in practice the maxim of his hungry ancestor, "Italy is an artichoke, to be eaten leaf by leaf." Others make fear, the fear of seeing the Piedmontese monarchy dissolve in a Republic, the spur which drove him on. To others, again, his desire to be avenged on Austria for her thirty-years long attempt to foil and browbeat him, or his desire to vindicate himself from that deep-rankling suspicion of treachery in 1821, seems the ruling motive. Those with a leaven of enthusiasm in themselves protest that he was disinterested and patriotic; others cite his piety and mysticism, his belief, — call it superstition or call it faith, — that this War of Independence was a task set him by God, and therefore to be performed bravely and without murmurs, be the sacrifice what it might. His best biographer tells how deeply Charles Albert was affected by the visions of a nun, a conventual Joan of

[1] The original reads: "*pose l'Italia in grado di fare da sè*." The expression, "*L'Italia farà da sè*," originated with Charles Albert at the time of the dispute with Austria over salt and wine, and was the national watchword until the disaster of 1848-9 proved it to be fallacious: Bersezio, ii, 33.

[2] *Correspondence*. ii, 205.

Arc, through whom Heaven whispered its wishes to him.[1] Not one but many, perhaps all, of these considerations had their influence in shaping his resolve: but to suppose that, had he resolved otherwise, he could have spared Piedmont the war with Austria is to overestimate his power. Had he resisted any longer the patriotic hurricane which was blowing through his realm, he would have been broken, and civil war or revolution would have wrought havoc after his fall. But for a brief interval after the declaration of war Charles Albert was the idol of his people. He had responded to their compelling wish, and they did not stop to inquire into his motives. He was the Sword ordained by Heaven; they could but follow where he flashed, and thank God that the Italian Cause had such a leader.

Florence heard of the Milanese revolt on March 19th, and by the 21st the excitement had reached so high a pitch there that a crowd, composed largely of students and other young men, beset the palace of the Gonfaloniere with demands for "arms and all else necessary for their immediate departure for the defense of the frontier." The Gonfaloniere (or mayor), Bettino Ricasoli, had, of course, no authority to comply, but he went immediately to the Palazzo Vecchio and laid the matter before the Cabinet there sitting. Ridolfi, the Prime Minister, hurried to the Pitti Palace, and conferred with the Grand Duke. Within two hours the city was placarded with a manifesto in which Leopold, after announcing that "the hour of the complete resurrection of Italy had come unexpectedly," informed his subjects that he had given orders to the regular troops to march at once to the frontier, and that volunteers would be enrolled and sent after them as fast as possible. He himself seemed to burn with zeal for the "holy cause of Italy," in behalf of which he promised to conclude negotiations then pend-

[1] Beauregard. 132-4.

ing for an offensive and defensive league among the Italian States. Without delay the Tuscan troops marched northward. Every city and town hummed with warlike preparations. The university students at Pisa and Siena formed a legion of their own, and their professors enlisted with them. The patriotic furor drew volunteers of all classes into the ranks, and, as invariably happens, there were black sheep among them. But the general temper was disinterested. Every day witnessed the setting forth of some band, in motley uniforms, and with incomplete equipment. They went gayly, as to a holiday party; singing and shouting from village to village till they reached the frontier, where they found neither quarters nor provisions, and where their lack of discipline and the unexpected hardships led them to grumble or to commit depredations.[1] Nevertheless, the war spirit blew hotter and hotter, and the government strove to guide it as wisely as their inexperience would permit.

Rome imitated Florence after but the interval required for the courier to post from the Arno to the Tiber. The Roman populace, led by Ciceruacchio, surged through the streets, clamored to be allowed to join their brothers, and attacked Palazzo Venezia, the residence of the Austrian ambassador. On the Campidoglio, they sang a *Te Deum*; in the Coliseum, they listened to the harangue of Father Gavazzi, the burly Barnabite friar, who, like another Peter the Hermit, preached a crusade, and had a large white cross worked upon his cassock. At night, the city blazed with illuminations, as in Carnival time; thousands of *moccoletti* (little candles) sparkled and flickered in the darkness, and myriads of voices babbled and shouted and sang. Pius disapproved, but he had not yet the courage to resist. His ministers, while formally deprecating the insult to the Austrian ambassador, gave orders for eight regiments and three batteries to march

[1] Trollope, 100; Ranalli: *Istorie Italiane* (Florence, 1855), ii, 84.

frontierwards under John Durando, with Massimo d'Azeglio and Count Casanova as his adjutants. A legion of volunteers, numbering within a few days 12,000 men, was enrolled. Princes, and plebeians, and members of the intermediate classes flocked to the recruiting quarters. Money flowed in like a tide in spring; women of the nobility offered their jewels, women of the peasantry their hoard of copper, or, having no pennies, whatever keepsake had a marketable value; even the cardinals gave up their horses for the artillery. Shame on him who seemed listless, woe to him deemed hostile to the great cause. The Jesuits had to close their schools and habitations in obedience to the general outcry, though it was plainly the Pope's duty to protect them so long as no charge could be verified against them. But Pius was still unwilling to stand up bravely against the popular current. He rebuked the enemies of the Jesuits, "whom he had with supreme pleasure always regarded as indefatigable co-workers in the vineyard of the Lord," and almost in the same breath[1] he admonished the "Peoples of Italy" that to use victory well was a greater and harder thing than to conquer, and that they should endeavor through harmony to secure peace and justice for Italy. When the volunteers, for whom a commander had been found in the person of the Neapolitan Colonel Ferrari, set out for the "holy war," Pius blessed them, and they too went gayly, boisterously, wearing the cross on their breast, cheering the tricolor ribbons tied above the Papal banner, and believing that they were indeed crusaders who had the full sympathy of their Pope. But Pius, bewildered by the suddenness of this latest emergency, only consented in order to gain time for reflection and to ward off a crisis; he had no intention of allowing his eager subjects to cross the frontier; and, lacking resolu-

[1] Pius's defense of the Jesuits and his paternal address to the Peoples of Italy were both published on March 30.

tion himself, he hoped that Chance would unfold some
escape from the evil consequences of his irresolution.[1]

Outwardly, therefore, from the Alps to the Tiber,
Italy was ablaze with patriotism; nor did the flames stop
there, but, leaping Tiber and Garigliano, they whirled
southward over Bomba's kingdom, and reached the sea.
Naples had enjoyed her Constitutional government well-
nigh fifty days when she heard of the overturn in Vienna
and Milan; fifty days, — a brief space in the life of a
people, too brief, indeed, for a people to recover from ten
times fifty years of degradation, yet long enough for those
mercurial and impulsive Neapolitans to begin to fritter
away their just-won victory. They suspected the King's
honesty, though they cheered him still; they grumbled
because the improvement which they had expected did not
show itself; their newspapers, allowed freedom, ran to
license, blackguarding everybody and everything, including each other; there was a babel of sound, a confusion
of purposes, and, as usual, he who screamed loudest had
the most hearers. Like the other Italians during the
past two years, the Neapolitans had gained their desires
by shouting: no wonder, then, that they imputed an
irresistible virtue to noise, and deemed strong throats
instead of wise heads to be the attribute of statesmanship.
Twice already they had yelled unpopular Cabinet Ministers into retirement, and they had already clamored for
changes in a constitution which had scarcely had time to
be understood. So do children dig up in the afternoon
the seeds they planted in the morning, to see if they have
taken root. We need not wonder that the Neapolitans
were but children in government and self-control. The
beggars found that the Constitution did not mean more
macaroni and cheese for them, therefore they concluded
that they must hurrah for a more generous constitution;
the tradesmen could observe no increase in business nor

[1] Minghetti, i, 359-61; La Farina, iii, 296-300; Farini, ii, 14-25.

decrease in taxation, so they had their reason for complaining; the employees turned out of office, the myriad would-be employees to whom no office was given, — they also had their grievance; the ministers grumbled at being decried by the irresponsible demagogues of the cafés and street corners, and these in their turn berated the ministers and all the rest who had a different plan from their own. Some there were, of course, who, keeping head clear and tongue quiet, foresaw the evil consequences of this clatter and discord. "Among the people which shouts, the King who deceives, and the ministers who do not know what they are doing, an honest man has no place,"[1] said Charles Poerio, the Liberal leader, who too soon resigned from the Cabinet.

Bomba himself chuckled over all these evidences of the inability of his subjects to profit by their newly-acquired privileges. The pet he had given them, the Constitution, was a lion's cub, which needed but time for claws and fangs to grow; the King's policy was to wait patiently, sustaining his rôle of patriot until simulation were no longer necessary. In Bozzelli, the minister in whom the Liberals had set great hopes, he found a pliant tool: for the late exile, the ex-martyr to the Liberal cause, could not withstand the seductions of power and the King's flattery, and erelong Bozzelli became odious to the very men with whom he had conspired and suffered during the best part of his life. And yet the people seemed still to have the upper hand. When their clamors drove the Jesuits out of Naples, the King pretended to be highly gratified to be rid of his best friends. When changes were proposed to him, he was scrupulous in pointing out that he could not approve of them because they were contrary to the Constitution, and his dearest wish was to obey that sacredly. But in spite of his strictness, he soon found a pretense, with Bozzelli's con-

[1] Settembrini, i. 272.

nivance, for forcing one of the few honest and able members of the Cabinet to resign, — Saliceti, whom Bomba feared because he thought he looked like Robespierre, and whom Bozzelli felt was a dangerous opponent.

Added to these difficulties which inexperience, factiousness, dissension, and distrust threw in the path of Constitutionalism, was the civil war between Naples and Sicily. The Sicilians, after freeing themselves in January, had refused every offer of compromise. Lord Minto, on behalf of the King, had tried to patch up a reconciliation, but they rejected all his advances and declared that thenceforth Sicily should be an independent State. They had had enough of a sovereign who bombarded their cities and massacred their citizens; they had trusted for the last time the perfidious Bourbons, who made oaths only to break them. The Neapolitans, who had had quite as good cause as the Sicilians to execrate the Bourbon régime, nevertheless seconded Bomba's determination to subdue Sicily, and they were as angry as the King himself at the attempt of Naples's richest province to break utterly away. And while they jeered the troops that came back beaten from Palermo and Messina, they scolded the government for its slowness in dispatching a force sufficiently strong to annihilate the rebellion.

Into this world of confusion came the news from the north and temporarily focused on a single point the energy of the conflicting factions. The masses demanded war; the more prudent Liberals hailed the sudden upthrust of the question of Italy's emancipation as a cause in which all minor disputes would be merged. From every side the pressure upon the government to declare war on Austria became irresistible, and at length on March 26 Bomba, from his palace terrace, signified his consent to the frantic multitude below him. Then was there such rapid arming, such enrolling of volunteers, such delirium of patriotic hopes, as we have witnessed at

Rome and Florence. To old William Pepe, just returned to his native land after more than a quarter of a century of exile, was given the command of the troops that were to march overland to the Po; other regiments were embarked on the royal navy, to coöperate with the Piedmontese and Venetian fleets at the head of the Adriatic. Volunteers, too impatient to wait for the march of the regular army, set out without delay. Princess Belgiojoso, a Milanese gentlewoman, "with masculine purpose and feminine vanity," equipped two hundred recruits at her own expense, and doubtless regretted that she could not put on trousers and be their captain. A new ministry, composed of such unimpeachable Liberals as Dragonetti, Troya, Imbriani, and Pietro Ferretti, was formed, — making the third remodeling of the Cabinet in less than two months, — and it announced its desire to coöperate in the national war. The King basked in great popularity; it seemed as if he were almost reluctant at being prevented, by the internal conditions of his realm, from riding at the head of his troops on their glorious enterprise. When General Pepe suggested that it would naturally be disagreeable to his Majesty to make war on the Austrians, one of whose archduchesses he had married, Bomba retorted curtly, "You are mistaken: I have always detested the Austrians."[1]

Lest posterity should doubt Bomba's skill at dissembling, — a skill hereditary in the House of Bourbon, — it will be well to transcribe the proclamation which he addressed to his "best beloved people" on April 7: "Your King shares with you that lively interest which the Italian cause awakens in all minds; and it is therefore determined to contribute to its safety and victory with all the material forces which our peculiar position in one part of the kingdom leaves at our disposal. Although not yet established on certain and unchangeable terms, we con-

[1] La Farina, iii, 311.

THE WAR OF INDEPENDENCE DECLARED. 139

sider the Italian League as existing in fact, because the universal consent of the princes and peoples of the Peninsula causes us to regard it as already concluded, as the Congress which we were the first to propose is about to meet at Rome, and we propose to be the first to send thither the representatives of this part of the great Italian family. Already has an expedition been sent by us by sea, and already has a division begun to move along the Adriatic coast to act in concert with the army of Central Italy. The fate of our common country will be decided on the plains of Lombardy, and every prince and people of the Peninsula is bound to assist in taking part in the struggle, which ought to insure its independence, liberty, glory. We, though pressed by other particular necessities, which keep occupied a large portion of our army,[1] intend to assist with all our land and sea forces, with our arsenals and the treasure of the nation. Our brothers await us on the field of honor, and we will not fail there where the great interest of Italian nationality will be fought for. Peoples of the Two Sicilies, draw round your prince! Let us remain united in order to be strong and feared, and let us make ourselves ready for the contest with that calm which is born of the consciousness of force and courage. Let us trust in the valor of the army to take that part in the magnanimous enterprise that befits the largest principality of the Peninsula. To display all our vigor abroad, we have need of peace and concord at home, and we count on the excellent spirit of our fine National Guard, and on the love of our people, for the preservation of order and the observance of law: as our people ought always to count on our loyalty, and on our love for the Liberal institutions, which we have solemnly sworn and which we intend to maintain at any greatest sacrifice. Union, abnegation, and firmness, and the independence of our most beautiful Italy will be

[1] Referring to the troubles with Sicily.

achieved! Let this be our sole thought; let so generous a passion silence all others less noble: and twenty-four millions of Italians will certainly have a powerful fatherland, a common and very rich patrimony of glory, and a respected nationality which will have great weight in the world's political scale."[1]

If Epaminondas had been in the habit of issuing proclamations, though they might have been less florid, they could hardly have conveyed a more genuine impression of patriotism than this Bourbon proclamation conveyed. How sincere Bomba was we shall soon see: for the present, we need only bear in mind that his subjects put faith in him, believing that Naples, too, was to win her crown of glory in the War of Independence.

By the end of March, 1848, the whole Peninsula throbbed in unison, as it had never throbbed before. A common cause uplifted it; hopes, indefinite but mighty, made it drunk; nothing seemed unattainable since Piedmontese and Tuscans, Romans and Neapolitans, were all concentrating on Lombardy and Venetia, which had already risen and driven from most of their cities the detested Barbarians. One would fain stop here, and picture the beautiful image of Italy free and independent as the Italians saw it in their enthusiasm in those days of early spring. Powerful is the spell of romance; fascinating are the ideals which shimmer aurora-like upon the black concave of a nation in darkness. But History's supreme value consists in this, that it records the process by which men came to distinguish mirage and unsubstantial dreams from fact and truth, to sift visions from reality. Delightful are many illusions, but Truth alone is precious, Truth alone can permanently satisfy us, and to discover Truth we must search the sequel.

Looking back now, we can see plainly what was hidden from the Italians, — the vagueness of their aim, the in-

[1] See *Correspondence*, ii, 383-4, for text and translation.

adequacy of their means, their lack of leaders. Had ever another great cause such incoherence, such headlessness? Charles Albert, the visible Sword of the War, devoted and sincere, but mystical, procrastinating, dreading Republicanism on the one hand, regretting Absolutism on the other; the Tuscan Grand Duke, flurried out of his easy-going neutrality to take sides against his kinsmen and his caste; the Pope, the symbol and Banner round whom all should rally, a mere parish priest projected from the twelfth century into the nineteenth and still believing, or affecting to believe, that there was nothing incompatible between the mediæval and modern system; finally, Bomba of Naples wilfully perfidious, but for the moment masking his deceit, — these the leaders of the National War. And the people who were to do the fighting, — how they were split up by factions and numbed by inexperience! Nevertheless, so overmastering is a national passion, the Italians took slight note of this in those early days. They were convinced that the mere desire for independence would suffice to dissolve every obstacle; they believed that all things were possible. Sicily alone, engrossed in her own struggle for freedom, sent no contingent to the patriotic hordes gathering along the Po.

CHAPTER VII.

FROM GOITO TO PASTRENGO.

WHEN in youth we first read of great wars, our attention is so absorbed by the chronicles of exciting and valiant deeds that we fall readily into the blunder of supposing that in war-time every one was a patriot, and that the great issues were wholly decided in the camp or on the field. We overlook the fact that the army of fighters constituted but a small minority of the population, and that those who stayed at home were busy at their accustomed labors; that the gay world had its theatres and balls just as though no thousands were dying in battle and in hospitals, and as though another army of civilians were not amassing provisions, clothes, ammunition, and money for the sustenance and success of the campaign. Historians encourage us in this half view, doubtless because it is easier, if not more agreeable to them, to describe martial exploits than to interrupt their narrative with unheroic details. In cases where a war was practically the expression of a single ruler's will, — of an Alexander, a Charlemain, a William the Conqueror, — it is right and sufficient to keep his gleaming helmet always in sight; but in modern times the political situation often determines the military, and cannot be ignored. Yet to blend the two, to show how a victory in the field reacted on the policy of the government and on the enthusiasm of the citizens, or how the lukewarmness or dissensions or incapacity of the civilians chilled the ardor of the soldiers, — this is no easy task. Yet, although we have now got far enough away from the Revolution of 1848 to see that the military operations then were of secondary importance compared with the political causes which conditioned them, nevertheless, obedient to the human tendency to idealize the Past, — to worship deeds and to slight thoughts which are the parents of deeds, and which deeds but partially express, — it is the combats in the field, rather than the disputes in the council and the agitation in the market-place, that have been best remembered. Let us, at least, endeavor to ascertain the influence of each, in order that we may see both the woof and the warp wherewith the Time-Spirit wove one of its temporary garments.

By daybreak on March 23 Radetzky's troops had stolen quietly out of Milan, the Marshal himself, according to one account, being driven off in a carriage loaded with hay, the better to avoid the shot of some chance marksman in the villages through which his retreat lay. His plan was to march with all speed eastward until he should fall in with the Austrian garrisons, which, he believed, still held the country between Mantua and Verona. The Milanese, astonished to find themselves free, broke out into exultations which, though natural, consumed most precious time which should have been spent in the pursuit of the retreating enemy. As it was, only a few bands of volunteers set out to cut off the Austrian stragglers. At Lodi (March 25) Radetzky heard that Venice had revolted, and realized the danger of his position. Lombardy in insurrection round him, Venetia menacing in front, he was like a hunter on the prairies who sees a horde of Indians sweep towards him from all directions. But Radetzky was a grim fighter, and now desperation toughened his courage. He pressed on without delay, striking terror among the country-people by shooting them down and burning their dwellings, until he reached Montechiaro, a strong post on the river Chiese, a few miles southeast of Peschiera. There he was rejoiced to learn that his lieutenants were still masters of the Quadrilateral.

The river Po, rising in the Alps which divide Piedmont from France, flows eastward to the Adriatic. It is the backbone of Northern Italy, and into it rivers, like ribs, descend from the Alps on the north. Of these rivers the Ticino formed the boundary between Piedmont and Lombardy, and the Mincio, draining Lake Garda, separated Lombardy from Venetia. Thence passing eastward, you meet first the Adige, then the Bacchiglione, the Brenta, the Piave, the Tagliamento, and the Isonzo, which all flow into the Adriatic, the Isonzo being the boundary between Venetia and Goritz, the first province on that side of the Austrian Empire. Except at the passage of the rivers, the plain of Lombardy was too flat to offer points favorable for defense, but in Venetia Austria found a natural stronghold which she had taken precautions to fortify; that stronghold was the Quadrilateral, a district not quite rectangular, having at its four corners the formidable towns Peschiera, Verona, Mantua, and Legnago. Peschiera, situated at the southeastern bight of Lake Garda, was further protected by the last spurs of the mountains which rise along the eastern bank of that lake. The river Mincio, flowing thence almost due south, makes a natural fosse or protection to the western side of the Quadrilateral, until, near Mantua, it overflows in many marshes and pools, passable in but few places over causeways. The river then bends southeastward and merges in the Po, furnishing a defense against attack from the south. Legnago and Verona guarded the Quadrilateral on the east. Verona itself was an almost impregnable fortress, and between it and Peschiera the mountains completed the circuit of defense. Such the famous Quadrilateral, a wonderfully strong military base, interpolated in the otherwise open plain of the Po. It was large enough to permit of the massing of a vast army, yet small enough to allow troops to march from any one of its corners to another within a single day.[1] It blocked the passage of an enemy who wished to go from Lombardy to the Adriatic, and, moreover, it was in direct communication with Austria by way of the Adige valley, through Tyrol.

Radetzky, reassured at learning that the Quadrilateral was safe, paused, therefore, at Montechiaro to let his men breathe and to collect the Austrian forces which had escaped from the Lombard cities. His general plan was to hold the Quadrilateral until reinforcements could reach him from beyond the Alps, and from the Isonzo, where a corps of reserves had been assembling for several weeks past.

On March 24 the first Piedmontese regiments crossed the Ticino in two columns, one commanded by General Bes, the other by General Bava. General Passalacqua was dispatched immediately to Milan to represent the King before the Provisional Government; but on the 26th, when Bes entered that city with the Brigade Piedmont, a regiment of cavalry, and a battery, he had by no means so cordial a welcome as he had expected. Already the Republican element among the Milanese began to show its repugnance to the possible transfer of Lombardy to Charles Albert. "You drive out an emperor only to give yourselves up to a king," was the taunt the Republicans thrust at those of their fellow-citizens who leaned towards fusion with Piedmont. But not only the Republicans, all the Milanese were so puffed up by their Five Glorious Days that they looked on the tardy coming of the Piedmontese as almost superfluous. They had themselves fought and won, and while the issue hung in suspense, no help had come from Turin. "Is it not rather late,"

[1] From Peschiera to Verona is only about twelve miles; from Verona to Legnago, twenty-five miles; Legnago, to Mantua, twenty miles; Mantua to Peschiera, twenty miles.

they asked, "to bring succor after the need has gone by?" Indeed, so extraordinary had been the liberation of Milan, and of the other Lombard cities, that the Lombards became extravagantly over-confident. They believed that the war was over; that Radetzky was scurrying pell-mell across the Alps; that it was only a question of where the triumphant Italians would deign to draw their frontiers on the east. One suggested Trieste, another Illyria, another would be satisfied with nothing less than the eastern coast of the Adriatic, once the fief of Venice. The same extravagance prevailed in military affairs. Radetzky's troops, the best equipped and drilled in Europe, had been beaten by citizen-soldiers armed but with mediæval pike or modern blunderbuss, and none recognizing an officer superior to himself; therefore, discipline and long and expensive preparations were unnecessary; the patriot-hero had but to show himself, and Radetzky's Croats would turn tail and run. Bes, finding the Milanese in this temper,[1] quitted the city on the 27th and proceeded to Treviglio, where he joined the Lombard volunteers, who, under Manara, had set out to harass Radetzky's rear.

Charles Albert himself left Turin on the evening of March 26, and three days later he entered Pavia amid the wildest enthusiasm of the population. He announced to the Lombards that he "came without condition to terminate the great enterprise which Milanese valor had so happily begun." Mindful of his promise, he would not go to Milan now, but by rapid stages he pushed on to Cremona. There he learned that Radetzky was not so utterly beaten as the popular confidence supposed, and it became necessary for the King to lay out a definite plan of campaign. His army consisted of two corps, the first,

---

[1] *Memorie ed Osservazioni sulla Guerra dell' Indipendenza d' Italia* (Turin, 1849), 2. This work is by Charles Albert, and therefore furnishes first-rate evidence from the Piedmontese standpoint.

under Bava, having nominally 18,000 men, the second, under Sonnaz, having 16,000, and the reserves, under Victor Emanuel, Duke of Savoy, having about 9,000 men. Charles Albert assumed the supreme command; Franzini, Minister of War, was his Major-General, and Salasco his Chief of Staff. Although her army had long been Piedmont's boast, and although Charles Albert had the strong warrior instincts of his Savoyard line, consecrating his zeal pretty equally to military and religious affairs, the test of war soon showed many unavoidable defects in his troops. In the first place, not one of them had ever seen actual service; they belonged to a generation which had grown to maturity since Waterloo. In the second place, the Piedmontese system of allowing the infantry to return to their homes after only fourteen months' apprenticeship, though they were liable to be called out at any time up to their thirty-fifth year, tended to soften them and to break up discipline. Soldiers with wives and children go reluctantly to the hardships of the camp and the dangers of battle. The Piedmontese army, therefore, was weakest where it should have been strongest, — in its infantry, which, though brave enough, lacked endurance and cohesion. The cavalry was considerably more efficient, and the artillery was a really strong arm, even when measured by the standard of the best in Europe. But the most ominous defect was the inexperience of the generals. Only a few of these had ever been in action, and these few had fought more than thirty years before, when they were only subordinates, in Napoleon's last campaigns. They had the theory of war from their manuals, and perhaps they had somewhat too much of the assertive self-confidence of men whose knowledge of an art is wholly theoretical. No one could impugn their average willingness and bravery, but these are qualities which, without corresponding decision and knowledge, cannot be trusted to win battles. Strange as it seems, the members of the General Staff were also ignorant of the topography of the seat of war; they had no proper maps, no reliable information concerning the places Austria had for thirty years been fortifying. They did not know, for instance, that the fortifications of Mantua had been strengthened since 1797; and they did not supply this want by organizing a trustworthy service of scouts.[1]

When, therefore, Charles Albert learned at Cremona that Radetzky had encamped at Montechiaro, he decided to make a rapid dash on Mantua and then follow the Mincio northwards to Peschiera. This movement would either cut off Radetzky from the Quadrilateral or compel him to retreat behind the Mincio. At Goito, on April 8, occurred the first important skirmish of the campaign. Radetzky had already abandoned Montechiaro and concentrated his forces near Villafranca, determined to prevent the Piedmontese from crossing the Mincio. But at Goito, Bava's brigade fell upon the Austrian brigade under Wohlgemuth, and though the contest was hot and the Austrians blew up the bridge, some of the Piedmontese sharpshooters crawled over its ruined parapet, dislodged the Austrians at the other end, and enabled Bava to transfer his command to the eastern bank. The losses — 126 Austrians and 50 Piedmontese — suggest no great affair; but the moral effect of the victory at Goito was immense, not only on Charles Albert's army, but on all Italy. It proved that Italians could stand firm under fire, and it excited the ambition of the Italians of the Centre and South to have their share of feats of glory.

But the fight at Goito, and a little skirmish at Mon-

[1] For details concerning military affairs see Charles Albert's *Memorie;* Rüstow's *Italienische Krieg von 1848-9* (Zürich, 1862); Pinelli's *Storia Militare del Piemonte* (Turin, 1855); Le Masson's *Custozza, Venise,* and *Novara;* Mariani's *Guerre dell' Indipendenza Italiana;* and Schneidawind's *Graf Radetzky.* The various prejudices of the authors are quickly seen, and can be allowed for.

zambano and Borghetto on the following days, made it clear to Charles Albert that he had a serious task before him. The military promenade, the chase, that the Lombards had predicted, turned out to be a war. Radetzky withdrew the bulk of his troops into the fortresses of Peschiera, Verona, and Mantua, leaving only a few regiments in the plain. He would not gratify the Piedmontese by coming down into the open and risking a general battle. This wariness on his part placed Charles Albert in a dilemma: he must either lay siege to the fortresses, or, plunging through the centre of the Quadrilateral, he must effect a junction with the Venetians, say at Padua, and there await an attack by Radetzky on his rear. In the former case he must delay until heavy siege guns could arrive and trenches be dug, — a delay which would check the enthusiasm of his troops; in the latter case he would leave Lombardy unprotected, and expose his column in passing to a charge on either flank. A great commander, like Napoleon, would have made the dash, despite the greater risk; for he would have realized that it was of the utmost importance for the *morale* of an army like the Piedmontese for it to be kept active. Veterans can endure a siege, while inexperienced soldiers lose heart and discipline during a tedious suspense which offers few chances for bravery. Charles Albert, having nothing of the Napoleonic genius, decided to besiege the strongholds rather than to push on and hazard being cut off from communication with Piedmont. On April 11 he fixed his quarters at Volta, and while waiting for heavy artillery and reinforcements, he directed assaults now against Peschiera (April 13), and now against Mantua (April 19), in the hope that the Italians shut up in those cities would rise and overpower the garrisons busy repelling the Piedmontese. But these hopes proved vain: the Austrians not only warded off their assailants, but also checked any internal revolt.

While the Piedmontese army was thus engaged, operations which might, if properly guided, have put Radetzky in extreme jeopardy were going forward in the North. The valley of the Adige was, as I have stated, Radetzky's sole line of communication with Austria: to capture that, and so to deprive him of succor and escape, was of more importance than to capture Mantua or Peschiera; because if the valley of the Adige had been closed, the blockade of the Quadrilateral would have been complete, and the Piedmontese might have sat down patiently before the fortresses and starved them out. But this vital movement was intrusted to a force quite inadequate to carry it through. The Lombard Volunteers, a corps only a few thousand strong, undisciplined and badly generaled, moved up Lake Garda and proceeded to Trent and the Lower Tyrol. The volunteers expected that the small Austrian garrisons would run before them, and that the natives would rise in mass to welcome and join the pioneers of liberty. But the Austrians held their positions stubbornly, reinforced by detachments which Radetzky sent from Verona, and the natives were too cautious to risk their fortunes with the national cause until they should see a certain indication that it would conquer. The desultory guerrilla warfare which went on during several weeks, enlivened by occasional skirmishes which proved the courage of the volunteers, failed to accomplish the great purpose in view. The Provisional Government at Milan, whether from inability or from a dull perception of the gravity of the issue at stake in Lower Tyrol, neglected to send supplies; the Piedmontese generals, though appealed to for aid, were slow in replying, because of the ill-defined relations between them and the Lombard troops. Since the Lombards had not been regularly enrolled as a part of Charles Albert's army they were not bound to obey his command unless they chose; obviously, therefore, he could not assume responsibility for their actions unless they formally recognized his authority. General Allemandi, disgusted and disheartened, resigned, and James Durando assumed command of the Volunteers; but the favorable moment had passed, and Radetzky had thenceforth little anxiety for the valley of the Adige.[1]

It must not be supposed, however, that the full significance of these blunders was understood at the time. The war fever still raged; enthusiasm, hopes never ran higher than during this month of April. Whatever might be the dissatisfaction in the camp at the slowness of the campaign, the people of the Centre and the South gave themselves up to rejoicings for the anticipated victory. Twelve thousand Roman volunteers under John Durando and Ferrari came marching buoyantly up through the Legations. On a great chariot which they drove before them they built an altar, above which a tall pole bore the Pontifical colors. Monks, with pistol and sabre at their girdle, made a guard of honor for this imitation of a mediæval *barroccio*, and the multitude of "Crusaders," uniformed fantastically, but all wearing a tricolor cross, followed them. By April 20 they had reached Ferrara, where they came to a standstill until the Pope should give them permission to cross the Po and have their target-practice at the Austrians. The Tuscan contingent, numbering about 6,000 between regulars and volunteers, and a battalion of Neapolitans had, at about the same time, come up with the Piedmontese army, and were stationed at Montanara and Curtatone, with the stream Osone at their backs. Far greater reinforcements were expected from Naples, King Bomba having promised that 40,000 of his men should participate in the War of Independence; but as yet hardly one third of that number had set out, under General Pepe, for the south bank of the Po.

By April 25th, therefore, a month after the declaration

---

[1] The best account of the operations of the free corps is in Dandolo's *Volontari Lombardi*.

of war, Charles Albert seemed to have sufficient forces within hail to justify the confidence of the most optimistic patriot. The effective of his own army had been brought up to about 60,000 men; Pepe's 14,000, not yet come; the 12,000 or 13,000 Romans; the 6,000 Tuscans, and the 5,000 Lombard skirmishers in the Tyrol, made an aggregate of over 90,000 Italians opposed to about 55,000 Austrians in the Quadrilateral. Charles Albert's numerical superiority, however, was deceptive. From his own force we must deduct 17,000 men whom he left on the right bank of the Mincio; and we must remember that as yet he could dispose of neither the Pontifical nor the Neapolitan troops. Great as was the lack of cohesion in the Piedmontese army itself, a considerable part of its regiments being filled by this year's recruits or by reserves who had had no military discipline for six or eight years, — men who had been trained with the old flint-lock musket and who found the new percussion-cap arm strange,[1] — still greater was the task of establishing concerted action among volunteers and contingents from the other States, who, though nominally under Charles Albert's general control, still preserved a certain independence. Radetzky's army, on the other hand, had a single master and excellent discipline. Setting apart 15,000 men to garrison the four fortresses, and 5,000 to keep the Adige valley clear, he had under his immediate command 35,000 troops which he could mass at a day's notice on any point the enemy threatened. And so long as he adhered to his plan of avoiding a pitched battle, the strength of his position more than compensated for his inferiority in numbers.

Fortunate would it have been for Charles Albert if he had had only the military affairs to direct. To organize his own army, to weld the free corps into a compact and

---

[1] The percussion-cap was substituted for the flint-lock in 1843: Bersezio, iv, 12.

efficient body, to devise a campaign and carry it out rapidly, — these would have been tasks to try to the utmost a commander far abler than he was; but beside these, he had to struggle against political and diplomatic obstacles of a very threatening kind. He discovered only too soon that, however noble his purpose of helping his brother Italians to drive out the Barbarians, he must reckon with the other princes of Italy and with Europe. And, indeed, his position was anomalous. He was making war on Austria, while pretending to be merely preserving order in Austria's rebellious Italian provinces. What motive, what excuse could he give? Kings do not make war and stake the very existence of their realm out of pure disinterestedness. What was the reward he expected to receive? Was he, under the guise of patriotism, fighting to annex Lombardy and Venetia to Piedmont? If so, what were Leopold of Tuscany, and Pius IX, and Bomba of Naples to gain by sending troops to aid him? Could they desire to see the House of Savoy establish over Northern Italy a kingdom which would menace themselves? They had all been swept along so irresistibly by the revolutionary current during the past two years, that they had had no leisure to foresee whither they were tending. When their subjects had shouted for mild reforms, they had granted them; but before the reforms could be fairly tested, there had come the cry for a constitution, and that, too, had been conceded; and then, before the text of the Constitution had been digested, war was demanded, and they had declared war. Now they asked themselves, what would be their condition in case the war should prosper. Change there must be, if Austria's tyranny were finally abolished from Italy; how would the change affect each of them? Amid the general vagueness, Gioberti's scheme still captivated many imaginations. Italy free, her States independent, but bound together in a confederation over which the

Pope should preside, that pretty phantom still seemed realizable; but when examined near by, when men came to discuss its details, it proved to be, what it had always been, empty, vain, and lifeless.

The negotiations for the Customs League had a few months before been hailed as a sign that Gioberti's project was feasible; but the compact had never been concluded. Now, at the outbreak of the war, Pius endeavored to form a defensive league which should embrace the Roman States, Naples, Tuscany, and Piedmont. He proposed that a Congress of representatives from those States, and from the provinces in insurrection, should convene immediately at Rome to take measures for common defense, for the political reorganization of the Peninsula, and for the definition of the rules which should guide the several States in their mutual and international affairs.[1] Leopold entered cordially into the project, and Bomba professed an equal desire that it should be successful: the former, whose resources were meagre, wished to avail himself of the strength of the stronger members of the proposed league; the latter, as sovereign of the most populous realm in Italy, expected to exert in the new partnership an influence matching his importance. Pius dispatched to Charles Albert a special nuncio, Monsignor Corboli Bussi, — the most enlightened and sincere ecclesiastic who ever served that pope, — to urge that Piedmont should at once send representatives to the Congress. The King replied that he must first consult his ministers. The ministry bluntly pointed out that the first duty before them, and every patriotic Italian, was to get rid of the Austrians; that achieved, Piedmont would not only take part in, but she would hasten the meeting of a general congress.[2] At the same time, Marquis Pareto besought the transpadane princes to

[1] Letter of Pius IX to Leopold, March 28, 1848.
[2] Bianchi, v, 180.

hurry forward their auxiliaries, and to instruct their officers to act in harmony with Piedmontese headquarters. How the course of subsequent events might have been affected had Charles Albert immediately adhered to the League, we can only surmise: it could not have brought him a real increase of military power, but it might have given pause to the charge that he was fighting, not for Italy, but for his own aggrandizement. He seemed to justify the envious tongues — and there were many of them — which accused him of being willing to use the troops of the other princes, although he intended that the glory and the advantage should fall to him alone. But even admitting that selfish interest may have had weight with him, he could adduce strong reasons in support of his action. As he had been the first to declare war, and as he furnished the largest army, he had naturally the right to the supreme command; if he took Leopold, Pius, and Bomba into military partnership, the campaign would lack unity of purpose; if the Congress met before the issue had been decided, it would stir up political disputes and long-smothered feuds, and divert the Italians from their most urgent concern, the expulsion of the Austrians. Therefore, he deemed it less dangerous to appear self-seeking than to consent to a compact pregnant with discord.

Equally unsatisfying was his attitude towards the Lombards. He had come to their aid without demanding pledges or conditions, and tacitly agreeing that the fate of Lombardy should be decided only at the end of the war. But he soon found that his operations in the field suffered through the incompetence of the Provisional Government. Not only did this fail to provide transportation and supplies for his troops, and to organize troops of its own, or even to take proper care of its volunteers, but it lacked moral influence over the population, which was settling back into a do-nothing state, where it watched the struggle between the Piedmontese and the Austrians as if itself were not concerned in the result. The King saw the need of an arrangement by which he might extend his authority, but he could not, in honor, take the initiative. Nevertheless his agents encouraged that party in Lombardy which began to agitate for immediate fusion with Piedmont. The Provisional Governments in each of the Lombard cities took steps early in April to form a Central Government to act until an Assembly could be elected to discuss the ultimate organization of the country. Although in this new body there was a majority — including President Casati — favorable to Piedmont, yet a minority in it, and in the public, stubbornly insisted that Lombardy should be independent and Republican; and this minority had the noisier if not the abler advocates. Clubs and newspapers started up to fight for one side or the other; as if that was a time for word-battles, when Radetzky held the Quadrilateral and the National Spirit needed every encouragement! Charles Albert had reason to feel not only that Lombardy gave him no adequate support, but also that a Republic might at any moment surge up behind him; and yet he had too much respect for his pledge to coerce the Lombards to make terms.[1]

His relations with the Venetians were less dubious only because he had less direct contact with them. Immediately after the proclamation of the Republic at Venice, most of the cities on the mainland that had formerly acknowledged the authority of the Doges voted to renew their old allegiance. The government, presided by Manin, took measures to push the war in Venetia, and to prepare for a general election. But while Venice was resolved to guard her independence, and had been recognized as an independent State by the Piedmontese Consul [2] (April 11), she nevertheless turned to Charles

[1] C. Casati, ii, 238-9.   [2] *Memoriale Veneto*, 27.

Albert for assistance. He sent General Albert La Marmora to her to superintend her military organization, and a special envoy, Rebizzo, to watch her political transactions. He had, however, no real authority over her, for she was under no obligation to follow the advice of his agents, and he had no assurance that her gratitude would lead her to political union with Piedmont when the war was won. Here and there a city — Vicenza, for instance — expressed a desire for immediate fusion, just as Brescia among the Lombard cities had done, but such an expression revealed only an ominous diversity of opinions and for the present interfered with military concord.

Such was the coil of difficulties which involved Charles Albert in his dealings with his Italian neighbors, with those who were supposed to be engaged in a common patriotic enterprise. His relations with the Great Powers were strained still tighter. The ministers of Prussia and Russia had withdrawn from Turin soon after the opening of hostilities. The British minister, after having warned the King against making war, kept reiterating, now that war was joined, reproofs and dismal predictions. He intimated that the Subalpine King had forfeited all claims to the sympathy of law-loving Europe, by his disregard of treaties, — those bugaboos with which diplomacy is wont to frighten little offenders, but which the great culprits laugh at; he painted the danger which engirdled Piedmont: he suggested that Charles Albert's best hope lay in abandoning his misjudged adventure before more harm were done.

Abercromby's new attitude shows how the position of England and Palmerston towards the cause of Italian independence was misunderstood. No one can deny that for nearly two years past Palmerston's support had greatly encouraged the Italians; he had constantly instructed his agents to advise the rulers of Italy to concede reforms demanded by the times; he had sent Lord Minto to give this advice greater weight, and to confer with the Liberals; but he seems not to have perceived that the Italians were aiming at something far beyond mere concessions and reforms, — that they were being stirred by the Spirit of Nationality, that they were thirsting for independence. So he did not foresee that the encouragement he gave them would precipitate a revolution. He thought that the grievances they complained of could be remedied by improvements in legal and administrative matters which would not necessitate political changes. But when the fires of revolution leapt up in all parts of Europe, Palmerston was too genuine an Englishman to approve of them. Liberalism with him did not mean incendiarism. He had no faith in Liberty won at the barricades; he believed in progress by slow development, not by sudden violence; he was a monarchist who saw Chaos and Anarchy behind Red Republics. When, therefore, Charles Albert embarked in a war which, if successful, must recast the political face of Italy and disturb all Europe, the British Foreign Secretary, instead of sanctioning the conflict to which his own words had previously been an instigation, wished to restore the old order of things as quickly as possible. Thus towards the patriots in Italy, and the champions of nationality elsewhere, his attitude was conservative; and Charles Albert, who had counted upon securing at least the moral support of England, had to endure, on the contrary, her chilliness and chiding.

The French Republic gave him still greater anxiety. Just as he was quitting Turin for the seat of war, news came that a troop of four thousand French Republicans were marching on Savoy with the intention of kindling a rebellion, and though they were immediately routed by the loyal Savoyards, yet the attitude of the French government was not reassuring to him.[1] He suspected that the Republic wished to confirm its position by engaging

[1] *Correspondence*, ii, 308.

in a foreign war which should divert Frenchmen from home politics and satisfy their immemorial craving for "glory;" and indeed the massing on his western frontier of the so-called Army of the Alps justified his alarm. For thirty years France had envied Austria her predominance in Italy; now that Austria was stricken to the knee, France had her opportunity. To Mazzini and other Italians in Paris, the French ministers had said: "If Italy's soil, her boundaries, or her liberties are attacked, if your arms are unable to defend her, we offer for her salvation, not merely the good wishes, but the sword of France."[1] They protested that French affection for Italy was disinterested, but when we read the secret dispatches of President Lamartine we are compelled to entertain doubts. Platonic love has never been a characteristic of Jacques Crapaud. On April 6 Lamartine wrote to Bixio, the French minister at Turin, that events in Italy disquieted him to the point of thinking about the possible descent into Piedmont of the army of observation, either in response to a call from Charles Albert, or without any invitation.[2] Bixio replied that the Piedmontese would regard such a movement as a hostile act, and would oppose to it all the resistance in their power.[3] "All Italy would cry out," he wrote a little later (April 20), "that 'France, of whom we have no need, has come down upon our plains for her own interest and not for ours. She has lied; for she wishes to take Austria's post, and she resuscitates that insensate policy which her Republican government has repudiated in words but reproduces in acts.'" Bixio therefore counseled his government to wait patiently until the Piedmontese army should meet with a reverse: then, he said, the Italians would be quick in appealing to France.[4] But Lamartine seems from the start to have reckoned on Savoy and Nice as the plums which

[1] C. Casati, ii, 240. [2] Bianchi, v, 275.
[3] Ibid. [4] Beauregard, 170; Bianchi, loc. cit.

should fall to France in the general shaking of the boughs. France, he told the Piedmontese minister, "cannot be the only Power to stand with her hands in her pockets. The Republic, as a rule, does not intend to meddle in the internal affairs of other States; but it wishes, and it has the incontestable right, to hold itself in readiness to defend oppressed nations, and to prevent the European equilibrium from being upset to the advantage of the oppressing States. Austria complains quite as much as your government, and with more reason, at the concentration of our troops toward the Alps; since she understands full well that, in case you were worsted in the war you have undertaken in Lombardy, those troops would be ordered to march against her."[1] For the present, indeed, France had to stand with her hands in her pockets; for Palmerston exerted his influence to keep her quiet, and other considerations deterred: but though Lamartine protested that his intentions were pacific,[2] he held the Army of the Alps at marching orders, and kept Charles Albert in suspense. The King dreaded the contagious influence of the Republic upon the Italians, who were just in a state to catch any virulent political disease. The Provisional Government at Milan had addressed an appeal to France;[3] Venice had done likewise: and though the French government had sent no official reply to either, yet it was natural to suppose that, had it no other motives, the French Republic would favor the establishment of a republic in Lombardy and Venetia. With good reason, therefore, did Charles Albert distrust French intrigues and dread French interference.

In Austria the Imperial government somewhat recovered its energy after the first panic at Metternich's downfall. The news of the insurrection of Lombardy and Venetia roused great indignation, even among those races which were themselves angry at the House of Hapsburg,

[1] Bianchi, v, 277.   [2] *Correspondence*, ii, 378.   [3] *Ibid*, 354, 370.

and the common cry was that the Italian provinces must be reconquered and punished. But the outlook was so black during the early days of April that Ficquelmont, who had succeeded Metternich as head of the Cabinet, deemed it necessary to compromise. He sent Count Hartig on a special mission to Italy with instructions to make peace on the following terms: Austria should retain Venetia, but give up Lombardy, which should assume two hundred millions of the Austrian debt, pay the cost of the war, and conclude a commercial and customs treaty with Austria.[1] Ficquelmont besought Palmerston to urge Charles Albert to suspend hostilities until these negotiations could be arranged, and Palmerston, eager to avert a European war, gladly consented to do so. Lamartine also seems to have supported this project. But when the British minister sounded the Piedmontese Cabinet, they replied that they would resign rather than discuss such a dishonorable proposal, and when Hartig put forth a feeler at Milan, the Provisional Government curtly refused to listen to him.[2] The temptation thus resisted was alluring: the war had progressed far enough to show that it would require more troops, money, and time than had been expected; Radetzky might maintain himself in the Quadrilateral for months; a temporary reverse might dishearten the army; every day increased the political entanglements at home and the diplomatic complications abroad. If Charles Albert made peace, he could almost certainly count upon annexing Lombardy to his kingdom; he would be free to deal with the internal affairs which were pressing upon him; his army would go home with the prestige of victory. But his honor was at stake; and his honor, pledged to redeem Northern Italy from the Ticino to the Adriatic, would not suffer him to desert Venetia. The fact that Austria was willing to treat at

[1] Bianchi, v, 260.
[2] *Correspondence*, ii, 306, 320, 322, 332, 342, 349–51, 401.

all encouraged the belief that she felt Radetzky's position to be even more precarious than it seemed to the Piedmontese; not only honor, therefore, but common-sense, prompted the refusal of the proffered half loaf when the whole loaf might be had for a little effort. Hartig, failing at the very outset of his mission, contented himself by issuing a proclamation to the Lombardo-Venetians; a more specious and pusillanimous manifesto — with its references to the "good monarch" and "father," Ferdinand, and to the love Austria had always borne to her Italian subjects — was never indited by a nonplussed diplomat.[1]

These were the difficulties which, in addition to the military question, pursued Charles Albert night and day. If glory or selfish ambition was his motive, he learned soon enough of what inglorious elements, of what weariness of body and petty torments of soul, that which is called fame, that which ambition thirsts for, is composed. But he had rather the air of one to whom a charge full of hardship and cumber has been given, of one who submits to the task Providence has assigned to him, but who, while submitting piously, feels none the less that the burden is heavy and the path steep. "The King seems to commit his future victories to the mercy of God," writes Costa, his equerry and intimate. "His nights are passed in prayer. Sleeping in a closet adjoining his chamber, I heard him, two days ago, utter such sighs that, thinking him ill, I looked through a crack in the door. There he was on his knees, praying with all the fervor of his soul."[2]

Whilst the King was thus wrestling with other antagonists than Radetzky, the slowness of his campaign began to be freely criticised both by the army, eager for decisive victory, and by the great multitude of those stay-at-home critics who in war-time always display wondrous

[1] Text in *Correspondence*, ii, 380–91.   [2] Beauregard, 158–9.

courage and infallible generalship so long as they are not within range of the cannon's roar. The enthusiasm throughout the Peninsula was still very great, despite the disappointment which many felt when they perceived that the expulsion of the Austrians would require more time than they had anticipated. Of the issue, nobody doubted; nor had sober second-thought yet come to rebuke the over-confidence of the majority. On April 26 Charles Albert, who had by this time received large reinforcements, and who realized the need, both from the political and military point of view, of driving the campaign to a conclusion, crossed the Mincio. He planned to complete the investment of Peschiera, the ordnance having come up, and to make an assault on Verona, in the hope that the Veronese would rise at his approach. Radetzky, who had thus far adhered to his intention of declining a pitched battle, knew the need of preventing the Piedmontese from cutting their way across the Adige above Verona, and he accordingly ordered General d'Aspre to hold the village of Pastrengo. On the 30th the second corps of the Piedmontese army, commanded by General Sonnaz, moved forward to dislodge him, but, it being Sunday, Charles Albert insisted that his troops should attend mass before going into battle, so that eleven o'clock had struck before active operations began. By that time D'Aspre was on the alert. The Piedmontese rushed to the charge with their war-cry, "Ever forwards, Savoy!"[1] but though they outnumbered the Austrians, the latter had a strong defensive position, and for several hours the battle raged. Charles Albert exposed himself with the nonchalance of a man who fears nothing in this world or the next. His troops fought gallantly, his officers carried out their instructions promptly; by four in the afternoon the Austrians were in retreat, having abandoned Pastrengo and the neighboring villages,

[1] "*Sempre avanti Savoja!*"

and withdrawn in disorder to the left bank of the Adige. To pursue them without pause, even to the very gates of Verona, should have been the immediate business of the victors: but the King, perhaps fearing an ambush, perhaps underestimating the preciousness of a few hours at such a time, passed the famous order, "For to-day this is enough," and held back his victorious army from its prey.

CHAPTER VIII.

THE FIRST MASKS FALL.

As the news of Pastrengo sped southward, it met news of another sort; the Pope, it was reported, had deserted the National Cause. The report proved to be but too true, as any one could assure himself by reading Pius's latest allocution. How had it come to pass that Pius, who so recently had blessed the departing Crusaders and had prayed God to bless Italy, drew back just at the moment when his blessings were bearing fruit? Had he made a feint of patriotism in those earlier weeks? Or had some evil genius suddenly possessed him? Remember the incompatible nature of his twofold power, and you can surmise what had happened. Never did circus-rider undertake such an equestrian feat as this good-natured, unathletic priest had striven to accomplish ever since July, 1846. He had striven to ride two horses, — one, the Church, stationary during the past three hundred years, the other, the State, now unhitched and restless to gallop forward. Either both must move or both must stand still, unless the timid rider was to be thrown to the ground. Pius had at last realized that his position was untenable, and, true to his clerical instincts, he thought it would be easier to check the motion of the State than to spur the Church from her immemorial fixedness.

We speak of national enthusiasm sweeping everything before it, but this figure is only true in part. Watch a tide coming in: the waves leap forward, this wave breaking a little farther up the beach than its predecessor, and the next farther still; but the undertow below the surface you do not see, although in time this undertow shall conquer the shoreward flood and drag it back. At Rome, the party of Reaction — the Gregorians and Sanfedists, and every ecclesiastic in whose brain mediævalism was stamped as indelibly as the footprints of antediluvian monsters on primeval mud — had become less and less openly combative in proportion as Liberalism got control: but they were not destroyed, — far from it, — neither were they idle, though their activity had to be more subtle and cautious than formerly. From the moment when Pius, bowing to popular clamor, allowed Papal troops and volunteers to march northward, the Reactionists bewildered him with cunning doubts. They insinuated calumnies against Charles Albert, in order to undermine his prestige as the military leader of the patriotic war; they threw out artful questions as to the legality of the Pope's engaging in an offensive campaign, and by these questions they hoped to scare him into withdrawing his moral support from the Italian cause. Pius himself, though unendowed with statesmanlike breadth and foresight, was yet sufficiently keen to perceive the equivocalness of his actions. He had not declared war on Austria, yet he was encouraging his subjects to arm with the evident purpose of joining those Italians who were fighting Austria. The excuse he gave at first was that he intended to limit his troops to defending the Papal frontier in case this should be attacked, but when Durando and the Papal army reached the Po they soon showed that they had no intention of remaining there in idleness. Durando, assuming that he acted in accordance with Pius's sanction, issued a proclamation in which he implied that they had really set forth on a crusade, a war of Christians against barbarous and immoral enemies, and that, in fighting for Italy, they were serving the Pope and God.[1]

[1] Proclamation issued at Bologna, April 5; text in Minghetti, i, 365–6.

When Pius saw this manifesto he became furious, and could with difficulty be dissuaded from publishing a disclaimer which would have immediately crushed the hopes of his patriotic subjects. The *Official Gazette* of April 10 announced tersely that "when the Pope wishes to make declarations of his sentiments, he speaks *ex se*, never through the mouth of any subaltern."[1]

The ministry, with the exception of their President, Cardinal Antonelli, were unanimous in favor of war; Antonelli for the present dissembled his policy and seemed to sympathize with them, because it would be well, in certain emergencies, to have the protection of the Liberals. To calm the Pope's scruples, they pushed the negotiations for an Italian League, in the belief that Pius, as a temporal prince, might furnish a military contingent to the League without prejudicing his character as Pontiff. But Piedmont, by refusing to discuss the matter, deprived him of this means of satisfying his amphibious conscience. Meanwhile, Durando and his troops grew restive; they had good reason to believe that the Pope was at heart willing that they should share in the National war, and they cared little for the petty quibbles which had sprung up to make him diffident. Durando had been ordered " to put himself in correspondence as soon as possible with Charles Albert's headquarters, and to act in harmony with it."[2] What did that mean except that the Papal government fully expected that the Papal army would participate actively in the campaign? When the ministers assured Pius that his indecision threatened to wreck the internal peace of the State as well as to exasperate the troops, he replied that, even though his army should cross the Po, he could easily order it to retreat, in case he should decide not to take part in the war. On April 18, therefore, Prince Aldobrandini, Minister of War, wrote to Durando: "I have just shown your note

[1] Minghetti, i, 367. [2] Farini, ii, 53.

to the Holy Father, who has replied to me that you are authorized to do whatever you judge necessary for the tranquillity and welfare of the Pontifical State."[1] At the same time the minister wrote to the Legate at Bologna: "Your Eminence will well understand that in putting ourselves in concord with Charles Albert's headquarters we intend to work for the safety of Italy, and likewise for the greater interest of the Pontifical government. It will be for your Eminence, should you deem necessary in the interest of the government itself some step yet more daring (*ardito*), to give the General the requisite orders."[2] Whatever Pius intended by his equivocal message, Durando construed it with patriotic eyes, crossed the Po, and began operations on Austrian territory.

The Reactionists plied the Pope with their insinuations and terrors. The Austrian ambassador urged and threatened. Vague rumors were circulated that, if Pius persisted in attacking Austria, there would be a religious schism among the Catholics in Austria and Germany. His mind, once intimidated, saw cause for alarm in everything. He trembled at the hint that Austria could easily capture Ancona from the sea; he trembled lest Bomba's troops, in passing through his territory, should seize the Marches; but he trembled most at the sound of that word "schism." His first duty was to preserve inviolate the Church which had been intrusted to him; the pontiff eclipsed the patriot in him, — eclipsed the patriot, but not the prince. He began to discern, now that he thought his ecclesiastical supremacy was threatened, that his temporal power was indivisibly joined to his spiritual power; he had been good-naturedly abrogating some of his prerogatives as prince, not dreaming that in so doing he might diminish his authority as pope; now it flashed upon him that whatever weakened one side of his dual nature

[1] Farini, ii, 55.   [2] Minghetti, i, 364.

weakened the other. He saw, we may imagine, revolutionary Europe, as in a frightful vision, breaking up into chaotic fragments, dissolving princedoms and privileges, and rolling headlong towards anarchy. If princedoms dissolved, could popedom endure? Was not political anarchy the twin of religious anarchy, of atheism? In comparison with the considerations which embraced the destiny of the world, the triumph of the Italian cause was a small concern. The moment had come when he could falter no longer. Schism? — the very word was distracting!

Events hurried on. With the Papal troops actually in the field, and rumors of schism echoing through the Quirinal, the Pope must declare his position. This he was expected to do at a Consistory of the Cardinals on April 29, and his ministers, having a foreboding of what his declaration would be, drew up an address in which they endeavored, by stating the case frankly, to counteract the influence which the Reactionaries through their insinuations and threats had obtained over him. The ministers, speaking only as advisers of the temporal sovereign, besought him to consent to his subjects' participation in the war. The times and public opinion, they said, demanded this, and though war was always an evil, in this case it was the least of the evil alternatives from among which they had to choose. If Pius forbade the war, he would endanger the temporal existence of the Holy See, because popular enthusiasm had gone too far to be checked without turning into wrath. But if the Pope declared that, while desiring peace, he was unable to prevent war, he would confess himself to be the ruler of a realm in which he was powerless to enforce his commands.[1] Pius was moved by this remonstrance, but he gave his ministers no intimation as to what he had determined on. The country was sup-

[1] Text of remonstrance in Minghetti (i, 368-71), Pasolini (97-9), Farini, (ii. 86-90).

posed to have a constitution, and the ministers to be responsible for the policy of the government; yet here a vital question was at issue, and the ministers were allowed to know nothing of their sovereign's intention. Pius said that he did not wish it to appear that his allocution before the Cardinals had been drawn up by laymen; nevertheless, from his manner they still hoped. On the 29th he read his allocution in the Consistory; the ministers, like the public, had to wait for its publication in the Roman *Gazette*. Grubbing through the rough Latin as best they could, they found there the transcript of their fears. Pius, after animadverting to and condemning the rumors of schism, announced his purpose in the following sentence: "Although some persons now desire that we, together with the other peoples and princes of Italy, make war against the Austrians, we deem it proper to disclose clearly in this solemn meeting of ours, that that is wholly foreign to our intentions, since we, however unworthy, exercise on earth the functions of Him who is the author of peace and lover of charity, and according to the office of our supreme Apostolate we follow and embrace all races, peoples, and nations with equal zeal of paternal love."[1]

The ministers, realizing that their power of usefulness was shattered, placed their resignations in Cardinal Antonelli's hands. Antonelli himself pretended to lament that, as cardinal, his duty forbade him to imitate them; he even insisted that, although he must obey the Pope in spiritual matters, he desired to have no more political affairs thrust upon him. He felt so deeply the trammels of his scarlet gown, and envied them their freedom to act! Early on the following morning the Pope summoned them to a council. He appeared astonished that they had been disturbed by his allocution. "It is true," he exclaimed, "that I have refused war, because I am

[1] The allocution is printed in Farini, ii, 92-8.

Pope, and as such I ought to regard all the Catholic peoples with equal affection, and as sons: but you have not noted that passage in which I said, 'If among our subjects there are some who allow themselves to be drawn by the example of the other Italians, how could I restrain their ardor?' Is not this the very thought that I have always repeated to you? You are not responsible for my allocution; you have not signed it."[1] Evidently Pius was as blind to the attitude which a Cabinet in a constitutionally governed country must maintain, as to the effect his declaration would produce upon his own subjects and all Italy. The ministers persisted in resigning, but consented to discharge their routine work until a new Cabinet could be formed. As soon as the allocution was understood in Rome, a storm of maledictions burst upon the Pope and the Clerical Party. The populace, still lead by Ciceruacchio, who was now as wrathful as he had once been friendly towards Pius, took possession of the streets. The Civic Guard joined them. The Castle of St. Angelo was seized, the city gates were locked, sentinels were posted at the door of every unpopular cardinal's palace. The orators inflamed the political clubs with angry speeches; the mildest demanded Antonelli's discharge, the fiercest cried out, "Down with the Pope! Down with the Papacy!" For two days a revolution seemed unpreventable.

Pius, beginning to learn the effect of his allocution, vacillated between resentment and alarm: he was incensed that subjects to whom he had granted so much should ungratefully and impudently criticise any act of his; he was alarmed lest, in their fury, they might carry out their mutterings against himself. He talked of quitting Rome, of leaving the reprobates to destroy themselves by their wickedness. While he was making frantic efforts to gather a new ministry, the old ministers

[1] Minghetti, i, 376.

strove to prevent a catastrophe in Rome, and to mitigate, if that were still possible, the evil which Pius's address would do to the national cause. They represented to him that he had taken from Durando and the Papal troops, now beyond the Po, the character of recognized belligerents; so that, if captured by the Austrians, they might be shot down as bandits or outlaws. To provide against this danger, Pius dispatched Farini to Charles Albert's headquarters, instructing him to request the King to assume command of the Papal forces, and so to assure them the same treatment which the Piedmontese had at the enemy's hands.[1] The ministers proposed, further, that Pius should make a journey to Milan to offer himself as mediator between Italy and Austria. They reckoned on his being received with enthusiasm everywhere; that the people would interpret his visit as a sign that, whatever he had said in the Consistory, he had not deserted Italy; that, in a word, the moral effect of his sympathy might still be preserved to the patriotic cause. Pius himself agreed to the plan; but when Minghetti and Pasolini called upon Piazzone, the agent of the Milanese Provisional Government, he proved lukewarm, and intimated that the Pope might expect a cold reception among the Lombards.[2] So that hope had to be abandoned.

Pius still seemed greatly astonished at the hostile demonstrations his allocution had awakened. "Evidently the Romans do not understand Latin," said he to the ministers; "therefore I will speak to them in Italian. Give yourselves no anxiety; remain at your posts; tomorrow you shall see that I will completely reassure you." And walking in the Quirinal Garden with Recchi and Pasolini, he repeated to them that he would correct the mistake. He even sent a servant to the printing office to fetch the copy of the new order he had written; but the servant failed to bring it. The next day (May 1)

[1] Farini. i. 114.   [2] Minghetti, i, 282-3.

the city walls were placarded with the expected proclamation; it was in Italian and quite clear, but, to the disgust of the ministers, it merely reiterated those passages in the allocution which had given the greatest offense. Long afterwards it was learned that the address as written by Pius had been amended and its meaning changed by Cardinal Antonelli; the Cardinal, unscrupulous though he was, could hardly have made the changes without the Pope's consent, but whether the Pope consented willingly, or was deceived by Antonelli, no one now can say.[1] On May 2 Count Mamiani, a writer and thinker of ability, who had only recently been permitted to return to Rome from exile, accepted Pius's request to form a new Cabinet. He stipulated that he should be allowed to follow the policy of his predecessors towards the National War, and that the temporal interests of the State should be wholly intrusted to lay ministers. On May 4 he organized his ministry, and thanks to his own popularity as a Liberal, the violent symptoms of the Roman populace began to subside. But Pius's great prestige was gone, and gone irrevocably. Whoever shall write the history of the decline and fall of the Roman Papacy will assign April 29, 1848, — the day in which the Ninth Pius issued his antipatriotic allocution, — as the date when the temporal sovereignty of the Pope ceased to have the support of a majority of his subjects. For a generation before that, indeed, the popes had maintained their temporal power only through foreign influence; then for eighteen months Pius had, by a different policy, secured the loyal adherence of the Papal population: from April 29, 1848, down to the present time a majority, constantly increasing, has been implacably opposed to the Papacy.

The publication of the allocution was also the turning-point in the Italian National movement. It mattered relatively but little that the Papal contingent should be

[1] Pasolini, 102-3.

withdrawn from the war, but it mattered immensely that the moral support of the Pope should be withdrawn. Pius had been worshiped for nearly two years as the political redeemer of Italy; his position at the head of the Catholic world gave a peculiar sanction to the cause he espoused; Catholics who fought against that cause might well ask themselves whether they were not in some fashion fighting against him; Italians had reason to believe that in upholding the principles which he approved, they were engaged in an undertaking which really was, what the rhetorical orators called it, a crusade. But his disavowal relieved the Austrians of the imputation that they were attacking the head of their Church; it deprived the Italians, not only of the moral sanction of the Pope, but also of his unique services as the centre and unifier in whom the differences between princes and peoples and the conflicting interests of the various provinces might be reconciled. They were exhilarated by one hope, one aim, — the independence of Italy. The allocution taught them that in the very heart of the Peninsula was a ruler who would sacrifice Italy in behalf of the Papacy. So they learned, as Pius himself had learned, that the existence of the Papacy was incompatible with Italian Independence, that the interests of the pope-priest would inevitably, in case of conflict, determine the action of the pope-prince. Churchman that he was, he had simply thrown over everything to save, as he supposed, the Church; that he deemed this necessary proved, as did his astonishment at the wrath he thereby excited, how little he knew the times in which he lived, and how completely he lacked the statesman's equipment.

The allocution had a twofold effect on the Italians: it exasperated one party, it chilled another. The former, who had been looking upon Pius as a Julius II or an Alexander III, — a fighting pontiff, eager to direct all the enginery of the Church against the foes of Italy, —

accused him of duplicity and desertion. They quoted against him Dante's famous arraignment of that pope "who made, through cowardice, the great refusal."[1] They ceased forever to respect him. The others, while deploring his action, still felt bound to obey it, as the command of their spiritual chief. The Reactionists, who had frightened Pius by their evil whispers, of course rejoiced; they at least knew its significance, and indulged no delusions. To Charles Albert, the Pope's defection was a severe blow; for he had strengthened himself in the belief that Pius's coöperation gave a sacred character to the National enterprise, and he understood the political importance of retaining Pius as a figure-head or symbol. But the King had no thought of wavering, despite the backsliding of the Pope.

To emphasize his assumption of the rôle of peacemaker Pius sent an autograph letter to the Austrian emperor, in which he appealed to disinterestedness which, it is safe to say, no European monarch in these latter ages has allowed to govern his conduct. "Let it not be unacceptable to your Majesty," wrote the Pope in a tone of unsophisticated entreaty, "that we address ourselves to your piety and religion, exhorting you with paternal affection to cause your arms to cease from a war which, without having the power to reconquer for the Empire the minds of the Lombards and Venetians, brings with it that fatal series of calamities which are wont to accompany it, and which are certainly abhorred and detested by you. Let it not be unacceptable to the generous German nation that we invite it to lay down hatred and to convert into useful relations of friendly neighborliness a domination which would be neither noble nor happy were it based solely on the sword. Thus we trust that the nation itself, worthily proud of its nationality, will not stake its honor in sanguinary attempts against the Italian nation, but

[1] *Inferno*, iii, 60.

will rather find its honor in nobly recognizing the latter as a sister, as both are our daughters and very dear to our heart, agreeing to occupy each its natural boundaries on honorable terms, and with the Lord's blessing."[1] This pacific appeal, brought to Ferdinand at Innspruck, whither he had fled on account of renewed turbulence in Vienna, met with the reception that was to be expected. The Emperor referred Monsignor Morichini, the bearer of the letter, to his ministers, with the remark that "Austria possesses her Italian provinces by virtue of the same treaties which have reconstituted the temporal power of the Pope."[2] Wessenberg, one of the Imperial ministers, treated the Pope's intercession as an object of derision.[3] Temporal popedom, therefore, had no more "divine right" to be, than had any other petty duchy to which the Treaty of Vienna allotted a separate existence. Austria, having made a tool of Pius, had that contempt for him which one has for tools that can be used no more. He had forfeited his influence alike over Italy and over Austria; let him now try whether the Reactionists into whose hands he had played could keep him on his throne.

Whilst Italy was still venting her indignation at Pius's "great refusal," the news of another defection staggered her: the King of Naples withdrew his support from the National war. The counter-revolution in Naples came about sooner and more suddenly than Bomba himself expected: that from the first he desired it, and stealthily connived at it, no one can doubt, but there is doubt as to whether he had directly so large a share in causing it as has been charged against him. The truth is that his perfidy was only one factor in the result. He had but to wait and be patient, not interfering, or, if he interfered, to do so quietly, and the hysterical populace would succumb from sheer exhaustion. Cowardice being Bom-

[1] Farini. ii, 129.   [2] Bianchi, v, 103.   [3] Beauregard, 210.

ba's dominant trait, as it had been that of his father Francis and of his grandfather Ferdinand, his course throughout was that of a coward. Fear led him to grant the Constitution, to accept a more liberal ministry, and to issue his patriotic manifesto; fear likewise kept him from being hasty in recanting. Cowering in his palace, like a rat in a corner, he simply trembled and watched his chance.[1] We can understand every one of his actions by referring them to cowardice, which, whatever may be said against it, makes its victims wonderfully alert.

The Troya Ministry of April 3 had Liberal intentions, but lacked experience and authority. Six or eight men, however devoted, cannot lift a whole people to a higher political level; one strong man can lead a people down; but the process of elevation is necessarily slow. Now at Naples every one looked for the immediate realization of his desires. The Constitution was popularly supposed to be a sort of charm or talisman, — an Aladdin's lamp, — to possess which made character or effort superfluous. You had but to wish and to rub, and lo! it would create a perfect government. The Neapolitans, like most persons, mistook the Land of Cockayne for Utopia. Consequently, their ministers were in no wise able to satisfy them. They were unsupported by a sane and constant public opinion; they had not ready-made men fit to fill the thousands of offices in the various departments of government; they had not the candid coöperation of the King. Political clubs wrangled, newspapers snarled, any man had lungs enough to set flying calumny or suspicion. The seat of government was situated, as I have before remarked, not in the brain but in the larynx, and of all peoples this side of Arabia, the Neapolitans have the strongest throats. The Cabinet, therefore, did not or could not preserve sufficient order to hear themselves speak, or to be heard. They strove to fulfil their prom-

[1] Cf. Nisco, 212-3.

ises by sending commissioners to negotiate the formation of the Italian league, and they hastened preparations for the departure of the Neapolitan troops to the north. But they felt an invisible influence continually opposing them. Every day Bomba's eagerness for war grew slacker, and he had in the Cabinet itself an underhand coadjutor. Ruggiero, Minister of Ecclesiastical Affairs, maintained that the King ought to understand what his share of the plunder was to be, before he sent his army to Lombardy; otherwise, he would discover too late that he had served as cat's-paw for Charles Albert's ambition. Unofficial statesmen, whose Parliament-house was this or that café, and each of whom spoke with all the emphasis of irresponsible egotism, proclaimed one or other of the many political follies which bubbled to the surface in that stormy year. One preached socialism, another communism, a third insisted that the government should open National workshops; the poor Constitution which, at best, was like Joseph's coat of many colors, was attacked on every side, — one doctrinaire insisting on cutting out this patch, another insisting that the sleeves did not fit, until there was not a shred left which suited every one. Dardano, from his throne in the Café of Progress, announced that nothing but the Constitution of 1820, with such additions as he decreed, would satisfy him; La Cecilia, gliding from throng to throng, whispered that only a Republic would secure his sanction; and, one and all, these demagogues had their little rabble of partisans.

General William Pepe set out on May 4 to take command of the Neapolitan contingent, which numbered only 15,000 men instead of the promised 40,000; his instructions were to remain quietly south of the Po until he should receive orders to advance. This incensed the populace, and sharpened their suspicion that the King was false. A Camarilla, whose roots were in the Royal Palace and whose branches spread among the priesthood, plotted reaction; Bomba, meanwhile, pretending ignorance of its existence, but holding himself ready to reward it if it succeeded. The Pope's allocution gave great comfort to these Retrogrades, who further circulated the report that Pius intended to launch the ban of excommunication against the National war. Out of confusion such as this anything, except good or wisdom, might spring; it remained for Opportunity to determine which of the warring elements should prevail.

The sane, patriotic minority looked forward to the assembling of Parliament as an event which, by concentrating attention on common interests and by strengthening the Liberal Ministry, must give pause to the hurly-burly of factions. The elections passed off without disturbance, and on May 12 the deputies began to assemble at the capital. They met informally at the Town Hall of Montoliveto, a precinct of the city, to arrange for the ceremonial at the opening of the Chambers. The King himself drew up the order of exercises and prescribed the form of oath which the deputies were to take. Just here came a difficulty. Bomba insisted that they should swear to be loyal to the throne and to uphold the Constitution; but one of the stipulations of the Troya Ministry on taking office had been that the Constitution should be amended. The deputies, therefore, claimed that in swearing to uphold the Constitution it should be understood that they referred to the Constitution as it might be amended by the Chambers. A dispute arose as to what was intended by the word *svolgere*, which had been used in the programme of Troya and his colleagues; the deputies held that it meant plainly enough "to modify" or "to develop." The King demurred. The ministers thought they had persuaded him to change the required oath, when, on the 14th, he issued a bulletin in which the form of oath appeared unchanged. All day long there were negotiations between the deputies and the ministers, and between the ministers and the King. The popular representatives grew suspicious and stubborn; the King would not recede; the ministers resigned. In the hall at Montoliveto extreme opinions began to flash out. One deputy declared that they ought to take no oath until after the Chamber had convened and the credentials of each member had been duly verified. Finally, a compromise oath was drawn up and sent to the ministers, who still served as intermediaries, for the King's approval. The King replied that the deputies wished to arrogate to themselves powers to which they had no right. Thereupon Petruccelli set the assemblage in an uproar by shouting, "We are betrayed!" The populace, which had gathered outside the hall, now showed signs of tumult, not allayed when another deputy, Zuppetta, appeared on a balcony and protested that all the deputies would die rather than permit the King to betray the law of the Constitution. Bomba, whose emissaries kept him informed of the course of events, took alarm, and tardily consented that the oath should be amended to suit the popular demand. But when his peacemakers reached the hall they found it already in confusion. La Cecilia, a Mazzinian, followed by brawlers of his sort, had broken in upon the deliberation of the deputies, and had, with wild words, exhorted them to come to no agreement with the King until all the strongholds of the city had been turned over to the National Guard. As soon as La Cecilia's proposition had been put to vote and carried by a majority of the deputies, the multitude, maddened by the suggestions of treason and fearing a *coup d'état*, began to construct barricades. At three in the morning Bomba, thoroughly scared, sent a last messenger to inform the deputies that they might dispense with the oath-taking altogether. But it was too late.

At daybreak, Via Toledo and all the other streets leading into the square in front of the Royal Palace were barricaded, and behind the barricades glowered squads of National Guards and of angry citizens. In the square, Swiss regiments were massed in battle array. But there were still a few cool heads eager to prevent a conflict; these besought the King to order the troops back to their quarters. Bomba replied that he would do so, but that first the barricaders must disperse, as it would be unseemly to have it appear that his soldiers were afraid of a popular mob. A proper reply; but when these peacemakers begged the insurgents to retire, they were not listened to. After long suspense, about eleven in the morning, a shot, fired, it is said, by some one at the Via Toledo barricade, precipitated the struggle. The troops charged and were repulsed; then they turned cannon against the barricades, and, blowing a breach through them, gradually drove the insurgents from point to point, until, late in the afternoon, they had routed the last squad of resisters. Thereupon followed such an orgy of cruelty as accompanies the taking of a hostile city by half-savage Croats or Cossacks of the Don: houses were sacked and burnt, men and women were slaughtered; the innocent and guilty being alike hunted down by the Swiss soldiery. The deputies who, in session at Montoliveto, had organized a meaningless Committee of Public Safety, were allowed to disperse unmolested, not, however, before they had drawn up a protest against the act of blind and "incorrigible despotism" which forced them to suspend the labors for which the country had elected them.[1]

Bomba learned that night that his faithful troops had killed above 500 of his "best-beloved subjects;" and that a thousand prisoners had been put under arrest. He immediately issued a proclamation dissolving the Parliament, commanding the disarmament of the National Guard, and recalling the Neapolitan contingent from the National war. He promised to maintain the Constitu-

[1] Text in Nisco, 220; Mancini, who drew up the protest, was sentenced to the galleys for twenty-five years.

tion, though he treated the deputies as rebels who had attempted to overthrow his throne. Henceforth, however, he had no fear of the Liberals, and consequently no scruples. This insurrection of the 15th of May had proved him master, and though he let the empty simulacrum of a Constitutional Government stand for a little while, it was because it no longer caused him hindrance or alarm. His influence, and that of Naples, upon the National Cause whose development we are following, ceased from that time and need hereafter receive but little attention from us. We need only remember that after Bomba threw off his simulated patriotism, he devoted himself body and soul to the punishment of those men who had from January to May, 1848, frightened him into posing as a reformer, and to the extirpation of every offshoot of Liberalism in his kingdom. What his methods were, and what his success, was told two years later, and even Diplomacy, even the Machiavellians who then ruled Europe, were horror-struck at the tale. It was of Bomba and his permanent reign of terror after May, 1848, that Gladstone said "the government of the Bourbons at Naples is the negation of God."[1] Through lack of evidence we may absolve him from the charge of having directly planned the *coup d'état* of May 15, not because his conscience rebelled at that infamy, but because his cowardice counseled him to wait for a propitious moment; but we cannot absolve him from his perfidious intent, nor from his wily instigation of civil discord, nor from his unconcealed exultation, as from his palace window he encouraged his troops in their murderous work, nor from the infamous retaliation which he took when his Swiss mercenaries had enabled his cowardly hand to strike without fear of resistance.[2]

[1] See Gladstone's *Letters to Lord Aberdeen*, 1850.
[2] For the counter-revolution of May 15, see Pepe: *Révolutions d'Italie* (Paris, 1850), iii, chap. 9; La Farina, iii, chap. 24; Settembrini, i, chap. 21.

In General Pepe the order to lead back his army to Naples kindled indignation. His first impulse was to disobey, but fearing that the troops would not follow him, he resigned his command to General Statella. Repenting, however, he canceled his resignation and bade Statella inform the King that the Neapolitans' foremost duty was to their fatherland, to Italy. His resolution, unjustifiable by any technical standard of military allegiance, was loudly applauded at Bologna, where he had his headquarters for the moment. But the troops hesitated between obedience to their general and obedience to their king: the officers' wives wrote to their husbands that they would be punished by death or exile if they persisted in their disobedience; the common soldiers, having been taught that their one duty was to their sovereign, very naturally set his commands above romantic attachment to the Italian cause. One division deserted and went home, Pepe distrusting the troops still loyal to himself too much to order them to attack the deserters. Very rapidly other regiments melted away, until at length he had but a few battalions willing to stand by him. With these, in the second week of June, he crossed the Po and marched to Venice, to take a conspicuous part in the defense of that city.[1]

The withdrawal of the Neapolitans came at a critical moment. General Nugent had been hurrying with reinforcements from Illyria, to effect a junction with Radetzky. He had taken Udine, left a detachment to block Palmanova, crossed the Piave, beaten the Venetian volunteers at Cornuda, and was already preparing to attack Vicenza, when Pepe received his orders to return. Had Pepe been allowed by May 20 to throw his 15,000 men into Venetia, he might have held Nugent in check for a long time; if, indeed, he failed to rout him completely. The effect of such a movement must have been very per-

[1] Pepe, iii, chap. 10.

ilous for Radetzky, who would thereby have been deprived not only of nearly 20,000 men, but also of all hope of getting help by way of Venetia. Still more disastrous was Bomba's defection to the war as a national undertaking. Henceforth the war could not be regarded as an effort of all Italy to expel the Austrians; for Bomba had bluntly signified that Naples had no concern in it, and the Pope had refused to give it his official sanction. Instead of harmony there had been discord; instead of national patriotism, local selfishness. The paralysis of reaction, beginning at the extremity of the Peninsula, had crept up almost to its middle; the masks had fallen, disclosing the true features of Pius and Ferdinand. The peoples of the South and Centre had got self-knowledge; they had learned, and bitter was the learning, that they who had so enthusiastically shouted for independence and unity were still bound more tightly than they supposed by their devotion to clique and faction and by traditional feuds. Not yet had they learned that patriotism means the love of country, and not the success of party. With the collapse of Constitutionalism at Naples ends the period when the revolution which was openly acknowledged after Pius's decree of amnesty in July, 1846, and which had with rapid strides brought the Italians face to face with Austria on the battlefield, had the ascendant. We shall now enter the period when the Italian cause ceased to be national, and when the revolution, split up into fragments, made a final desperate resistance to the forces of reaction.

BOOK FIFTH.

DISINTEGRATION : DEMOCRACY : DISASTER.

> Non sien le genti ancor troppo sicure
> A giudicar, sì come quei che stima
> Le biade in campo pria che sien mature :
> Ch' io ho veduto tutto il verno prima
> Il pruu mostrarsi rigido e feroce,
> Poscia portar la rosa in sulla cima ;
> E legno vidi già dritto e veloce
> Correr lo mar per tutto suo cammino,
> Perire al fine all' entrar della foce.
> DANTE, *Paradiso*, xiii, 130-8.

CHAPTER I.

FUSION VERSUS CONFUSION.

CHARLES ALBERT'S victory at Pastrengo, on April 30, enabled him to complete the investment of Peschiera. A week later (May 6) he made an assault on the outposts of Verona; but though his men fought gallantly, the unfavorableness of the ground, seamed by vineyards and plantations, the strength of the Austrian intrenchments, and the lack of accurate topographical information on the part of the Piedmontese staff, compelled the King to sound the retreat. His troops, covered by the reserves under the Duke of Savoy, withdrew in such good order to their camp at Sommacampagna that the Austrians deemed it prudent not to pursue them. This encounter, called the battle of Santa Lucia after the scene of the hottest fighting, taught Charles Albert that Verona was not to be captured by a spurt; it also awakened in the soldiers distrust of the ability of their commanders. There now ensued a period of comparative inactivity, during which the right wing of the Piedmontese army battered at the walls of Peschiera and watched the neighborhood of Verona, while the centre lay along the left bank of the Mincio, and the right wing kept watch upon Mantua. So long a line could nowhere be a strong one; merely to man it took nearly all of Charles Albert's available force, leaving him no corps with which, were he so disposed, he could make an independent offensive movement. He relied, therefore, upon being able at short notice to concentrate the bulk of his army at any point that was threatened.

But while he was preventing the Austrians from breaking into Lombardy, Nugent with his corps of reinforcements was marching steadily out of the east, recapturing town after town between the Isonzo and the Brenta. Unless he were checked, nothing could stop him from effecting a junction with Radetzky. The Venetians realized soon enough that they had set too great confidence in their volunteers who, though not deficient in bravery, proved again and again that they were no match for the Austrian regulars, either in battle or in strategy. Nor did Durando, who, disregarding the Pope's allocution, had led the Roman troops into Venetia and placed himself under Charles Albert's orders, succeed in barring Nugent's advance.[1] Only for a moment at Vicenza was this second Austrian army brought to a stand, and rather than delay there, it made a détour and came up with Radetzky's outposts on May 22.

With the prospect of aid from the east, Radetzky determined to relieve Peschiera, now hard-pressed for food. Accordingly he marched very quietly and swiftly out of Verona and reached Mantua almost unperceived by the Piedmontese scouts. His plan was to cross the

---

[1] Nugent, disabled at this time, was succeeded by Prince Thurn.

Mincio, ascend its right bank, and appear in front of Peschiera before Charles Albert should have time to mass an army against him; or, if he failed in this, he hoped to draw the Piedmontese towards Mantua, engage them there, and so allow opportunity to a division from Verona to rescue the garrison at Peschiera. The Marshal eluded observation, and reached Mantua almost before the Piedmontese were aware of it. On the morning of May 29 he sent forward about 16,000 men to cross the Mincio; but they unexpectedly came upon the Tuscan contingent, about 6,000 strong, which held the villages of Curtatone and Montanara, on the extreme right wing of the Piedmontese army. General Laugier, who commanded them, had received assurances from General Bava, stationed at Volta with a considerable force, that in case he were attacked by superior numbers Bava would hasten to support him. But there was some misunderstanding; the messengers failed to deliver their dispatches, or Bava to act upon them, and for many hours the Tuscans fought a brave fight, until at length, their small field-pieces disabled, their ammunition exhausted, and themselves completely overpowered, they retreated in disorder. Nearly half their force was killed, wounded, or captured, among them being the legion of university students, who displayed unflinching valor, and died rejoicing that they had the privilege of giving their lives to their country. Not inaptly was Curtatone called the "Tuscan Thermopylae," — a defeat surpassing many a victory in glory. The resistance of the Tuscans probably saved the Piedmontese army, for had Radetzky been able on May 29 to hurl his main force on the Piedmontese at Goito, as he reckoned on doing, he might have defeated Bava before aid could have come to him. As it was, the Austrians, having turned the right flank of the Piedmontese, could now carry out their attack on the rear; but the stand made by the Tuscans gave time for Bava to realize his danger, to communicate with headquarters, and to receive strong reinforcements. When, therefore, Radetzky on the following day (May 30) advanced upon Goito he was met by the main body of Charles Albert's army and repulsed, after a hard battle. The Austrian troops in great disorder retreated on Mantua unpursued by the Piedmontese, who had suffered too severely in the engagement to be able to do more that day. In the moment of victory a messenger brought the King the announcement that Peschiera had surrendered on that very morning to the Duke of Genoa. Two such victories in a single day compensated for many a tedious gloomy week and revived the flagging expectation that the Italians would shortly drive the Barbarians out of Italy and establish independence. Never did success seem to them more sure than on the first of June, 1848.

But this month of May had seen the development of new political complications as stubborn as Radetzky himself. The anomalous relations of Lombardy towards Charles Albert became more and more untenable. The Provisional Government gave him little military support. "We can hardly procure wagons for our wounded, who are all heaped on straw," wrote Castagnetto, the King's private secretary.[1] The country people regarded the Piedmontese almost as meddlers, not as liberators, and begrudged them provisions; and they continued to stand aloof and watch the duel between Piedmont and Austria, as if their own fate did not hang on the issue. In the cities, especially at Milan, there was endless talk, capable of producing no good and much harm. Mazzini had arrived in Milan early in April, and though he announced that he would not press his doctrines until the war should be decided, still his presence gave encouragement to those Republicans who insisted that nothing but a united Republican Italy would satisfy them, and it lent plausibility

[1] Bianchi, v. 234.

to the Monarchists, who insinuated that Mazzini, in spite of his protestation, was intriguing against the King. The other wing of Republicans, headed by Cattaneo, harangued for an Italian Federation, composed of independent Republican States. The Provisional Government, willing but not forcible, though strongly in favor of union with Piedmont, felt in honor bound to abide by its pledge that the destiny of Lombardy should be settled only at the end of the war. But discord spread apace. The government could not silence the clatter of tongues, much less could it command obedience. Any rabble had only to collect in front of the Palace and threaten and shout in order to bring Casati, the President, to the balcony to utter pacifying words, whose effect lasted but an hour. The provinces of Bergamo, Brescia, and Cremona made demonstrations in favor of immediately offering themselves to Charles Albert.[1] Gioberti came to Milan, and from his window in the Bella Venezia hotel he poured forth his florid and fascinating eloquence in behalf of Piedmont and fusion. Austrian emissaries were secretly feeling their way towards reaction by stirring up dissension; the King's partisans labored earnestly, but unofficially, to persuade the government to bring the question to a popular vote. At length, on May 12, a proclamation was issued, stating that in view of the condition of the country there would be a plebiscite on May 29 to decide whether Lombardy would accept fusion with Piedmont or not. To appease a part of the objectors there was inserted into the resolution to be voted upon a clause providing that a Constituent Assembly, elected by universal suffrage, should be convoked in all the provinces which should agree to the fusion, in order to discuss and establish the bases and forms of a new monarchy under the House of Savoy.[2] This provision naturally caused anger in Piedmont, where the first Subalpine Parliament

[1] Ottolini: *Rivol. Lombarda,* 236.   [2] C. Casati, ii, 254–5.

had assembled on May 8. The Piedmontese held that they had already their Constitutional Government, and that if the Lombards wished to unite with them, they ought to accept the government which Piedmont had. To ask to share a neighbor's hospitality and then to insist that he shall run his house according to your preferences seems presumptuous, to say the least. A further wrangle came over the question of the future capital. The Turinese, intensely loyal to their city, could not listen calmly to the suggestion that Milan might be selected by the Constituent Assembly as the capital of the new kingdom.

If shipwrecked buccaneers instead of baling their swamping life-boat should fall into a quarrel over the booty that each should have when they came to land, they could hardly display more folly than did those partisans in 1848, not only in Italy, but in every country where the revolution gave the principle of Nationality a chance to establish itself. But the passions which proved so disastrous were necessary products of past feuds; even selfishness and headstrong will were symptoms of hope, however sadly they might be misused then; for it is with races as with men, — only those that have no will are beyond regeneration. This, however, was the bitter knowledge the peoples of Europe were to learn after their wilfulness in 1848 had plunged them into disaster; in no wise did it, at the time, teach them self-restraint. Whilst they bellowed for the best things of the day after to-morrow, they let to-day, with its good things, glide irretrievably by.

Still, despite irritation in Piedmont and dissension in Lombardy, the party of fusion had evidently a majority. England, suspicious enough of this whole Italian imbroglio, yet whispered to Marquis Pareto, "Let the fusion be made quickly." Other diplomacy, both in Italy and outside, had for the moment no great deference paid to it on this matter. Piacenza, by a vote of 37,000 to 379, had set the example of "fusing" with the Subalpine Kingdom. Parma and Modena, each long since abandoned by its dukeling, soon followed suit. Several of the cities of Venetia, realizing, now that Nugent's army had cut its way from the Isonzo to the Piave, that they could not win unaided, were also for throwing themselves upon Charles Albert's protection, but the Republicans still had the upper hand at Venice, and sought to postpone a decision until a Constituent Assembly could be elected. At Milan, the fomenters of discord, many of whom were afterward known to be on Austria's pay-roll, concocted a counter-revolution to explode on May 29, the day of the plebiscite; but beyond causing President Casati alarm, and making the streets noisy for a few hours, they got nothing by their plot. On June 9 the Provisional Government announced that 561,002 Lombards had voted for immediate incorporation with Piedmont, and only 681 for delay. How large a minority of Republicans abstained from voting can only be conjectured. The result of the plebiscite did not at once put an end to the ephemeral character of the government, because nothing could be permanently settled until the stipulated Constituent Assembly had been convened; yet it seemed a great point gained, that Lombardy had formally united her lot to that of Piedmont.

In watching the progress of this Italian struggle we must continually shift our point of view. In the retrospect, the causes which led to failure are much more conspicuous than they were to the actors in that drama, who had the future still before them. We, who see the beginning and the end, can confidently say that the end could not have been otherwise: the lava torrent rolled from the volcano of revolution, followed the channels of least resistance, and cooled and hardened when its heat and impetus were spent; but we have to imagine the lava as still molten, still plastic, and its force as still uncomputed, if we would understand this historic episode. And therefore, while we now can point out the very spot where the stream began to divide or slacken, we must try to see how Charles Albert's struggle looked to contemporary observers in May, 1848. We see the internal confusion, the blow dealt by the Pope's withdrawal, the perfidy of Bomba, the ominous advance of Nugent across Venetia, the gesticulations of politicians in and out of Parliament, the gliding to and fro of sectaries and Austrian agents; but Europe at that time saw that Lombardy had for two months been redeemed from Austrian despotism, that the Duchies were free, that Venice seemed impregnable, and, above all, that Charles Albert had shut Radetzky up in the Quadrilateral and had an even chance of starving him out. Moreover, grave events had come to pass north of the Alps. Another revolt had sent the Austrian Emperor out of Vienna, to seek refuge at Innspruck; Bohemia was in rebellion, clamoring for independence; the Magyars were rising, the Croats were up. Never had the Austrian Empire been so near dissolution. In Germany, too, the elements of revolution and nationality had triumphed; a new nation or confederacy was striking its roots at Frankfort. In France, the land of swift political vibrations, the government of February had already been overthrown; Cavaignac's soldiers had shot down the Red Republicans, and he was practically the dictator. Amid an upheaval so great, no wonder that the probability of Charles Albert's success was overestimated even by the shrewdest politicians.

We have seen that, during April, Austria made her first effort to induce her Italian provinces to accept a compromise. Hardly had Hartig's mission failed before Emperor Ferdinand, or rather his advisers, because he was already sinking into imbecility which soon caused his abdication, began to cast about for an armistice.

The situation in Austria was so black that they saw no chance to save the Hapsburg Empire proper but by abandoning Lombardy and Venetia, and recalling Radetzky to put down the rebellion in Bohemia and Hungary.* Accordingly, Baron Hummelauer was dispatched to London to request Palmerston to act as mediator. Palmerston, bent on warding off a European war, and anxious to prevent the revolutionary movement from culminating in the establishment of several Continental republics, or in anarchy, gladly accepted the office. "The Austrians propose," wrote Lord Ponsonby from Vienna (May 12), to the Foreign Secretary, "that the Milanese should appoint an 'hereditary Viceroy' totally independent of Austria and of every other Power; — hereditary only to preserve fixity; that they shall select the second brother of the Duke of Modena, who shall bring, as it were, a marriage portion of the Duchy of Modena; that Parma shall also be incorporated with Lombardy, Austria resigning the right enjoyed by treaties of a contingent succession to that Duchy; that the Lombards shall take upon them absolutely a certain portion of the Austrian debt, and shall contribute also a certain proportion to the expense of any military aid which may be required by the Lombards; Austria is also willing to give up everything, except such portions of the territory of the Venetian Kingdom as are necessary for the defense of the Tyrol and other parts, and for the free intercourse between Vienna and Trieste. The Viceroy is to be under the suzerainty of the Emperor."[1] To offer such generous terms at the outset showed that Austria believed her condition desperate, and it justified the expectation that she would make even larger concessions rather than come to no bargain. And, indeed, after Hummelauer reached London, he stated (May 24) that Austria was ready to give up Lombardy altogether on condition that she should

[1] *Correspondence*, ii, 454.

assume her share of the Austrian debt, and that Venetia, while still appertaining to the Empire, should have a constitutional government and an independent administration, presided over by an Austrian archduke.[1] Palmerston charged the British diplomatic agents to urge the Italians to listen to these proposals. He held over the Piedmontese the danger of French interference, — a scarecrow that served him equally well in dealing with Austria. If the French army, whether invited or not, descended to the scene of war, it could undoubtedly drive Austria out of the Quadrilateral; that being the case, Austria, besides being deprived of Venetia, would suffer the expense of a protracted campaign and the ignominy of defeat; whereas she could retire now with honor, and make terms that would compensate her for the cession of the coveted province. He reminded Piedmont, on the other hand, that the war had already proved a much more formidable undertaking than she had expected; that some mishap might cancel the successes thus far won; and that, if France stepped in, she would demand payment for her services, and that the Italians would discover too late that they had merely substituted a French for an Austrian master. Nevertheless, Palmerston saw that, as matters then stood, the Italians would consent to no terms which excluded Venetia from the boon of independence, and he therefore declined (June 3) to engage his government officially in negotiations which were foredoomed to fail.[2]

Austria, meanwhile, secretly approached Charles Albert on the subject, though she openly was much more exasperated against him than against the rebellious Lombards and Venetians. The Piedmontese ministry, getting wind of the affair, informed the King that they should resign if he saw fit to accept the compromise. Being interpellated in Parliament, Minister Pareto flatly replied: "It

[1] *Correspondence*, ii. 479.　　[2] *Ibid*, 532-3.

has never entered into the intentions of the King or of
his Cabinet to treat so long as one Austrian remains in
Italy. Sooner than break this promise the ministry will
resign. The Lombards may rest assured that nothing
will ever be arranged without their concurrence or knowledge."[1] Charles Albert was too loyal to the Constitution he had granted to think of overriding his ministers'
decision; yet the temptation was very great, and though
he put it by, he was not blind to the fact that it might
be more prudent to entertain Austria's proposition. Indeed, there is reason to believe that the ministry repelled
the earlier overtures of Hartig before consulting the
King.[2] How he regarded later similar overtures may be
seen from the following letter of his, written at Roverbella on July 7 to Franzini, who had just had a consultation with Abercromby, the British minister: "You understand perfectly what I think about the aggrandizement
which I believe we ought to desire for our country, taking
into consideration, above all, our finances and the forces
which our army can put into action. . . . On my conscience, I believe, then, that if we can obtain through
England's mediation the cession of Lombardy as far as
the Adige, with the two Duchies (Parma and Modena),
we shall have made a glorious campaign, and that a State
as small as ours against the colossal Austrian Empire will
have made superb acquisitions almost unheard of in history. . . . To desire more is a temerity, I dare say it,
almost insane. It is to wish to risk the loss, the everlasting ruin of the Italian cause. . . . You see now what
my position is with a responsible ministry which has given
a pledge to the Chambers. Whilst the union with Lombardy is not yet absolutely concluded, and there are at
Turin, as at Milan, such exorbitant pretensions, I cannot
at the head of the army take the initiative. I can only

[1] Beauregard, 232.
[2] Charles Albert: *Guerra dell' Indipendenza*, 140.

represent in conscience the state of things which, certainly, is fitted to open one's eyes. But if they wish me to risk all, I have my honor of a soldier foremost, and I will go on until a bullet causes me to end with joy a life of ups and downs, and wholly consecrated, sacrificed to my country."[1] And the King did fight on, however his judgment might demur, and he called his Cabinet's refusal "generous," though he doubted its sagacity. Had mere ambition guided him, this was his opportunity to close a war which added Lombardy and the Duchies to his kingdom and which gave his army a fair meed of glory; but he had a motive higher than ambition, and his honor was at stake.

France watched these negotiations closely, protesting the while her disinterested sympathy for the Italian cause, but hinting that, if her good offices were to be secured, she must have a guarantee that a part or the whole of Savoy should be ceded to her in case Piedmont annexed Lombardy and the Duchies.[2] Austria, involved in ever-thickening dangers at home, did not abandon her hope of terminating the war in Northern Italy. In June she sent another special agent, Schnitzermeraay, to Milan, to treat directly with the Provisional Government. In so doing she snubbed Charles Albert, for Lombardy had already voted for fusion with Piedmont; she virtually recognized the Provisional Government, and she separated the fate of Lombardy from that of Venetia. Schnitzermeraay brought a letter from Wessenberg, the Austrian Minister of Foreign Affairs, in which he proposed to negotiate on the ground that Lombardy should be independent, and he asked the Provisional Government to use its influence towards an armistice.[3] When Casati and his colleagues were approached by the Austrian negotiator, they replied,

---

[1] Beauregard, 233–4; *Correspondence*, iii, 63.   [2] Bianchi, v. 282.
[3] Wessenberg's letter is dated June 13; see Ottolini: *Rivol. Lombarda*, 264–5.

"The government rejects at the outset this proposal, declaring that it is impossible to make of an Italian matter a Lombard matter."[1] They added that, having already united with Piedmont, they had no authority to act without instructions from Turin.[2]

But whilst Diplomacy was endeavoring after this fashion to patch up a peace, one man on the Austrian side showed great contempt for concessions. That man was Radetzky. His eighty years had not cooled his warlike spirit, nor numbed his activity; rather had they hardened his native stubbornness. No sign of weakness, no cry of distress came from him. He did not even listen to the Imperial instructions to be ready to welcome the first overtures for an armistice. By the arrival of the reserves his army now numbered about 45,000 men, exclusive of the garrisons in Verona, Mantua, and Legnago, and he was promised reinforcements as fast as they could be equipped by the Imperial government, whose finances were sapped by being forced to pay wages to 20,000 loafers at Vienna in order to keep them quiet.[3] Only once after his repulse at Goito on May 30 was his position seriously threatened, and that was when the Piedmontese, by capturing Rivoli (June 10), seemed about to cut off his communications through the valley of the Adige. But as usual, the Piedmontese paused after their first victory, and allowed Radetzky time to intercept their advance. Even the loss of Peschiera had cost him less than 2,000 men. He now laid out a daring plan which, thanks to his celerity and the tardy information of his enemies, proved successful. Hurrying his army eastward, he attacked Vicenza, where he was met with a second army of reserves 15,000 strong, under Welden, which had come down through Tyrol. He forced Vicenza, after the bravest resistance of the campaign, to capitulate, and then, with equal swiftness, he returned to Verona. Vicenza capitulated on the very day

[1] Ottolini, 206.   [2] Bianchi, v, 283.   [3] *Correspondence*, ii, 618.

that Charles Albert drove the Austrians from Rivoli; had he been aware that Verona was left at that moment with but a small garrison, he might have marched on that city and prevented Radetzky from reëntering it. But his scouts brought the news to him too late, and when, still hoping to improve this splendid opportunity, he turned from Rivoli to Verona, he found that the Austrian Marshal had outsped him. This was the turning-point in the war. The loss of Vicenza left Venetia open to the Austrians, and deprived the Italians of the 15,000 troops under Durando, who had there surrendered; it allowed Radetzky, having nothing more to fear in the East, to concentrate his whole attention upon the Piedmontese in his front.

For the present, however, torpor overcame Charles Albert's movements. The tardy reconnoissance towards Verona, with the bad news from Vicenza, seemed to paralyze him. But the truth is that he was held immobile, not so much by his lifelong infirmity of purpose as by his realization of the inadequacy of his means. The struggle had in very fact become a duel between little Piedmont and colossal Austria; that grand wave of patriotism which, in March, had swept through the Peninsula had subsided. The Neapolitan contingent, except a few companies, had gone home; Durando's Romans, too, had gone home on parole, not to fight for three months; those of the Venetians who had not been killed or captured were shut up in Venice; the Lombard volunteers, — never above ten thousand,[1] — had proved of little service; the Tuscans who had escaped from Curtatone were in garrison at Brescia. For a war that was national and had for its object the liberation and indepen-

---

[1] Mariani (i. 625) states that Lombardy furnished 14,000 volunteers during the campaign, and that 25,000 Lombards were on the muster rolls of the regular army. These figures give an exaggerated notion of Lombardy's effective contribution to the war.

dence of Italy, the Italians had given him but scanty support. Lombardy, out of her three million or more inhabitants, had furnished only a few thousand fighters at one time; the Papal States, with three millions, had sent fifteen or sixteen thousand, some of whom were mercenaries; Tuscany, with a million and a half, had had six or seven thousand in the field. Measured by their quotas, the patriotism of these States seemed ineffective. A cause for which only one man in fifty will risk his life cannot be said to have stirred the souls of a whole people. And yet it would be unfair to judge the Italians merely by this numerical standard. We must take into account their inexperience in political and military matters, the difficulty which always attends the sudden arming of a large force, the lack of leaders to drill volunteers, the lack of weapons, uniforms, and provisions. And, moreover, the ease with which the first victories had been won inspired a fatal over-confidence. Too great reliance was placed on the invincibility of volunteers; throughout Europe men seriously affirmed in 1848 that the old methods of war were superseded, and that henceforth citizen troops, undrilled and equipped only with a righteous purpose, would overpower, almost without effort, the best-drilled standing armies. And in Italy the mutual jealousies and the masked unwillingness of the princes contributed to check military organization. Up to the beginning of June, every one believed that success was certain; yet a month earlier than that the discordant note went sneaking through the Peninsula that this was Charles Albert's campaign, and that he had troops enough to fight it out. Why engage in a war of which he would reap the glory? The strident chatter of the Piedmontese newspapers doubtless helped to spread this pernicious notion; the refusal of the Piedmontese ministry to join the League helped to spread it; Gioberti, in his harangues at Milan, Florence, and Rome, helped to spread it. And the ancestral feuds and jealousies sprang up in a crop of rank suspicions and distrust. The Venetians insinuated that Charles Albert had delayed sending them aid to repel Nugent, because they would not give themselves up to his rule. Every officious captain of volunteers complained that he had not received due support from the royal headquarters, because the King's staff envied the prowess of the free corps. Whenever disaster came, the horrid charge of treachery followed it: it was whispered that Ferrari had been beaten at Cornuda because he did not wish to win; that Durando had left Treviso to its fate because he was disloyal, and he had lost Vicenza through wilful disobedience; that Bava had failed to reinforce the Tuscans at Curtatone because he was at heart a traitor. Such insinuations, once winged, flew far. And, even in the Piedmontese army itself, grumblers and busybodies blamed the mistakes and threw doubts upon the ability of the generals. In these ways the reaction from the first exaggerated expectations vented itself. Looking back, men saw all the chances which had been missed, and they did not separate the failures that had been due to incompetence from those which were inevitable. So wide a chasm between their hopes and their achievements must be the result of deliberate guilt; and in their disappointment they sought only for scapegoats, without respect for justice. Popular chagrin is as unreasonable as popular enthusiasm.

To Charles Albert all these things were as a nettle-shirt, whilst he waited motionless there in the presence of Radetzky's united armies. If he looked eastward, Verona and Mantua beetled in front of him,—two fortresses not to be captured in a week nor a month, but well supplied with men and cannon, and directed by a wily commander who had already outwitted the best strategy of Piedmont. If he looked south, he saw no prospect of succor. If he looked west, he saw Lombardy disorganized and Piedmont distrustful. He was, moreover, experiencing a difficulty peculiar to every commander-in-chief in modern times. Of old, when a king made war and led his army, his operations depended solely on his judgment; but since the establishment of constitutional government, the king or general in the field must constantly have an eye to the political effect of his tactics. He needs a new levy or another subsidy, — and this must be voted by Parliament; whether Parliament will vote it or not depends upon the view the representatives take of public opinion, which, in turn, is rapidly swayed by the reports from the field. So the modern general must, in a measure, play to the gallery, even risking defeat by a too hasty movement, rather than allow public opinion to grow lukewarm through his apparently ill-considered inactivity. He has, in a word, to conquer not only the hostile army in battle but the Opposition in Parliament.

The Piedmontese deputies soon gave Charles Albert anxiety enough. Freedom of speech was to them who had lived hitherto with a gag in their mouths like his first jack-knife to a boy, — they hacked and cut at everything to assure themselves and the world that they really had a tongue to use. They proposed bills to abolish many antiquated abuses and to reform ancient institutions, — a worthy purpose, no doubt, but ill-timed, when matters of immediate and vital importance had to be dispatched by raw legislators, and when every matter beat up opinionated disputants. But the notification to the Chamber of the vote of Lombardy for fusion drove these disputants to the verge of civil war. The majority of the ministers and their supporters wished to have the annexation of the new provinces ratified as soon as possible, in order that the royal authority might be substituted for their flaccid provisional administration; but some of the Radical deputies protested against any act of union until the end of the war, and most of the Piedmontese members were in a frenzy lest Milan should be the capital of the new kingdom. The plebiscite in Lombardy had simply declared that a Constituent Assembly should establish the basis of the government under the crown of Savoy; now one party urged that the Assembly would have competence to select the seat of government, while the other maintained that it would have none. Not only did the Cabinet threaten to resign, but there seemed to be a doubt whether, even if the fusion were agreed upon by a majority of the deputies, the country would accept it. At length, however, a compromise was reached, by the framing of the bill of annexation in which there was no mention of the future capital, and the jurisdiction of the Constituent Assembly was restricted to the limits named in the Lombard vote of May 29; that is, its duty would be "to discuss and settle the bases and forms of a new Constitutional Monarchy under the House of Savoy." On June 28, by a vote of 127 to 7, the union of Lombardy and four Venetian provinces was therefore accepted.[1]

When the representatives of these Venetian provinces — Vicenza, Treviso, Padua, and Rovigo — appeared before the Piedmontese Chamber to announce their mission, they had been startled by the rebukes of Brofferio, the implacable Republican deputy. "Your cities," he said to them, "have little regard for concord in separating themselves from a city with which till now they have had a common destiny. Until Venice has spoken, every other voice from her provinces is untimely and malign."[2] Nevertheless, in spite of the reproofs of Brofferio and the anti-fusionists, the Venetian provinces were declared united to Piedmont by the same act which accepted the union of Lombardy, on June 28. Their secession from Venice marked the beginning of the end of the Provisional Government in Venice herself. When Manin, on

---

[1] *Correspondence.* iii, 13-14. [2] Brofferio, part III, 119.

March 22, had proclaimed the Republic of St. Mark, he had apparently fixed the form of government, and the cities on the mainland at first adhered to it. But as soon as it was seen that Lombardy, too, was free, many Venetians realized that there would be a complete reconstruction of Upper Italy. Lombardy postponed the determination of her affairs until the end of the war; whereas Venice, by her natural but premature decision, had isolated herself. Whatever might be the outcome of the struggle, she at least had announced that she had made her choice, and would remain independent and Republican. The first reverses in the field, however, warned her that she needed assistance, and then it was that she appealed to Charles Albert for troops; hers was an appeal to help a neighbor in distress, without promise of compensation, and he responded to it, though less promptly and effectively than the Venetians expected. As the need of terminating the uncertain administration in Lombardy became urgent, Piacenza, Parma, and Modena having already declared for fusion with Piedmont, the advocates of fusion in Venetia labored to break the political isolation in which their country was placed. Their first move was to have Venetia declare her lot inseparable from that of Lombardy: but this proved a mere declaration, and nothing more. Lombardy held her plebiscite: Venetia did not stir. Nugent's corps of reserves had already taught the Venetian cities that the War Department at Venice had not forces enough to defend them: and then those cities, having asked for an immediate decision of the question of fusion, when this was postponed, acted on their own responsibility and voted to unite with Piedmont.

Venice was now left almost alone. On June 18 the Austrians began to draw their trenches round Mestre, thus practically cutting off communication between the City of the Lagunes and the mainland. The party for fusion increased its agitation, being helped, according to report, by money furnished by Piedmontese agents; but the jeopardy in which the Venetians found themselves would have sufficed, without the application of disingenuous and underhand means, to warn them to seek an alliance with the Power which was drawing all the Northern Italians into its protection. The demands of the Fusionists to put the question to a vote became more and more imperative, — even the National Guard joined in them, — and the Provisional Government, having put off the convening of the National Assembly as long as possible, announced that it would meet on July 3. The Assembly alone had authority to decide this momentous question, but no one could predict with certainty what its decision would be.

Accordingly on July 3, having previously attended mass in the Church of St. Mark and listened to an exhortation from the Cardinal Patriarch, one hundred and thirty-three [1] deputies, accompanied by a great throng of citizens, ascended the Giants' Staircase and took their seats in the Hall of the Grand Council. If ever the monuments of a splendid Past might inspire men of a later generation with a sense — a hallowing sense — of the glory and dignity of which those monuments were the products and are the witnesses, it would be in that Hall of the Grand Council, when those representatives of free Venice met there to determine her fate. Let a deputy look where he would, he saw reminders of the strength and beauty of the State which his ancestors had raised to a unique position among the nations of the world. Venice, though built on the shifting mud where sea-gulls made their nests, yet had, through the indomitable courage of her sons, a foundation more permanent than that of rock-born cities; she counted her life not by

[1] Sixty deputies, from districts occupied by the Austrians, were unable to attend.

decades nor by generations, but by ages; she had been strong when her neighbors were weak; she had been civilized when Paris and London were but half-barbarous settlements and the site of Berlin was a morass; in her great days she had bowed neither to pope nor to emperor; and she had ever been surpassingly beautiful, floating there on the Adriatic for fourteen hundred years, as delicate and wonderful as a nautilus, yet firm as marble and stancher than the stanchest ship. And now, after fifty years of servitude she was again free, robed in the glory of her incomparable Past, and resolutely facing the strange world and perils upon which she had reawakened. No son of hers on that 3d of July could sit in the Great Hall and not feel that his action must not only match the solemn exigencies of the Present, but also be worthy of the city to which forty generations of his ancestors had consecrated their lives, and to which Dandolo and Morosini, and many another as just and brave as these, had brought the offering of their individual fame.

When the Assembly had been organized, and the credentials of the deputies had been examined, President Manin read a report on the condition of the country. He was, as all knew, an inflexible advocate of the Republic, but he spoke with absolute impartiality, as befitted the chief magistrate, summing up the course which the Provisional Government had followed, and stating how matters then stood. He warned them that it was the duty of the national representatives to determine whether the moment was opportune for changing the character of the government, and, in any case, to substitute a permanent for the provisional administration. Then the session adjourned. At nine o'clock on the following morning, having listened to reports from the Ministers of Foreign Affairs, War, and Finance, the Assembly prepared to take up the vital political questions: "Does the crisis demand an immediate decision?" "Shall Venice vote for fusion with Piedmont?" Tommaseo, Minister of Instruction and, next to Manin, the most popular champion of the Republic, first mounted the tribune, and in temperate but earnest language he insisted that it was neither inevitable, useful, nor becoming that they should then and there decide. Those who insinuated that Charles Albert would be more willing to help them if they merged their State in his kingdom, imputed to the King a stain which all the blood he had honorably shed in the Italian battles could not wash out. He had come of his own accord, without conditions, to liberate Lombardy and Venice; what right had they to treat him as a broker who demanded prepayment for his services? If his motives were not generous, if they were selfish and mercenary, then he was more to be abhorred than perfidious Bomba himself. At least let them assume that Charles Albert was honorable, — let them not affront him by such imputations. He would respect them more, he could not aid them less, if they maintained their independence till the end of the war; then, when their action would not seem to be due to self-interest nor fear, they could decide calmly and wisely. Venice had declared herself a Republic; but no declaration was immutable, nor could her determination to wait be construed as anti-Italian. What gain, indeed, could she secure from immediate fusion, since it must be several weeks at the shortest before Charles Albert would be in a position to drive the Austrians out of Venetia?[1] Thus argued Tommaseo, very plausible and at times eloquent, though his manner was that of a writer rather than that of an orator. The deputies listened attentively, but they did not applaud.

When he had concluded, Paleocapa, Minister of the Interior, an eminent engineer and partisan of Piedmont, rose to reply. His studied simplicity, his frequent asseveration that he spoke only as a "practical and positive

[1] Text in Rovani: *Daniele Manin* (Capolago. 1850). 167-74.

man," his directness and ease, were more effective than Tommaseo's more academic rhetoric. He showed that a decision must be taken at once. In one breath, he said, you affirm that Venice is impregnable; in the next that you are ready to be buried beneath her ruins, — whereby you imply that she is not impregnable. You talk of the great sympathy our cause has awakened throughout the world; but in Italy, only Charles Albert has recognized our Republic; outside of Italy, only Switzerland and the United States have recognized it. You dream of help from France; but how can French succor reach you, unless you make an alliance with the princes across whose soil French troops must pass? "France herself is in a critical position, and whilst she promises liberty to Poland, to Italy, and to other peoples, let us not dissimulate the fact that she has great trouble to preserve her own liberty. Whatever may be our inmost desires, we appear to our kinsmen to have isolated ourselves, and to persist in our isolation. Lombardy has sent us men, Lombardy gives us money, Lombardy gives us guarantees, Lombardy opens her arms and says to you, *Be brothers!* And we are timid and vacillating and reply to her, *We will decide whether to unite with you when the war is over.* To Lombardy Austria offers independence, but she indignantly rejects the offer. *My cause,* she says, *is common with that of Venice, and shall be, to the last drop of my blood, to the last penny in my purse.* And Venice replies, *I prefer to wait.* You appeal to our ancient liberty; you do well to revive the memories of the great days of our Republic: nevertheless, let us not mistake; the Republic, such as it could be established in our days, is a democratic republic, the only possible one in the actual social conditions of Europe, — this republic is much farther removed from that aristocratic republic of which you have recalled the name and banner, than it would be from a Constitutional monarchy which had truly a free Constitution. And since you refer to that independence which you owe to the maturity and wisdom of your fathers, remember also their prudence, their practical wisdom, their actions mature but always conformed to the real needs of the country, without abstractions, without flights, without a policy too vaporous and cloudlike, — a policy which, like the clouds, can turn too easily into a tempest." [1]

From the bursts of applause which interrupted Paleocapa's speech and broke out at its conclusion, it was evident that he had the sympathy both of the deputies and the bystanders. Then Manin, after stating that, like the previous speakers, he spoke not as a minister but as a simple deputy, said: "I have to-day the same opinion which I had on the 22d of March, when before the Gate of the Arsenal and in St. Mark's Place, I proclaimed the Republic. I still have it, and all then had it. Now all have it not. I utter words of concord and love, and I beg not to be interrupted. It is a fact that to-day all do not have it. It is also a fact that the enemy is at our gates; that the enemy awaits and desires discord in this land, unconquerable as long as we are united, most easily conquered if civil war enters here. I, abstaining from any discussion of my opinion or of the opinions of others, ask to-day assistance, ask to-day a great sacrifice, and I ask it of my own party, of the generous Republican party. To the enemy at our gates, expecting our discord, let us to-day solemnly give the lie. Let us to-day forget all parties; let us show that to-day we forget to be Royalists or Republicans, but that to-day we are all Italians. To the Republicans I say, The future is ours. All that has been done, and all now doing, is provisional. The Italian Diet will decide at Rome." [2]

Manin's magnanimity was loudly applauded, and it

[1] Rovani, 159-67.
[2] Ibid, 177-8. I translate exactly; the speeches of Tommaseo and Paleocapa I epitomize.

deserved to be, so rare was party abnegation then and always. By a vote of 130 to 3 the Chamber decided that the political status of Venice must be settled immediately, and by a vote of 127 to 6 the proposition to fuse with Piedmont was carried.[1] On the following day a new Provisional Government was chosen, to administer affairs until the Parliament at Turin should formally ratify the act of union. Manin, though pressed to continue in office, declined. "I have made a sacrifice, I have not denied a principle," said he; "I could not be minister for a king, except on the side of the Opposition."[2] A deputation, consisting of Donà, Dolfin, and Grimani, proceeded to the camp to inform Charles Albert of the step Venice had taken. They found him at Roverbella, still inactive and still hesitating.

A month had passed without gain for the Piedmontese. The troops lay sweltering in their tents, or marching on dress-parade, — Charles Albert had a fondness for frequent reviews; thousands were in the hospital; many had already succumbed to dysentery and the heat. The Lombard midsummer and the indecision of the King and his staff were surely drying up the strength and the enthusiasm of the army. In every knot of soldiers the question was, "Why don't we advance?" Camp wits asked whether the cavalry horses had the gout. Every officer's mess was a debating club, in which one plan after another was discussed. One would-be Jomini maintained that they ought to attack Verona from the north, another that they ought to blockade Mantua, a third that by making a circuit and capturing Legnago they could fall upon Radetzky in the rear. And in the King's own Council all these and other opinions were ventilated. Moreover, mutterings reached him from Turin. Brofferio, the Radical deputy, tried to introduce a vote of censure upon the bad management of the campaign, nor could he be re-

---

[1] *Memoriale Veneto*, 67. [2] *Ibid*, 68.

strained except by the representation of the Cabinet that a discussion in open Parliament of the military situation might precipitate disaster. Negotiations for an armistice were still languidly carried on by English and French diplomacy, and Mamiani, the leader of the Roman ministry, was trying to take up the broken thread of the league between Rome and Piedmont.

Over against all these uncertainties stood one reality: Radetzky, with an army already larger than that of the Piedmontese, held the Quadrilateral and Venetia. Verona confronted Charles Albert on the left, Mantua on the right, — two huge obstacles which could not be overcome by soldiers' chatter or deputies' vote, and which, until they had been overcome, must bar the road to victory. After contemplating them for a month, and measuring their strength, Charles Albert might well write to his Minister of War that it would be wise to accept the terms offered by Austria, — to take Lombardy, abandon Venetia, and make peace.[1] But his honor was involved, and obeying that, he was willing to risk everything. Neither he, nor the Northern Italians had forgotten the Peace of Campo Formio, and he would not be a party to a similar compact of shame. After spasmodic and ineffectual manœuvres against Verona, he at last, on July 13, resolved to lay siege to Mantua, — an undertaking which might require four months' perseverance, so strong was that fortress. Accordingly the main body of the Piedmontese army was concentrated round Mantua, where the mephitic exhalations from the marshes combined with the torrid heat and the inadequate supplies to sap the vigor of the troops. Not long, however, were they allowed to remain unmolested among the malaria and mosquitoes.

Radetzky, whose army now numbered nearly 90,000 men, deemed the time had come to take the offensive.

---

[1] See quotation on p. 195.

He had 50,000 under his immediate command at Verona, 20,000 were guarding Mantua, and a fresh corps of 20,000 was sweeping down the valley of the Adige. Charles Albert's troops numbered about 60,000, of whom the left wing (15,000), under Sonnaz, occupied the heights from Sommacampagna to Rivoli; the centre, about 10,000 strong, stretched from Peschiera to Goito; the right wing, commanded by Bava, was encamped on both banks of the Mincio, blockaded Mantua on the south, and reached to Roverbella. A dangerously long line, as any novice could see! Radetzky's plan was to drive the main body of his army like a wedge between the Piedmontese left wing and centre, and, having isolated Sonnaz, to turn upon Bava, hurl him towards Mantua, and cut off his retreat. Sonnaz, attacked at Rivoli (July 22), held his ground, but knowing that he could not long resist the superior force massed against him, he withdrew during the night to Sommacampagna, and, on the following day, to Peschiera. The King, on the 23d, decided to concentrate his centre and right wing on Villafranca. But the messengers were slow, the heat terrific, and much time was lost in sending for Bava to come and give his opinion. On the 24th the Austrians were repulsed in their attack at Sommacampagna, but they crossed the Mincio at Salionze, and caused Sonnaz to retreat on Volta. On the 25th a general battle was fought, the battle of Custoza, in which, despite their fortitude and valor, the Piedmontese were beaten. All went against them. At the outset the troops commanded by the King's sons had to wait so long for their breakfast, owing to the incompetence of the commissariat, that they set forward only at eleven o'clock, when their attack had already been prepared for by the enemy. The staff, having as usual but imperfect information of the position and strength of the Austrians, wasted regiments by driving them against whole divisions. As the inequality in forces became more apparent, they looked for Sonnaz's corps as eagerly as ever Wellington looked for Blücher's at Waterloo, but word came that Sonnaz could not possibly arrive before six o'clock. But the Piedmontese could not hold out till then, fighting one against two, and exhausted from hunger, thirst, and heat.[1] Accordingly a counter-order was sent to Sonnaz, to leave a garrison at Volta and to rejoin the main army at Goito.[2] At five o'clock the Piedmontese retired in good order to their positions round Villafranca; at half past two next morning they marched back to Goito. There a terrible calamity befell them: the commissary department had taken flight, and for another day the soldiers had no food.

Sonnaz, being sent back to capture Volta, which he had failed to garrison, fought throughout the night (26–27) and being finally repulsed, he was powerless to maintain discipline among his retreating battalions. Heat and hunger and fatigue were eating out the life and courage of the Piedmontese; and the Austrians, well-provisioned and elated, were closing in on them. The King, seeing that all would be lost unless he could gain respite for revictualing his troops, sent envoys under a flag of truce to ask on what terms Radetzky would consent to a suspension of hostilities. "The King shall retire behind the Adda, surrender Peschiera, give up our prisoners, recall his troops from the Duchies, and make peace," was the Marshal's uncompromising reply.[3] Hard terms, indeed; bitter terms, when contrasted with the sweet hopes of a week ago; and yet, as Colonel La Marmora said, it were

[1] The thermometer stood at 98° F. Deaths from sunstroke were reported in both armies.

[2] This order was believed by many Italians to have been forged by the Austrians to prevent Sonnaz from bringing his corps to the rescue of the main army; but Minghetti (ii, 40) states that it was written in pencil by General Cossato, and taken to Sonnaz by the Duke de Dino, one of the Piedmontese aides.

[3] Minghetti, ii, 43.

wise to accept them. But Charles Albert could not bring himself so suddenly to what seemed an ignominious pact, and rejecting the proposal, he resolved to retreat until he should come to a position favorable for a last stand. Westward, therefore, he led his jaded, demoralized troops. They marched by night, and when Radetzky, marching by day, overtook their rearguard, they had still enough pluck to resist until the main army was again in motion. The Marshal, unaware of the utter prostration of his adversary, was cautious in advancing; for the desperate valor of the Piedmontese at Sommacampagna and Custoza led him to suppose that they were still formidable.[1]

The collapse of an army is oftentimes relative to its previous excellence; the Piedmontese army, while it had not been excellent in drill nor fortunate in its leaders, had been uniformly brave; but after making a last desperate effort at Custoza, it could not recover. Charles Albert hoped each day that the panic would subside sufficiently for him to call on his troops for a final rally, but panic in an army, like nervous collapse in an individual, though it strike suddenly, requires a long and tedious cure. Nor did he reach any defensible position, where he might turn about and check his pursuer. Like the fabled chagrin-skin, Lombardy seemed to shrink under his feet. He had abandoned the line of the Mincio when the retreat began, hoping that at the Oglio he might make a stand; alas, almost before he realized it, his confused regiments had passed the Oglio and were still struggling westward. Then he looked to Cremona; but before he had paused there a day the batteries of the Austrian vanguard began to boom; his position became untenable, and he had to resume his backward march.

---

[1] He says in his official bulletin that he "never saw an army fight with such resolution and bravery" as his own; whence we can infer the quality of the Piedmontese fighting. *Correspondence,* iii, 90.

Then he counted on the Adda, as a last ditch behind which he could reform his squares; but the Adda, too, slipped away from him. At Codogno (August 2) the British minister, Abercromby, after an interview with Charles Albert, went to Radetzky's quarters to ask on what terms he would consent to a truce; the Marshal would now listen to nothing short of the complete restitution to Austria of all her Italian territory.[1] Those terms could not be accepted.

The King had now reached the parting of the ways: prudence and military wisdom counseled him to withdraw to Piacenza, where strong fortifications behind the Po would protect his army, cover Piedmont, and force Radetzky into a long siege; but chivalry pointed to Milan. "Having gone as brothers to succor and defend brothers who had shaken off the foreign yoke," writes the King, "it was our duty to achieve our undertaking, to keep our word to the end; we could not retreat on Piacenza, except by deserting Milan without a struggle, without a capitulation which should mitigate the vengeance of the Austrians. As Piedmontese, the sole reasonable road of safety was clear to us in passing the two frontier rivers; as Italians, we sacrificed a part for the whole, a province for the nation, and we had that gratitude therefor which all know."[2] Accordingly, on the afternoon of August 3, the Royal army, fagged in body, discouraged in heart, began to encamp under the walls of the Lombard capital.

The news of the disaster at Custoza had at last roused the Milanese from the easy-going confidence with which they had watched the progress of the campaign. They had, indeed, undertaken to furnish the army with provisions, and they had talked of equipping a Lombard corps: if they fell short in fulfilling their obligations, as they unquestionably did, it was through the deficiency of men able in organizing rather than through their intentions.

[1] *Correspondence*, iii. 110.   [2] *Guerra dell' Indipendenza*, 83.

Dishonest contractors and sutlers — those buzzards that prey upon every army — were often to blame for the failure of provisions; as was inexperience for the military delays and blunders. Not until the middle of July, — much time having been wasted in deciding what style of helmet the dragoons should wear,[1] — had a Lombard division been sent to the front, and that consisted of only twelve battalions, ill-drilled and insubordinate, and poorly generaled. "Aim at the commissioned officers, but spare the generals; they are too useful to *me*," was Radetzky's order to his sharpshooters.[2] Whether he actually gave this order or not, the irony implied in it touched none of the Italian officers more nearly than the Lombard.[3] Now when the news from the front portended an invasion of Lombardy by the Austrians, the Milanese displayed some of that energy which had astonished Europe in the preceding March. On July 27 the government of Milan issued a report in which it attempted to quiet alarm by stating that by the latest advices the King had 60,000 men at Goito; the following day an equally incorrect manifesto appeared.[4] But the truth soon overtook these delusive assurances, and as each successive courier told how Radetzky's advance kept pace with Charles Albert's retreat, every one could compute the dwindling distance between the Austrian army and Milan. The Milanese, or at least many of them, startled from their security, at once cried out that they had been betrayed, and they vibrated between fury and consternation. Just at this time the Provisional Government resigned, — Lombardy having been formally handed over to Royal Commissioners, — but before resigning it created a Committee of Public Defense, composed of Gen-

[1] Ottolini : *Rivol. Lombarda*, 258.   [2] *Ibid*, 259.
[3] This criticism does not apply to the commander-in chief of the corps, General Perrone, a Piedmontese, who seems to have made the most of his poor material.
[4] Mariani, i, 582–3.

eral Fanti, Dr. Maestri, and a lawyer Restelli, and it appointed General Zucchi to the supreme command of the Lombard National Guard. This Committee worked with desperate haste to prepare against the invasion; it mobilized the National Guard, it proclaimed a levy in mass, it decreed a loan of fourteen millions, it collected forty thousand shirts to be given to Charles Albert's tattered soldiers, it stored flour for eight days, and cattle for fifteen days, it distributed half a million cartridges to the Guards, and held as many more, together with about fifteen tons of powder, in magazines. Laborers were employed in large numbers at double wages to work on the fortifications.[1] There was bustle and nervous energy enough, but all too late: three or four days being too brief a time in which to organize an effective resistance and to convert raw volunteers into soldiers.

On the morning of August 4 the Austrian vanguard, under Strassoldo, began to assail the Piedmontese outposts at Ca Verde, about four miles from Milan on the highroad to Lodi. At the booming of the cannon, the Committee of Public Defense wished to sound the tocsin, as a signal that the country was in danger and that the citizens should barricade the streets, but General Olivieri — President of the Royal Commission which had just arrived, and which now had technically the government of the city in its charge — refused, on the ground that it was premature to spread general alarm. This conflict between the two committees boded ill for harmony, and was the cause of subsequent most deplorable excesses. As the cannonade increased, the Committee of Defense set the town bells pealing: men, women, and children swarmed in the streets and raised barricades all the more swiftly for their practice at that work during the Five Glorious Days. The King's troops, after withstanding the onset of the Austrians until nightfall, were withdrawn into the

[1] Ottolini, 296-7.

city and stationed along the bastions. Charles Albert, who throughout the day had as usual exposed himself in the posts of most imminent danger,[1] also retired within the walls and took up his quarters in the Greppi Palace.[2] There he held a council of war, at which the futility of resistance was made clear. The Piedmontese believed that Milan was not well-provisioned; they knew how easily its fortifications could be battered down by the Austrian cannon; their own heavy artillery had, by mistake, gone to Piacenza; they suspected that the Milanese, who had been so tardy in their display of energy, would quickly cool when the bombardment began. Seeing slight chance of a successful resistance, and fully impressed with the devastation which any resistance would involve, the Council therefore advised the King to treat with Radetzky. Accordingly, Generals Lazzari and Rossi, accompanied by De Reiset and Campbell, the French and English consuls, — who went to ask for a suspension of hostilities in order that their countrymen might quit the city, — set out for the Austrian headquarters. After the Piedmontese envoys had had a long conference with the Marshal, the consuls were admitted and were told by Radetzky that he had agreed to the surrender of Milan, and that foreigners had therefore nothing to fear. Lazzari and Rossi returned to the King at six o'clock on the following morning, bringing the terms of capitulation, to be ratified and dispatched to Radetzky at four o'clock that afternoon.[3]

The Milanese, awakening that morning in the expectation of hearing the cannonade renewed, were surprised at the silence. The Municipal Government, the Committee

[1] When begged by his officers to retire out of range of the Austrian guns, he said sternly : "It seems to me that the situation is grave enough for you not to give me advice. If I stay here, I know what I am doing." Beauregard, 314.
[2] Now occupied by the Banca Nazionale, No. 6, Via Alessandro Manzoni.
[3] C. Casati, ii, 383–7.

of Defense, and the General Staff of the Civic Guard, having been summoned to the Greppi Palace, were there informed of the negotiations which the King had made, and of the urgent reasons for making them. After listening in astonishment, Restelli, one of the Committee of Defense, poured out a violent protest and hurled the charge of treachery at the King's generals. Then the Lombards quitted the building; but a great crowd had already gathered outside, and it beset the committee-men for news. Zucchi, much agitated, and losing self-control, cried out, "All is lost, gentlemen!" and hurried away. The excitement among the multitude grew intense. Shouts of "Treason," "Death to Charles Albert," boomed along the streets, now filling with denser masses. The Royal Guard at the entrance to the King's quarters could hardly beat off the angry throng.

Thereupon Litta and Anelli, two members of the Consulta,[1] hastened to the King, who asked them what the Milanese wished. "Either war or death," replied Litta; "nor can any of us, Sire, guarantee your life if you refuse to fight." Charles Albert replied that, without adequate munitions or a firm desire on the part of the citizens to defend the city, it was suicidal to prolong the struggle, and that the municipal authorities had themselves just acknowledged that the terms were alike honorable and unavoidable. "Your Podestà himself has assured us that the people prefer peace to the horrors of war," added the King. "It is not true," fiercely broke in one of the National Guard; "the people burn for war: we remember 1821." At this allusion to that early episode, which had branded an indelible suspicion on his reputation, Charles Albert knitted his brows, and then asked: "Well, what would you have me do?" "Fight," was the reply. "And

---

[1] When the Royal Commission assumed its duties, the old Provisional Government was asked to serve as an advisory body until the crisis was past.

are you all ready to shed your blood for the country?" asked the King. "Yes." "So be it; I will gladly give mine for you." When this decision had been reached, the popular leaders rushed into the streets to spread the news; but while they madly cheered, they determined that it was as important to hold the King prisoner in his palace as to go out and confront the Austrians.[1]

Litta and Anelli, on the one hand, and Charles Albert on the other, at once issued proclamations stating that the defense would be prosecuted to the end. The mob under the windows of Casa Greppi, however, would not be reassured. It howled, and threatened, and reiterated the venomous cry of treason. When General Bava appeared on the balcony, the masses below called for the King; and when Charles Albert showed himself, he was greeted with musket-shots and insulting yells. At length, after nearly half an hour of tumultuous frenzy, the mob became somewhat quiet, and seemed to be persuaded that the King meant to keep his word. Meanwhile, the sane citizens, learning that the capitulation had been revoked, and taking as calm a view of the situation as was possible to them in such a moment, realized that Milan was indeed unprepared for a bombardment. It was well enough to shout "Death rather than surrender;" well enough to clamor for the privilege of being buried beneath the ruins of the city; but reason refused to confound the madness of desperation with the heroic resolve of patriotism. The loud-mouthed mob, merely in a competition of noise, could not rival Radetzky's cannon; what, then, had it to oppose to Radetzky's shot and shell, and to his 60,000 troops? Convinced of the folly of resistance, these sane citizens urged the Municipal Government to accept the terms of surrender before it was too late. Accordingly, a deputation, consisting of the Podestà, three Assessors, and the Archbishop, proceeded to the Austrian encampment.

[1] C. Casati, ii, 395-7.

Four o'clock had passed, and the Austrian artillerymen were preparing to open fire, when the deputation reached the Marshal's quarters at San Donato. He agreed to ratify the terms he had already proposed, and the convention was signed by General Hess, on the part of Austria, by Podestà Bassi, for the Milanese, and by General Salasco for the King.

Meanwhile another paroxysm of frenzy swept over the mob. Neither they nor the King knew yet of the second embassy to Radetzky, but instead of preparing for the Austrian attack, they raged before the Greppi Palace. It became evident that, not satisfied with penning up Charles Albert as a hostage, they had murder in their wild brains. General Bava wished to summon a regiment to disperse the mob, but Charles Albert forbade him; he did not wish, he said, to sacrifice the life of one of his soldiers for his own. Then Bava with great difficulty, having been mauled and beaten, made his way through the dense throng, and went to his quarters to give orders to the Piedmontese army during the expected bombardment. He found his officers and men so exasperated at the indignity their king had suffered, that he could hardly restrain them from rushing to the rescue. Had that befallen, had the Piedmontese troops been unleashed upon the furious Milanese, a massacre must have ensued which would have estranged Lombardy and Piedmont for many a year. As it was, the recollection of this terrible day was graven deep enough into the memory of both peoples.

In an inner room in Casa Greppi, worn by the bodily fatigue of the past ten days, and gloomy in spirit over the irreparable disaster, sat Charles Albert; his emaciated face more haggard than ever, infinite weariness in his eyes, yet still kingly, still unafraid. He sat there awaiting his death, while the howls of the multitudes outside grew fiercer and nearer, as a martyr, calmly expecting the bolts of his cell to be drawn and wild beasts to rush in upon him. He had hoped to save his sons by keeping them away from the trap in which he was caught, but the Duke of Genoa succeeded in reaching Casa Greppi, and, having in vain offered himself as a hostage in place of his father, he remained there to endure the worst. A few of the King's officers, with sabres drawn, guarded the approach to his room. The little squad of sharpshooters who had stood at the entrance to the palace had long since been driven back by the mob; one of them had been killed on the threshold leading to the King's apartments; the others held the landing of the staircase and were grimly resolved to die before their King. Night came, and still Radetzky's cannon were silent. The little party of Piedmontese wondered at the delay; the roars of the mob swelled louder and louder. About nine o'clock, Podestà Bassi, returning from signing the articles of capitulation, at the peril of his life reached the beleaguered palace and told the news. It was thought that his words might allay the populace, and accordingly he went out on the balcony to speak. One of the Piedmontese held a lantern, so that the Podestà's face could be seen; but that did not prevent a shower of missiles and bullets from assailing him. In his agitation he could only say, "I am your Podestà:" then he added the single word "capitulation," which fell upon that maddened multitude like a lighted fuse on a magazine. The Royal sharpshooters had seized a favorable moment for closing and barring the heavy street-door of the palace; now the rioters began to collect fuel and gunpowder to blow it open, and to destroy the building. The danger was imminent, but cut off from his troops, what hope had Charles Albert of succor? Fortunately, Colonel Alfonso La Marmora, escaping by a window in the rear of the palace and thereby avoiding the mob, hurried to Porta Orientale, took two battalions of the brigade Piedmont stationed there, and returned at double-quick pace to the scene of peril. The rioters fell back at the sight of the troops and slunk into the adjoining streets, where they could howl unmolested. La Marmora burst into the King's quarters and brought him safety. Charles Albert walked away from Casa Greppi, while his officers rode beside him, and rejoined General Bava in the Collegio Calchi-Taeggi.[1] There he snatched a few moments' repose, while preparations were making for his army to evacuate Milan. At two o'clock on the morning of August 6 he stood at Porta Vercellina and watched his troops, numbering scarcely 25,000 men, pour in confusion out of the city. He was the last to leave, except the division under the Duke of Genoa, which stayed behind to consign Milan to Radetzky at noon that day. By the terms of the capitulation, the Piedmontese army withdrew by the shortest route, through Magenta and Buffalora, beyond the Ticino. Ninety thousand Milanese, dreading the first severity of Radetzky's conquest, accompanied them.[2]

Never was there a sadder ending to a noble enterprise which had, until within a fortnight, promised success. Bitterer even than the defeat at Custoza was that terrible Saturday in Milan. That the King and troops who had for three months been fighting almost single-handed against the common enemy of all the Italians, and who, renouncing the road of salvation, went to Milan to make a last stand, should be greeted as traitors, should be in-

[1] Massari: *Alfonso La Marmora* (Florence, 1880), 47; Massari states, however, that La Marmora escaped by the street-door, and not by the window.

[2] The best account of this episode is in Beauregard (chap. 11), and C. Casati (vol. ii, chap. 13). Minghetti, also, is clear as far as he goes. Consult also Mariani, Ottolini, Massari, etc. In the various accounts of an occurrence so chaotic, the details are often confused and contradictory. The Committee of Public Defense published, under the date "Italia, 16 Agosto, 1848," a pamphlet entitled *Gli Ultimi Tristissimi Fatti in Milano*, in which they gave their version of the episode.

sulted and threatened even with massacre, — this was a sting of ingratitude almost without parallel in modern times. Well might Minghetti say, in recalling that hideous 5th of August: "We envied, indeed, those who were slain at Goito, at Custoza; they had the consciousness of giving their life for their country and their king, and with it the hope of final victory; we were on the verge of plunging into the horrors of anarchy or into those of civil war, without glory and without hope."[1] It was natural that the sudden revulsion from over-confidence to disaster should bring gloom and chagrin to the Milanese, but that it should have so frenzied them that they fell a prey to cruel and unfounded suspicions proves how pernicious the wrangling and rant of demagogues of all parties had been: unable to explain the defeat of Charles Albert, though the explanation was evident, they seized on the insinuation of treachery, — the last resort of rogues and madmen, — and vented their fury on the supposed traitor. So, at the time of the cholera, the panic-stricken Neapolitans tore alleged "poisoners" and "anointers" to pieces; so, during the witchcraft delusion, the Puritans tortured and killed many innocent victims. The charge of treason against Charles Albert is too preposterous to need refutation; had he wished to betray Lombardy, he would never have made the military error of going to Milan: by going there, he was able to stipulate better terms for the Milanese. He might, indeed, have prolonged the contest for two or three days; but in that case it is probable that Radetzky would not have allowed the Piedmontese to retire with their arms and munitions; without these, all hope of resuming the struggle must have been abandoned.

On August 9 an armistice was concluded, by which Charles Albert agreed to evacuate Lombardy, Venetia, and the Duchies, and to withdraw his fleet from Venice.

[1] Minghetti, ii, 57.

His troops were allowed to take with them their baggage trains and their artillery. If, at the expiration of six weeks, peace was not ratified, the armistice might be continued at the consent of both parties, but should either determine to renew the war, he must announce his intention eight days before opening the campaign.[1] This armistice was called after the name of General Salasco, who signed it in behalf of the King. While Radetzky proceeded to restore the Austrian administration in the reconquered provinces, the Piedmontese army rested from its terrible experiences along the western bank of the Ticino. Charles Albert himself, plunged in gloom, took up his quarters at Alessandria. The great desire of his life had been frustrated; his hopes were dead; from all Italy the winds bore to his ears that loathsome word, *traitor;* even Death, which he had sought in the thickest of every battle, had, like his friends, deserted him; and yet, though tempted to abdicate and find in some convent that release from care which he longed for beyond all things except death, he consented to stand at his post, that he might save his country from the ruin which impended.

[1] Text in Mariani, i, 616, note 1.

CHAPTER II.

DEMOCRACY INVADING.

IF the dramas of history were as symmetrically proportioned as are the ideal dramas of Shakespeare, we might suppose that, with the defeat of the Piedmontese army and with Radetzky's return to Milan, we had witnessed the close of the last act of Italy's tragedy in the year of revolutions. After thirty years of plotting and hoping she had finally met Austria face to face, and after sudden victories she had been suddenly beaten. The logic of the Italian movement had been wrought out to a conclusion. That movement began in each State as a protest of Liberal subjects against their local tyrant; but the ease with which the tyrants had been overthrown in 1820, 1821, and 1831, and the inevitable interference of Austria to restore them, taught the Liberals that they must overthrow Austria before they could permanently secure the concessions which they wrested from their rulers. Thus their local endeavors broadened and came to concern not merely Piedmont or Rome, but the entire Peninsula, — came to be National, and to aim at the destruction of the National enemy, Austria. After 1831 all but the most hare-brained conspirators recognized the futility of casual revolts; but what Liberal, however sanguine, could expect that Italy, parceled among half a dozen princes, could be united in a National war against the Arch-tyrant? United? That was the very possibility which Metternich's régime was organized to strangle. Nevertheless, after Pius's election in 1846, as Liberalism advanced, every local gain that it made was a stimulus to the National Spirit; until, in March, 1848, it seemed to have brought about a genuine harmony between the Italian Peoples and their Princes. Then the Spirit of Nationality, without waiting for the just-granted Constitutions to be put in operation, without giving time for the genuineness of that harmony to be tested, impelled the Italians against Austria; and for a while victory seemed theirs. But too soon localism began to weaken the National impetus; Pius drew back, Bomba defaulted, Leopold hesitated, all leaving Piedmont to fight the battle alone. Radetzky recovered his balance, and having gained new strength, he beat Charles Albert step by step back across the Ticino. Thus had the Physical Force of Italy proved inferior to the Physical Force of Austria; apparently the Italians must submit to the inevitable, resolving, while they submitted, that when the next day of reckoning dawned, they would have might as well as right on their side. But nothing went according to rule in that year 1848. Hopeless as the struggle seemed, it was not yet over. Nationality, though mutilated, was still to make a mad effort, and the spirit of Revolution was still to run its fiery course in each of the States where it had not already been quenched. These two movements, though distinct in origin and purpose, were yet so interrelated as at times to seem blended in one. To drive Austria out of her recovered territory, and in any event to confirm the result of the Revolution in Piedmont, Tuscany, and Rome, were therefore the two great purposes which henceforth swayed the Italians.

In Piedmont, partisanship had developed rapidly during the brief session of Parliament. The discussion of the question of Fusion had stirred the deeply-embedded fibres of local jealousy; the proposal to expel the Jesuits had inflamed theological prejudices; the criticisms on the conduct of the war had enraged the military party against those carpet knights who, from their easy-chairs in the

Chamber or in their newspaper offices, presumed to censure and vituperate the real soldiers in the field. Early in July, Balbo and his colleagues had resigned, owing to the lack of support incurred by their measure for the temporary administration of Lombardy. For three weeks, the King cast about vainly for another Cabinet. Revel tried to form one, but failed; then Collegno, by dint of persuasion and compromise, succeeded. On July 28 the new ministry, presided over by Casati, — as a recognition of Lombardy's entrance into the kingdom, — assumed office, and almost immediately it induced the Chamber to confer dictatorial power upon the King until the military situation should improve. The news of the disaster in Lombardy, of the King's retreat on Milan, and of his capitulation, set Piedmont in an uproar. Every one had counted upon victory as certain; the certainty of defeat now aroused consternation and wrath. Casati at once resigned. The Political Club, which had come to have great influence, being composed of the Radical deputies and of unofficial members, passed resolutions condemning the armistice and assuring the King that the country would rise in mass and enable him to prosecute the war rather than submit to an inglorious peace. But when Brofferio hurried to present these resolutions to Charles Albert, he barely escaped being cut down by the Royal officers, who were incensed that he, who had in Parliament assailed the army, should presume to come among them on such an errand. A glimpse at the disorganized troops sufficed to convince even the fire-eaters that it would be madness to insist upon a resumption of hostilities before the *morale* and strength of the army had been restored. And yet Marquis Pareto, late Minister of Foreign Affairs, declared that the Salasco armistice was unconstitutional, and therefore not binding, because it had not been countersigned by a member of the Cabinet:[1] nevertheless, Pareto himself privately

[1] *Correspondence*. iii, 182, 187.

admitted that the majority of the country desired peace. The clubs might talk war as loud as they chose, the public did not respond; at Genoa only seven men, and at Turin only thirty signed the list opened for the enrolment of fresh volunteers.[1]

There now began a struggle between the Aristocratic and the Radical parties for mastery. The former not only desired peace, but they also hoped that the collapse of the war, which they regarded as the culmination of Liberalism, would put an end to the innovations of the past two years and allow the Old Régime to recover its ascendency. Hostile to Constitutionalism from the first, they could now throw on it the blame for the recent calamity, and point to the good old days of paternalism and prosperity. The Radicals, on the other hand, maintained that the war had failed because Constitutionalism had not gone far enough, and that, instead of retreating, it was necessary to advance. Let the leaders of the people be given free play, let the great Democratic instincts of the country be aroused, and the war might be resumed and brought to a victorious end. They accused the Royalists of having declined to organize the popular elements in Lombardy and Venetia, and so to have deprived themselves of an inexhaustible source of strength; they censured, also, the King's unwillingness to seek aid from Republican France, while that aid might still have been effective. Between these extreme parties, there hovered the Moderates, who would neither turn back into Absolutism with the Retrogrades, nor plunge forward into greater ruin with the Radicals. The King, while personally smarting for revenge, yet knew too well that the moment for reopening the conflict had not come. He had led back hardly 25,000 men from the war; desertions were still frequent; no regiment was in fighting order; of one regiment only 600 men out of 2,700 remained in

[1] *Correspondence*, iii, 141.

the ranks. Against his will, therefore, Charles Albert inclined towards peace, and he formed a ministry which though patriotic was conservative. He detested Radicalism, but he would not, like Bomba, listen to the Reactionists and stifle the Constitution which he had sworn to uphold. The new ministry, formally announced on August 19, was presided by Marquis Alfieri and had among its members Generals Perrone, Pinelli, and Dabormida, and Count Revel.

Slow-footed and circumspect Diplomacy, which had been left behind by the recent swift-paced events, was now, thanks to the lull in hostilities, able once more to draw within speaking distance. During the critical days of Charles Albert's retreat, the Casati Ministry had dispatched one of its members, Ricci, to Paris to inquire on what terms the French government would agree to send an army to aid Piedmont. At Paris, Ricci met Guerrieri, whom the expiring Provisional Government of Lombardy had also dispatched to ask for French intervention. The King's minister refused to recognize the legality of Guerrieri's mission, but they both appeared before General Cavaignac and stated their purpose, leaving Cavaignac in doubt as to what he should do. Before he came to a decision, however, the report of the capitulation of Milan reached him, and a special messenger announced that Charles Albert, having been forced into an armistice, no longer needed French military assistance. Palmerston, who had never abandoned his aim of averting a European war, now proposed to Cavaignac that England and France should renew their efforts at mediation, and to this proposal Cavaignac consented (August 10) all the more willingly because he wished if possible to keep France at peace.[1] Accordingly, on August 16, Mr. Abercromby, the British minister, and M.

[1] Bastide to Normanby, Aug. 10; Normanby's reply, Aug. 11: *Correspondence*, iii, 122, 126.

de Reiset, the French chargé d'affaires, went from Turin to Alessandria and had an interview with Charles Albert. The bases of the mediation which they offered were similar to those laid down by Hummelauer on May 24.[1] Austria should relinquish Lombardy and the Duchies, but retain Venetia, promising, however, to grant the Venetians an independent administration; the frontier between the new kingdom of Upper Italy and Austria should run from Lazise on Lake Garda, between Verona and Villafranca, and meet the Po at Bergantino, thus giving the Italians the fortresses of Peschiera and Mantua, and the Austrians Verona and Legnago. Charles Albert, having listened to the terms, remarked on "the necessity of securing the future destinies of Venice and of preventing it from being said that Piedmont, having made satisfactory conditions for herself, had neglected both the cause of Italy and the interests of the Venetians." To this Abercromby replied, that neither his government nor the French would consent to suggest any agreement which might justify a charge of dishonor against the King, or be unjust to the Venetians.[2] They would not, however, discuss any modification of the terms they presented. Charles Albert, having pondered the proposition, formally accepted it that same day in a note addressed to the two envoys. The constitutionality of this acceptance, written by Count Revel, was subsequently impugned, because the Casati Ministry had already resigned, and the ministry which Revel was forming had not yet been announced; but in crises like this, when diplomatic etiquette must be waived, happy is the King who has a minister unterrified by punctilio.

Palmerston and Cavaignac, having secured Charles Albert's acceptance, at once opened negotiations at Vienna. There, however, instead of frankness and dispatch, they encountered equivocation and delay. Aus-

[1] See *ante*, p. 193.   [2] *Correspondence*, iii, 204.

tria had begun to realize that she was more than a match
for Piedmont, and having reconquered her insurgent
provinces, she did not wish to give them up. Her only
dread was lest France should decide to go to the rescue
of the Italians; for she knew that Cavaignac and Bastide,
the French Foreign Minister, wished to prevent a war,
but that a large element of glory-loving Frenchmen were
eager for any excuse to take the field. Therefore she
procrastinated, offsetting the menace of French intervention by the hint that the German Confederation
would march an army into France if the French marched
into Italy. Only on September 1 did the reply of Wessenberg, the Austrian Foreign Minister, reach London.
He stated that mediation was unnecessary, because
Charles Albert had agreed to negotiate directly with
Austria, and further, that the Piedmontese had not fulfilled the terms of the Salasco armistice by withdrawing
their troops and fleet from Venice.[1] Palmerston was for
a moment ruffled by what seemed to be disingenuousness
on the part of Charles Albert, but on applying to the
Piedmontese Ministry he found that Wessenberg's assertion was false. Radetzky had, indeed, attempted to
open direct negotiations with the King, but the latter had
informed him that he had already accepted England and
France as mediators.[2] In regard to the failure of the
Piedmontese to carry out the conditions of the armistice
at Venice, it was shown that the King's government had
repeatedly ordered the recall of his troops and fleet;
but that these orders had not been obeyed, because the
Venetians had reëstablished a Republic and refused to
allow the Royal messengers to deliver their instructions.[3]

By this uncandid ruse Austria gained a whole fortnight's time in which to strengthen her armament in
Italy. But Bastide, growing anxious at the ill-feeling

[1] *Correspondence*, iii, 246–7, 259–60.   [2] *Ibid*, 306–7.
[3] *Ibid*, 294–5.

which these delays created in the French war-party,
wrote peremptorily to ask whether Austria accepted the
mediation. To this Wessenberg, on September 3, replied
yes, but Austria, he said, reserved the right of first establishing
with the mediating Powers the conditions
which should furnish the basis of the negotiations;[1] and
he added that, before any settlement could be reached,
Piedmont must keep her pledge. Here was an excuse
for further postponement, and time was Austria's most
efficient ally at this juncture. The terms to which Austria
now laid pretensions were "the ancient treaties"[2]
which had assigned the river Ticino as the eastern boundary
of Piedmont; in other words, the war and the radical
change in the position of Italian Nationality were to
be disregarded. Baron Wessenberg willingly agreed
that the armistice should be renewed for one month from
September 21, — the date of its expiration, — but the
negotiations made no progress. Wessenberg declared that
Austria was quite able to pacify her reconquered provinces
without outside interference, and that as for a settlement
with Charles Albert, he was ready at any time to
submit that to arbitration. To read his dispatches, that
of September 17, for instance, one would imagine that
it was not Austria but the other parties who had been
shilly-shallying for six long weeks.[3] The old suggestion
that a Lombardo-Venetian kingdom, having an archduke
for king, and enjoying as much independence as Bohemia
or Hungary enjoyed, was again raked up, and it pleased
Bastide, whose countrymen had from the outset looked
suspiciously on the possible formation of an Italian monarchy
which should include Piedmont, Lombardy, Venetia,
and the Legations.[4] Great stress was laid on the
fact that the rural populations of the reconquered provinces
had welcomed Radetzky's return, but Palmerston

[1] *Correspondence*, iii, 320. [2] *Ibid*, 331.
[3] *Ibid*, 419. [4] Bianchi, v, 336.

could not be hoodwinked: he insisted that the plebiscite, which had shown by an overwhelming majority that the Lombards wished to unite with Piedmont, "must carry more weight with it as an expression of national sentiment than can be attached to any demonstrations of farmers and peasants, who may have thought that by cheering the arrival of Austrian troops they were likely to conciliate conquerors and to escape ill-usage."[1] Palmerston further attempted to convince the Emperor's advisers that, since they could never hope to win the affection of the Lombards, and must therefore maintain their hold by a large army, it was for their interest to withdraw voluntarily, when their withdrawal could not be attributed to fear or compulsion, and when they could get ample compensation in money for the loss of a valuable province.[2] But the Imperial Cabinet knew that England would limit herself to giving advice, and, therefore, although the Foreign Secretary's advice was excellent and proved to be prophetic, they did not heed it. Their dilatoriness during the summer and autumn served the interests of the Empire better than a decisive policy could have served it. Like Radetzky's Fabian tactics in the Quadrilateral from April till July, it enabled them to gain time, and with time, strength. That the House of Hapsburg should have preserved its realm intact during the convulsions of that year is one of the marvels of modern history. It succeeded in so doing, chiefly because of the mutual hostility of its rebellious subjects; but much credit was due to its diplomats, who by temporizing and tergiversation kept the other Powers of Europe from interfering in behalf of Austria's oppressed races.

The internal condition of Piedmont during this long suspense became more unruly. The war-party were like

[1] *Correspondence*, iii, 399.
[2] See a notable dispatch from him to Ponsonby (Nov. 11); *Correspondence*, iii, 506-7.

passengers rescued from a sinking ship, who, at first thankful to escape with their lives, as soon as the imminent prospect of drowning has passed, begin to regret that they have not saved their jewels and money. The horror of the campaign became less vivid; the great prize which they had just missed seemed more and more precious. Only a few weeks ago they could have had all Lombardy and Venetia as far as the Piave; now they had only the smart of defeat. They saw so clearly that but for this or that blunder the National War would have ended in a triumph! Was it not possible to try again, now that experience had taught them how to avoid all blunders? Reasoning thus, they were not to be sobered by facts: let the treasury be empty, let the remnant of the Piedmontese army be disorganized, let Radetzky's forces be as strong as they might, these enthusiastic warriors believed that if they were listened to victory would be sure. And they were listened to, because they made the most din. Two thirds of the population of Piedmont unquestionably desired peace, but the other third was noisily bellicose.

Charles Albert himself longed for a last opportunity to prove that he was no traitor. Bitter was it to him to acknowledge that his maxim, "Italy will work out her own salvation," was fallacious; bitterer still, to be told by his ministers that in another campaign the command of the army must be intrusted to a general of greater ability than himself. Colonel La Marmora was sent to Paris in search of such a general. Cavaignac received him coldly: he could not officially depute one of the French officers to take command of the Piedmontese troops, as that would give umbrage to England and Austria, but if Bugeaud or Changarnier chose to go on his own responsibility, no objections would be raised. Bugeaud and Changarnier declined, and La Marmora returned from his bootless errand.[1] Equally sterile were the secret

[1] Massari: *La Marmora*, 52.

negotiations between the King's Cabinet and the French government to arrange a military alliance between Piedmont and France.[1] The date of the expiration of the armistice drew near, and yet the King was in no condition to reopen the war; he had come to realize both his own isolation and the inability of the mediating Powers to bring Austria to terms. Therefore he consented perforce to the extension of the truce.

The political situation grew from day to day more threatening. The Genoese, always turbulent, could hardly be restrained from open revolt. At Turin, the Lombard exiles, exasperated by the reports of the cruelties with which Radetzky restored Austrian despotism in the reconquered provinces, roused the anger and sympathy of the Piedmontese. The war-party, composed of Radicals and Democrats, stormed. The King had an interview with Brofferio, which was accepted as a sign that he was leaning towards the Radical policy; he renewed his relations with Gioberti, who at the moment was the most popular public man in Italy. "Even if I have to put on the red cap," the King was said to have exclaimed, "I will have my revenge."[2] The sessions in the Chamber took on a lurid hue. Again and again the Radicals attacked the ministry, whose moderation, based on necessity, they jeered at as unpatriotic and cowardly. Even a frank statement by Dabormida, the Minister of War, that the condition of the army rendered impossible an immediate rupture of the truce, did not appease them. By a narrow vote the ministry escaped censure, but Dabormida resigned. The Chamber itself was but an annex of the Political Club, which became, says Brofferio, its President, "a sort of very imposing popular government,"[3] and which corresponded with similar clubs in other parts of the Peninsula. Only too evident was it, that the men who thus clamored for still larger political

[1] Bianchi, v, 342-3.   [2] Brofferio, iv, 203.   [3] *Ibid*, v, 5.

freedom, who felt hampered in a limited monarchy and yearned for the ample elbow-room of a republic, had not yet learned how to employ the constitutional rights which they already enjoyed. That revolutions never go backward is the old saw of the political doctrinaires, being verified again in Piedmont at the close of 1848; for under this cloud of war-talk Radicalism was rapidly uncoiling itself.

Radetzky's conduct in Lombardy belied both his own promises and the specious report that Austria's sole intention was to conciliate her subjects lately in rebellion. "We have already granted to all the inhabitants of the Lombardo-Venetian Kingdom, without distinction, full pardon for the part they may have taken in the political occurrences of the present year, commanding that there shall not be practiced against them any inquisition or punishment, except in respect to those considerations necessary for the confirmation of public employees. Likewise, it is our sovereign will that the inhabitants of the Lombardo-Venetian Kingdom have a Constitution corresponding not less to their respective nationality and to the needs of the country, than to their union with the Austrian Empire."[1] Thus ran the Imperial proclamation, on which the Imperial Minister Wessenberg passed the comment that "history furnishes no example of an insurgent people being treated with more consideration and more generosity." Radetzky, however, interpreted the Emperor's order after his own fashion. He governed by martial law: he levied a contribution of fifteen million francs on a few of the rich Milanese, 1,200,000 francs from Pompeo Litta, 800,000 francs apiece from the Borromeo and Princess Belgiojoso;[2] and, believing in the efficacy of terror as a means of maintaining order,

---

[1] Text in *Correspondence*, iii, 408.
[2] The list of persons fined is given in *Correspondence*, iii, 634-5; Radetzky raised more than twenty million francs in this way.

he was not solicitous to prevent cruelties on the part of his soldiers. His régime leaned towards chastisement rather than reconciliation, and was therefore unwise, because if Austria determined to keep Lombardy and Venetia, it was for her interest to allay the hatred engendered against her during the past few months. But it must be said in palliation of Radetzky that for a while after his return he had to guard against possible uprisings. The free corps and a few of the fortified towns did not at once surrender: Garibaldi, with three thousand volunteers, prosecuted a guerrilla fight round Varese and Como; Arcioni and D'Apice skirmished in Valtellina till they were forced to seek safety in Switzerland. Venice alone, with her islands and a margin of the mainland, still held out.

On August 7, the day when Charles Albert's shattered army returned to Piedmont, his three commissioners, Castelli, Colli, and Cibrario, formally took possession of Venice, and the tricolor banner with the shield of Savoy was hoisted on the masts in front of St. Mark's. As if Fate had only mockery for the melancholy King, he was hailed sovereign at Venice in the very moment when his power to rule there was cut off. Rumors of the Piedmontese disaster sifted among the populace and caused great alarm, and on August 11 throngs collected before the residence of the Royal Commissioners and demanded news. It was too late for equivocation. A clerk read from the balcony of the palace an account of the capitulation of Milan. The people demanded to know their own destiny. Castelli then told them that the Piedmontese troops and squadron would probably be withdrawn. Cries of "Treason" and "Death to Charles Albert" greeted him. "We want Manin! Long live Manin, the savior of the country!" shouted the Venetians. After half an hour's delay the short, stout figure and grave face of Manin appeared on the balcony. "The

Commissioners," he said, "have resigned; the day after to-morrow the Assembly will meet to nominate a new government. During the next forty-eight hours I will govern. . . . Now disperse; we must have silence and calm to provide for the needs of the country."[1] And the multitude, so great was its trust in Manin, retired without further demonstration. Thrice fortunate is the man who can inspire such confidence; capable of high deeds is the people who can appreciate and obey such a man.

On August 13 the Assembly convened and wished to make Manin dictator, but as he declined, it elected him, Rear-Admiral Graziani, and Colonel Cavedalis triumvirs, to have full power over military and political affairs, but it reserved to itself the right to decide upon the final destiny of the State. The Triumvirs at once devoted themselves to their great task. Money had to be raised, now by increasing the tax on tobacco and other luxuries, now by forced loans from the banks, now by appropriating all the gold and silver plate. The Venetians contributed liberally, though some of them murmured; women brought their jewels, men offered their cash, to the National Treasury. On one loan the Ducal Palace and the Procuratie Nuove were pledged as security. The army was increased both in numbers and discipline, and the navy was improved so far as improvement was possible in the small vessels which composed it. Tranquillity and harmony for the most part prevailed, although the sacrifices were heavy and the outlook unpromising. Partisans of Austria there were even here, but they dared not speak up; and when critics of the government and professional grumblers began to sow discontent, the Triumvirs, with commendable energy, dissolved the political club in which the brood of dissidents nested. Firm and just and honest was the rule of the Triumvirate. "There can be but two parties now," said Manin: "Italians and Austrians."

[1] Frrera: *Manin e Venezia* (Florence, 1875), 98.

But of course the great question for Venice was, What Europe would do with her, since Europe did not allow small States freedom ,to follow their inclination or their interest. Manin had sent Tommaseo without delay to Paris to bespeak the assistance of the French government, and Tommaseo was received by both Cavaignac and Bastide with words of sympathy, often reiterated in the subsequent months. To Lord Palmerston, the First Triumvir wrote (August 20) a letter full of sound argument and shot through with emotion, — an unusual material in the web of Diplomacy. He appealed to English generosity and common-sense, and even to British commercial interests, and in order to allay Palmerston's well known repugnance to a Democratic régime, he assured him that the Triumvirate was only provisional, without a political color that might prejudice the ultimate form of government, and bound solely to busy itself with internal quiet and external defense, so long as the danger lasted.[1] Manin urged England and France to unite in persuading Austria to include Venice in the terms of the Salasco armistice, in so far, that is, as military operations were concerned; but despite the request of the mediating Powers, which pointed out that, as the fate of Venice was involved in the negotiations for peace, it was better for both sides to suspend hostilities which could result in no permanent advantage to either, Austria persisted in keeping up a desultory warfare on the Venetian outposts which she had blockaded since June 18, — Austria, who had recognized the Provisional Government of Lombardy two months before by negotiating directly with it, treated Venice as a rebellious city, to be dealt with as the Imperial government saw fit, and without interference from foreign powers. France and England, however, disregarded this assumption and included Venice in their diplomatic parleys. In order not to estrange Piedmont,

[1] Text in Errera, 138–43.

Manin repeated to the King's ministers his statement that the lot of Venice would be decided by popular vote at the end of the war. Indeed, the indefatigable Triumvir left no means unemployed for propitiating those Powers from which Venice might hope for succor, and by which, if the worst came to pass, her destiny would be sealed.

Yet the picture we have of Venice during those autumn months though noble is pathetic. The city itself, bustling with martial preparations, began to feel the pinch of civic sacrifices, while the conviction that she was doomed to be abandoned became more and more certain, despite the encouragement of Manin and his colleagues. The Piedmontese troops and squadron sailed away (September 8); French men-of-war, which had come (September 15) with a flourish as of protectors, lay inactive while Austrian ships harried the provision-boats, and finally completed the blockade of Venice by sea; winter approached, with its prospect of scanty food and fuel, or the alternative of a bombardment. At Paris, Tommaseo and Pasini — the latter had been intrusted with a special mission to uphold the Venetian cause in the expected international conference — wrote and talked and pleaded, now getting a ray of hope from some diplomat's cordial smile, and now dashed by ministerial reticence or evasion, but never able to send their government a statement which could relieve its suspense.

Pasini's instructions were simple. Venice would agree to any terms which did not rivet her again to the Austrian Empire, or convert her into a monarchy under an Austrian or Estensian prince.[1] On reaching Paris early in September, Pasini found the Powers disposed either to abandon Venice altogether, leaving Austria to recapture her by force; or to convert her into a free port; or to use her resistance as an argument for compelling Austria to

[1] Bonghi: *Vita di Valentino Pasini* (Florence, 1867), 386.

consent to the liberation of the Venetian provinces.¹ The second proposition was soon dropped, as it was evident that Venice, from her peculiar site, could not maintain herself as a Hanseatic port, unless she were allowed a strip of mainland. Lord Palmerston, even thus early, seems to have looked upon her restitution to Austria as inevitable, although he did not fail to cite her resistance as a reason why Austria should delay no longer in accepting the scheme of mediation which England and France had framed. Bastide, on the other hand, cherished the plan of constituting Lombardy and Venetia an independent republic, — a plan which would remove the apprehension of the French over the possible union of those provinces with Charles Albert's kingdom. Piedmont, as we have seen, would be satisfied for the present with the annexation of Lombardy, but the Lombards in Paris, instead of coöperating with the Venetians or the Piedmontese, urged that though Venetia were restored to Austria, Lombardy should be allowed to exist as a republic.

In this diplomatic tangle Pasini felt his way cautiously but firmly, keeping always in hand as a guiding clue the resolve to save Venice. But as the weeks passed and brought only expressions of sympathy and of hope that Venice would not be disappointed at the final settlement, he realized that the Western Powers had little intention of giving material aid to her. In order to learn the truth, he wrote to Palmerston, requesting him to suggest to the Venetians how they could put an end to the evils which afflicted their country.² Palmerston's reply (October 18) left no doubt as to the policy of the British government. After declaring his lively interest in the fate of Venice, and remarking that, had the recent campaign turned out favorably for Piedmont, the reconstruction of Northern Italy might have conformed more closely to his own preference and to the desires of the Venetians,

[1] Bonghi, 349.   [2] *Correspondence*, iii, 489.

he reminded them that victorious Austria could not be expected to concede to the Italians provinces which they had been unable to wrest from her. If the city of Venice still held out, it was because the mediating Powers had urged Austria to defer vigorous operations against her until negotiations had been concluded. "The proposals which have been made to Austria," he continued, "do not contemplate the severance of the city of Venice, or of any part of the Venetian territory, from the Imperial Crown. . . . It is evident, therefore, that, Austria being at liberty to employ her naval and military means for the purpose of reëstablishing her authority in the city and State of Venice, any armed resistance on the part of the Venetians must be fruitless, and could only lead to a needless effusion of blood and to a bootless sacrifice of life. . . . I would beg to suggest that the wisest thing which the Venetians could do would be to enter into communication with the Austrian government with regard to the future condition of the Venetian State."[1]

Pasini showed this "terrible reply" to Bastide and Cavaignac. The latter protested that he should deem himself dishonored on the day when he sanctioned an arrangement leaving a single Austrian soldier south of the Alps, and that France desired the emancipation of all Italy.[2] Bastide likewise disowned participation in Palmerston's views. "There is, I know well enough," he wrote, about this time (November 17) to Manin, "a policy which would make Venice the ransom for Lombardy; this policy is not mine; I will never accept a treaty of Campo Formio. If, then, I were sure to remain in power I would tell you to have full confidence; but France touches a crisis which may bring forward other men and other principles. I can only answer for my own good-will and that of my government."[3] It was but too plain, therefore, that Venice need expect no real aid from

[1] *Correspondence*, iii, 509-10. [2] Bonghi, 351. [3] Errera, 100-1.

the mediating Powers. Like a fugitive slave, she must submit to being restored to her brutal master; the judge who gave the decision was sorry, of course, — he pitied her sufferings, and admired her brave dash for freedom, — but he could not suspend the operation of the law.

The desperate snarl in which diplomacy was involved during those autumn months was a symbol of the confusion which prevailed throughout Europe. In some respects, the great French Revolution of 1789 had been less alarming than were these revolutions of 1848. For in 1789 the upheaval at first concerned France alone, and did not threaten the feudal régime in Germany, Austria, and Italy; but in 1848 all Europe, from the Douro to the Don, was shaken, and men dreaded lest the very bases of social order should be shattered in the general convulsion. They now knew, too, the nature of revolution: how in a few swift tiger-bounds it plunges into chaos, where Robespierres and Terror reign. In their consternation they heard again the click of guillotines raised in every capital in Europe, and they saw royal heads roll into the clotted sawdust. Events chased each other so fast that the bewildered spectators, unable to read their significance, could only draw from them fresh fuel for their fear. Pledges given to-day were conditional on the unforeseen accidents of to-morrow. In such a whirlpool, Diplomacy struggled ineffectually. Her slow feet could not keep pace with the rush of events. The electric telegraph, recently invented, had not yet been generally adopted; railways were few; communication was still made, especially in Italy and over the Alps, by courier and post wagon. It took nearly four days for a letter to reach Paris from Turin; eleven or twelve days' journey separated besieged Venice from London; special messengers spent five days from Berlin, and six days from Vienna, to London. In the interval, battles might be fought, ministries overturned, sovereigns deposed or expelled. These delays account for many of the blunders both of the revolutionists and of the established governments. Thus, before the second flight of the Austrian Emperor from Vienna, in October, was known in Italy, the favorable moment for acting upon it had passed. Amid the almost universal shifting, I discern only two fixed points: Palmerston at London, determined to prevent, at whatever cost, a European war; and Radetzky, at Milan, resolved to repel all comers, whatever mediation might suggest, and however the perplexed Imperial Cabinet might vacillate from day to day. The inertia of the Old Régime was slowly wearing out the vehement but separate assaults of the Revolution. If Austria — that is, the Hapsburg dynasty — could only keep afloat for a few months, it might outride the storm; for Croats and Magyars and Slavs, instead of discharging a simultaneous broadside into the imperial slave-ship, were battering each other. In Germany, the ghost of the Empire would soon be laid. In France, as Bastide foresaw, the government was toppling, all parties discordant, and the masses only eager that bottom should be reached in order that some stable edifice might be erected. It was a time of avalanches and earthquakes, in which self-preservation was the only fixed instinct.

In such a time it was as inevitable that political ideals should hurry to an extreme as that flames, having broken out on the ground-floor of a building, shall climb to its upper stories. We have seen how rapidly Radicalism gained ground in Piedmont after the publication of the Salasco armistice, and how Venice reverted to her democratic government. We shall now see that a similar process was going on in Tuscany and Rome. In Tuscany the Moderate Cabinet, of which Marquis Ridolfi was the head, soon failed to satisfy the more aggressive politicians. There as elsewhere, the first war enthusiasm had brought out several thousand volunteers, who with the regular troops had gone gayly to the front; but the Tuscans, over-confident like the rest of the Italians, complacently folded their hands, and, imagining that they had discharged their obligations so far as furnishing a contingent to the National War was concerned, they gave themselves up to the common impulse to chatter and wrangle over internal politics. Even the disasters at Curtatone and Montanara, in which the flower of the Tuscan youth had been cut down, did not convince them that their first duty, their imperative business, should be to push forward their military organization; unless indeed, they wished the campaign to collapse. But while they certainly had no such wish, they wasted the precious days and weeks in idle patriotic demonstrations, which added not another file to the regiments in the field. Grand Duke Leopold, though placed between two motives, — his kinship which drew him towards Austria, and his autocratic traditions, which urged him to save all that he could of his authority, — still avowed his loyalty to the Constitution, and his sympathy for the patriotic cause. Yet he could not but reflect that, if Charles Albert conquered Radetzky, the new kingdom of Northern Italy, with ten million inhabitants, would prove a dangerous neighbor for little Tuscany with her million and a half; consequently, it is not surprising that in his heart he had no very fervent desire for Charles Albert to succeed, unless Tuscany herself could be strengthened, as was by some suggested, by the annexation of territory. Leopold was solicitous, therefore, to renew negotiations for the Italian League, as a means whereby the possible encroachments of Piedmont might be resisted.

On the 26th of June the first Tuscan Legislative Assembly met in the Great Hall of the Palazzo Vecchio, — that Hall on whose walls Leonardo da Vinci and young Buonarotti once painted frescoes which, like the splendid era of republican Florence, had long since vanished, —

and then began that babel of official speechifying which
our great modern historian has called, with more truth
than urbanity, "government by gabble." The deputies
echoed the complaints of the unofficial assemblies in the
market-place or the cafés, when they accused the ministry
of lukewarmness in prosecuting the National War.[1] As
if half a dozen gentlemen seated round a green table
possessed any spell by which they could instantaneously
convert a loquacious and unmartial people into a silent,
disciplined army! But deputies and populace little
thought of this; they were mesmerized by the common
fallacy of the age that government is an omnipotent, full-
pursed creature, that can make the poor rich, and the
idle industrious, irrespective of the character of the people, of whom government is, in reality, only the obedient
servant.

On July 30 a mob broke in upon the session of the
Chamber, which hastily adjourned, leaving the rioters —
who were led by "three individuals known to the police
as thieves and vagabonds" — to proclaim the downfall
of the grand-ducal dynasty and the establishment of a
provisional government. In the course of the day order
was restored; the deputies resumed their deliberations
and decreed the mobilization of 6,000 Civic Guards, but
Marquis Ridolfi announced that he and his colleagues
had resigned.[2] The Grand Duke had great difficulty in
forming another cabinet; because Ridolfi had represented
well enough the general views of the Moderate party, and
it would be deemed suicidal to seek for ministers among
the Radicals. At length, after much importuning, Gino
Capponi — the most venerable of living Tuscans, whose
popular nickname, "the Patriarch of Liberty," was well
deserved — entered on office (August 20). In the inter-

[1] See the reply of the deputies to the speech from the throne, *Correspondence*, iii, 102-5.
[2] *Ibid*, 113.

val, a very grave event had come to pass. Early in August General Welden occupied Emilia, and threatened Bologna with a large force of Austrians; Tuscany was thrown into consternation lest he should invade her territory for the purpose of seizing Massa, Carrara, and the Lunigiana, which had voted a few months before to annex themselves to Tuscany. The Grand Duke in alarm appealed to Sir George Hamilton, the British minister, to intercede. Hamilton therefore wrote Welden that, if he would refrain from violating the Tuscan frontier, the Grand Duke would agree that no levy in mass nor other military preparation should be made in that part of Tuscany, but that the government, "in order to calm the public excitement, rather than to secure their own existence," asked to be allowed to send some troops to the frontier "for a show of resistance." He added that "the Grand Duke in accepting the sovereignty of Massa, Carrara, Lunigiana, etc., declared expressly that he assumed such sovereignty till definitive territorial arrangements should be made in Italy, and to prevent those provinces from falling into a state of anarchy."[1] Welden immediately replied that he consented to the terms,[2] which, while they postponed the Austrian invasion, revealed Tuscany's helplessness to repel foreign aggressors.

Capponi, the blind patriot, had scarcely taken the helm of government before there exploded at Leghorn a revolution which proved that the Grand Duke's authority was equally powerless against its internal enemies. Leghorn had long been the most turbulent city in Italy, composed of stevedores, porters, and loafers, and a floating population of sailors and strangers, to whom had recently been added swarms of emigrants from Lombardy and Naples, not all bad, but all having a grievance, and being, therefore, predisposed to agitation. The Livornese, moreover, had enjoyed during the past year the political

[1] *Correspondence*, iii, 150–1.   [2] *Ibid*, 157.

tuition of Guerrazzi, — one of that most dangerous class of fanatics, who, though intelligent themselves, recklessly sow among the ignorant masses doctrines which those masses work out in brutality and bloodshed. On August 23 Father Gavazzi — that same Barnabite whom we last saw playing Peter the Hermit to the Roman Crusaders — arrived in the harbor of Leghorn; but the Tuscan government had previously forbidden him, on account of his demagogic proclivities, to set foot on Tuscan soil. Nevertheless, the rabble rowed out to his ship and brought him ashore amid great applause. When the Lieutenant-Colonel of the Civic Guard went to inquire by whose command a guard of honor had been stationed before Gavazzi's hotel, he was curtly informed that "His Highness the People" had so ordered. The matter being telegraphed to Florence, the Cabinet hoped to conciliate this new sovereign by permitting Gavazzi to proceed through Tuscany to Bologna, whither he was bound. On the 24th the burly friar, having bellowed an incendiary message to a great crowd in the market-place, was drawn in a gilded coach to the railway station, and thence he set forth in triumph. But at Signa he left the train, perhaps to avoid another ovation, and was quietly dining, when there came grand-ducal carabineers who ignominiously escorted him by the shortest road to the frontier.

When the Livornese learned how their hero had been insulted, they rose in wrath, seized the arms of the Civic Guard, imprisoned the Governor, and were for declaring a Provisional Government; but the more prudent of them suggested that a messenger be sent to Florence with the offer to the ministers that Leghorn would cease rioting on condition that amnesty were granted and that Gavazzi's companions, who had been arrested, were released. While awaiting an answer, the Livornese elected a Governing Committee composed of Guerrazzi, Mancini, La Cecilia, and Gualberto Roberti. Capponi and his colleagues, still bent on taming the tiger by mildness, granted the rioters' demands. The distribution of arms and ammunition to the Civic Guard, however, was construed by the Livornese to mean that the government intended to preserve order by martial law, and they flew into another frenzy. An officer gave the word to fire upon them: five were killed and many wounded, which merely exasperated the survivors, who beset the Guards' quarters so fiercely that the Guardsmen turned and ran. Leghorn was now in the hands of the mob, which, it must be said, both at this time and afterwards, showed a scrupulous respect for property; never countenancing robbery nor pillage, nor menacing the lives of the citizens except for political reasons. All Tuscany was alarmed. The government saw that it must resort to sterner measures, and therefore dispatched Colonel Leonetto Cipriani to occupy the insurgent city with troops. The Livornese, nothing terrified, threw up barricades and prepared to oppose his entrance, but before coming to blows they sent off Malenchini, now a member of the Governing Committee, to Florence, to offer to submit, provided the Cabinet would promise to push with greater vigor the armament for the National War, and would declare amnesty to the revolters, besides making several internal reforms. The government replied that while they would enter into no negotiations with the rebels, they would act as leniently as possible if Cipriani were peaceably received in the city, and that they would refer the other matters to the deputies. On the strength of this reply, Cipriani with about 2,000 troops was admitted into the city, but when he issued a proclamation forbidding public meetings and closing political clubs, up flared the rebellious monster and fell upon the troops. After a bloody encounter, Cipriani was forced to retreat to the fortress of Porta Murata, where his men refused to make any further head against the rebels.

Leghorn now indulged in one of those wild orgies which ever since 1793 European Republicans of the red variety have been pleased to deem inspiring. A French *vivandière*, dressed in tricolor and wearing a Phrygian cap, was worshiped as Our Lady of Liberty; crowds of rioters swarmed in the streets, shouting death and destruction to everybody except themselves and Italy, — a lawless, threatening crew, yet never bloodthirsty, like its Parisian prototype. Torres, a soldier of fortune, who had led a volunteer corps in Lombardy, was hailed as a hero and given command of the city for a few hours. Then Ghilardi, just returned from the war with a battalion of Tuscans, was acclaimed leader of Leghorn's forces. Cipriani, meanwhile, had gone away, powerless to execute his orders. The helplessness of the government had now been so thoroughly demonstrated that it was even proposed to hire 4,000 Swiss mercenaries, and only a feint was made to preserve the Grand Duke's dignity. Yet Guerrazzi could now do what the government had failed to do: he went down to Leghorn, where his immense popularity was unabated, and on his own responsibility governed the city until the accesses of violence had passed. Then the ministers appointed Tartini to be governor, but the Livornese rose against him, and another conflict began. The Grand Duke ordered the formation at Pisa of a camp of Civic Guards from all parts of Tuscany; a few thousand of them came, loitered there awhile, and then deserted. So this show of force also proved farcical. Then all communication between Leghorn and Florence was cut off, but as this measure virtually acknowledged that the Livornese were their own masters, it neither troubled them nor strengthened the government. Charles Albert, being appealed to for aid, sent a regiment of Piedmontese troops to Leopold, but on the express condition that they should not be called upon to act against the people. At last, early in October, the ministry consented, much against its will, to the nomination of Montanelli as governor of Leghorn, and he was received with wild delight by the victorious rebels: for Montanelli was, next to Guerrazzi, the most popular of the Democratic leaders, and his reputation had been increased by his bravery in the late campaign, where he had been left for dead at Montanara, and he had only recently recovered sufficiently from his wounds to take up his political work. Under him, Leghorn became tranquil; but the credit not only of the Capponi Cabinet but also of the Moderate party was ruined. What availed it for the ministers to announce that they were negotiating for the convocation of an Italian Diet at Rome, or that they were resolved to push forward military preparations? What availed it that they tried to bridle the press and to put down political agitators? At Leghorn the rabble had triumphed, for, by the appointment of Montanelli, Democracy had been officially recognized, and in other towns the disposition to riot had become chronic.[1]

Unable to stagger longer, Capponi and his colleagues resigned (October 12). The Grand Duke wished to replace them by men of similar stamp; but Ricasoli, Salvagnoli, and D'Azeglio, to whom he applied, after looking over the field, reached the conviction that, like Capponi, they would lack the support of the country. Under the windows of the Pitti Palace the populace shouted for Guerrazzi and Montanelli; deputations came from Pisa, Lucca, Arezzo, and Leghorn, to press the claims of those Democratic idols; but Leopold hesitated. For him to accept Guerrazzi as a minister was as if Louis XVI had given a portfolio to Marat or St. Just. Nevertheless,

[1] For the affair at Leghorn see La Farina, iv, 54–63; La Cecilia: *Ultima Rivoluzione Toscana* (Capolago, 1851), part I; Capponi: *Settanta Giorni di Ministero*; Guerrazzi: *Apologia* (Florence, 1851); *Correspondence*, iii, 266, 280, 315, 321, 331, 347, 393, 498, 506, 510.

Leopold had but one other alternative, — abdication; therefore he sent for Montanelli, and instructed him to form a ministry. On November 1 the new cabinet was announced, Montanelli being its President and Minister of Foreign Affairs, and Guerrazzi Minister of the Interior. Its programme was unexpectedly mild; and the Grand Duke and Moderates dared for a moment to hope that King Demos, having had his lawless way thus far, would now turn docile.

Upon the ministers the responsibility of office had its usual effect. They found that a change of the watch at mid-tempest had no quieting effect on gale or billow. They found, too, that some of their former associates began to complain of their conservatism; which meant that the ministers preferred to go to the devil at a dignified pace in their state coach, rather than at a frantic gallop. The treasury was empty, the army a mere phantom, the police weak and unrespected; newspapers were blatant; demagogues were incendiary and slanderous: all of which things would not correct themselves any more readily under a Democratic than under a Liberal ministry. Every citizen, whatever his politics may be, is the natural enemy of the tax-man; popularity great as Montanelli's, therefore, could not make Democratic taxes agreeable. The peasantry, instigated by the priests, looked sullenly at the townsmen's efforts to govern, and refused to submit to the conscription. Demagogues and journalists shrieked at the suggestion that tongue and pen should not utter every wild thought; as if Liberty meant self-control, or respect for the common weal!

Montanelli had already made himself famous as the author of a scheme which, he insisted, would heal all the wounds of Italy. He proposed that a Constituent Assembly should meet at Rome to determine the political constitution of the Peninsula, and to take measures for prosecuting the War of Independence, the former aim to be held in abeyance until the latter had been achieved. He made the promotion of this scheme one of the conditions on which he accepted office. But it was evident that a Constitutent Assembly, elected by universal suffrage, might vote for a complete change in government; it might dethrone the princes and set up a republic, or it might merge a small State like Tuscany in the proposed kingdom of Upper Italy. Guerrazzi, at his first interview with the Grand Duke, sounded Leopold on this subject, and discovered that he had accepted Montanelli's project with all its consequences. "But have you reflected that this Constituent Assembly may deprive you of your crown?" asked Guerrazzi. "I have," replied Leopold; "and though I should be ready even for this for the welfare of my people, still, to speak frankly, I do not fear it, because my family has deserved well of Tuscany, and I think that I have added something of my own to my father's merits: therefore, the people when consulted will not wish to exchange me for some one else, and I believe it will vote for the Constitutional Principality and for me." Guerrazzi then assured His Highness that, if he ever repented of this decision, he, Guerrazzi, would endeavor so to arrange matters that the ministry might be dissolved with credit to the Grand Duke's reputation.[1] From that time on Leopold was more friendly towards the domineering Guerrazzi than towards the genial Montanelli; and though the latter remained nominally at the head of the Cabinet, Guerrazzi was its real leader. The revolution had traveled far when the descendant of Maria Theresa clasped hands with the demagogue of Leghorn!

In the Roman States the drift towards Democracy had been equally steady. The unceasing friction between Church and State engendered more and more heat. The situation at Rome was perpetually paradoxical. Pius had discountenanced the war, but his subjects might fight if

[1] Guerrazzi, 126-7.

they chose, and he would ease his conscience by protesting that he was unable to restrain them. His pacific mission to the Emperor had been greeted with derision. He had raised his voice as the fountain of orthodoxy, and yet he was leaning on Mamiani, a philosopher whose works were pilloried in the *Index*, a patriot who had never submitted to the dishonorable terms of Pius's amnesty. Only a man of high courage and unselfishness would have consented to act as buffer between the Pope and the Revolution at that desperate juncture. How Mamiani was hampered, how he was deceived and discredited by Pius's shuffling behavior, would take long to tell. Pius ignored his ministers so far as possible, regarding them only as dummies to keep the people quiet, or as scapegoats on whom he could throw the blame for his own perverseness. He charged a monsignore with the formulation of a presslaw; he consulted the cardinals on temporal matters; he listened more and more willingly to the insinuations of the Retrogrades; and the Retrogrades, among whom was many a sly partisan of Austria, kept playing on that dread of schism which had already drawn from him the fatal allocution of April 29. Mamiani strove to reorganize the internal administration, to restore the bankrupt treasury, to foster the National War spirit, to revive the Italian League: but to what purpose? At home he was everywhere blocked by ecclesiastical unwillingness and by the Pope's lack of candor; abroad, the Papal legates, instead of obeying his instructions, took their orders directly from the Quirinal. If Mamiani protested that, as responsible minister, he should have control over the temporal affairs of the government, it required only a little clerical jugglery to show that the affairs which he deemed *temporal* were really *mixed* or wholly *ecclesiastical*, and therefore beyond his jurisdiction. He was too honest to submit to this cheap trick, and his frequent protests so irritated Pius that he cast about for a more pliant tool. Minghetti, whom he first sounded, disapproved of the Pope's attitude towards the National War. Pellegrino Rossi, to whom, also, overtures were made, was unpopular both with the Retrogrades and the Radicals. For the present, therefore, Pius had to tolerate Mamiani: but when Parliament met, on June 5, there was a crisis. The ministry, having drawn up an address from the throne, submitted it to Pius for his approbation. He kept it for correction, and so altered it that the ministers, on receiving it back, preferred to resign rather than to assume responsibility for it. Parliament, already assembled, was waiting impatiently for the sovereign's message. Pius, in high dudgeon that the ministers should presume to criticise his emendations, hurled abuse at them, accused them of treachery, and dismissed them. But presently he bethought him of the consequences of his anger: who would guarantee to save him from the infuriated people as soon as his treatment of his Liberal advisers should be known? Anger gave way to fear, and fear made it easy for peacemakers to patch up a temporary reconciliation. The disputed address was not read, but in its stead a hastily-scrawled, colorless greeting from the sovereign to the Parliament.

It was hoped that the deputies might bring solid support to the ministry, that their presence in Rome might check the incessant agitation; but these hopes were unfulfilled. The deputies, though for the most part worthy men, had neither experience nor political wisdom; they were beset by the mania for chatter which was epidemic throughout Europe that year. The hall in the Palace of the Cancelleria, where they met, was as noisy as a music-hall when instruments are tuning, — fiddles squeaking, viols droning, flutes piping. and Prince Canino's big trombone drowning all the rest. It made no difference whether the topic were great or small, Canino burst in with his stentorian tones and Radical ideas. And outside, the Clubs, instead of growing quiet, grew more uproarious; every street corner or café had its orator; every piazza resounded with an antiphony of demagogic harangues and popular cheers. Gioberti came and had such a greeting as had been reserved for Pius himself only a few months before. And all the while Reactionists and Sanfedists were stealthily plying the Pope with scruples and provoking disorder among the masses. The news of the capitulation of the Roman troops at Vicenza caused consternation, which increased when the report came that the Austrians had occupied Ferrara. Against this audacity Pius protested, but with slight effect, for Welden marched to Bologna a few weeks later, announcing himself to be the friend of the Pope and threatening all who opposed him with a fate similar to that of the inhabitants of still smoking Sermide. Again Pius protested; the deputies demanded a levy in mass and an appeal to France for troops; the Sanfedists, some of whose myrmidons followed Welden's corps, said nothing, but took heart. Bologna rose and repelled the Austrians (August 8), and then Radetzky declared that the violation of Papal territory had been unsanctioned by him. Just in the midst of this crisis (August 1) Mamiani and his colleagues, unable to endure longer Pius's indecision and amphibiousness, resigned. Count Fabbri succeeded to the premiership, a well-meaning old gentleman, whose only policy it was to obey the Pope implicitly and to commit the safeguarding of the State "to Most Holy Mary and the chief Apostles."[1] Alas, not even those august patrons intervened in behalf of the Vicar of the Church which had lavished so much tallow and incense and entreaty upon them. Sedition reigned at Bologna, discontent at Rome; the deputies clamored for war, the ministers replied that the sovereign alone could grant that demand, and the sovereign held fast to his pacific rôle.

[1] La Farina, iii, 559.

On August 26 he prorogued Parliament for ten weeks; on September 16 good-natured but ineffectual Fabbri retired, and Pellegrino Rossi became Prime Minister.

Rossi had not accepted office without much persuasion. Besides being unacceptable to the extremists of both parties, he had a Protestant wife, and some of his writings were in the *Index;* but Pius assured him that that did not matter. The Radicals frowned at him because he had been Louis Philippe's ambassador; the Retrogrades sniffed heresy and revolution in his Liberal opinions; but Pius, who, like some women, could not conceal his likes and dislikes, had a personal attachment for him which counterbalanced every objection. Rossi, therefore, took up the heavy burden. His colleagues seemed perhaps a shade more conservative than Mamiani's, but their opinions counted for little, as he was himself the head and hands of the Cabinet. His programme had two aims, — it aimed at promoting the National Cause by cementing the much talked of league, and at maintaining order at home. To achieve the first he renewed negotiations with Piedmont and Tuscany, and he hoped even to entice Bomba into the patriotic federation; but Piedmont, as usual, was evasive and procrastinating. In dealing with internal affairs, Rossi displayed a vigor hitherto unseen. He was just, but inflexible. He warned the tumultuous that they should be checked and punished, and to show that he was in earnest, he caused two or three companies of carabineers, on whom he thought he could rely, to patrol the streets of Rome. Unlike Mamiani, he had affiliations with no political club, but he published in the official newspaper articles fraught with political wisdom that the Romans would have done well to heed. He appointed General Zucchi to reorganize the army; he took measures for the immediate introduction of railways and the electric telegraph; he planned reforms in the judicial, financial, and police departments.

In brief, Pellegrino Rossi was a strong, clear-headed man, who went his way fearlessly, firm in the belief that an honest application of constitutional government was the only method by which the State could be saved from reaction on the one hand and anarchy on the other; and that the majority of sensible citizens would be drawn to its support as soon as they should see it working effectively. But a strong, unwavering man, who showed favor to nobody and refused to compromise or to cajole, was just the person whom every one who hoped to benefit by the reign of disorder found most obnoxious. Sanfedists hated Rossi because he circumvented their attempts to overthrow the Constitution; Radicals hated him because he was a Moderate; the lawless hated him because under his rule they could not cover their crimes with a mask of patriotism. Every one had a grievance, from the fat abbot, forced to contribute some of his wealth to the tax-gatherer, to the cabman, who grumbled that a concentration of the law-courts would give him fewer attorneys' fares. His haughty bearing sufficed to make him unpopular with those who had no more definite grudge against him. The rise of the Democratic ministry in Tuscany sharpened the desires of the Democrats at Rome. They, too, began to clamor for Montanelli's Constituent Assembly, and in extolling that, they turned angrily upon Rossi who opposed it.

As November 15, the date for the convocation of the Chambers, drew near, ominous mutterings were heard among the masses, and the demagogues emitted in the newspapers articles full of calumny and violent instigations. Rossi was advised to take the precaution of going accompanied by a body-guard, but this he refused. "If they wish to kill me," he said, "though they were prevented to-morrow, they would find some other day." On the morning of the 15th he received warnings, — one, it is said, from a priest, who had been told at the confessional of a plot, — but Rossi, like Cæsar, could not be deterred by omens or entreaties. Attended by Ringhetti, Under-Secretary of Finance, he drove to the Palace of the Cancelleria. A sullen mob crowded the square, and pushed into the entrance of the palace, where a file of police was drawn up. Rossi's carriage stopped in the courtyard, and, having got out, he strode resolutely to the staircase, a few yards distant. The evil-looking crowd pressed round him, uttering imprecations and jostling him. He had ascended only a few steps when some one struck him in the back with an umbrella, and just as he turned his head a villain made a slash at his throat with a knife and cut the left carotid artery. In an instant the minister fell on the stone stairs, his life-blood pouring out in a swift stream. Round him was the utmost confusion. The party of assassins rushed shouting into the street; the police cowered and did nothing; deputies ran to and fro, each asking the others what had happened; and in the general consternation Rossi was carried upstairs to the apartments of Cardinal Gazzoli, where he quickly expired. Meanwhile, in the Assembly Hall, President Sturbinetti had called the deputies to order, and with untimely phlegm he bade the clerk read the minutes of the last session. Some one protested that that was not the moment for dull routine; at which a voice shouted sarcastically, "Why so much ado? Is the King of Rome killed?" No one dared to silence that shouter. Astonishment and dread paralyzed the deputies, who, however, were too agitated to be kept long listening to the clerk's reading. They dispersed into the city, over which, while day lasted, a pall of suspense lowered. But after nightfall bands of plebeians gave themselves up to savage exultation. Now as formerly Ciceruacchio led them, but they sang a different tune. It was no longer "Long live Pius," but "Long live Brutus the Second," and "So die the betrayers of the People!" They yelled, as only an Italian crowd can yell, a wild song with the refrain, —

"Blessed is the hand
Which struck the tyrant low;"[1]

and under the windows of their victim's widow they chanted a *miserere*. Misguided Demos! not upon it, but upon the demagogues who encouraged it, — and they were of many kinds, — should fall the blame for those lurid orgies over Rossi's murder. And had not Pius himself, by coquetting with popularity in the early days and by playing fast-and-loose during all days, done his share towards unleashing the demon which lurks in every ignorant mass? He who sows the seed cannot deny the flower.

At the Quirinal the news of Rossi's death produced dismay. Only one minister, Montanari, remained at his post. The courtiers hid themselves, leaving the Pope almost alone, but for the diplomatic corps, which hastened to the palace. Outwardly, Pius seemed calm, perhaps with the numbing calm of terror. He bade messengers summon Pasolini and Minghetti. What a comment this, on the rotting Papacy! The Pope, in his hour of danger, could trust not his cardinals nor prelates, but two young laymen who had frankly opposed his antipatriotic policy, and who now risked their lives in his behalf. Minghetti warned Pius that his only hope lay in abandoning the fatal neutral position he had adopted since April 29, and in loyally promoting the National Cause. Pius demurred; Minghetti asked for time to consult his friends. In the morning (November 16) when he returned, he found the Presidents and Vice-Presidents[2] of the two Chambers at conference with the Pope. Muzzarelli, President of the Upper Chamber, began by disparaging Rossi, and intimated that his death, after all, was not of

---

[1] Pasolini, 145, note 1.
[2] Muzzarelli and Pasolini, of the Upper Chamber; Sturbinetti and Rusconi, of the Lower.

great importance. Pius interrupted him. "What!" he exclaimed, "a monsignore dressed in that color, a man whom I placed at the head of the Superior Council, dares to come here and make me an excuse for such an assassination!" Then Sturbinetti broke in with a story that he had seen cab-drivers disputing among themselves which of them should take Rossi's body out to Porta Leona where the carcasses of dead beasts were thrown. Pius, to close this horrible talk, asked Rusconi if he would accept the office of premier. Rusconi declined, alleging incapacity. "Thereupon Sturbinetti broke in again," I quote Rusconi's account of this memorable interview, "in the same tone as before, attenuating the importance of the murder and repeating that it was not worth while to become desperate over Rossi's assassination. At such approbation the Pope was so agitated that the muscles of his face quivered in a frightful manner. Then, at the spectacle of his terrible agitation, I remembered to have read that the Pope in early life had been subject to epileptic fits. And fearing that the Pope's condition produced by so violent an emotion might be followed by apoplexy, I took courage and said frankly: 'Your Holiness, I see that this conversation hurts you. If you consent, we will retire, and await your orders to return.' The Pope accepted this advice, and we four went out, leaving the Pope alone in the room."[1]

In an antechamber they found Minghetti, Sterbini, and others, and they discussed the question of the future ministry. The majority suggested that Galletti, who had twice been Minister of Police, and who was in favor with the populace, should be proposed for Pius's confirmation. Meanwhile crowds were collecting outside of the Quirinal, and presently Galletti himself, accompanied by Sterbini, had an audience with the Pope. They demanded on behalf of the people that Pius should agree to the immediate

[1] Pasolini, 145, note 1.

convocation of the Constituent Assembly and that he should come out squarely for war. To this Pius replied bluntly that he would consent to nothing under compulsion; and the popular spokesmen returned to the piazza. Then the multitude burst out into wrath. Some of the rioters set fire to one of the entrances of the palace; others climbed up to the roof and towers of the neighboring buildings and fired volleys into the palace itself; others ran in search of a cannon, and, having dragged it into position in front of the main portal, they prepared to bombard. A musket-shot killed Monsignor Palma, a prelate who happened to be in a room near that in which Pius himself had taken refuge. There was no possibility of long defending the Quirinal, as only a few Swiss were on guard there, and should the infuriated mob break in, no one could answer for its deeds. Pius, therefore, decided to treat with the rebels, but in doing so he protested to the diplomatic corps that whatever he might be coerced into accepting he should not feel bound to abide by. Galletti was sent for and charged with the formation of a Cabinet; and when this was announced to the rioters they dispersed with shouts for Pius.

Galletti named Rosmini for President and Minister of Instruction; Mamiani for Foreign Affairs; himself for the Interior; Sereni for Grace and Justice; Sterbini for Commerce; Campello for War; Lunati for Finance. The next day Rosmini, the gentle philosopher, declined, and the Pope appointed Muzzarelli in his stead; but the real leaders in the Cabinet were Galletti himself and Sterbini, a demagogue of the vilest kind, whose hideous face, disfigured by the blotches of vice, was a fit index to his depraved character. Rome was now in the hands of the populace, guided by such men as these. On November 20 the Chamber of Deputies reassembled. Galletti had promised that the first act of the ministry should be to investigate Rossi's murder and punish the guilty: but he dared not propose this when the session opened. A member named Potenziani moved that a committee be appointed to bear to His Holiness the expression of the devotion and unalterable attachment of the deputies. Up jumped Canino and opposed the motion, declaring that the "true and legitimate sovereign" of the country was the Italian people. The motion was lost. A majority of the representatives of the Papal States thus denied their allegiance to the Pope.

Pius now thought only of flight. His Swiss Guards had been removed from the Quirinal; his commands were impotent; his very life hung at the mercy of a populace to whom he had given only too much cause for vindictiveness. He consulted the foreign ambassadors. Duke d'Harcourt wished him to take shelter in France; Martinez de la Rosa, the Spanish minister, offered him a safe escort to the Balearic Isles; Count Spaur, the Bavarian envoy, who also acted in behalf of Austria, urged him to accept Austrian protection. Pius listened to all, seemed to wish to accept the hospitality of each. At five o'clock on the afternoon of November 25, having put on the plain gown of an abbé, he quietly left the Quirinal in a carriage with Countess Spaur. D'Harcourt remained for several hours in the Pope's writing-room, burning a lamp and occasionally speaking aloud, to have it believed that Pius was still there. Only the next day did the Romans learn that their sovereign had fled, and that he had taken refuge at Gaeta, under the protection of King Bomba and to the satisfaction of Austria.[1]

Thus did the Revolution complete its astounding work of driving the upholders of the Old Régime into exile: Louis Philippe and Metternich, William of Prussia and the Emperor of Austria, and now the Pope himself, must all that year scamper before the peoples they had abused. We have followed the course of events in Italy closely

[1] See La Farina, Farini, Minghetti, and Pasolini.

enough to see the strides by which Democracy neared its goal. We have seen Charles Albert and Pius the twin idols of Italy's admiration, and the twin targets of her scorn. The failure of the war, instead of putting an end to sectional jealousies, increased them; for the Radicals asserted that the National Cause had been betrayed by the Princes, and now the Radicals insisted on having their turn at the wheel. More Democracy, not less Democracy, more agitation, not less agitation, would, they affirmed, still save Italy. "The war of the Princes is done; now for the war of the People!" exclaimed Mazzini, in his fervid way, after Charles Albert's defeat. "Good news," said Cattaneo, the Lombard Republican, as the report came that Radetzky was marching back on Milan; "good news; the Piedmontese have been beaten. Now we shall be our own masters; we will fight a people's war, we will chase the Austrian out of Italy, and set up a Federal Republic."[1] Thus can party hatred stab patriotism.

The Princes had failed; the Peoples would now make their fight. Their Constituent Assembly should in some miraculous fashion educe unity and strength, arms, money, soldiers, discipline, self-control, and unselfishness from elements which had hitherto lacked them. The Princes, in their selfish ambition, had refused the Italian League; the People would show them the wonders and virtues of the Constituent. But let us not waste sarcasm. The men who honestly believed in these possible marvels were under the spell of an impulse stronger than any individual will: they were unconsciously carrying to its logical conclusion the purpose of the Revolution. That spirit which informs mankind always throws with greater force than is needed just to strike the mark.

The process of descent from moderation to excesses was very similar in the different Italian States. In Pied-

[1] Arrivabene: *Memorie* (Florence, 1880), 253–4.

mont, Genoa was in constant tumult; in Tuscany, Leghorn; in Pius's realm, Bologna; and then Democracy invaded the capitals, and seized the reins of power. Who would have predicted a year before, that by the end of 1848, Balbo and Alfieri, Capponi and Ricasoli, Mamiani and Minghetti and D'Azeglio, — the leaders of Italian Liberalism and the champions of the National Cause, — would be discredited; and that Gioberti, turned Democrat, Guerrazzi, and Sterbini would rule in their stead? Truly, the only miracle, the only romance, is reality.

CHAPTER III.

REPUBLICS AT ROME AND FLORENCE.

WHEN the Pope's flight was known in Rome it caused few demonstrations of joy. Those who desired tranquillity — and they were the more numerous though the less noisy — were stupefied; even the Radicals paused for a moment, as if astonished and fearful at this result of their audacity. Pius left a note in which he bade Marquis Sacchetti to inform Galletti of the flight, "engaging him with the other ministers not only to protect the palaces, but much more the persons belonging to them," and recommending "to the aforesaid gentlemen the quiet and order of the whole city."[1] The ministers, naturally assuming from this that the Pope still regarded them as his legal representatives, issued a proclamation declaring that Pius, misled by fatal counsels, had quitted Rome; in spite of which they would maintain order, and they asked the public, both at the capital and in the provinces, to coöperate with them. Mamiani, who had hitherto refused to serve in the Cabinet, now deemed it his duty to accept, becoming, as his ability entitled him to become, its foremost member. In the Chamber of Deputies, Prince Canino demanded that the ministers should then and there proclaim the "sacrosanct Italian Constituent," to which Mamiani replied that they would do their utmost to cement the Italian Confederation. Galletti, who wished to be everybody's friend in order that he might get everybody's vote, interposed in a speech in which he alternately praised Mamiani and Canino, and

[1] Text in Farini, iii, 1–2.

then showed his impartiality by disagreeing with the proposition of each. The line of division, however, was plainly drawn. Mamiani and the Constitutionalists endeavored to revive the old scheme of a Federal League of Princes; Canino and the Radicals clamored for the Constituent according to the gospel of Montanelli. Even at this desperate crisis the former, it will be seen, were ready to make a brave fight to save their sovereign.

But Pius in no wise responded to their devotion; but acted in all ways to insure its defeat. Once at Gaeta, although he talked reconciliation, he did whatever was certain to weaken the vigor of his supporters and to exasperate internecine strife. He pretended that his coming to Gaeta was a matter of chance, and thereby he wished to appease the Spanish and French ambassadors, each of whom had understood that the illustrious refugee was to honor his country with a visit. Pius was, indeed, completely under the influence of Cardinal Antonelli and King Bomba, who hastened to Gaeta to do him homage. On November 27 the Pope issued a brief in which, after asserting that he had left Rome because his spiritual authority had been threatened, he declared that all the acts which were due to the coercion he had suffered were illegal and void. Nevertheless, he still felt compunction in his heart for his beloved but misguided subjects, and he therefore appointed a governing committee of seven members[1] to administer the State in his absence. This brief, which so bluntly repudiated the Galletti Cabinet and its provisions for maintaining order, was received by the more violent Romans as spurious, by the others as unconstitutional, because it had not been countersigned by a responsible minister. Only four of the Committee nominated by Pius were in Rome,

[1] These were Cardinal Castracane, Monsignor Roberti, Prince di Ruviano, Prince Barberini, Marquis Bevilacqua, of Bologna, Marquis Ricci, of Macerata, and General Zucchi.

and of these Prince di Ruviano declined; the others,
although nominally accepting the charge, gave no sign of
energy; nor is it probable that, had they moved, any one
would have seconded them, for the clerical element at
Rome was despicably timid throughout the Revolution,
and Cardinal Castracane, Monsignor Roberti, and Prince
Barberini had no influence over the Liberal and Radical
elements. The ministers, after endeavoring to persuade
this committee to acknowledge them and getting no response,
resigned; but both Chambers united in begging
them to remain in office, and they consented. On a
motion of Dr. Pantaleoni, a Liberal who had been on
friendly terms at the Quirinal, it was voted to send a
deputation to Gaeta to implore His Holiness to return to
his capital. The deputation, which consisted of two
members from each of the Chambers, and of the octogenarian
Prince Thomas Corsini, Senator of Rome, set
out on December 5, but on reaching the Neapolitan frontier
they were stopped by Bomba's police, who had orders
to permit no deputation bound for the Pope to pass.
Accordingly, they had to wait at Terracina until they
could announce by letter the purpose of their mission
and receive a reply from Cardinal Antonelli, who, with
crocodile grief, deplored that they could not be allowed
to visit the Holy Father. Had Pius been sincere in his
professed solicitude for the restoration of peace among his
subjects, he would at least have received the bearers of
these overtures; but there is no evidence that his professions
were sincere. The pious jargon which he used on
all occasions belongs to the pontifical rôle, and does not
necessarily express the inmost convictions of him who uses
it. I would not imply that Pius was wilfully hypocritical;
he believed stanchly enough every dogma of his Church,
and he was as superstitious as a Calabrian peasant; he
desired virtue, peace, and all other good things to prevail,
but he made his fatal mistake in imagining that his

particular whim, his pet hobby, was virtue. This error is hereditary, so to speak, in the pontifical line, a natural outcome of pretended infallibility. Pius, being infallible to himself, could not admit that he had made any blunders. He had always been right, his subjects always wrong, and whenever they differed from him they were the victims of wicked men. Therefore, he prayed daily for their return to virtue, that is, to obedience to him, he and virtue being synonymous. Conciliation meant that they should come to him and on their knees implore forgiveness.

Whatever were Pius's utterances, therefore, his acts after his arrival at Gaeta cannot bear the interpretation that he was eager to conciliate his subjects. On the contrary, he seems to have taken satisfaction in the thought that, if the Revolution were allowed to run its course at Rome, it would quickly develop into anarchy, amid which the fractions would annihilate each other, and so clear the field for his return. No doubt the murder of Rossi and the attack on the Quirinal were calculated to scare and madden a sovereign of far greater courage and self-control than Pius ever possessed; but even in the face of such violence, a sovereign who really desired to save his "beloved people" from wilder ruin would not have repelled the offers of those still loyal, temperate subjects who wished to make a stand against the partisans of anarchy. Had Pius been merely a temporal prince he might have had scant sympathy from a Europe in which every princeling was then anxious for his own crown; but Pius, thanks to the two-headed, monstrous nature of his office, could slip into his spiritual robes and parade before the Catholic world as injured in his ecclesiastical sovereignty. The blunders he had made were political, the sedition in his realm was political, yet now he had the effrontery to pretend that the differences between him and his subjects involved his spiritual supremacy. Pius threw himself on the protection of the Catholic world, feeling secure that, after the revolutionary hurricane had blown itself out, his restoration would follow as a matter of course in the general reconstruction. Meanwhile, he could view complacently from his Gaetan refuge the factions in Rome at their work of mutual extermination. Ecclesiastical princedoms, says Machiavelli, "are acquired either through valor or fortune, and are maintained without either the one or the other: for they are upheld by antiquated rules in religion, which have been so potent, and of a quality that they would hold those princedoms intact, no matter how they act and live. They only have States, and do not defend them; they only have subjects, and do not govern them."[1]

When, therefore, the delegates returned to Rome and announced that the Pope would have no dealings with them, the Radicals were greatly encouraged; the Moderates, deprived of whatever strength came to them from the presumption that they were acting in sympathy with the sovereign, were proportionally depressed. The need of a government whose authority would be respected became urgent, and, since the committee appointed by the Pope failed to exercise any power, the deputies established a Junta which, being created by them — who were the *de facto* representatives of the popular will of the State — might command the respect of the people. Prince Corsini, Senator of Rome, Zucchini, Senator of Bologna, and Camerata, Gonfaloniere of Ancona, were appointed on the Junta; but as Zucchini withdrew, Galletti, "who never refused any office," was substituted for him. Mamiani still persevered in his effort to save the Constitutional monarchy through the convening of a Federal Assembly; but the partisans of Democracy grew bolder. Tumults spurted up in Rome and in the provinces. The Civic Guard was won over to the cause of the Constituent

[1] *Il Principe*, chap. xi.

Assembly. Intriguers, busybodies, loafers, doctrinaires, fanatics began to pour into Rome from all parts, and to swell the tide of discord. Mamiani dared to propose that the ministry should have for two months full powers to expel all foreigners who fomented disturbances; but Canino, as usual, stormed against the motion, and, as usual, Canino carried the day. On December 20 the Junta issued a proclamation announcing that it would bend its energy to attain the speedy election of the Constituent. Thereupon Mamiani resigned (December 21), — a man who had twice taken his post at the desperate breach, and had twice retired, not from lack of courage but from lack of support. The ministry was reformed, but without acquiring any new members of weight or dignity. Sterbini, the favorite of the rabble, now dominated its counsels. On December 26 the Chamber of Deputies was dissolved; the Upper Chamber had already dribbled away into oblivion. On the 29th the ministers announced by manifesto that on the following 5th of February a National Constituent Assembly, to be chosen by universal suffrage, and to have full power to determine the political destiny of the State, would meet at Rome.

Pius did not miscalculate the effect that his flight would produce on European diplomacy. As prince of three million Italians, more or less, it made slight difference whether he stayed or fled; but as Pope, his flight swelled to the bigness of an international concern, and all the Catholic Powers immediately busied themselves with it. Cavaignac, seeing a chance for France to meddle in an affair in which Austria had for years had the monopoly of meddling, and desirous also to propitiate the French Clericals, gave orders (November 27) for the immediate dispatch of 3,500 troops to Civitavecchia. If the Pope's person were in danger, General Molière, who commanded this force, was to protect him, but he was in no wise to interfere in the political quarrels at Rome. If

Pius were a captive, France would dispatch an army sufficiently large to liberate him.[1] At the first intimation of this intended intervention Mamiani drew up a protest which was indorsed by the deputies and transmitted to the French government. After denying the right of foreigners to interfere in the disputes between a people and their prince, and after asserting that the spiritual authority of the Pope had not been menaced nor impaired, Mamiani quoted that article of the French Constitution in which it was distinctly stated that the arms of France should never be employed to the detriment of the liberty of the peoples.[2] The French general, finding the Pope already safely lodged at Gaeta, made no offensive move on the Roman State; but the French government at once set about intriguing to gain ascendency over Pius, in order that it might have the credit of restoring him to his throne. Gaeta became a hotbed of diplomatic schemes. France, Spain, Naples, Austria, Piedmont, and even distant, puny Portugal, sent their talkers thither to circumvent each other. Spain proposed that the Catholic Powers should hold a conference and determine how Pius might be reëstablished at Rome and his supremacy guaranteed. This was a question, the Spanish spokesman declared, which the whole Catholic world had the right to settle, regardless of the preferences of the Romans. Gioberti replied to this on behalf of Piedmont, that it was a temporal and not a spiritual matter, and that the public opinion of Rome and Italy ought to be respected. Naples urged that England, Prussia, and Russia should be admitted to the conference, since they were parties to the Treaty of Vienna, which was the basis of Europe's political status. Russia advised that 10,000 Austrian troops and 10,000 Neapolitans should march on Rome and put an end to the insurrection. Charles Albert at first attempted to persuade Pius to take up his residence in Pied-

[1] Bianchi, vi, 18.   [2] La Farina, iv, 42-8.

mont; but Pius was sore against the King, not only because Piedmont had repelled the previous negotiations for the Italian League, but also because he had misgivings that the King coveted Papal territory. To the Piedmontese envoys he announced that, having already confided the adjustment of his affairs to the Catholic Powers, he would await their decision. And he persisted in his refusal to have any official dealings with those Constitutionalists who still labored at Rome to save his cause. Even Pasolini, for whom he personally felt honest friendship, and to whom he was indebted for unswerving loyalty, he refused to receive. Privately, some of the Constitutionalists did see him, and urged that if he would but promise to support the National War, and to carry out sincerely the Constitution at home, it would be easy to effect a reconciliation between him and his angry subjects; but to this he would not consent. Even Ricci and Bevilacqua, two members of the Governing Committee which he had appointed, made similar recommendations, and after being kept long in suspense, were similarly dismissed.[1] When the Romans set up their temporary Junta, Cardinal Antonelli hurled a condemnatory manifesto at them and it; and when, finally, the Constituent was proclaimed, Pius launched a "monitory" in which he declared the Constituent to be a Satanic device, and warned Catholics under pain of excommunication to abstain from taking part in the elections.[2]

In this way did Pius paralyze the endeavors of that remnant of his subjects who, still faithful to him, strove to avert an irreparable disaster; in this way, as if it were his unavowed wish that the lawless faction should have free scope to commit crimes which would alienate the sympathy of Europe from Italian Constitutionalism, and justify not only foreign intervention but also the

[1] Farini publishes their memorial, iii, 66–75.
[2] *Monitorio* of Jan. 1, 1849; text in Farini, iii, 118–22.

severest measures of repression when he returned to Rome. That he consciously willed this, I cannot affirm, but that all his acts tended to this result, no one can deny. With Antonelli whispering into one ear and Bomba whispering into the other, what means of access had the Holy Ghost to Pius's conscience? The Holy Ghost, we are forced to admit, left no sign of his inspiration throughout all these pitiable trials of craft between petticoated priests and smug-faced diplomats. By his allocution of April 29 Pius had given warning that he was Pope first and then Italian; by his attitude at Gaeta he reannounced this fact; with the addition that, compared with his Papal authority, he cared so little for Italy that he had no scruple to call in foreigners to punish his aggrieved subjects. This was the logical outcome of that amphibious nature of the Papacy. The conflict between the interests of the pope-priest and the pope-prince was bound to be fought to a conclusion, and what that conclusion must be some far-sighted Italians already dimly apprehended.

The slaying of Rossi, the Pope's flight, and the visible swamping of monarchical authority in the Roman States, gave impetus to the Democratic movement in Piedmont and in Tuscany. In Piedmont the political clubs surpassed the Parliament in influence, and the clubs were dominated by Radicals, whom no measure proposed by Perrone's Cabinet could satisfy. In the Chamber of Deputies, Gioberti led the Opposition, and against his florid eloquence and his popularity, ministerial logic and ministerial caution struggled in vain. Next to him in weight was Brofferio, who, like Prince Canino at Rome, had inexhaustible lungs and an irresistible propensity to use them; but Brofferio, be it said, was a politician to be taken much more seriously than any one could take the Bonapartist demagogue. The Cabinet existed under sufferance, knowing well that its term was brief, and perhaps anxious for the casual stroke which should end its feeble throes. On December 3 it brought in a bill to forbid university students from joining political clubs; that suggestion was sufficient to bring down on it the invectives of the defenders of free speech and juvenile patriotism; the Chamber voted against the ministers, and they resigned.[1] After the King had vainly tried to compose a new cabinet under Massimo d'Azeglio, with members from the Moderate party, he made a virtue of necessity and summoned Gioberti. At last the big-browed, magic-voiced abbé, he who had been the prophet of Italy's resurrection, and had outsped even Pius himself in popularity, was prime minister of the king who had once sent him into exile and prohibited the circulation of his books. He made up his Cabinet chiefly from members of the Left side of the Chamber,[2] but although the ministry was called Democratic, the real Democrats soon began to arraign its genuineness. But whether it were genuinely Democratic or a counterfeit, that ministry was looked on as the last partition which separated Piedmont from anarchy.

Seldom has a prime minister been confronted with a more hopeless task than that which now confronted Gioberti. The vital question, in which all others were bound up, was how to reopen the war and secure victory. The armistice still held, renewed from time to time, until the coming of winter forced both contestants to postpone operations for a few months; but in Piedmont the conviction spread day by day that another trial of arms was inevitable. Mediation, to be sure, still dragged on its snail-like course, professing to hope that an adjustment might be reached, although Austria had by unmistakable

---

[1] *Correspondence*, iii, 655.
[2] Gioberti, President and Foreign Affairs; Ricci, Finance; Tecchio, Public Works; Rattazzi, Grace and Justice; Cadorna, Education; Sonnaz, War; Buffa, Agriculture.

hints made it probable that she would yield no foot of her recovered territory. How could Italy be brought into condition to resume the battle? Last spring the entire Peninsula thrilled with patriotism; the peoples were really stirred, the princes all pretended to be stirred; and yet no sufficient harmony could be attained. What hope of harmony now, when internal politics had everywhere sunk into the virulent stage, when the recollection of recent defeat was a check to enthusiasm, when Charles Albert was hated and Pius IX despised, when all the instruments of war had been tried and found wanting? The prospect of success, so far as success depended upon the resources and public opinion of Italy, was at least tenfold smaller than it had been in March, 1848. What were the favorable elements in Europe now that had been lacking then? There were none. To a calm observer it was already evident that the tide had turned in favor of reaction. Louis Napoleon had just been elected President of the French Republic (December 20), and while no man could yet fathom the cold-blooded villainies which he was preparing, every one realized that the attitude of France towards the Italian cause would more than ever be regulated by personal ambition. In Austria, the feeble-minded Emperor Ferdinand had abdicated (December 2) in favor of his young nephew Francis Joseph; the insurrection at Vienna had been put down; Latour's murder had been avenged; and Jellacich, with his army of Slavs, was moving on rebellious Hungary. The chief hope for Italy lay in that struggle of the Magyars for independence; if they succeeded in holding their own, much more if they beat back Jellacich, the Austrian army in Lombardy and Venetia might be summoned to send reinforcements to save the Empire, in which case the Italians could fight at an advantage. But this was as yet only a possibility. Radetzky actually held the Italian provinces with an iron hand, and the Austrian Empire seemed in far less peril than it had twice been in during that year. Indeed, the period of panic among the established governments of Europe had passed, and reaction was steadily regaining ground.

To deal with these manifold difficulties, Gioberti brought unlimited self-confidence, an unusual capacity for work, persuasive eloquence, and immense popularity. The war, he saw, must be either Piedmontese or Italian, and he did not hesitate in deciding that it should be Italian. He aimed to secure the coöperation of Tuscany and Rome in order that the original National character of the contest might be revived. But there were now two clearly defined parties in Italy, — the Democratic and the Monarchical. With which should he ally himself, which should he use, to drive out the Austrians? The Democrats proclaimed that the Princes had failed, and that Italy's salvation must henceforth be wrought by the efforts of the Peoples. Venice was already a Republic; Rome was a Republic in all but name; Tuscany was hurrying towards Republicanism; Gioberti himself had been lifted into power by the Democrats of Piedmont. How could he restore the prestige of Constitutional Monarchy, and incite his countrymen once more to rally to a royal standard? The task was stupendous, but he did not shrink from it.

His ministerial programme, announced on his taking office (December 16), surprised the Moderates and disappointed the Radicals, by its temperance. "Italian Nationality," he said, "turns on two hinges, which are, the independence and the union of the Peninsula." The former, he continued, could be achieved only by arms, and therefore the ministry would apply all their energy to make ready the armament, and all their prudence to choose the right moment for renewing the struggle. The mediation of France and England should in no way prejudice the Italian cause, for if it failed to provide absolute autonomy to Italy, the Cabinet would never accept its terms. Union could be cemented only by the Confederation of the various States; therefore, he added, "We embrace willingly the ensign of the Italian Constituent. We shall take care earnestly to arrange with Rome and Tuscany the means most appropriate and prompt for convoking such an Assembly, which, besides giving Italy civic unity without prejudicing the autonomy of our various States and of their rights, will make it easy to profit by the forces of all in behalf of the common redemption. . . . The development of our institutions is based chiefly on the accord of Constitutional Monarchy with the Democratic spirit. . . . Constitutional Monarchy alone can give to our country unity, force, and power against internal disorders and foreign attacks. But Monarchy, separated from the popular will, does not respond to the needs and desires which to-day spur and enkindle the nation. Therefore we gladly welcome the wish expressed by many for a Democratic Ministry, and we shall exert ourselves to bring it about. We shall be Democrats, occupying ourselves especially with the laboring and unfortunate classes, and taking measures for protecting, instructing, improving, and ennobling the poor masses, raising them to the estate and dignity of a people. We shall be Democrats, preserving strictly inviolate the equality of all citizens before the common law. . . . Democracy considered in these terms cannot alarm any one, and ought not to make any one jealous. . . . Its most specific character lies in this, that it is supremely conciliatory."[1]

The doctrine of conciliation is with rulers and ministers often very popular; but it usually is interpreted by them to mean that the opposition shall defer or surrender to their views, while they concede nothing. Real conciliation, however, is not to be arrived at when two great antagonistic principles clash; then, either one or the

[1] Full text in *Correspondence*, iii, 673-5.

other must prevail, and that which loses is ultimately
blotted out. The victorious principle may, indeed, win
gradually by a series of apparent compromises, or it may
win by a single decisive stroke; but in either case there
is no conciliation. And in the contest into which Gioberti
now plunged, conciliation was unattainable; the
hostile principles might be held in abeyance for a time,
they could never be blended; for the Democracy which
he proclaimed was not the Democracy which the Democrats
had at heart; the Constituent Assembly he proposed
differed in essence from theirs. Nevertheless, he set
strenuously to work to rehabilitate Constitutional Monarchy
in the eyes of the populace and to persuade the
Democrats that he was furthering, if only by words, their
own programme.

He did not err in reckoning the Pope's flight and
evident tendency towards reaction as the most serious
impediment to a revival of Italian concord. Pius must
be dissuaded at all hazards from making his grievance
an international affair. Gioberti, therefore, dispatched
Martini on a special mission to Gaeta, to offer Pius the
sympathy and protection of Piedmont, and to beg him
to allow Piedmont, rather than a foreign government, to
act as mediator between him and his unruly Romans.
But Pius at first refused to receive Martini at all, except
as a private visitor; and in an interview with him, he
berated Piedmont equally with the other Italian States.
Growing heated, as he told over the story of his wrongs,
he angrily declared that he "had no trust in any Italian
government; that he held the demagogues in abomination,
the Moderates in suspicion; that he hoped for foreign
aid; that the Church was not Italian, but Catholic,
that is, universal; that the Pontiff, beyond being the
prince of his own subjects, was head and father of all
the faithful; that he should hold the Austrians dearer
than the Italians, in case the former were the upholders

and the latter the enemies of his authority."[1] Finding Pius in this intractable mood, Gioberti dropped the submissive tone for one of firmness, yet still deferential, and intimated to His Holiness that, if Austria were summoned to interfere in the States of the Church, Charles Albert would formally protest, and that only his reverence for the Pope would prevent him from regarding such interference as a cause of war. To the Pope's foreign counselors, who were competing for the privilege of escorting him to Rome with their regiments, Gioberti stubbornly opposed logic and justice; repeating to them that the difficulties between Pius and his subjects were of a political nature, having nothing to do with his spiritual rights, and that, therefore, no outsider had a fair excuse for meddling. When, he said, they asserted that the Pope was neither a Roman nor an Italian prince, they committed the absurd blunder of implying that the Roman States did not belong geographically to Italy. "If this were so," he added, "Italian Nationality would be lost, Italy would become in certain fashion subject to the whole world, and the Pontiff — the honor of our Peninsula — a burden and, so to speak, a pledge of servitude." Words unanswerable, because true, as the history of Italy from the days of Charlemain could prove; words which described not only the contemporary, but the past conditions for a thousand years, during which the Papacy, with its dual nature, its legerdemain of temporal and spiritual, had been the one insuperable obstacle to the formation of a united Italy, and the perpetual cause of foreign intervention and tyranny. The Spanish minister, to whom Gioberti sent this message, simply denied that there was such a thing as Italian Nationality, or that Piedmont or Naples had more interest than Spain or any other Catholic Power in the Pope's temporal concerns; as for consulting the preference of the Romans

[1] La Farina, iv, 109.

themselves, those Powers no more dreamt of doing that than of consulting oxen how they preferred to be yoked.

Against these rebuffs Gioberti persevered; but Pius was now hopelessly under the influence of the Reactionists, who, flocking to Gaeta from all parts of Europe, cut the last thread of sympathy between him and the Italian cause. Just as he had refused to countenance the efforts of the Roman Moderates on his behalf, so he thrust away the proffered mediation of Piedmont, and resolved to appeal to foreigners for assistance. That vision of an independent Italy, united under the presidency of the Pope, — that Guelf revival which Gioberti had preached, — would never come to pass to the end of time. Pius himself pricked that gleaming bubble by demonstrating beyond cavil that the Papacy was a mediæval institution, incapable of being reformed, incapable of adapting itself to the conditions of the nineteenth century. The love of worldly power was as strong in him as in any petty ruler of his age; and when he found that Constitutionalism at Rome meant the curtailing of his autocratic privileges, he eagerly turned to foreigners who would, by their bayonets, allow him to revive and maintain that mediævalism which was indispensable to Papal rule.

Gioberti, however, though he rightly regarded the winning back of Pius to be of supreme importance, did not limit his activity to Gaeta. He conducted negotiations with the Provisional Government at Rome, in the hope of disposing the Romans to seek of their own accord a reconciliation with the Pope, and so to avert a foreign invasion. He opposed the convocation of the Constituent and the proclamation of the Republic, towards which the Romans were sweeping, for he knew that Monarchical Europe would never permit a republic to stand. In these endeavors he came into conflict with Montanelli, who sent emissaries from Florence to urge the Roman Democrats to complete as quickly as possible their arrangements for the meeting of the Constituent. For the success of Gioberti's policy, he needed to secure the coöperation of Tuscany, but Tuscany was under the Montanellian spell, the Grand Duke himself professing acquiescence to his prime minister's scheme. Leopold, as I have stated, looked suspiciously on Charles Albert's acquisition of Lombardy and Venetia, and no doubt Montanelli hinted to him that the Democratic Constituent would not consent to the formation of a large subalpine kingdom. Moreover, since the Constituent was to choose a general to command the National army when war was resumed against Austria, its choice would not fall on Charles Albert, but probably on the great popular captain, Garibaldi.[1] In a dispatch, remarkable alike for depth, directness, and friendly temper, Gioberti strove to allay Montanelli's jealousy of the aggrandizement of Piedmont, and to convince him of the inevitable ruin into which the Democratic Constituent would drive the patriotic cause. He warned him that it was the part of statesmanship to strive for what was feasible, not for the impossible, and that Rome and Tuscany, even should they achieve their Democratic union, would be powerless without Piedmont; for Piedmont alone, among the Italian States still consecrated to the struggle for independence, had an army, and that army could never be persuaded to fight in behalf of the Democratic policy. The benefit which the whole Peninsula would derive from a strong Kingdom of Upper Italy, to serve as a shield against foreign incursions, was too clear to need demonstration; only the secret enemies of Italy, or those Italians who were the victims of political delusions, had made an outcry against it. "Let the Tuscan minister bethink him of the terrible responsibility which weighs on his head! On him depends perhaps the salvation or the ruin of Italy!"[2] To Gioberti's appeal Montanelli was deaf;

---

[1] Bianchi, vi, 89. [2] *Ibid*, 91-4.

deaf also to the proposition to postpone the question of the Constituent until the war should be concluded. With the tenacity of a zealot he believed that his scheme alone could save the country.

That Montanelli, the mercurial professor, patriot, and political Lothario, who loved his latest hobby best, should insist on the Constituent or nothing, need not surprise us. But what of Leopold, who had a crown to lose? At the outset, as we saw, he accepted Montanelli's plan in desperation, flattering himself that his past record as a mild prince had endeared him to the Tuscans to a degree that would withhold them from dethroning him. Then the Pope's flight seems to have given him a hint which for the time being he carefully kept in his own bosom. He appeared not unwilling that the Constituent should be convened; Montanelli had told him that if it were convened at Florence under his auspices, it would increase his popularity; now that it was to meet at Rome, Leopold might not only hope to be its honorary president,[1] but also to manipulate it to confer on him the permanent sovereignty of Central Italy. Comparative order reigned in Tuscany until the elections, when the ministers, by going in person to the districts where tumults broke out, quickly restored quiet. On January 10 the Chambers met, and in an address to them Leopold praised the Constituent, as a "principle of force and harmony," that was to determine the "final formula" of government for Italy.[2] The deputies in Parliament, and the Democrats outside, at once set up a cry for the proclamation of this political cure-all. Leopold now showed some diffidence; he had qualms of conscience about sanctioning a scheme which the Pope had condemned. Then Guerrazzi reasoned with him, reiterating the well-worn arguments, touching dexterously the chord of self-interest. Leopold still wavered; the British minister, he

---

[1] Guerrazzi, 128.   [2] *Correspondence*, iv, 40.

said, was opposed to the project. Guerrazzi sought out Sir Charles Hamilton, brother of the minister, in an adjoining room, and won him over. The Grand Duke, apparently convinced, gave his autograph consent to the proposition (January 21), which the ministers introduced without delay in Parliament. There no voice was raised against it, so ominous was the aspect of the multitude which swarmed in the galleries and in the piazza before the Palazzo Vecchio.[1] Nothing now remained but for Leopold to sign the bill which both Chambers had passed; but he procrastinated, and under the pretense of needing rest, he finally departed to Siena (January 30), whither his family had already preceded him.

At Siena the party of reaction made a demonstration in his honor, shouting, "Down with the Constituent!" "Down with the Clubs!"[2] The ministers at Florence, alarmed at the flood of indignation rising upon them, for the populace suspected them of treachery, sent a note to request Leopold to return, and by his presence to silence the suspicions caused by his delay in approving the bill. Leopold replied that as he was ill he could not come immediately, but that he would be glad to see any member of the Cabinet. Montanelli accordingly posted to Siena: it was high time that, like the man who danced with the bear, he should "keep his eye on his partner." Being ushered into the Grand Duke's chamber, he found that serene personage in bed, his head bound up, his general manner that of a sick man. The fervid premier began his exhortation, duly informing his master that, unless the bill for the Constituent were forthwith signed, a revolution could not be prevented. The patient listened to language that few descendants of Maria Theresa had had thrust upon them by any servant: no doubt he squirmed under the grand-ducal bedclothes, but he offered no reprimand; only announced languidly that he was then

[1] Guerrazzi, 135-6.   [2] *Correspondence*, iv, 117.

too ill to conduct business of state. The following morning he reassured Montanelli as to his health, saying that he felt a little better, and that, after trying to eat something, he would take a drive to get what benefit he could from the fresh air. Shaking Montanelli cordially by the hand, Leopold, with wife and attendants, entered his coach, and drove out for his airing. So he passed without suspicion through Siena's clattering streets, and when his coach was last seen, it was rolling full-speed along the highroad to the Maremma (February 7.)[1]

A few hours later two notes were handed to Montanelli from Leopold. In the first he stated that he had no intention of quitting Tuscany, and that if his servants took the Maremma road they would receive instructions where to rejoin him with his baggage; he assumed, of course, that no opposition would be made to their departure. In the second letter he gave the reasons for his flight. Not fear, but conscience, he said, had led him to this decision. When the Tuscan Parliament had voted unlimited powers to the members of the prospective Constituent, he had been troubled with religious doubts, to resolve which he had written secretly to Pius; and Pius had replied that the ban of excommunication which he had launched against the partisans of the Constituent in the Papal States applied to those partisans elsewhere. Therefore, Leopold could not expose his own soul and the souls of his misguided subjects to the danger of hell, to which the Holy Father condemned them if they disobeyed his monitory.[2] Thus did the Pope, by the exercise of his spiritual authority in a matter purely temporal, control the political action of an independent prince in a neighboring State.

But Leopold had not only the "moral" support of the Pope to comfort him; he had also the promise from Austria of military support, which, even to a person of his manifest piety, must have helped him to bear his tempo-

[1] Trollope, 159–62.   [2] Text in La Farina, iv, 86–7.

rary trials with composure. The following note from Radetzky to the Grand Duke bears the date February 2, 1849. "Royal Highness: According to precise orders received from the Imperial government and from the Emperor our sovereign, it is gratifying to me to signify to your Imperial Highness, that, if you will in everything and throughout everything conform to what has been already announced to your Highness by the Aulic government, in a dispatch dated the 26th of February last, your Highness need only abandon your States on *terra firma*, and place yourself in safety at Santo Stefano; and I, as soon as I have subdued the demagogues of Piedmont, will fly to your aid with 30,000 of my brave troops, and will replace you on the throne of your ancestors. If the courier who will give this present letter into your own hands brings back no answer, I shall consider the affairs as arranged."[1] Radetzky's geography was a little misty, in that he mistook Santo Stefano for an island; but that did not obscure the significant parts of his letter. What the terms were which Leopold had concerted with Austria, we can easily surmise; the vital fact is that the Tuscans, after a brief period during which they could only speculate as to their sovereign's whereabouts, learned that he had alighted at Santo Stefano, a little port on the Tuscan coast, whence he might, if fluttered farther, take ship for Elba, or other refuge more remote. How long he had been playing his double game with Montanelli and Guerrazzi we have no sure means of knowing, — traitors and swindlers do not set down in a diary the moment when they conceive iniquity, nor the measures by which they hope to compass it, — but that Leopold's deceit was recent, is as highly improbable as the deceit itself was natural. He, like his brother monarchs, had been caught up in a great, grim danger; the instinct of self-preservation led them to dissemble, to promise all things, to con-

[1] Trollope, 155-6.

ciliate by smiles and favors the monster which threatened them; to keep faith with that monster lay no more within their interpretation of honor, than if they were at the mercy of maniacs or cannibals. Doubtless, it is owing to this view of the case that we have no apology from Leopold or any of his henchmen; his mission in the world was to play the fox, and, having escaped from the hounds with pelt and brush entire, he may be said to have fulfilled his mission.

On that same 7th of February, whilst the grand-ducal coach was rumbling down into the fens, Montanelli hastened back to Florence, bearing with him Leopold's two letters. No man was more astonished than Guerrazzi, astonished and enraged, for he realized that he had been duped by the fugitive prince; he, the bold, quick-witted, iron-willed man, who had flattered himself that he held the dukeling safe in his hand! Florence broke into an uproar at the news. On the following morning the multitude surged into the Piazza; demagogues harangued under Orcagna's Loggia, — what had that portico not seen and heard, as it stood there in mute beauty for five hundred years? The deputies in session in the Palazzo Pubblico were listening to Montanelli's explanation, when an angry mob burst into the Chamber. In vain the President tried to keep order; the spokesmen of the populace would not be still. Many deputies, dreading violence, stole away to the anteroom, and bloodshed seemed imminent. Then Guerrazzi sprang into the tribune, and in tones which the rabble had not yet forgotten to fear, called for quiet, in order that business might proceed. The startled deputies returned, and after Guerrazzi had presented the resignation of the ministers, a deputy named Trinci moved that a Provisional Government consisting of three members should be elected. The motion was carried unanimously, Guerrazzi, Montanelli, and Mazzoni being the triumvirs chosen. Then ringing of bells, firing of salutes, and the removal of the grand-ducal arms from the public buildings, amused the Florentines for the rest of the day.[1] Sudden tempest and spasmodic sunshine, — such was the stuff of which their revolution was made. After a lapse of three centuries and a quarter, Florence could again call herself a republic.

Meanwhile the Roman State had been hurrying towards the same goal. The Provisional Government busied itself in recasting the laws and in fending off anarchy: the former seemed idle diligence, since the approaching Constituent was to make everything over; the latter was a work of immediate necessity, in which, however, the government incurred the hatred of the turbulent classes, which protested that martial law administered by Sterbini, their late idol, was no whit more satisfactory than it had been under Gregory. The elections now occupied the attention of the country. In the cities and towns, Pius's ban had little effect; indeed, many of the bishops refrained from officially publishing it. All except the most ignorant citizens refused to believe that the Pope had power to consign them to eternal damnation for voting for a candidate to the assembly. The clubs took care to nominate men of their own stripe, and sent a swarm of stump speakers to buzz their political doctrines in the ears of the multitude. As became that epoch of upheaval, there were many strange and inconsistent combinations, some ludicrous, others verging on the tragic. Aristocrats vied with democrats in extolling Republicanism, priests threw off their allegiance to their high priest Pius, and ardently upheld the National Cause. Nor were the emissaries of Pius and the Reactionists idle, although they worked in the open only so far as it was safe. General Zucchi attempted to win back the Papal troops to the Pope's side, but failed; Monsignor Bedini, a special agent from Gaeta, appeared at Bologna, to organize

---

[1] *Correspondence*, iv, 118–19.

a revolt among the Swiss mercenaries, but his plot was discovered and frustrated. Among the superstitious peasantry vulgar impositions, adapted to the credulity of those priest-ridden unfortunates, were resorted to. Notes written by angels, forbidding the peasants to vote, dropped mysteriouly into their huts; statues of the Madonna winked their eyes, or wept, or gave other signs of grief and displeasure; visions were reported, prophecies circulated; to all of which miracles, which the priests manufactured, the priests could of course give an orthodox interpretation. In some cases curates, in order that the age of those eligible to vote might not be verified, refused to open the baptismal registers.[1] At Rome the balloting lasted three days, and by night the ballot-boxes were carried in procession through the streets, to the accompaniment of torches and brass-bands.[2] And thus one hundred and forty-two representatives were at length elected, without grave disturbance, but with infinite hubbub.

On February 5 they assembled at the Capitol and marched to the Palace of the Cancelleria, where Armellini delivered an address of welcome. After narrating the steps by which Pius IX had fallen from grace, he reminded them that they were seated among the tombs of two great epochs. "On one side," he said, "are the ruins of the Italy of the Cæsars, on the other side, the Italy of the Popes; it is for you to erect a durable edifice on this rubbish." When he had concluded, Prince Canino jumped up and shouted, "Long live the Republic!" and as soon as his stentorian voice was silent, Garibaldi took the floor. "What good is it," he asked, "to waste time over empty forms? To delay a moment is a crime. Long live the Republic!" But Sterbini, once the loudest demagogue of them all, now felt that there was need of prudence, perhaps to allow himself time to shift to the

[1] La Farina, iv, 122-4.   [2] Farini, iii, 162.

winning side; and he consequently insisted that the first business before the Assembly was to examine the credentials of its members, and to organize according to parliamentary rules. Not until February 7, therefore, did the future Constitution of the State come up for discussion. Then among many speeches only two policies were discernible: either to delay final action until the Italian Constituent should meet, or to take at once a decisive step. Mamiani, with great vigor and courage, upheld the former plan. He bade his countrymen not to be led away by false parallels; the uprising of the French people in 1789, for instance, had been successful only because France had a vast army with which to defend her republic; but Rome was weak; in Italy she could count on only the doubtful support of Tuscany; what could those two small States accomplish against the hostility of the great Powers? In Rome, he said, there was possible only the government of the Popes, or the government of Cola di Rienzi. Noble and beautiful was the ideal of a republic, but the Romans were not yet educated for it; unjust and brutal the temporal sway of the Popes had often been, yet it might be possible to make it genuinely Constitutional, whereas to abolish it prematurely would be suicidal. At all events, the question of the Pope's temporal sovereignty had become an international question, and the Assembly must remember that, whatever course it chose to pursue in regard to it, the Catholic world would have to be reckoned with. Let them not set vain hopes on the support of Revolutionary Europe, for the Revolution was everywhere failing. To this wise counsel Masi, Prince Canino's secretary, replied with extravagant assertions and turgid rhetoric, which drew forth loud applause. He was followed by Filopanti, a professor of mathematics, who harangued after the fashion of Danton, — all that they needed, he said, was "audacity! audacity! audacity!" — and moved that the

temporal power of the Papacy be abolished, but that
guarantees be given for the free exercise of the Pope's
spiritual functions. For him, too, there was great applause.
Audinot supported Mamiani, hoping that by the
creation of a provisional government the fatal decision
might be postponed. But the sentiment of nine tenths
of the deputies was against delay. They had been elected
to establish a republic; naturally, therefore, nothing else
would satisfy them. If some of them had doubts, if they
hesitated to take the plunge, they were whipped up to
the point of recklessness by their more daring comrades.

At length Canino mounted the tribune, and after declaring
that there could be no reconciliation between the
Papacy and Italian liberty, he exclaimed, "But do you
not feel this sacred ground tremble beneath your feet?
It is the souls of your ancestors, who chafe with impatience
and cry in your ears, 'Long live the Roman Republic!'"
These words were greeted with cheers, followed
by demands that Filopanti's motion be put to a
vote. Mamiani strove to have his own motion take
precedence, but further discussion on that side was
stopped by Monghini, a young deputy from Ravenna,
who shouted: "Either Pope, Provisional Government, or
Republic! Of the Pope, I should be ashamed to speak;
the Provisional Government would be a prolonged agony;
therefore there remains only the Republic." Which
terse statement, after kindling the deputies and the
crowds in the galleries, flew forth to inflame the crowds
outside. Sterbini, having now clear indication of the
safe direction in which to jump, rose and proposed that,
as soon as the form of government should be decided, the
republic should solemnly be proclaimed on the morrow
from the great portico of the Capitol. After further
contest over parliamentary quibbles, in which Mamiani's
motion was set aside, and Audinot's amendment was lost,
the Chamber voted on Filopanti's motion; 120 deputies

favored it, 10 opposed, and 12 abstained from voting. Then Galletti, President of the Assembly, promulgated in its name the following decree, which, he said, "marks a solemn era, establishes a right of the people, and establishes a principle until this moment so greatly desired in Italy, but never before incarnate. 1. The Papacy has forfeited in fact and of right the temporal government of the Roman State. 2. The Roman Pontiff shall have all the guarantees necessary to secure his independence in the exercise of his spiritual powers. 3. The form of government of the Roman State shall be a pure Democracy, and it shall take the glorious name of the Roman Republic. 4. The Roman Republic shall have with the rest of Italy such relations as the common Nationality requires."[1]

It was two hours past midnight on February 8, 1849, when the members of the Constituent, having taken this fateful step, adjourned from their labors. On the forenoon of that same day they reassembled at the Capitol, where Galletti, amid the enthusiasm of the populace, the ringing of bells, and the salute of cannon, proclaimed the new republic. The yellow and white flag of the Papacy was hauled down and the tricolor banner of Italy hoisted.[2] The Revolution was at last in the saddle. Shake our heads as we may at the crudeness and extravagance of the majority of the deputies, smile as we must at their mimicry of the French Revolutionists of 1789, yet we cannot fail to be thrilled by the sublime recklessness with which they voted out of existence an institution formidable since the days of Hildebrand. They were right, everlastingly right, in announcing that the Papacy had been, was, and always would be the enemy of Italian liberty; that was the one grain of fact which they winnowed

---

[1] *Correspondence*, iv, 128-9.
[2] For the proceedings of the Assembly, see Farini, iii. chap. 11; La Farina, iv, 125-32; *Correspondence*, iv, 118, 124, 128.

from the whirl of political chaff; and that fact they proclaimed in scorn of consequence. The Capitol at Rome has witnessed many strange spectacles: men of all nations have met there, the fate of many nations has been decided there; the yells of the hordes of Brennus and Alaric, the acclamations of Cæsar and Constantine, have floated from it across the Forum; but seldom has it been the scene of a stranger spectacle than on that February morning in 1849 when seven score deputies, for the most part long-haired and bearded, with the stocks and broad-collared, wide-flowing coats and bulging trousers of the time, made a festival over the downfall of the Papacy.

On February 7, the day when his rebellious subjects were planning his deposition, Pius held a consistory of the cardinals at Gaeta, in which it was determined to appeal immediately to Austria, France, Spain, and Naples for troops to restore the Pope to his dominion. The efforts of Gioberti had failed, — Piedmont was not even asked to take part in the holy work; Pius, instigated by Antonelli and Bomba, insisted upon summoning foreigners to settle his family quarrel. The proclamation of the Republic at Florence and Rome likewise destroyed Gioberti's hope of securing harmony among the Italian States through the preservation of the Constitutional Monarchy. Henceforth, monarchical Piedmont could expect little genuine sympathy or effectual assistance from the Democrats on the Arno and the Tiber.

CHAPTER IV.

NOVARA.

THE news from Rome, Florence, and Gaeta reached Gioberti almost simultaneously. Better than any one else could he realize the damage done to the Italian cause on that fatal 7th of February; nevertheless, not yet disheartened, he planned a last heroic effort for rescuing Central Italy from anarchy. He would send a division of Piedmontese troops into Tuscany to put down the rebellion and restore the Grand Duke, thence to advance into the Papal States and restore Pius to Rome! To the Republicans who now controlled affairs on the Arno and the Tiber there were opposed a majority of Tuscans and Romans who had no military force with which to assert themselves. Gioberti believed that these friends of Constitutionalism would welcome Piedmontese intervention, and that the turbulent class would slink away without lifting a hand against his resolute, disciplined regiments. It was, indeed, a bold stroke, the highest flight of statesmanship to be recorded throughout this crisis. It would teach European diplomacy that Piedmont was willing and able to uphold order throughout the Peninsula; it would render unnecessary interference by Austria or France; it would insure the coöperation of the Central Italians in the National War which, as all signs indicated, would soon be resumed.

In great secrecy Gioberti made his preparations. He chose Alfonso La Marmora to lead the Piedmontese contingent, — an excellent choice, both because La Marmora, though young, was an officer of courage and discretion, and because he had friendly relations with the foremost Tuscan Liberals. Charles Albert saw the political value of the scheme, and therefore consented to it, though he shrank from any course which might appear to justify the charge that he had designs upon the territory of either the Grand Duke or of Pius. To the King's envoy at Gaeta, Gioberti wrote protesting against the Pope's appeal to foreign Powers. He assumed that that decision sprang from the Reactionists and not from the Pope himself, and he pointed out that among the Italians only the Republicans were hilarious at it. "I rejoice," he said sarcastically, "at this singular accord between Joseph Mazzini and the most eminent Antonelli, and I console myself by thinking that the rest of Italy holds a quite different opinion. . . . My principal scope is to restrain demagoguery and to save our institutions, and to this aim I must direct all my acts. The Piedmontese Parliament will never permit Austria to intervene in the affairs of Rome. We have a hundred thousand men that can fight the Austrians in the Roman States just as well as on the banks of the Mincio and the Adige."[1] These words, of course, wrought no change in the Pope's present attitude, but Gioberti expected that, as soon as his plan should be successful, — as soon as he could announce to Pius, "You may return without fear to your capital, and Piedmont will guarantee you against further internal disturbances," — even Antonelli and the Reactionists would be forced to recognize the loyal disinterestedness not less than the strength of the King.

To the Grand Duke at Santo Stefano, Gioberti offered the immediate intervention of the Piedmontese troops, promising that they should act solely in his behalf, and that at his request they should be withdrawn. To this, Leopold replied by autograph letter, thanking Charles Albert and begging him to send succor without delay. "I

[1] Farini, iii, 192-3.

have sacrificed all to my duty," he concluded, "and having refrained through conscientious scruples from signing the law authorizing the Constituent, I perceive that the good God visibly protects me. Your aid is evidence to me thereof; be courageous in this last battle for the honor of God, and accept my eternal gratitude."[1] Yet almost before the ink of this letter had time to dry, Leopold wrote another to the Emperor of Austria congratulating him on his recent accession to the throne, and explaining that his own recent policy, so contrary to the Austrian traditions of his House, had been due not to preference but to coercion.[2] Leopold, indeed, had almost reached the moment when he might, without risk, throw off his mask of duplicity. On arriving at Santo Stefano he had declared that, as he had neither quitted his dominions nor intended to quit them, the Triumvirate established at Florence had not even a semblance of legality to excuse it; and yet he refused to nominate a new government to administer public affairs during his absence, and he refused to empower General de Laugier, who commanded the remnant of the regular Tuscan troops, to put down the rebellion. Bomba invited him to accept shelter at Naples. St. Marc, a French adventurer, brought him word from Gaeta that if he permitted the Piedmontese to interfere in Tuscany Austria would attack Piedmont. So he feigned solicitude for the possible injury which might befall the Italian cause if he accepted Charles Albert's succor, and, while still pretending friendliness towards Piedmont, even talking of accepting protection there, he made ready to send his family to Gaeta. The foreign ambassadors who had joined him at Santo Stefano adjured him that, if he deemed it necessary to place his family out of danger, he should himself remain in Tuscany in order to provide without delay for the restoration of his authority. Leopold, who had already taken the

[1] Bianchi, vi, 100. [2] *Ibid*, 103.

precaution to embark on the British man-of-war *Bulldog*, kept the representatives of august Diplomacy rowing to and fro between his ship and the shore for nearly a day, he promising, they exhorting, he recanting, they imploring. When they found that he was bent on departure, they urged for the last time that it was his duty to leave behind him a duly accredited government, and to deprive his absence of the semblance of abdication. He smiled, temporized, but did nothing; and when the ambassadors had been rowed ashore, the *Bulldog* weighed anchor (February 21), and bore Leopold to the rookery of Gaeta. Villamarina, the Piedmontese minister who had conducted negotiations at Santo Stefano, wrote to his government: "It is impossible to represent the mass of deceits, baseness, and cowardice that this prince has displayed in this affair."[1] The purpose was unmistakable: Leopold, like Pius, wished Austria to interfere; he knew the unmartial character of his subjects well enough to know that they would cower at the approach of Radetzky's 30,000 "braves."

Leopold's apostasy would not have deterred Gioberti from sending La Marmora into Tuscany, but opposition in Turin itself suddenly dashed that plan. Gioberti, as we saw, had been lifted into power by a Democratic wave, but when the Democrats discovered that he favored none of their pet schemes, they turned against and beat upon him. His great popularity, coupled with his eloquence and political dexterity, sufficed to keep him erect against their attacks from December till February: now, however, rumors of his proposed intervention in Tuscany reached the ears of his opponents, and they demanded an explanation from him in Parliament. Gioberti replied in a fervent speech, showing that the revolution at Florence and Rome was not truly Democratic but the work of adventurers and reckless men, who, while they did not repre-

[1] Bianchi, vi, 107-9.

sent the patriotic majority, spread discord and terror, and threatened irreparable harm to the National Cause. At these allegations, the members of the Left took fire, and Brofferio, their spokesman, essayed then and there to wither the prestige of the Prime Minister; but the Right quenched his invective with shouts. On the following day (February 12), however, Brofferio renewed the attack, branding as infamous the plot of a Democratic minister to stifle the heroes of liberty at Rome and Florence; that was a business, he said, in which Austria had hitherto enjoyed a disgraceful monopoly; shame, and thrice shame, upon the Italian minister who had conceived such an outrage against brother Italians! Gioberti, still relying upon his supremacy, rose and replied, and when he deemed that he had said enough to counteract the effect of Brofferio's tirade, he demanded a vote of confidence. The Chamber hesitated, and then passed to the order of the day. Gioberti, though virtually beaten, refused to accept this as reason for resigning. The populace was still with him, and for a week it escorted him in triumph through the streets, cheered his palace windows, hissed Brofferio and even threatened to sack his house. But when the news came that La Marmora was actually at Sarzana, preparing to conduct his little army across the Tuscan border, the storm broke out afresh. The Democrats in the Chamber redoubled their attack; the members of the Cabinet declared that their chief had undertaken his policy of intervention without their consent. Gioberti, in answer, protested that he had laid his plan before them, and that, having secured their approval to it, he had also secured the King's acquiescence. The ministers persisted in their disavowal; the haughty premier hinted at resignation. But this threat could not scare his antagonists, whose anger blinded them to every other consideration except the ouster of this dictatorial man. Gioberti, believing himself indispensable, handed his resignation to the King, and the King, despite a petition signed by fifteen thousand citizens, accepted it. He had, from the first, borne under sufferance the Premier's imperious ways, chafing, as a sovereign whose ministers had been so recently mere servants must chafe, at being only the instrument of a superior will. "Louis XIII," says Beauregard, "complained that Richelieu left him nothing to do but to cure king's evil. Charles Albert, so long as Gioberti's ministry lasted, could not say even so much as this."[1]

With Gioberti's downfall disappeared the last important minister of that year of revolutions. How many like him had been hailed as indispensable to the salvation of Italy, and like him had been ruthlessly flung aside! Greater than any of his predecessors in Piedmont, greater than Capponi and Ricasoli at Florence, greater than Rossi and Mamiani at Rome, his elevation had been as high, his ruin as swift and complete, as theirs. His fate proved anew that in revolutionary crises it is not by logic nor eloquence of tongue, but by sword and grapeshot that the strong man can tame an unbridled people and lead it to victory; not in the Council Chamber but in the saddle is the post of him who would control a revolution which is the sudden unleashing of the physical forces of a nation. Gioberti, measuring himself with the other politicians at Turin, had quickly discerned his superiority, and believing that he alone could repair the disaster of the summer of 1848, he had used every art and conciliated every element by which he might attain power; but, once in office, he cast off partisan tethers and showed himself a statesman. As the Moderates had called him renegade when he clasped hands with the Democrats, so the Democrats called him renegade when, perceiving that the last hope of Italy lay in the preservation of Constitutionalism,

---

[1] Beauregard. 440; see also 437 et seq.; Brofferio, iv, 66-74; Alf. La Marmora: *Un' Episodio del Risorgimeto Italiano* (Florence, 1875), 16-19.

he proposed to quell the Democratic rabble in Florence and Rome. That was, indeed, the one act of real statesmanship during those stormy months, — an act too bold and heroic to be understood by doctrinaires of any party, and consequently it hastened the overthrow of its author. Not then, nor for a long time thereafter, could Gioberti's great qualities be justly appraised. Men remembered his vanity, his ambition, his disregard of hostile opinions, his ill-disguised condescension even towards his friends; too many had been worsted by his eloquence, or had seen their individuality overwhelmed by his, for them to be able to judge him without passion. He was guilty of the one sin which politicians hold unpardonable, — he refused to be the slave of Party; for he made Parties, he did not obey them. The almost boundless confidence he inspired among the masses was towards him personally, rather than his policy. By a word, a gesture, he exercised over the multitude an influence to which many would-be leaders could never attain, however persuasive or flattering they might be. His popularity exceeded, for a time, that of any other Italian. In Rome itself they lauded him above the Pope, and declared that Pius had roused the enthusiasm of Italy because he was at first believed to be Gioberti's disciple. But the deification of the living is always the severest test to which human nature can be subjected, and in Gioberti's case the wonder is, not that it puffed up his self-esteem, but that it did not utterly spoil him. He had that attribute which distinguishes the statesman from the mere politician or doctrinaire, — he constantly advanced. As fast as facts vitiated his theory, he threw the old theory over and framed another more comprehensive. Disillusions could neither embitter nor depress him. When he found that his Neo-Guelfic dream was unrealizable, that Pius was but a simple parish priest misplaced on the Papal throne, and that the conflict between Church and State was irreconcilable, he adopted

a different policy. So, too, when events taught him that
the redemption of Italy could be achieved only through
Constitutional Monarchy and not through Democracy, he
abandoned Democracy. He could learn from experience,
— the mere politician, the doctrinaire cannot do that.
The State papers which he wrote during his brief term
of office bear evidence that he had solved the problem of
Italian unification. That he was prevented from entering
the Promised Land himself was due to the overwhelming
resistance of the times and men, but he sketched the route
for his successors, and they, after desperate toil, followed
it to the goal. We, who look back after fifty years have
clarified the atmosphere, can discern that as Gioberti was
ahead of his countrymen when he published his "Primacy" in 1843, so he was ahead of them when, in 1849,
beclouded by partisan abuse, he fell from power. Time,
the great arbiter, has justified him.

Gioberti retired, his colleagues remained. General
Chiodo superseded him as President of the Council, —
the sixth premier in less than a year. This appointment
of a military officer indicated, not less than the retention
of ministers approved by the war-party, that Piedmont
had begun to look upon a renewal of the conflict as inevitable. Gioberti himself had held this view, and had
worked night and day to remodel the army. Charles
Albert, brooding over his defeat of the previous summer,
and smarting under the calumnies which assailed him
from all sides, longed for a last chance to prove his sincerity either by victory or death. On the opening of the
Chambers (February 1) his speech had a warlike ring;[1]
intimating that, unless Austria speedily consented to the
propositions of the mediating Powers, Piedmont would
make an end of temporizing. Austria had, indeed,
treated mediation much as Louis XI treated his doctor,
ridiculing and scorning it when the prospect was fair,

[1] *Correspondence*, iv, 106-7.

but imploring its assistance when danger threatened. She expressed her gratitude to England and France for their kind offers, — and immediately invented an excuse for rejecting them. If the peacemakers, growing impatient, demanded a prompt statement of her intentions, she replied that they should have it in two or three days, which stretched to as many weeks, when some new phase could be counted upon to justify further postponement. Neither Drouyn de Lhuys, who was now French Minister of Foreign Affairs, nor Palmerston was deceived as to the motive behind Austria's dilatoriness, but they both set the preservation of peace foremost, and were slow to construe Austria's disingenuousness as an affront to themselves. The Imperial Cabinet, in which Prince Felix Schwarzenberg now took the lead, had finally consented to be a party to a conference to meet at Brussels, and settle the fate of Northern Italy, but he delayed the Imperial envoy's appointment from week to week. At length, on February 22, Austria formally announced to Palmerston that the only basis on which she could begin to negotiate was the maintenance of her territorial limits as laid down by the Treaty of Vienna;[1] in other words, she intended to keep Lombardy, Venetia, and the Legations, and to ignore both the Italian national sentiment and the change wrought by the late revolution. To Palmerston, who, as early as January 18, had informed the Lombards and Venetians that Austria did not intend to relinquish any of her Italian territory,[2] this announcement was no surprise; it merely saved him the bother of keeping up the pretense that the conference would be held, but he still hoped to be able to restrain Piedmont and Austria from another encounter.

Charles Albert, however, thirsting for revenge and vindication, willingly threw himself into the current which, by divine appointment, as he believed, was hurrying

[1] *Correspondence*, iv, 131.   [2] *Ibid*, 23.

towards war. The Democratic party had for months clamored for another duel with Austria, and now both the Moderates and the Reactionists regarded war as preferable to the unsettled and expensive armed truce. Austria on her side did not dread the issue; she was gaining upon her rebellious subjects in Hungary, and she had strengthened Radetzky's army in Northern Italy to the point where she felt confident of his ability to repel the Piedmontese. She would not be the aggressor, but she pursued a policy which should exasperate the King to attack her. Radetzky had governed Lombardy by martial law, sparing no cruelty, extorting a levy of forty million francs from the nobles, inciting the lower classes against the aristocracy, confiscating the property of those who had emigrated during the previous summer, and threatening to desolate any town which murmured against his orders. And as if to emphasize her purpose of driving Piedmont to desperation, Austria prepared to resume the bombardment of Venice, even before the projected conference at Brussels, which was to settle the Venetian question by arbitration, had been abandoned. With both Piedmont and Austria thus eager for a death-grapple, Palmerston's pacific messages produced no effect. By the end of February no one could longer doubt that, unless France and England forcibly interfered, — a possibility which their action during the past seven months rendered highly improbable, — the armistice would soon be denounced.

But what resources had Piedmont accumulated for another conflict? During the first campaign she had equipped 140,000 men, including the reserves; she had raised an extraordinary loan of 60,000,000 francs, and had housed 25,000 Lombardy emigrants, — huge burdens for a country of four and a half million inhabitants to carry.[1] The numerical losses during the war, especially

[1] Beauregard, 370, note 1.

during the retreat, had been immense, but not more discouraging than the demoralization of all parts of the army, and the dissatisfaction which prevailed among all classes of civilians. Nevertheless, each minister of war had vied with his predecessor during the autumn and winter in reconstructing the army. Arsenals rang with smiths' hammers; factories hummed with the weaving of uniforms and tents; barracks swarmed with recruits; the shouts of the drill-sergeant, the tramp of regiments were heard throughout the land. By dint of unremitted activity, 117,000 troops were ready for the field at the beginning of March, 1849. The number was imposing, but the quality, in spite of many improvements, was poor. The new soldiers were often mere lads, whom a few months' drill did not suffice to make stanch; in the reserves were middle-aged men, long unaccustomed to military duty, and always reluctant to quit their families; the veterans of the last campaign had bitter memories of hardships and failure. The lack of competent officers could not be supplied, nor could the political animosities which were raging in Parliament and the clubs be kept from infecting the troops. Worst of all, the commander-in-chief was a foreigner. Having failed to induce a French general of repute to take command, the Piedmontese government offered the position to Chrzanowski, a Pole, who had distinguished himself in the Polish insurrection in 1831, and who had since been a soldier of fortune out of a job. He had but slight acquaintance with the Italian character, and only a superficial knowledge of the topography of Northern Italy. Inordinately conceited, he wanted in tact in dealing with the Piedmontese generals, whose professional jealousy was naturally aroused to see themselves at the beck of a supercilious stranger. In person insignificant, with perhaps a bantam strut instead of dignity, he inspired no enthusiasm among the common soldiers, who had as yet no proof of his military genius.[1] And it was more than unfortunate, as Cavour remarked, that their commander-in-chief should be a foreigner whose very name they could not pronounce. We must remark, however, that, before the campaign opened, Piedmont hoped and wished to believe that the little monkey-like Pole, with his red-rimmed eyes, was the prodigy his friends had painted him and he deemed himself.

From Charles Albert's pride as king and ambition as soldier, no greater sacrifice had been wrung than this of relinquishing his command to a subordinate and a stranger; but the disasters of the first campaign had convinced him that the sacrifice must be made. Eagerly he watched the remoulding of his army, and he accepted gladly the reports of those of his officers who with more zeal than judgment declared that it was again in a condition to fight. Able and loyal generals, James Durando among them, nursed no such illusions, and expressed their doubts frankly to the King;[2] but he whose heart was set on revenge or martyrdom, preferred to listen to those who saw the situation as he wished to see it. And, indeed, an army of 117,000 men, with 156 field-cannon and 2,000 siege-guns, was formidable enough on paper; Napoleon had won his greatest victories with a smaller force than that. On March 12 Charles Albert proclaimed the dissolution of the armistice, according to which eight days must elapse before hostilities were begun.

Piedmont, relying upon her own strength, was thus going to her final duel with Austria; but while she had no allies, she counted upon rekindling the enthusiasm of the other Italians and of securing from them assistance which might prove effectual. The Cabinet dispatched Camozzi to organize an insurrection in Northern Lombardy; it warned Venice, which had been blockaded dur-

[1] Rüstow, 385–8.   [2] Beauregard, 435–6.

ing the winter, to be ready to make an attack on her besiegers; it authorized Lorenzo Valerio to proceed to Florence and Rome and to urge the Republicans in those cities to coöperate in a war which had the common independence of Italy at stake. In Tuscany, since the proclamation of the Triumvirate on February 8, Guerrazzi had been the foremost figure. He owed his elevation to demagoguery, but he did not propose that demagogues should control him, and so he came to be regarded by orderly citizens as the last dike between them and the flood of anarchy. There were tumults in many places, but, except at Empoli, they passed off for the most part in noise. Florence gave itself up to political revels. A huge liberty-tree was erected in the Piazza della Signoria, round which the rabble danced and shouted like collegians at a bonfire; smaller liberty-trees planted in the smaller squares had each its bacchantic worshipers; a liberty-cap decorated the head of Ferruccio's statue outside the portico of the Uffizi, and in the portico itself tables were spread for a great civic banquet, at which the tongues of orators needed not to be loosened by wine. Mazzini, who had reached Florence on the day of Leopold's flight, harangued the multitude from the steps of Orcagna's Loggia. He would have them immediately declare the Republic and vote for "Unification"—the term "Fusion" stuck in his throat—with Rome, and having stirred up the populace, he strove to persuade the Triumvirs. But Guerrazzi was by no means eager that Tuscan autonomy should be merged in that of Rome, and he insisted that until the Tuscan Assembly were elected the Provisional Government had no authority to take so radical a step.[1] Nevertheless, he bowed to popular clamor in so far as to agree that the representatives to the Roman Constituent should be chosen at the same time with the Tuscan deputies. When the masses still shouted for the proclamation

[1] Guerrazzi: *Apologia*, 230.

of the Republic, he replied to them, "Very well; bring me to-morrow two thousand young Florentines equipped and ready to fight for the Republic!" "You shall have thirty thousand!" shouted the enthusiastic crowd. But on the morrow not a soldier appeared.[1] Nevertheless, Guerrazzi had a brief martial exploit. It happened that for a fortnight after Leopold's flight General de Laugier, with about three thousand troops, — all that remained of the Grand Duke's army, — lay at Massa, ready to undertake to put down the rebellion, if only his master would authorize him so to do. From time to time the Florentine shouters were dismayed by rumors that De Laugier was marching on their city. Accordingly, Guerrazzi, having mustered as many Civic Guards as he could, set forth to give battle; but on drawing near to the position where he expected to encounter the enemy, he ordered his men to advance, not with bayonets but with sprigs of olive stuck in the muzzles of their guns. Fortunately, De Laugier's troops had already disbanded, and he himself, on whose head a price had been set, had taken refuge across the Piedmontese border, with the forty or fifty men who still stood loyally by him and the Grand Duke. So this pretty little theatricality was not spoiled by any of the obtrusive violence of real war. While Guerrazzi was thus reaping the honors of a bloodless campaign, however, Florence was thrown into commotion by the news that a host of peasants, led by an Englishman named Smith, was marching on the city. Beacon fires blazed on the adjacent hills; musket-shots were heard just beyond the walls; the citizens rushed to the threatened gates, — San Frediano, Romana, San Gallo, and Pratese; the church bells rang to arms, above all the great bell of the Palazzo Vecchio boomed. Montanelli rose from a sick-bed, and hurried to the scene of confusion. But after a skirmish the peasants withdrew, and by morning

[1] Guerrazzi, 241.

order and equanimity returned. Florence has been the prey of conquerors of divers kinds, but it was not written in the Book of Fate that she should be captured by "an Englishman named Smith."

After Guerrazzi's return to the capital, Montanelli went off to win his share of military renown by organizing a cordon of defense along the northern frontier, upon which the Austrians, who had just occupied Ferrara, seemed to have wicked intentions. The country swarmed with political clubs, from each of which, as from the little vents in the neighborhood of a volcano, gas and vapors spurted. The peasantry, taking their opinion from the priests, remained loyal to the Grand Duke. A large part of the aristocracy and educated middle class, who had composed the Moderate Liberal party, saw no hope for the preservation of Constitutionalism, and no escape from anarchy, except in Leopold's restoration, but they had not yet the courage to make an open stand in his behalf. The Republicans had everywhere the ascendency in haranguing and in influencing the masses, and at the elections (March 15) their candidates carried the day. Just at this moment Valerio came to Florence with the tidings that Piedmont had broken the truce. He urged the Tuscan government to join in the war; but the Republicans had not yet forgotten Gioberti's scheme of suppressing them, and they were too excited over their internal affairs to give Valerio a hearty welcome. Besides, Tuscany had no army ready for service. But their sympathies in a war between Piedmontese and Austrians gravitated inevitably to the former, and Valerio could therefore proceed on his mission with the assurance that although the Tuscan Republic could give no immediate aid, it might in a few weeks furnish a body of recruits, and that, in any case, it saw that it had a common interest in Charles Albert's success.

At Rome the five weeks since the proclamation of the

Republic on February 8 had witnessed the efforts of the Republicans to find anchorage amid the swirl of the current setting towards chaos. The Assembly appointed an Executive Committee of three irremovable and responsible members to carry on the government. These were Armellini and Montecchi, both Romans, and Saliceti, a Neapolitan, whom Bomba had exiled because he was frightened by his fancied resemblance in features to Robespierre. They were well-meaning, if not able men, who delegated the routine business of the State to the Cabinet, of which Muzzarelli, Sterbini, Campello, and Saffi were the prominent members. They issued a programme in which they outlined a conciliatory policy, but the vehemence of the haranguers in Parliament and in the market-places showed only too clearly that the dominant faction had no idea that conciliation implied any concession on its part. In the Assembly Audinot was almost the last representative of Constitutionalism. Mamiani, Pasolini, Minghetti, and their comrades had either voluntarily retired from political life when the Pope refused to sanction their efforts, or they had been beaten in the elections. The clubs and the newspapers vied with each other in turbulence, and their strident voices passed for public opinion. Much of the popular excitement effervesced in street parades and similar shows, and in patriotic saturnalia borrowed from France. The sight of a Phrygian cap on the cross of the obelisk of the Piazza del Popolo sufficed to evoke a tornado of cheers. At St. Peter's, the Republicans held a religious service, in spite of the unwillingness of the ecclesiastics, who performed the ceremony under compulsion.[1] Patriotic hymns — including young Mameli's most popular ode, "Brothers of Italy" — were sung on every occasion. Military favorites — Garibaldi, more than all — shared with the political favorites and the lords of the rabble the ova-

[1] Farini, iii, 214–15.

tions of the multitude. In brief, applause was on tap; a sort of devil-may-care buoyancy was common to all Republican hearts, and kept them from being oppressed by the gravity of the future.

But beneath this froth there were strong purposes at work. The every-day affairs of State had to be attended to. Money had to be raised. The army, the judiciary, the police, must be reorganized. With a fearlessness that their enemies called vandalism and sacrilege, the new rulers laid the axe to the root of Papal abuses. The Assembly decreed, for instance, the abolition of the tribunal of the Inquisition, and appointed a committee of deputies to superintend the operation. "They went," says La Farina, "and between two women of ill-fame, playing cards, they found a Dominican friar, who gave them the keys. Then were set at liberty several wenches made stupid and numb by long imprisonment; two nuns guilty of illicit love; a Livornese guilty of blasphemy, who had languished there eighteen years; one who called himself Bishop of Egypt, who, condemned to perpetual seclusion during the reign of Leo XII, had wholly lost, in that horrible den, his power of walking; and many others, guilty of witchcraft, of sorcery, of miracles, of insult to Catholic beliefs. . . . At that spectacle the people broke into fury, and crying vengeance on so great an outrage, rushed to the Convent of the Minerva, the residence of the Father Inquisitor, and wished to burn it; but the Citizens' Guard and the gendarmes hurried to the spot, and after long efforts succeeded in quieting their minds and in allaying the tumult, so that no one was harmed."[1] This forbearance typifies the conduct of the Romans throughout their period of self-government. When we reflect upon the iniquities which Papal misrule had fostered, when we reflect upon their own excitability and their complete independence to do whatever their

[1] La Farina, iv, 160–1.

anger prompted, when we remember that many of their leaders were men who took for models the fiery spirits of the French Reign of Terror, we shall wonder at the general moderation of those Roman revolutionists. Had they willed it, nothing could have prevented them from wiping out the hated minions of the Papacy, from the few cardinals who still remained in Rome to the last mousing friar. In the provinces, political assassinations were indeed frequent, but the government, far from instigating or approving them, strove to put them down.

In its political measures, the Republic endeavored not only to establish itself by a solid administration at home, but to secure from republicans throughout Italy the recognition of its central and supreme position. It besought Tuscany and Venice to merge themselves in it, and though the former hesitated and the latter declined even to send a representation to the Constituent Assembly, the Romans bore a grudge to neither; they only redoubled their exhortations at Florence, and they voted a subsidy of a hundred thousand crowns to aid the Venetians in maintaining their siege. When Pius from Gaeta appealed [1] (February 18) to the Catholic Powers to lift him back into the throne from which he had run away, the Romans, undismayed, proclaimed in the face of Europe their right to be their own master.[2] Nor were they innocent of secretly fomenting Republican intrigues in Piedmont, especially at Genoa. Why, indeed, should they be more scrupulous than their antagonists in seeking for self-preservation? So there was at Rome genuine force, not merely for huzzaing, but for serious enterprises, — a force as yet turbulent and diffusive, which nevertheless was instinctively tending towards a compacter and more rational organization.

The arrival of Mazzini in the Eternal City gave the

[1] Text in *Correspondence*, iv, 149, 180–3.
[2] C. Rusconi: *La Republica Romana* (Capolago, 1852), 122–4.

Republicans what they most needed, — a chief whose preëminence none could gainsay, a director for that energy which was wasting through imperfect control, a living symbol of the cause. At Rome he was a prophet in the midst of his disciples. Here were men who, though they had never seen him, had for years been guided by his teaching; here were others who had long been his devoted emissaries, bearers of his instructions from London to Italy; here was a multitude ready to acclaim above all other heroes him who worshiped the People as the visible embodiment of God invisible. They bestowed upon him the Roman citizenship, they elected him a deputy, and when, on March 6, he appeared for the first time in the Assembly, he was assigned a seat beside the President. The applause, the cheers would not cease till he rose and spoke. His words, which illustrate Mazzini's peculiar gift of expressing mystical ideas in language so clear that neither he nor those who heard him stopped to analyze them, are worth recording. "All that I have, not done, but striven to do," he said, "has come to me from Rome. Rome was ever a sort of talisman to me; when still a lad, I used to study the history of Rome, and I found that whereas in all the other histories all nations were born, grew, played a part in the world, and fell never to reappear in their first vigor, one city alone was privileged by God with the power of dying and of reviving greater than before, to fulfil in the world a mission greater than the first she had fulfilled. I saw the Rome of the Emperors rise first, and by conquest extend from the confines of Africa to the confines of Asia; I saw Rome perish, blotted out by the Barbarians, by those whom today, also, the world calls Barbarians; I saw Rome rise again, after having driven out those very Barbarians, revivifying from her sepulchre the seed of civilization; and I saw her rise grander to move by the victory, not of arms, but of words, — rise in the name of the Popes, to repeat her great mission. I said in my heart: 'It is impossible that a city which alone in the world has had two great lives, one greater than the other, should not have a third. After the Rome which worked by the victory of arms, after the Rome which worked by the victory of words,' I said to myself, 'there will come the Rome which shall work by the virtue of example: after the Rome of the Emperors, after the Rome of the Popes, there shall come the Rome of the People.' The Rome of the People has risen. I speak to you here of the Rome of the People. Do not salute me with applause, let our felicitations be mutual. I can promise you nothing from me, save my coöperation in all that you shall do for the good of Italy, of Rome, and for the good of humanity, of Italy. We shall have, perhaps, to traverse great crises: perhaps we shall have to fight a holy war against the only enemy that menaces us. We will fight it; and we will win it. I hope, if God please, that foreigners may never again be able to say what many repeat even to-day, in speaking of our affairs, that this which comes from Rome is a fatuous flame, a light that flits among the graveyards. The world shall see that this is a light as of a star, eternal, splendid, and pure, as those which sparkle in our sky."[1]

In expression almost as precise as a scientific formula, in substance vague and elusive as a sufi's dream, Mazzini's oration seemed to the Assembly to be the utterance of truth, because it expressed what all were feeling. He did not explain the process — call it magic, rather — by which a people inexperienced in civic affairs, corrupt in public morals, ignorant, uncontrolled, was to be suddenly transformed into a community capable of self-government. The mediæval alchemist promised to transmute old pots and kettles into pure gold; Mazzini, the modern wizard, proposed, by repeating the mystic incantation, "God and People," to transmute ranters into statesmen, and rabble

[1] C. Rusconi, 302.

into soldiers, in the twinkling of an eye. And yet he knew well enough that this was contrary to the laws of the spiritual world. He himself had preached that progress is a development, not an instantaneous creation; that character and intelligence, whether private or public, come not by spasms, but by slow and painful accretions. Only last week he had admitted to Capponi, in Florence, that Italy was not yet ripe for the Republic;[1] nevertheless, he insisted that the Republic alone could lead her to final unity and victory, and that, though the experiment were foredoomed to fail now, it must be made, in order to sow the seed of ultimate success.[2]

In thus refusing to reckon with facts he was wholly in accord with the men who listened to him in the Roman Assembly. No wonder, therefore, that his corroboration of their wishes, added to his genius and the prestige of his career, gave him authority over them. Henceforth he held in reality, though not yet in name, the dictatorship of the Roman Republic; and when Valerio came to Rome to ask assistance for Piedmont in the war now imminent, Mazzini's patriotism outweighed his Republicanism. Deputies there were who still raised their voice against aiding a king who, they screamed, had once betrayed the National Cause, and whose motive was dynastic ambition; but Mazzini silenced these narrow, vindictive zealots. "There should be to-day," he said, "only two sorts of Italians in Italy: those who stand for the war of independence, for the emancipation of Italian soil from the Austrians, and those who do not stand for the war of independence. Republican Rome will fight side by side with Monarchical Piedmont." He appealed for arms, for money; and ladies who heard him stripped off their jewels and dropped them from the gallery to the President's table (March 18). A Council of War was appointed, and a manifesto calling for volunteers was indited (March

---

[1] Capponi: *Scritti*, ii, 59, 60.   [2] Farini, iii, 270.

21). Steps were immediately taken for the departure of Colonel Mezzacapa with a corps of ten thousand men. For a moment the enthusiasm which had burnt so brightly last year seemed to be rekindled. Immense hopes hovered again in every breast; the joys of brotherhood, the certainty of victory, the vision of Italy united and free, — these the themes in discussing which every one became a rhapsodist. And now, as a year ago, Rome turned her gaze northward, and waited for tidings from the seat of war.[1]

In Piedmont, likewise, somewhat of the old fervor was revived at the announcement that the truce had been broken. Even those who harbored no delusive confidence in success accepted the decision as inevitable, and felt relieved that the long and ruinous suspense was ended; as a patient submits to a surgical operation in which the chances are ten to one against his living; better one chance in ten, than none at all. Charles Albert's face for the first time in many months wore an expression of serenity, almost of joy, as of one who, after long persecution, is led out to martyrdom which for him has no dread, but offers an honorable escape from earthly trials into the peace and rewards of heaven. When he bade farewell to his wife, she asked him when they should meet again. "Perhaps never," he replied solemnly, and left her fainting, to quit Turin for Alessandria.[2] Among the masses, easily swayed by hope, these dismal forebodings could not dash the excitement caused by the bustle of martial preparations, the passage of regiment after regiment to the front, the glowing prophecies of those sages who always spring up at such times to prove by geography and arithmetic just how many days will be required to reach and take the enemy's capital. The newspapers and street orators, of course, talked very brave.

The Cabinet, through the Minister of War, addressed

[1] Farini, 288-9; Rusconi, 130-4.   [2] Beauregard, 459.

a note to the Powers giving Piedmont's reasons for renewing hostilities. She complained that, although the armistice had been purely military, Austria had proceeded to reëstablish the Old Régime in Lombardy and Venetia, ruling by martial law, levying extortionate tribute from the inhabitants, and, in general, disregarding the fact that the political destiny of those provinces was to be settled by arbitration. Austria had further brought back her vassal princes to the Duchies; and she had persistently refused, in spite of her promises to France and England, to negotiate a peace. Thus she had forced Piedmont for nearly eight months to bear all the burdens of war without any of its advantages, — a situation disastrous to the treasury and only too favorable to the promoters of revolutionary schemes. Therefore the King felt justified in breaking off the disingenuous armistice which, if prolonged, threatened so to exhaust his resources that he would be unable either to resist an attack from Austria or to save his kingdom from anarchy.[1] Austria retorted to these charges by a circular note in which she threw all the blame for the abortive mediation on Charles Albert's insincerity. She had been long-suffering; she had not even punished his attempt to seize her Italian provinces by marching to Turin as she might have done in 1848; now he was about to heed his wicked ambition and attack her again; but the Emperor, sure of "the sympathy of all those in whose bosoms the sense of right" was still present, and relying on his army, his people, and "the protection and assistance of the Lord of Hosts, who will never permit the just cause to be overcome," accepted Piedmont's challenge.[2] The time had passed, however, when pen-and-ink vindication could help either side. Even the special agents whom France

---

[1] Ferrari to Abercromby; *Correspondence*, iv, 200; also Ferrari to Ricci, ibid, 212.
[2] *Ibid*, 216-19.

and England sent to warn Charles Albert from his hazardous leap spoke to deaf ears. Diplomacy must now stand by and watch the solution, by powder and shot, of the problem to which she had devoted many months of ostentatious incompetence.

Chrzanowski, the Polish soldier of fortune to whom Piedmont intrusted her fate, had somewhat surprised the King's ministers by asking them at his first interview, whether they would have their war at *wholesale* or *retail*.[1] Unused to hearing military affairs treated like groceries or potatoes, they replied that they left it to his judgment to decide which would lead quickest to victory, the sole object they had in view. Then he explained that by war at "wholesale" the campaign might be concluded in a single battle; whereas by the "retail" method there would be less risk but more delay. The ministers, as was their duty, left the responsibility with him; and he laid out the plan of a campaign which was to be both "wholesale" and "retail," besides being both offensive and defensive. He distributed the Piedmontese army along the Ticino River from Oleggio, near Lake Maggiore, in the north, to La Cava, at the confluence of the Ticino with the Po, in the south. At only two points were there bridges by which the Austrians might invade Piedmont: at Buffalora on the highroad between Milan and Turin, and at the junction of the two rivers. But the officious little Pole did not apprehend that Radetzky would take the offensive; he feared, on the contrary, that the old marshal, scared at the renown of the Polish generalissimo, would retreat double-quick to the Quadrilateral. Chrzanowski, prepared, therefore, to throw his troops across Lombardy, overtake the Austrians, and beat them, before they had time to shut themselves up in the four fortresses, as they had done in the previous year. Accordingly, on March 20, he distributed his army as follows: the 5th

---

[1] "*Guerra grossa o in dettaglio:*" Beauregard, 446.

Division, under Ramorino, lay near La Cava; the 1st Division, under Durando, occupied Vespolate and Vigevano; the 2d Division, under Bes, was at Casalnuova and Cerano; the 4th Division, commanded by the Duke of Genoa, held Trecate; the 3d Division, under Perrone, stretched from Romentino to Galliate; the Reserves, commanded by the Duke of Savoy, were at Novara and along the road to Mortara; Solaroli's Brigade, forming the extreme left wing, was at Oleggio. South of the Po, at Sarzana, too far away to be of immediate service, was Alfonso La Marmora's Division, with orders to cross the Apennines and attack Parma; still nearer, the right wing, under Belvedere, occupied Castro San Giovanni on the road to Piacenza.[1] Deducting the 14,000 men under La Marmora and Belvedere, the main army had nominally 100,000 men, but its effective strength was less than that, probably about 80,000 men. Radetzky's entire force in Italy reached 130,000, of which, after leaving 40,000 to garrison the towns, and deducting 12,000 or 15,000 on the sick-list, he had still about 75,000 with which to take the field.[2]

On the morning of March 20 Charles Albert was at Novara. M. Mercier, special envoy from the French Republic, exhorted him even now to pause. "It is too late," the King replied, with a fatalistic tone. "I am in God's hands, and ready to accept his decrees." Mounting his horse, he galloped, accompanied by Chrzanowski and the staff, to the western end of the bridge which spans the Ticino at Buffalora. On the Lombard bank no signs of defensive preparations could be descried. Here and there a few Austrian uhlans appeared; then these vanished, and all was still. Chrzanowski's spirits began to rise; he felt certain that his expectations would be verified, that the Austrians intended to retreat to the Mincio without striking a blow, and he chuckled to think

[1] Rüstow, 397.　　　　　　　　[1] Ibid, 393.

how he had perfected his arrangements for overtaking them. The sun shone brightly, the bayonets of the troops glistened, and when the clock in the belfry of Trecate struck noon, the army sent up cheer on cheer. Yet the silence across the river was suspicious; perhaps the Austrians were lying in ambush there just out of sight. After a brief delay, the Duke of Genoa's division was ordered to advance, and when the first files reached the bridge, Charles Albert placed himself at their head and led them forward. With trepidation they watched their monarch ride impassively over the bridge, as if there were possibly no Austrian sharpshooters hidden in the bushes on the other shore. The anxiety was intense, but brief; in a few moments the King and his foremost companies stood safe on Lombard soil. Soon the entire division had crossed unopposed, and unopposed it scoured the Milan highroad as far as Magenta. From peasants it was learned that Radetzky, during the previous night, had withdrawn his troops in the direction of Pavia. Chrzanowski's spirits somewhat abated; realizing that it would be hazardous to push on before receiving news from the lower Ticino, he recalled the Duke of Genoa from Magenta, and returned with the King and staff to Trecate.[1]

At ten o'clock that evening an aide came to headquarters with the news that Radetzky had crossed the Ticino at La Cava with his entire army, and that he might, at that very moment, be heading towards Turin. Chrzanowski at once communicated the report to Charles Albert, but neither seemed to be disconcerted by it; they both believed that there was still time to intercept Radetzky at Mortara, which he must pass before he could penetrate into Piedmont. Accordingly, on March 21, the left wing of the Piedmontese army faced about and marched southward.

[1] Beauregard, 465-70.

But Radetzky's first advantage was really of vital significance. Being much better informed of the position and movements of the Piedmontese than the Piedmontese were of his own, he knew the weakness of the division under Ramorino at La Cava, and saw that he could best invade Piedmont at that point; therefore, he massed his troops at Pavia during the night of March 19-20. At noon on the 20th, when the King was advancing unimpeded into Buffalora, Radetzky was pouring his troops across the river at La Cava. But what of Ramorino? He had been stationed with only 6,000 men at the most critical point along the frontier. His orders were to take a strong position round La Cava, in case the Austrians showed a disposition to attack; if they did not, he was cautiously to cross the river and seize Pavia, unless he should fall in with a superior force. In case, however, the Austrians assumed the offensive and attempted to enter Piedmont, he was to check them so far as he could by skirmishing until reinforcements could reach him.[1] But unfortunately La Cava, situated at the junction of the Ticino and the Po, needed a double guard; for the enemy might cross the former river and take the highroad to Mortara, or he might cross the latter and endanger Alessandria. Ramorino, believing the latter the more probable, withdrew, with all but a few skirmishers, to the south bank of the Po, and intended to defend the passage there. But Radetzky, as I have just stated, chose the upper crossing, and throughout the afternoon of March 20 poured his army in three columns into Piedmont, almost without encountering resistance. If Ramorino's error proved most disastrous, — and it did so prove, and he was shot for it by order of a court-martial, — what shall we say of the greater error of Chrzanowski who, having only two gates to protect, massed 50,000 or more men near one and only 6,000 near the other? The

[1] *Portafogli del Gen. G. Ramorino* (Capolago, 1849), 18-20.

real blunder sprang from the Polish general's over-confidence that Radetzky would not dare to invade Piedmont.[1]

Radetzky, having a sure footing on the enemy's soil, and having destroyed the bridge at Mezzanacorte and so cut off Ramorino's division south of the Po, lost no time in ordering his troops forward. His plan was to throw the bulk of his army on Mortara, after capturing which he could move with equal ease westward on Vercelli and Turin, or northward on Novara. To prevent an attack on his flank, however, he dispatched a reconnoitring force to Vigevano. During the morning of March 21, therefore, the hostile armies were converging on Mortara, but the Austrians had the advantage in distance and in time. They were already near Mortara and Vigevano before Chrzanowski could bring up his divisions. At La Sforzesca, a village a little to the south of Vigevano, there was a sharp skirmish in which the Piedmontese had the upper hand; but while Chrzanowski was preoccupied with that affair, Radetzky, late in the afternoon, bore down with an overwhelming force on Mortara. Taking

---

[1] An examination of the evidence leads me to reject the theory that Ramorino deliberately betrayed the Italian cause. That charge was immediately brought against him, and public opinion, both military and civilian, was too much exasperated for him to have an impartial trial. That he was a blusterer, no one denies; he boasted that he would drive the Austrians out of Italy and capture Vienna, with 20,000 troops. He had many of the faults of the professional soldier of fortune; his career in Poland, in Mazzini's "invasion" of Savoy, and in the Spanish Peninsula, proved that he was cantankerous and unreliable, but not cowardly. His behavior at his execution equaled Marshal Ney's in heroism. Having been driven from the citadel to the edge of the parade-ground outside Turin, he insisted on quitting the carriage; thence he traversed on foot the vast field, "not like a man going to die, but like a general who goes to take command of his division. The troops presented arms and he returned the military salute, and went and placed himself in front of the platoon detailed to shoot him." The sight of his coffin, near which he was stationed, did not dismay him. He refused to sit down, or to have his eyes bandaged; but, having opened his coat and bidden the soldiers to come nearer, he himself gave the command to fire. In an instant the bullets crashed through his breast and brain. See *Il Portafogli*, etc., 108–9.

the Piedmontese almost by surprise, he drove them from the outskirts into the town, whence, after a desperate hand-to-hand conflict, made more fearful by the coming of night, he at last drove them out. So disorganized was the Piedmontese system of communication that it was already eleven o'clock, and then only by chance, when news of this disaster reached Chrzanowski at Vigevano. He rose at once and sought the King, whom he found asleep, wrapt in his great gray cloak, bivouacking in the open air with the Savoy Brigade. "What is to be done, sire, with troops which will not fight?" asked the Pole angrily; and then he repeated the account he had just received from Mortara. The King, whose pallid face was more pallid than usual from the chilly air, listened, said little, but shook his head with the expression of a man whose worst fears are realized and who has no remedy to suggest. The conference being ended, he wrapt himself again in his mantle, and lay down before the flickering camp-fire; immovable as a recumbent statue on a tomb, he lay there with closed eyes, till dawn broke upon a cheerless March drizzle. Forty hours ago, amid sunshine and the acclamations of his regiments, he had crossed the Buffalora bridge.

Three courses presented themselves to Chrzanowski in these dire straits: he might boldly retrace his steps to Buffalora and invade Lombardy, in the hope of compelling Radetzky to follow him; or he might swoop down to La Cava, cut off Radetzky's retreat, and attack him on the flank; finally, he might reunite the Piedmontese army, so far as that was still possible, and risk a general defensive battle. He chose the last alternative, and fixed upon Novara as the point of reunion. All day long on the 22d, therefore, the Piedmontese divisions marched towards Novara, Charles Albert riding with them on his light brown horse Favorito, his face sombre, the reins thrown on the horse's neck, himself scarcely observing what was passing round him. A mournful march, broken by no cheers, no boisterousness, gloomy as the day, and the landscape as yet untouched by spring. At nightfall the army reached Novara and camped beneath its walls.

Novara, a town which had then 20,000 inhabitants, crowns a slight eminence in the plain which stretches thence to the Adriatic. Its streets are narrow and crooked; its walls, even in 1849, were too old to resist a bombardment, — they still form a picturesque break in the level landscape, and have long since been converted into pleasant walks where, on summer days, whatever breeze is stirring can be found. The country is covered with plantations, irrigated by innumerable small canals fed from two larger streams, the Agogna on the west and the Terdoppio on the east. Here and there farm buildings and villas, accessible only by narrow lanes, are seen among the plantations. It is a country ill-adapted to military operations, because cavalry and artillery must keep to the highroads, and even infantry can move only with great difficulty through the canal-seamed fields. Of these highroads, which are broad and well-kept, one leads east to Lombardy; another, running almost due south, leads to Vespolate and Mortara; a third, diverging to the southwest, is the direct route to Vercelli.

On the morning of March 23 Chrzanowski stationed the Piedmontese army in a crescent just outside the southern wall of Novara. His right wing, under the Duke of Savoy. held the Vercelli road; his centre, composed of the divisions commanded by Durando, Bes, and Perrone, lay among the plantations between that road and the highway to Mortara; his left wing, comprising the Duke of Genoa's division and Solaroli's brigade, guarded the eastern approach. It was eleven o'clock before the Austrian vanguard marching up the highroad from Vespolate encountered the Piedmontese outposts at Olengo, — a cluster of peasant dwellings about two miles from Novara.

D'Aspre, the Austrian general, was advancing cautiously, not yet certain that he should find the Piedmontese army at Novara. He drove in the skirmish line and pushed forward nine or ten furlongs to La Bicocca, — another village of twenty or thirty houses and a fortress-like brick church, — before he assured himself that he had the main body of the enemy in front of him. Hurrying messengers southward to inform Radetzky and call for more men, he hurled his columns on Perrone's division, set to guard La Bicocca, and took it, after a stern encounter. But presently the Piedmontese were reinforced, and by a brilliant onslaught they recovered the village. Then fresh Austrians came up from the south, and round La Bicocca, whose importance both commanders recognized, the battle raged. To and fro the pendulum of victory swung, as now the Piedmontese and now the Austrians prevailed. At length the Duke of Genoa was ordered to storm that critical position. Down the highroad, which there runs straight as an arrow for a mile, he led his regiments to the charge. They hurled back D'Aspre's troops from La Bicocca, they drove them pell-mell to Olengo. It was the fatal moment of the battle when audacity was discretion. The Duke wished to pursue the enemy; his men were eager and exhilarated; D'Aspre might be routed before aid could reach him. But Chrzanowski, who had planned to fight only on the defensive and would not alter his plan to fit circumstances, summoned Prince Ferdinand to return.. D'Aspre reformed his shattered battalions, got fresh troops from the south, and again took La Bicocca. Again Prince Ferdinand, this time accompanied by the King, galloped to win back the lost ground; but it was too late, his soldiers were weary, the enemy, much strengthened and now confident, could not be dislodged. The charge failing, the Piedmontese began to retire in disorder to Novara. In the centre, too, Durando and Bes had been slowly beaten back. When darkness fell, the routed army of Piedmont was huddled in disorder under the walls of the town.[1]

Charles Albert, who, throughout that terrible day, had exposed his person with more than his habitual coolness, watched at the Mortara gate the final overthrow of his troops. Beside him stood Chrzanowski and Cadorna, the Minister of War. "What do you propose?" he asked them. Chrzanowski declared that nothing could be done; Cadorna, by silence, intimated that he likewise saw no hope. "Then all is lost, — even honor," the King exclaimed in anguish. He ordered a white flag to be raised, and dispatched General Cossato to parley with the victorious enemy. While awaiting Cossato's return, Charles Albert remained long on the city wall, praying that some stray bullet might yet bring him a soldier's death. But the firing ceased, night and rain closed in, and he made his way through the gloom to Casa Bellini, which he had quitted that morning with the determination to conquer or die. Ah, how he envied his generals, Perrone and Passalacqua, as they were carried past him, mortally wounded! how he envied the heaps of Piedmontese dead, lying where they fell round La Bicocca, their duty done, their rest earned, heaven itself seeming to weep for them.

The Bellini Palace is an unimposing three-story building, situated in one of the quietest little squares of quiet Novara, — a house whose bleared mirrors framed in gilded woodwork, now faded, and whose tarnished chandeliers bespeak the bygone elegance of provincial high-life. The drawing-room, on the second floor, which was Charles Albert's headquarters, had doubtless been the scene of many an entertainment; it was now to witness one of the most pathetic events of the century. The King had just returned thither, when Cossato arrived from his mission

[1] The Piedmontese lost about 4,000 in killed and wounded, the Austrians, 3,000. For details, see Rüstow, Beauregard, Mariani; also Radetzky's official report, in La Marmora, 139-73.

to the Austrian camp. The terms which he was authorized to report were crushing. "I will never agree to them," said Charles Albert. He summoned a council of war to meet at quarter past nine. There were present the King's sons, Chrzanowski, Alexander La Marmora, James Durando, and Cadorna. Charles Albert stood with his back to the chimney-piece, at his left were Victor Emanuel and Ferdinand. "Is there not still a chance to cut our way to Vercelli or Alessandria?" he asked. Each officer replied, "No." Then, after a painful silence, the King spoke again, in a low but firm voice. "My life," he said, "has been consecrated to the welfare of Piedmont and of Italy. I perceive now that I am an obstacle to that welfare. To remove this obstacle I have in vain sought throughout this day a bullet; in default of which, abdication remains for me. Gentlemen, I am no longer your king; there is your king, my son Victor." This announcement, though expected by all, sounded in the ears of all like a knell. Having affectionately bade each of his officers farewell, Charles Albert dismissed them, and remained for an hour alone with his sons. Then he recalled Cadorna to furnish him a passport, and as the minister was taking final leave, Charles Albert grasped his hand and said, "I have faith that better days will shine for our country. If ever my son renews the war, and I live, I shall snatch up a gun and return, to fight as a simple soldier."

Accompanied only by his courier, Gamallero, and his valet, Francis Valetti, he quitted Casa Bellini in a cabriolet at eleven o'clock that night. Novara was in the wildest confusion, the troops having broken through all discipline and given themselves up to riot and pillage, as if in a conquered city. The King's carriage luckily escaped detection, and was soon hurrying along the muddy highroad towards Vercelli. There it was stopped by the Austrian outposts, and as no horses could be procured until the next morning, Charles Albert passed the night in the carriage to avoid recognition. At daylight he set out again, and proceeded unmolested till he reached the neighborhood of Casale, where a large force of Austrians was preparing to bombard that town. An officer advised the King's postillion to take a roundabout road in order to escape the danger. Thereupon Charles Albert, wishing to save Casale from unnecessary harm, and regardless of his own safety, leaned his head out of the window and expressed surprise that hostilities should still be in progress, since an armistice had already been agreed upon. "May I take this news to our commander?" asked the officer. "Yes," replied the King; "tell him that I am Count de Barge, on my way to Oporto, and I give him my word of honor that it is true." The officer, seeing a handsome sword on the seat beside the King, asked if he might examine it. On its hilt was a mystic emblem of the lion couchant with a helmet on his head, the shield of Savoy on his back, and a serpent in his claws; engraved beneath was the motto, *J'atans mon astre*, "I await my star." The officer admired the workmanship, little suspecting who its owner was.

Without further delay Charles Albert drove on, and soon passed beyond the Austrian lines.[1] He seems not to have foreseen that, had he been recognized by the Austrians and seized as a hostage, they might have wrung grievous terms from Piedmont. He crossed the mountains to Nice, and on quitting his kingdom forever, the last hand that he shook was that of Count Santa

---

[1] La Marmora, 178-80. The story was told, and is repeated by a writer so generally trustworthy as Beauregard, that when Charles Albert was first stopped, he got out of his carriage and had a long talk with the Austrian General Thurn, who suspected the stranger to be the King. To make sure, he had a Piedmontese prisoner brought in, and the soldier was about to salute his sovereign, when he was warned by a signal from the latter, and steadfastly replied that this was the Count de Barge. La Marmora, in the pages cited, dissipates this pretty legend on the best authority, — that of Gamallero, the royal courier.

Rosa, the son of that Santorre who had gone into exile after the revolution of 1821. Almost without resting, he pursued his journey through Southern France and Northern Spain, and on April 20 reached his destination, Oporto. There, worn out in body, broken in heart, he took quarters in the Villa entre Quintas, from whose windows his tired eyes could look out upon the Douro and its beautiful hilly shores. Two or three faithful friends attended him, and the Bishop of Oporto gave him spiritual consolation. He hoped for a visit from his son, the Duke of Genoa, but that could not be. Day by day his strength failed, until, in spite of his efforts to reach the armchair by the window, he had at last to keep his bed, where amid prayers, or gazing at the pictures of the Virgin and St. Francis, — gentlest of religious guides, — his life ebbed swiftly away. He died on July 28, almost his last words being, "I forget everything, — I forgive every one." They bore his body with funereal pomp homewards, and laid it in the tomb of his ancestors at Superga. Parliament decreed to his memory the title of "the magnanimous King," and Time has bleached his reputation from the blemish which calumny and the frenzy of disappointed partisans cast upon it. His countrymen and the world have long since acknowledged the service which he rendered Italy. If greatness be measured by material success, then Charles Albert was not great: he lacked the singleness of view, the bold volition of those who win the world's triumphs; but no king ever had a higher sense of honor, none ever served duty more loyally, nor bore lifelong misunderstanding more patiently, nor more willingly sacrificed himself to his convictions. His complex nature, the untoward blending of warrior and ascetic, of autocrat and patriot, give to his character and career the deepest interest for students of the human soul. Many men more famous than he are more easily analyzed, and consequently the sooner forgotten. He is the nineteenth century Hamlet, but the task allotted to him was incalculably more difficult and important than the avenging of a father's murder. They show his death-mask at Turin; it is a face of extreme sensibility, noble, dignified, but unspeakably sad; features, you would say, which had lost the habit of smiling, but which might show much pity and resignation, and be lighted by a momentary gleam of thankfulness at the approach of death.

At Novara, after Charles Albert's departure, the new king bravely faced the ordeal before him. Early on the morning of March 24 the Austrians began to bombard the town, but Victor Emanuel had already sent Cadorna and Cossato to Radetzky and requested a cessation of hostilities. Radetzky, who had burned with implacable hatred for Charles Albert, denouncing him as a traitor and a perjurer, was inclined to treat his son more generously. He offered an armistice on condition that peace should be reëstablished with all possible speed. Piedmont must defray the expenses of the war, and of an Austrian army of occupation until peace were concluded; she must disband her Lombard troops; she must recall her squadron from the Adriatic; and allow three thousand Austrians to garrison Alessandria, with a similar force of Piedmontese; the King himself must sign this armistice, and pledge his honor to maintain it. Victor Emanuel prudently accepted these terms; by rejecting them he would have exposed Piedmont to disasters in comparison with which even the defeat at Novara might have seemed slight. Thus ended amid gloom, but without dishonor, the second attempt of Piedmont to redeem Italy from bondage to Austria.

CHAPTER V.

THE QUENCHING OF FLORENCE AND ROME.

THE disaster at Novara closed the efforts of Constitutionalists to liberate and unite Italy. Henceforth we shall not be concerned with the affairs of Piedmont. Her conflict with Austria was, for the present, ended. Beaten, torn by internal factions, crushed by debts, vilified and misinterpreted, her business it now was to recover her strength and her prestige, and above all, to preserve and extend Constitutional methods through all her breadth. A painful task, accomplished gradually through the loyalty of her new king and the consummate statesmanship of the minister who soon rose to second him. But the achievements of Victor Emanuel and Cavour do not fall within the range of this history; nor shall we even pause to watch the attempted revolution at Genoa and Alfonso La Marmora's austere but necessary suppression of it, nor Austria's imperiousness in the negotiations for peace. In the remainder of our work, we have to trace the final efforts of the Revolution to save some remnants of Italian soil from the clutches of angry Despotism, sweeping forward with a presentiment of victory. Constitutional Monarchy, represented by Piedmont, had made the fight, and succumbed; Democracy, which still held Venice, Florence, and Rome, was now to be tested.

The campaign had been so brief that it had allowed no time for organizing a general insurrection in Lombardy: nevertheless, the Piedmontese emissary, Camozzi, stirred up Bergamo to strike for independence; Brescia, of its own accord, revolted against the Austrians. The Bergamasques submitted as soon as they saw their struggle was hopeless;[1] the Brescians, on the other hand, held out for several days. Their bravery is among the shining exploits of modern Italians, and deserves more than a passing mention. Having shut the Austrian garrison up in the Citadel, which commands the town, they elected a Committee of Defense, consisting of Drs. Contratti and Cassola, and prepared to maintain their freedom. It was wonderful to see their energy in providing themselves with weapons, in manufacturing powder, and in erecting barricades: for although the Committee directed them, it was hampered by the Municipality, a more timid and prudent body, and by a considerable number of citizens who had felt too often the iron hand of Austria to wish to jeopard their lives again. False bulletins reached Brescia from the seat of war; in some it was announced that Radetzky had been crushed and was retreating at breakneck speed to the Mincio, while others reported that Charles Albert had again played the traitor and lost a great battle, after which Chrzanowski, having been acclaimed dictator of Piedmont, had attacked the Austrians and forced them to sign an armistice in which they agreed to surrender Lombardy and Venetia forever. These lying messages strengthened the Brescians in their determination to resist. They cursed Charles Albert, they lauded Chrzanowski and the Republic; and presently, when Nugent appeared before the city with a force of two thousand men, they laughed at his call to surrender, and easily repelled his assault. A little later, however, in the night of March 30–31, Haynau arrived with 12,000 troops, and having succeeded in effecting his entrance into the Citadel, he summoned the Brescians to give themselves up. They replied to him that, according to the terms of the armistice which Radetzky had been

[1] See Camozzi: *Cenni della Guerra d'Insurrezione Lombarda del* 1849 (Capolago, 1849).

granted, the Austrians were to withdraw from the country without molesting it. Haynau did not undeceive them in regard to the fraudulent bulletins, but bluntly announced that, unless Brescia were surrendered within two hours, he would proceed to bombard it. The Brescians, nothing daunted by this threat, resolved to fight. During the afternoon of March 31, while bombs poured down from the Citadel, Haynau's regiments stormed the principal gates and after nightfall captured Porta Torrelunga, and gradually drove the defenders of the barricades into the heart of the city. "I should never have thought," wrote Haynau to Radetzky, "that so bad a cause could be sustained with such perseverance." The night was given up to those atrocities with which Austria was accustomed to celebrate her conquests. Men were slain in cold blood; women were ravished and then slain; dwellings were pillaged, and no attempt was made to put out the conflagration kindled by the bombs. The next morning a part of the Brescians wished to fight on till death; but the majority, aware of the hopelessness of the contest, and dreading the punishment that would be compounded against them for every hour's resistance, voted to capitulate. Haynau dealt with the unfortunate city, not as if it was thenceforth to be conciliated to the rule of Austria, but as if it was a town in a foreign land, that a barbaric captain blasts on his march. He governed it by martial law, permitting his soldiers to kill and plunder; he caused women to be flogged; he executed victims merely suspected of having participated in the revolt; he levied an indemnity of six million francs, besides a contribution of 300,000 francs to be paid to the Austrian soldiers who had been wounded, or to the heirs of those who had been killed, during the conflict. And thus, by a method which he called "salutary terror," he convinced the Brescians of the immense love which their good father, the Emperor, felt towards them: for himself, he

earned by his ferocity an infamous notoriety surpassed
by that of no other Austrian of his time.[1] The names
of nearly three hundred of his victims are recorded, and
among them we find old men of fourscore, and girls under
twenty, priests, mothers, and children. When in the following year Haynau visited London, the draymen at the
brewery of Barclay and Perkins were so incensed that he
should dare to come among decent human beings that
they fell upon and thrashed him; and when the Austrian
government claimed redress, Lord Palmerston replied
that "Haynau was looked upon as a great moral criminal;
and the feeling in regard to him was of the same nature
as that which was manifested towards the Mannings,
with this only difference, that General Haynau's bad
deeds were committed upon a far larger scale and upon a
far larger number of victims."[2]

The capitulation of Brescia put an end to the last serious resistance of the Lombards, who had henceforth to
submit to that régime of punishment which Austria
applied to her revolted subjects. It was in Florence,
Rome, and Venice that Italians still talked of independence and made a show of fighting for it. The Tuscan
Assembly met in Florence on March 25. Two days
later, news having come from Novara, the country was
plunged into dismay, and the deputies in secret session
voted that the peril of the moment demanded the appointment of a dictator, and that the man for the dictatorship
was Guerrazzi. The extreme Democrats preferred Montanelli, but the events of recent weeks had proved him to
be a man of less vigor than Guerrazzi; perhaps he himself realized his inferiority to his fierce Livornese rival;
at any rate, he refused to lead the anti-Guerrazzian fac-

---

[1] See Cassola: *Insurrezione di Brescia* (Capolago, 1849); La Farina, iv, 256-64.

[2] Marquis of Lorne: *Lord Palmerston* (London, 1892), 125. The Mannings had recently been convicted of exceptionably diabolical murders.

tion, and was content to go as special envoy to Paris and London. His departure did not, however, restrain his followers from agitating against the new dictator. In several stormy sessions which followed, they urged that the republic should be formally declared, and that it should unite with Rome, until, on April 2, Guerrazzi presented to the Assembly a declaration in which he demanded that the head of the State should have full powers, that the Assembly should be prorogued till April 15, that the dispute about the form of government should be postponed until Tuscany's independence was assured. "Deliberate," he said; "choose whom you will for head; words are nothing, things are everything. I shall be happy to show how one who truly loves his country ought to obey." After heated debate, his propositions were carried by a vote of 43 to 29, and he was ratified in the dictatorship.[1]

There now ensued a triangular conflict in which the contestants, while mutually opposing each other, had all the same purpose in view. That purpose was the restoration of Leopold: for while there was still much haranguing about liberty, every sober citizen knew that Tuscany could not long defend herself against an Austrian invasion, and that the coming of the Austrians would mean the restoration of the Grand Duke on whatever terms he might please to dictate. The Reactionists had from the first cherished no other wish than this; but the Liberals hoped to save the Constitution out of the impending wreck, by bringing back Leopold without the interference of foreign arms. The third competitor in this contest was Guerrazzi himself. He, too, saw that it would be impossible to maintain the independence of Tuscany against the veto of Europe, and accordingly he prepared to arrange matters in such wise that, at a propitious moment, he might be the instrument of the Grand

[1] La Farina, iv, 280-1.

Duke's restoration. If he played the part of General Monk successfully, might he not expect a fitting reward? Against all these conspirators, the uncompromising Democrats railed and worked. They would not be convinced that the game was lost; they talked vaguely about the invincible strength of a levy in mass of the Tuscan population, — as if the peasantry had not already shown their loyalty to their sovereign; they counted upon the moral support of England and upon the military intervention of France, — as if those Powers, which had not lifted a finger to save Piedmont, would discover a sudden reason for saving Tuscany; they clamored for the immediate union with Rome, — as if in a mere verbal compact there lay some mighty hidden virtue. But their chief object of attack was Guerrazzi, whose personality stood between them and the control of the government.

Guerrazzi, however, was too strong and stubborn a man to yield easily. He displayed great energy in dealing with the affairs of State, and made provision as if to defend Tuscany against foreign interference, for he did not yet avow his plan of restoring the Grand Duke. He maintained order, he tried to repair the bankrupt treasury and to galvanize the army: he went down to Leghorn and delivered a patriotic exhortation to a multitude in the cathedral. But the tide rose rapidly against him, and his enemies waited for an opportune moment to swamp him. It came very soon. He had collected at Florence a troop of Livornese volunteers, mostly tatterdemalions, and was equipping them with a view to sending them to the camp at Pistoja. The Florentines took umbrage at their presence, and whispered that Guerrazzi's real purpose was to use them as a Prætorian Guard. The Livornese were a lawless set, who had the unpleasant habit of frequenting taverns and not paying their scot, and even, it was alleged, of insulting the taverners' wives. A conflict between them and the townspeople seemed inevitable. Accordingly, Guerrazzi ordered their departure, but on April 11, when they were marching to the station to take the train, the Florentines fired some musket-shots at them. In a moment there was a riot. The Livornese retreated into the Square of Santa Maria Novella and defended themselves. Guerrazzi, hearing of the trouble, leaped on a horse and galloped to the scene where, at the risk of his own life, he succeeded, with the help of the National Guard, in separating the quarrelers. Nineteen were killed, and many more wounded in the brawl. The Florentines now dreaded that, as soon as the news of the encounter reached Leghorn, the masses of that ever-turbulent city would hasten to avenge their friends. Guerrazzi, therefore, gave orders that no armed band should be permitted to leave Leghorn, and at the same time he hurried the Livornese survivors out of Florence. The Florentine mob, heated by the affray, began to clamor against the Dictator himself, till the streets resounded with shouts of "Death to Guerrazzi!" "Long live Leopold!" During the night beacon fires again burned on the adjacent hills, and peasants flocked into the city.

It is evidence of the tenacity of mediæval traditions that the Florentines now turned not to the deputies still in Florence, but to the Municipio, — the town government, — for guidance in this emergency. The Municipio, composed of Constitutionalists, did not hesitate to assume responsibility not only for the restoration of quiet in the town, but also for the country's fate. On the morning of April 12 it issued a manifesto, announcing that in the name of the sovereign it assumed the direction of affairs, and it promised to obviate the danger of an invasion. Further, it added to its membership five of the most prominent Liberals, — Gino Capponi, Ricasoli, Serristori, Torrigiani, and Capoquadri, — in order to increase its authority. The deputies, on the other hand, met and declared that the session of the Assembly should be permanent; but although they were the representatives of the whole country, they could get no support. Gino Capponi was escorted to the Palazzo Vecchio amid cries of "We want honest men!" "Long live Leopold!" The populace uprooted the liberty-trees and even mutilated the statue of Ferruccio. Then the members of the Municipio entered the hall of the Assembly and announced that they had decided to engineer the restoration without the interposition of the deputies. Against this Taddei, President of the Assembly, protested; Guerrazzi likewise protested. "I had arranged things," he said, "for bringing back the Grand Duke in a more honorable way. But now it is important that no dissent be shown in the provinces; the adhesion of the Assembly is needed in order that this may not appear to be a course imposed by Florence and not agreed to by all Tuscany. I understand: you are proud of having taken the initiative, you do not wish to share with others the glory of the difficulties we endured, and the honor of the dangers we ran in curbing anarchy and the Republican faction."[1] Guerrazzi's sarcasm, however, could not move the members of the Municipio. Let whatever imputation be put on their acts he or any one else chose, they were resolved to prevent further disorder and to save the Constitution by warding off an invasion. So they proceeded to appoint a ministry and took upon themselves the title of Governing Commission. The reactionary masses, thirsting for a victim and fixing on Guerrazzi, collected in the Piazza della Signoria. With yells of "Death to the robber!" they threatened to break into the Palazzo and seize him. The new Commission hoped to get him out of the city and beyond the frontier; but it was too late, — the palace was surrounded by the angry mob, which would have torn him in pieces had he ventured forth. Accord-

[1] La Farina, iv, 288.

ingly, it was proposed that he should take refuge in the Belvedere fortress. Guerrazzi accepted the offer, and having hastened through the long corridor which connects the Uffizi with the Pitti Palace, he soon found himself in the fortress; thence in a few days he might quietly escape from Tuscany. But instead of being treated as he expected, he was crowded into a small cell with five other persons, and held there as a prisoner of State.

The disingenuousness by which Guerrazzi's fall was achieved brought him no sympathy. The Liberals who thus caged him would have pleaded that they could not hesitate in choosing between the sacrifice of one man and that of the Grand Duchy, and they would have insisted that they honestly desired to save his life. The truth is that Guerrazzi, of all the leaders of the Italian Revolution, was the least beloved. His personality drew no friends to him. Men followed him, they obeyed him, the masses even of turbulent Leghorn bowed to his will; but towards him personally they felt no devotion. He could inspire dread, he could compel obedience, but with his porcupine nature he repelled affection. At heart he was a misanthrope. Poverty and lack of appreciation in his youth stung him; he grew rich, he acquired fame, but bitterness rankled in him. He despised men, but instead of fleeing Timon-like from them, he sought his revenge in ruling them, and this, through his great talents, he was able to do. The very Grand Duke who feared and had persecuted him had to summon him to office. Once in power, Guerrazzi's ambition was to stay in power; he, too, would be an indispensable man, and by making Leopold's restoration hinge on his own connivance, he hoped to retain his ascendency. Grant that he acted from selfishness and not from patriotism, yet you cannot deny that his measures, whether as minister, triumvir, or dictator, were in the interest of law and order. He might at one time have provoked bloodshed; he might have paid off old hatreds by proscribing the men who had once tormented him. He did neither; to treat his enemies with sardonic contempt, to see them cringe before him, and to know that he could work his will with them, sufficiently gratified his vindictive spirit. So that when he fell no man regretted him, nor has any eulogy of him since been written; still we cannot forbear giving him the admiration which belongs to courage and tenacity. He coveted a great stake, and he dared to risk all to win it. That was a quality seldom met with among his easy-going Tuscan contemporaries, so fond of words, so ready to compromise.

The Governing Commission, having effected a bloodless revolution and having Guerrazzi caged in the Belvedere, flattered themselves with the belief that Leopold's gratitude would prevent him from abolishing the constitutional privileges which it was their one solicitude to preserve. They themselves swept away such products of the Democratic régime as they feared might offend his eyes, and they endeavored in perfect good faith to have it appear that Leopold's recall was the spontaneous wish of Tuscany. They sent an embassy to him, begging him to return at once and spare his people the shame of an invasion and himself the pain of seeing his rule founded on foreign arms, "which," they added, "you have always abhorred." Leopold replied with oracular vagueness that he would be to them what he had always been. Still he did not move from Gaeta. A second deputation went to him, and brought back an autograph letter in which he said, "The Tuscans may rest assured that I shall strive to seek the means most efficacious to heal them of the calamities they have suffered, and to restore the Constitutional government in such wise that the renewal of past disorders may not be feared."[1] The Provisional Government willingly gave a favorable interpretation to these

[1] La Farina, iv. 203-4.

phrases; but perceiving that some armed force was needed to put down the last vestiges of the insurrection, which persisted especially at Leghorn, they applied to Piedmont.[1] The Piedmontese, entangled in negotiations with Austria over the terms of peace, were loath, by interfering in Tuscany, to give Austria an excuse for rejecting their own terms. Nevertheless, they intimated that if the request were made to them by the Grand Duke, they would gladly listen to it. But Leopold was dumb, and then Piedmont, on the pretense of punishing the Livornese for injuries done by them to her consul, sent some men-of-war to Leghorn. Before they could act, however, matters had proceeded so far as to make action by them imprudent.

Leopold was dumb, and for a good reason. Whilst he was inditing ambiguous messages to the Florentines, he was engaged in quite a different sort of correspondence with Count Esterhazy, the Austrian ambassador at Gaeta, and with Radetzky. He besought Austria to send a corps into Tuscany without delay, and on April 25 he was cheered by the receipt of a communication from Esterhazy, who said: "Dispatches I have just received from Milan, by the hands of a trusty messenger, sent to me on a secret mission with this object, enable me to confide to your Imperial Highness, under the seal of secrecy, but in the most positive manner, that the wish you condescended to express to me a few days ago is in the way of being realized with vigor and instantly."[2] A little later Radetzky wrote that the Second Corps of the Austrian army would be at Reggio on May 6, ready to march on Florence and Leghorn. On May 1 Leopold ordered the dissolution of the Governing Commission and created Count Serristori Extraordinary Commissioner with full powers. Grand-ducal perfidy had now but little need for further dissembling. D'Aspre marched into Tuscany,

---
[1] Bianchi, vi, 469.   [2] *Ibid*, 482.

announcing himself to be the upholder of the sovereign, and commanding submission in his name. Only at Leghorn did he meet with a determined resistance, but Leghorn, after two days' fighting, had to capitulate (May 11) and suffer the usual horrors of an occupation by Austrian regiments. Leopold, clinging to deceit to the end, avoided a formal acknowledgment that D'Aspre had his sanction; but this was simply the weakest of evasions, for it deceived no one. On May 25 the Austrian general proclaimed the truth, that he was acting in response to the Grand Duke's appeal, and on the following day he entered Florence without molestation. For the first time in many years Austrian regiments were garrisoned along the Arno. The Constitution was annulled, Liberal institutions melted in the fire of reaction, and, when the old conditions had been as far as possible restored, Leopold came back.

The collapse of the revolution in Tuscany had no heroism in it to appeal to the imagination or to call forth respect. The bull-headed resistance of the Livornese and Guerrazzi's bold ambition were the only manifestations of strength. Leopold's dissimulation lacked even mediocre finesse; the gullibility of the Governing Commission might have been looked for in a parcel of Sunday-school children, but not in grown-up citizens of Machiavelli's birthplace. They could plead, indeed, that the Grand Duke's restoration was inevitable, and that they had at least averted unnecessary bloodshed, but they themselves had to admit that they had been duped. It was humiliating for men like Capponi and Ricasoli to confess that, "if the events of April 12 [the overthrow of Guerrazzi] must have this conclusion, it were better that they had never been brought about."[1]

Very different was the conduct of the Romans. The first report of the disaster at Novara filled the Assembly

[1] La Farina, 294.

with momentary alarm, but its leaders quickly infused confidence into them. Valerio, the Piedmontese agent, would not believe that all was lost; the situation, he said, demanded greater exertions, and he begged that the promptest assistance should be given to Piedmont. The Assembly voted that troops should depart that very night (March 29), and then it proceeded to elect a Triumvirate, composed of Mazzini, Armellini, and Saffi, with powers practically unlimited, although the Assembly itself remained in session to confirm their acts. Of the Triumvirs, Mazzini was the head, nay, we hardly exaggerate when we say that he was henceforth the autocrat of the Roman Republic. After nearly twenty years of plotting and propagandism, he at last found himself master of the Eternal City, on which his dreams had centred since his youth. If you would in imagination behold him as he appeared in life, you must put away all preconceptions as to typical conspirators; Mazzini, the greatest conspirator of them all, had not one of those outward tags by which to be recognized. He was now in his forty-first year, a man of small stature and slender frame. His head was cast in an intellectual mould, the brow high, the eyes deep set, the nose straight, the mouth firm; black hair and a short black beard framed his olive-tinted face. His habitual expression was serious, almost sombre, but when he was animated, his eyes burned with a strange light, and his features took on a terrible earnestness. There was no rant in his speech, nothing melodramatic in his manner. He would listen patiently while an opponent attacked his views; then he replied without petulance, yet wearing throughout the air of one whom no arguments can shake. So complete was his self-certitude that he could afford to be calm; it is fanatics of a lower order who fly into a passion when their views are endangered. Mazzini's vast personal influence sprang from his genuine sympathy and sincerity, and from his remarkable power of clothing speculative and mystical doctrines in language that every one could understand. His words were so plain that his disciples were often deceived into thinking that they grasped the thoughts behind the words. Theatrical in a high sense he unquestionably was, partly because he was too conscious of his own preëminence to be simple, and partly because he felt that this was indeed a world-drama in which he was playing a great rôle. Knowing the value of dramatic effect upon his countrymen, he did not hesitate to employ it. Those who fell within range of his fascination seemed to hear a prophet speak; his phrases, which twenty years' iteration had made hackneyed, still seemed to be utterances of the living Gospel. But there were many hearers in whose ears Mazzini's message sounded hollow, and either they expressed surprise that a man of his intelligence should fondle such vagaries, or they dismissed him as an unpractical enthusiast, or they berated him as a wicked schemer. "Charlatan" and "fanatic" are the titles which all the world's chief benefactors have some time borne. Although Mazzini was no charlatan, and only a fanatic in so far as, like every original man, he stuck to his principles through thick and thin, yet circumstances and his methods often seemed to justify those enemies who declared that he was both.

As the virtual dictator of Rome, he had now to step down from the high levels of idealism and to show his capacity for practical statesmanship. Consider the magnitude of the task before him. The Papal States, some four million souls, tossed by twelve months of revolution, bristling with factions, quite inexperienced in self-government, were to be remodeled into an orderly, compact republic. Against this consummation there warred not only internal discord, but the veto of Catholic Christendom; for, to the everlasting sorrow of the Romans, their destiny was involved in the temporal sovereignty of the

Catholic High Priest, who had been thrust upon them in by-gone ages, and whom the Catholic world insisted should continue to lord it over them against their will. And this High Priest, this Pope, who had recently had pious shudders at the thought of being a party to a war, was now beseeching Austria and Naples, France and Spain to make war in order to set him back on his throne. Common-sense showed that the Romans could not possibly withstand the armies of those four Powers; nevertheless the Romans, inspired by Mazzini's resoluteness, determined not to yield, and they saw several encouraging signs which took away from their determination its apparent recklessness. Foremost among fair omens was the still unsettled condition of Europe. It was not so evident to them as it is to us, that not only was the Italian cause hopelessly stricken at Novara, but also that by the beginning of April, 1849, the revolutionary movement throughout Europe had reached its death agony. They lived in the expectation that any day would bring the news of a decisive victory by the Hungarians, and this victory would paralyze, if, in fact, it did not demolish the Austrian Empire. They trusted with a blind confidence in the intervention of France. They reckoned on the ability of the Sicilians to prolong their struggle against King Bomba. They believed that if they could only maintain their independence a few weeks or months, Europe would be forced to recognize them, forced to acknowledge that they had the right to say how they should be governed. The stronger they proved themselves, the better the terms they could exact at the final settlement. Above all, they desired to be free, and they took the vehemence and justice of their desire as an indication that, somehow or other, the gods would bring to pass its fulfilment. Judged by the conditions which surrounded them, they were not, therefore, so rash as at first appears; they miscalculated, but where is the unerring prophet?

Mazzini and his colleagues lost no time in reorganizing every department of the government. The army, the empty treasury, the police, education, the courts, — they attacked all with vigor and decreed changes for their amelioration. They made the mistake common to reformers of trying to do too much, but this was inevitable, they had so many abuses to correct. They must make the Republic shine by contrast with the Papal régime; they must prove to all classes that the new form of government was, in very fact, as near perfection as it had been painted. Over against the minority of Republican zealots was the great mass composed of the indifferent or the antagonistic; the former must be allured, the latter, conciliated. The multitudes which had so persistently hurrahed for the Republic must not wake up to find that it could not add an inch to their stature, nor put any more pennies in their purse. Mazzini sequestrated some of the ecclesiastical buildings, and converted them into lodgings for the poor; he hired unemployed laborers to excavate the Forum; he apportioned public lands among indigent farmers; he poured out proclamations; he appealed to the sense of honor of the Romans to refrain from crimes; and, not content with quickening public opinion by exhortations, he decreed stern punishment for malefactors. In general, violent crimes were rare in Rome itself, although in the provinces assassinations for political motives were too frequent. At Ancona and Ascoli, lawlessness, instigated by the Retrogrades, kept decent citizens in a state of terror, until Felice Orsini was sent thither with authority to deal strictly. On the whole the Republicans treated their Clerical enemies with unexpected mildness. Occasionally a priest was set upon and beaten in the streets, or a vagabond monk was insulted, and in one case three Jesuits were massacred, but the government did not sanction these acts, and if it appropriated Church property, it did so under legal forms and for public uses. In this respect, Mazzini's administration need fear no comparison with that of Gregory XVI or with that of Pius IX after his restoration; it was the Vicar of Christ, and not the Republican Triumvir, who crowded the prisons and galleys with his political opponents.

In his effort to captivate popular opinion, Mazzini did not disdain to resort to cheap artifices. The masses at Rome were densely superstitious; religion in their minds being associated with the Church pageants which recurred every year at specified intervals. But during the absence of the Pope these ecclesiastical performances were interrupted, and what could the people infer except that since there was no pageant at Rome, there was, temporarily at least, no God at Rome? For God, to their thinking, was a vague invisible personage, to be prayed at and bowed to, whom, by some unexplained arrangement, the Pope carried about with him. With Pius at Gaeta, of course God could not be at Rome. Mazzini, therefore, determined to prepare a religious show by which the popular love of the spectacular might be gratified. It was customary on Good Friday to suspend a lighted cross in the dome of St. Peter's; this year, the lights instead of being white, were red, white, and green, — indisputably a portent that Heaven approved the Republic. For Easter none of the regular prelates could be induced to pontificate, but a patriotic priest named Dall' Ongaro consented to celebrate high mass at one of the four altars of St. Peter's reserved for the Pope. A multitude thronged the basilica to watch the ceremony, which was concluded by the priest's taking the Host, under the escort of men waving tricolor flags, up to the balcony of St. Peter's, whence the Pope always bestowed his blessing on the city and the world. Cannons boomed, the concourse in the piazza below knelt, and cheered the Republic when the Host was raised. Then instead of the white-robed Pontiff with the triple crown, and his attendants waving peacock-feather fans, Mazzini, in tightly-buttoned frock coat, appeared on the balcony beside the priest.[1] That was a unique spectacle, among all the strange spectacles of this checkered century, — the proscript who had but last year issued from his attic in London, now from the most conspicuous position in the world officiating in the place of the successor of St. Peter! The official organ of the Republic in reporting this episode declared that Christ in the Sacrament had blessed the free people! The canons of the basilica were fined for refusing to officiate in what they deemed a sacrilege, and what we must regard as a futile attempt to encourage patriotism in the masses through an appeal to their superstition. Mazzini should not have been the man to put on, even for that worthy purpose, and for a brief time, the canonicals of a mediæval religion which he not only did not believe, but which all the serious teaching of his life sought to destroy.

His proclamations fell thick as autumn leaves, one covering the other so fast that the bystanders had hardly leisure to read, and none to ponder. Yet here again he but adapted himself to what he conceived to be the temperament of the Romans, who might have misinterpreted silence to mean lukewarmness or inactivity. At the news of the insurrection in Genoa, he exclaimed: "The last prestige has fallen; the monarchical principle is condemned; may God and the People, who do not betray, triumph!"[2] The suppression of the Genoese revolt soon taught him, however, that Constitutional Monarchy had not fallen in Piedmont, and he was thereby deprived of the chance of seeing the Piedmontese rise in mass, every man a soldier, to sweep away the Austrians as the French had done in 1792. His extravagances, of which his enemies have made a target, were on the surface, and usually

[1] Balleydier: *Rivoluzione di Roma* (Milan, 1857), 310; Farini, iii, 320-1.
[2] Farini, iii, 314.

they were planned for a definite object; in substance, his policy was rational, shrewd, and courageous. But hostile Europe would not be propitiated by scenic parades; hostile Europe would not be daunted by rhetorical manifestoes; it was with her that the Republic must reckon, with her that it must prove its staunchness. And for this grim task, also, he girded himself.

The test came soon. One day a courier from Florence announced that the Tuscan Republic had collapsed, — news which instead of terrifying the Triumvirs called from them a defiant resolution. "We take this solemn oath," they announced, "to bury ourselves beneath the ruins of the fatherland rather than recede from the Republican principle we have proclaimed."[1] Swift on the heels of this messenger of ill-tidings came another, this time from the south: Palermo had capitulated, the republic in Sicily had been overthrown. I have purposely refrained from narrating the vicissitudes of the struggle between the Sicilians and King Bomba, because after the counter-revolution at Naples on May 15, 1848, the affairs of the Two Sicilies had no direct bearing on the development of the National movement which it is my aim to record. Sicily from the first restricted herself to the attempt to maintain her independence from Naples; wholly absorbed in her fight for Home Rule, she contributed but a few score volunteers to the Italian war. In Naples, after May 15, there was but a feeble resistance on the part of the Liberals to save the Constitution; so it was idle to expect aid from them for that war. Bomba did not, indeed, dispatch them suddenly: at his pleasure he allowed Parliament to meet, and at his pleasure he dissolved it, seeming to take a diabolical satisfaction in watching its long-drawn death agonies. Like the expert poisoners of an earlier age, he enjoyed his revenge the more because it operated gradually. How he made away with his oppo-

[1] Farini, iii. 334.

nents at Naples; how Sicily, having organized a provisional government, elected Charles Albert's son, the Duke of Genoa, to be king; how, when he declined this honor, Sicily set up a republic with the noble Ruggiero Settimo as President; how for a year she resisted Bomba's assaults; how Palermo and Messina and Catania, having been bombarded, surrendered, and were put through the ordeal by fire and sword, — these are events which deserve to be told, but cannot be told here. So long as Sicily held out, the Romans could feel that they had in that quarter an ally who, though not at present able to give them material aid, nevertheless helped to check the general flood of reaction by which they were themselves threatened. And now they realized that the subjugation of Sicily placed at Bomba's disposal regiments with which he could respond to the Pope's entreaty to invade the Papal States and put down the republic.

Pius, we have said, having officially declared that the trouble between himself and his subjects was not a political but a religious question, appealed to France, Austria, Spain, and Naples to show their devotion to Mother Church by interfering in his behalf. For two months, from mid-February to mid-April, Gaeta rustled with the whispers of diplomats. The intriguers of the Papal Court glided to and fro, carrying the hopes and fears of the Papacy under their scarlet or purple cassocks. It had to be decided, first, which of the four Powers should have the honor of being the Pope's champion, and second, on what basis the restoration should be effected. The four sons of Mother Church behaved towards each other with anything but brotherly love and trust; you might indeed have mistaken them for four bandits who, seeing a sumpter train approaching from a distance, fall to quarreling as to whose turn it is to kill the driver and seize the plunder. Pius would have preferred that Austria and Naples should do the job, because he knew that they worked thoroughly and without scruples; but he could not afford to ignore France and Spain. For a brief moment, between the rupture of the Salasco armistice and the battle of Novara, he had qualms lest Piedmont should whip Austria. In that case, Charles Albert would be the strongest ruler in Italy. Pius had snubbed him; what if the King should resent the snubbing? Evidently, the Pope would be at the King's mercy. Therefore Pius prepared to hedge; and if Charles Albert instead of Radetzky had been the victor of Novara, we should hear how Pius suddenly woke up to the King's unrivaled piety and how solicitous he was to conciliate Piedmont. Fortunately for his peace of mind, Novara left him free to choose a champion after his own heart.

The formal conferences opened at Gaeta on the 1st of April. The representatives of Austria (Esterhazy), Spain (Martinez della Rosa), and Naples (Ludolf), were inclined to respond immediately to Cardinal Antonelli's demand that the restoration should be a complete wiping out of all reforms and guarantees since the accession of Pius IX to the Papal throne. The French envoy, Duke d'Harcourt, declared that he could not consent to this plan, at least, until he received further instructions from his government, for he aimed to prevent Austria from forestalling France in the work of restoration. He had secret correspondence with the remnant of the Constitutionalists at Rome, urging them to overthrow the Republic and to recall the Pope; by so doing, they would deprive Austria of an excuse for interfering, and they might exact from Pius a pledge to respect the Constitution. France, he assured them, would sympathize cordially in this scheme. Whilst D'Harcourt was thus plotting with the Constitutionalists, Forbin de Janson, the French Secretary of Legation, plotted with the Reactionists at Rome, urging them to concoct a counter-revolution, and telling them that they would receive the support of the

French Catholic party. Both intriguers made the mistake of overestimating the strength of their respective accomplices. The Constitutionalists since the proclamation of the Republic had but a small representation in the Assembly, and slight influence over the public; moreover, they were men whom experience had taught to beware of the wiles of the Papal Court, and they would not stoop to restore the Papal régime unless they had the strongest guarantees that Pius would keep his word. The Reactionists, on the other hand, were numerous, but neither now nor at any other time during this crisis in the life of the Papacy did they display courage. They cringed and skulked and conspired in secret; they were never ready to stand up manfully for their principles or their sovereign. In the whole clerical and Sanfedist brood we find not one man who rose to the conception that everything should be sacrificed to Truth. Not from such elements, therefore, could any forcible opposition to the Republic be compounded. The Reactionists dared not declare themselves openly, but they used petty, underhand means to excite the bigotry of the lowest class. Statues of the Madonna wept or winked their eyes, and miraculous sweat appeared on the effigies of the saints;[1] as if by such cheap thaumaturgy Pius could be whisked back to the Vatican.

D'Harcourt's report of the situation warned the French Cabinet that it had no time to lose. Austria, already on the threshold of Tuscany, was as eager to proceed to Rome as the Pope and his Court were that she should. Louis Napoleon, the new president of the French Republic, saw the golden opportunity offered him, and he seized it, by determining to send a French army to suppress the Roman Republic. He had two motives, — he wished to propitiate the Clerical party in France by posing as the Defender of the Faith, and he wished to tickle all Frenchmen by a little martial pomp. The late Orleanist mon-

[1] La Fariua, iv, 420.

archy had discredited itself by subservience to Austria; the putative Nephew of his Uncle knew that the shortest cut to the admiration of Frenchmen was across a battle-field. The name of Napoleon, associated with conquest and glory, would not always serve to conjure with, unless the Putative Nephew could prove that that name still retained its virtue as a gratifier of Chauvinistic cravings. He could not be expected, therefore, to let slip this twofold offering of fortune; for he had already measured the imperial crown of his late uncle and discovered to his satisfaction that it exactly fitted his own brow; which he took to be the plainest omen that Fate intended his brow and that crown to meet. But he had not yet announced his discovery to the French nation, of which he was simply the president, sworn to uphold the Republic and the Constitution. How could he reconcile his wicked scheme against the Romans with Article V of the French Constitution? That Article declares that the Republic "respects foreign nationalities, as she means to have her own respected; that she undertakes no war for the purpose of conquest, and *never employs her forces against the liberty of any people whatsoever.*"[1] Surely no words could be plainer than these; but when have mere words daunted a would-be autocrat? Louis Napoleon applied to Diplomacy, and that venerable casuist, whose business it is to keep up appearances, and to fabricate pretenses which every one sees through, soon furnished him an interpretation to suit his wishes.

He did not, of course, disclose to his Cabinet his personal reason for approving the expedition against the Romans. True patriot that he was, he pretended to act wholly from a desire to enhance the prestige of France. On April 6 the ministry asked for a subsidy of 1,200,000 francs for troops which they deemed prudent to send to

[1] Tripier: *Constitutions qui ont régi la France depuis* 1789 (Paris, 1879), 315.

Rome. The Assembly contained a large number of members who were not only hostile to the Clericals but also genuinely Republican, and these at once suspected fraud. But the ministerialists bared their bosom and begged to have the purity of their heart inspected. The government do not intend, said Jules Favre, "to let France concur in the overthrow of the republic which actually exists at Rome; they act freely, untrammeled by other Powers, consulting only the interest, the honor, and the influence which appertain to France in every great European question."[1] Odillon Barrot, President of the Council, stated that they were guided wholly by their solicitude for the interests of France and for the cause of true liberty. The doubters were not yet satisfied. Emanuel Arago demanded that the government should make solemn declaration that it did not intend to sanction abroad what would never be sanctioned at home, — the violation of the principle of the sovereignty of the people. Odillon Barrot replied without blush or hesitation: "We will not go to Italy to impose on the Italians a government, whether Republican or other. There must be no misunderstanding on this point; we shall not employ the forces of France except to save the Roman Republic from the fatal crisis which threatens it."[2] Still, the doubters would not be reassured by the studied ambiguity of these replies. Ledru Rollin, leader of the Mountain, arraigned the ministers for proposing to break Article V; he arraigned them for having allowed Austria to recover her supremacy in Italy, and for leaguing themselves with her with the intention of forcing Pius back to Rome. "I demand that you answer categorically. Is the restoration of the Pope what you want? Have the courage to say so; come out of the clouds; rend the veil!" This challenge brought General Lamoricière into the tribune. He studied to be frank as evidently as his col-

[1] Farini, iii, 365.   [2] La Farina, iv, 434.

leagues had studied to be evasive. He wished it to be inferred from his remarks that the Cabinet, far from forming a partnership with Austria for the purpose of crushing the Romans, desired to frustrate her wicked designs. "You know," he said, "that if Austria without any interference from us were to escort the Pope back to Rome, a complete counter-revolution would follow; and then not only would the Roman Republic be lost, but the Liberal institutions and liberty of Italy, and the influence of France would be lost. If, after our soldiers have disembarked, Austria moves on Rome to destroy the Republic and reëstablish there with the Pope her own influence, we believe that the government should be empowered to send our troops to Rome to save what we can from the shipwreck, and, if not the Roman Republic, at least the liberty and influence of France in Italy." "And if the Romans refuse to receive the Pope, what will the French troops do?" called out Schoelcher, as Lamoricière finished; but the ministers did not reply, and the motion being put to a vote, 325 deputies favored and 283 deputies opposed it.[1]

Thus was France entrapped into giving her official support to an ignoble, sneaky expedition. Outwardly, she appeared as the champion of Italian liberty, a strong republic magnanimously helping a weak sister republic; her real purpose was to restore the Pope, maintaining the Constitution if she could, sacrificing it if she must, and this not even because she was devoted to Pius, but because she wished to succeed Austria in controlling the Papacy. The ministers who conceived and practiced this duplicity did not suspect that they were thereby holding the ladder for the ambition of Louis Napoleon. They appointed General Oudinot, son of Napoleon's marshal, to command the expedition of 8,000 troops, which embarked forthwith at Toulon. Oudinot's in-

[1] Farini, iii, 360-7.

structions were couched in terms as evasive as those the ministerial orators had used in Parliament. He was to reëstablish "a regular order of things on a basis conformable to the interests and rights of the population;" and although he was forbidden to recognize the existing republic, which the French ministry chose to regard as a combination of a few desperate demagogues who did not represent the real wishes of the inhabitants of the Papal States, yet he was cautioned to abstain, so far as possible, from appearing to direct the change in government which would soon be brought about by the "honest part of the population." Previous to setting sail, on April 20, Oudinot read to his troops a manifesto, in which he led them to suppose that they were bound, not on a mission of restoration, but on an errand of friendliness to show to the Roman Republicans the affection which French Republicans felt for them.

At Rome, meanwhile, the government continued the work of organizing a stable administration. On April 17 a committee presented the draft of a new Constitution, which provided for the election of two consuls, twelve tribunes, and an Assembly, and for laws which, on paper at least, looked wise. Audinot, almost the only member of the Constitutional party who still lifted his voice in Parliament, then pointed out that it was urgent that the Republic should state its position before Europe, declaring itself to be willing to negotiate with the Catholic Powers for the return of Pius to Rome and to guarantee him the free exercise of his spiritual functions, while it reserved to itself liberty and independence in temporal affairs. Accordingly, there was drawn up an address, lacking neither moderation nor eloquence nor common-sense, in which the Romans appealed to the conscience of Europe to recognize their right to govern themselves. Any other nation, they said, would endure ten wars rather than submit to one of the monstrous conditions by which the popes had maintained their rule; and they asked with what justice several millions of Italians must be subjected to the despotism of a sovereign whom they did not wish, and who profaned his religious authority in order to terrify his political opponents.[1] Europe, indeed, could not answer these questions; she did not try to answer them; the few million Romans were no more to her than are the crickets to the first frost of autumn. Official Europe wished to have done with revolution. The Pope must go back, irrespective of his subjects' preferences. The genuine French Republicans and the British Whigs of Palmerston's stamp would not commit themselves to the policy of abolishing Constitutionalism at Rome, but they would not insist that Pius should pledge himself to uphold the Constitution. They hoped that his benevolent heart and his good sense would teach him that conciliation would in the long run pay better than severity. What Pius's intentions were he set forth in an allocution which he took care not to publish until April 20, the day when Oudinot set sail from Toulon. The Pope recanted all his Liberal acts and disavowed by implication the efforts of Mamiani, Minghetti, Rossi, and every other Constitutionalist who had striven to keep him on his throne. He declared that the purpose of the reformers had been, from the first, to overthrow the Papacy. The Italian movement, if we believe him, was a conspiracy of heretics, atheists, and other bold, bad men, who, under the cloak of political sophisms, aimed at the destruction of religion and the appropriation to themselves of power and property. Listening to him, we might imagine that Gioberti and D'Azeglio, Capponi and Manin, not less than the obscurest volunteers in the National Cause, had plotted to turn Italy, and especially Rome, topsy-turvy in order that they might give themselves up to unlimited plunder and debauch. He made

[1] Farini, iv, 338.

no distinction in their intentions between the best and the vilest, although he reserved his fiercest epithets for the Republicans who had converted Rome into "a forest of raging beasts." As we read this Jeremiad, we could almost pity its author, — nay, we could pity him, but for the suspicion that his frenzy has been carefully rehearsed. What heart is so stony as not to be touched by the spectacle of one perfect man condemned by Providence to live in a world of villains? Think of his loneliness! Admire his fortitude! But just as our sympathy is going out to this modern Lot, we discover that he was not wholly alone. Heaven granted him to rest his eyes upon at least one man in whom even his fastidious and incorruptible virtue recognized a kindred spirit. Who was this prodigy that Pius called his friend? It was the King of Naples, "who" — I quote the Pope's words — "straining every nerve to promote the true and solid happiness of his people, so shines by religon and piety as to serve as an example to his own people." Pius IX found his ideal Christian in Bomba, the perjurer, the coward, the persecutor: we do not read that Jesus Christ gave a certificate of righteousness to Herod. Such excesses, whether in laudation or in censure, overleap their bound. Fact is fact and cannot be whiffed away by the bellowing of a Papal bull. Pius had real grievances, but he presented them in such wise that they could not appeal to any one who was not already as bigoted as himself. The allocution was important only because it left no doubt as to the sort of government he wished to have restored in his dominion.[1]

The news that a French expedition had set sail reached Rome on April 24, and created as much perplexity as alarm. The majority of the Romans preferred to believe, however, that the intentions of the French were honor-

[1] Full text of the allocution, which doubtless was written by Antonelli, in Rusconi, 434-51.

able. That same morning the first of Oudinot's ships entered the port of Civitavecchia, bearing a letter from Oudinot, which M. Espivent, his aide-de-camp, duly presented to Mannucci, the Mayor of the town. Oudinot announced that the French Republic, "sincerely well-disposed toward the Roman populations, desiring to put an end to the conditions under which for several months they have groaned, and to facilitate the establishment of a régime equally removed from the anarchy of recent days and from the inveterate abuses which before the elevation of Pius IX desolated the States of the Church," sent this expeditionary corps, which he hoped "would be welcomed and lodged as was becoming allies called by such friendly intentions." The Mayor asked for time to send to Rome for instructions, but Espivent would brook no delay. Thereupon the Mayor was for resisting, but Espivent, who was as well-stocked with manifestoes as a commercial traveler with samples, propitiated the other influential persons in the town by showing them a proclamation in which the French government declared that it was resolved not to impose on the Romans any form of government not desired by them. The Roman Assembly, notified by courier of these proceedings, protested against the threatened invasion and voted to resist it, but the citizens of Civitavecchia swallowed the French bait and refused to oppose the disembarkation, which took place on the following morning. The French troops landed, shouting, "Long live the Republic! Long live Italy!" and the beguiled populace cheered them in return.

Oudinot, having got safe ashore by this trick, issued a proclamation in which he revealed the fact that he had no intention of protecting a republic which France had never recognized, but that he raised a standard round which all friends of "peace, order, conciliation, and true liberty" must rally. Then the Civitavecchians, realizing that they had been duped, appealed to the honor and justice of the French generals and soldiers not to be the instruments whereby the intolerable abuses of the Papal administration should be riveted again on the Roman people. Oudinot, for reply, caused the placards on which this appeal was printed to be torn down; he seized the only press in the town; confiscated 6,000 muskets, which the Republic had bought in France; disarmed a battalion commanded by Melara; and declared the town to be in a state of siege. Shortly after, when Manara with his Lombard Legion wished to land and proceed to Rome, Oudinot forbade him. "What business have you Lombards to meddle in Roman affairs?" asked the French invader angrily. "And you, sir," replied Manara, "do you come from Paris, Lyons, or Bordeaux?" But Oudinot, not yet willing to deprive himself of whatever benefit he might reap from duplicity, consented to the disembarkation of Manara's men on condition that they should remain neutral until May 4. Nor did he openly avow his purpose when a delegation of Roman deputies waited upon him. He still let it appear that he came as a friend; in fact, he went farther, and feigned surprise and disappointment that the unselfish conduct of France should be suspected. He sent an agent, Colonel Leblanc, to Rome to confer with the Triumvirs, but Leblanc, either through indiscretion or under instructions, excited their alarm by harping on the determination of the Catholic Powers to restore the Pope. Mazzini, after listening to him, reported the interview to the Assembly, which immediately voted to commit the safety of the Republic to the Triumvirate and authorized it to repel force with force. But Captain Fabar, another French officer who had accompanied the delegation back from Civitavecchia, drew out of his pocket a proclamation in which Oudinot played on the other string, promising that the French should be as brothers to the Romans and that he would consecrate himself to the welfare of the latter's "beautiful country." Nor did Fabar omit to give warning that, as a force of Neapolitans and Spaniards was about to attack Rome, the only hope of saving the city lay in throwing open its gates to the French. The Triumvirs pointed out the discrepancy between Leblanc's tone and Fabar's, but the former was equal to the test. He had, he said, talked about Papal restoration merely to sound the temper of the Romans, and he disclaimed any official character for his remarks.[1] But he could not reassure the Triumvirs.

The time had come for a decision. Saffi and Armellini were in favor of assuming the good faith of the French and of trying to conclude an agreement with them; Mazzini, on the contrary, would not make a pretense of trusting them. The Assembly, coinciding in his distrust, voted, amid great enthusiasm, not to admit Oudinot into Rome. With a unanimity and vigor which had not been witnessed for many a day, the Romans prepared to defend their city. The deputies reviewed the National Guard in the Piazza a' Santi Apostoli; a committee of three, of whom Cernuschi, who had passed his apprenticeship in Milan the year before, was one, superintended the erection of barricades; the various bodies of troops were drilled; the walls were strengthened; deputies delivered patriotic harangues in every square; burly Friar Gavazzi exhorted priests and monks to throw the weight of their influence and example on the side of the Republic; noble ladies, among them the indefatigable Princess Belgiojoso, volunteered to nurse the wounded.

At Civitavecchia, Oudinot was lashing himself up to fighting pitch. As he had the misfortune of being the son of a distinguished marshal he was persecuted by the idea that he must by some brilliant exploit prove himself worthy of his father. He was also quick-tempered and

[1] Farini, iv, 3–6.

injudicious. He took it as a personal insult that the Republicans at Rome should have dared for a moment to contest his wishes. Who were they, forsooth, who bandied words with him, Oudinot, Duke of Reggio, commanding 8,000 soldiers of France? They were an inferior race, mere Italians, speechifiers and braggarts, who needed to be taught a lesson. In his contempt he exclaimed, "The Italians do not fight!"[1] From Gaeta, D'Harcourt wrote him to lose no time in moving on Rome and quashing the agitators. "Whatever is said, you will encounter no serious resistance at Rome; the majority of citizens will run to welcome you as soon as you show yourself."[2] Oudinot's messenger, Fabar, returning from the Eternal City, gave similar advice, confident that it would take but little for Frenchmen to destroy "the forge of Italian demagoguery." Oudinot needed no goading. He issued, on April 28, an order of the day in which he told his soldiers that they were about to put down a rabble of foreigners who had brought misfortune upon all Italy by arming themselves under the shadow of liberty. "The phantom of government which sits at Rome replies to my conciliatory words with reiterated boasts. Soldiers! let us accept the challenge, let us rush on Rome. We shall find neither the citizens nor the Roman soldiers our enemies. Both will regard us as liberators. We have to fight the outlaws of all nations who oppress this country after having lost the cause of liberty in their own. Under the French flag, on the contrary, Liberal institutions will have every expansion compatible with the interests and customs of the Roman nation."[3] Aggressors have short memories, otherwise this soldier of Republican France might have

---

[1] This phrase, which the Italians could not soon forget, was also attributed to Colonel Leblanc. Whoever said it, however, it illustrates the contempt then felt by the French for Italian valor.

[2] Farini, iv, 15.   [3] Ibid, 16.

recalled that in 1792 his own France denied the right of Europe to interfere in her affairs, precisely as the Roman Republicans were doing now. But to his Gallic vanity there could be no parity of condition between his Grand Nation and mere Italians. Accordingly, he posted a garrison at Civitavecchia and marched towards Rome.

On the morning of April 30 a lookout stationed in the cupola of St. Peter's discerned the French vanguard approaching from the west. He at once gave the signal, and the church bells clanged to arms. The French soldiers, hearing the peals, thought that they were only the usual noon-tide ringing. At about a mile and a half from the city walls, the road divides, one branch leading to Porta Cavalleggeri, the other to Porta San Pancrazio, and at this fork the French force separated, one column to attack the former gate, the other the latter. On posts along the way, the soldiers could read placards on which was printed in large letters Article V of the French Constitution, declaring that France would never interfere with the liberty of her neighbors; but what availed that pledge now, except to illustrate the emptiness of magniloquent phrases? Presently, each column encountered the Roman troops, and each column, after a stubborn fight, was driven back. By five in the afternoon the French were in full retreat, and but for Mazzini's refusal to pursue them, they might have been cut to pieces or captured. As it was they lost upwards of 300 in killed and wounded and more than that number of prisoners. To Garibaldi, who commanded the defense at the Villa Pamfili, fell the honors of victory, and that night there was great rejoicing at Rome. Oudinot, we may believe, when he had leisure to collect his fugitives and to count his losses, began to reflect that the Italians did fight.

The Romans took care to treat their prisoners with kindliness, giving to the French wounded attention similar to that which their own received. The Triumvirs issued congratulatory manifestoes and spared no effort to convert the popular enthusiasm, heightened by this success, into a solid and enduring instrument of defense. For the present, Oudinot lay inactive at Castel di Guido, convinced that until his division should be reinforced, it would be madness to risk another attack; and the Triumvirs allowed him to remain unmolested for the same reason that they had refrained from pushing their advantage on April 30, — they did not wish to exasperate France, but merely to prove to her that they would and could repel hostile interference. Almost immediately, however, they were threatened from another quarter. The Neapolitans, in two detachments, — one of regulars under Winspeare, and one of brigands and deserters under Zucchi, — were invading the Roman States from the south. Garibaldi went out against them and engaged in a skirmish at Palestrina (May 8-9), in which, though fighting with one man to three, he more than held his own. But the Triumvirs feared to send him assistance lest Oudinot should seize the opportunity to pounce on Rome, and he was consequently obliged to retire. At Fiumicino, at the mouth of the Tiber, a contingent of 4,000 Spaniards landed, there to combat malaria as best they could; in the north, the Austrians had invested Bologna, and were advancing along the Adriatic, but Oudinot warned them that as he intended to settle his quarrel with the Romans himself, they must keep out of Latium. Thus, in the early part of May, the Roman Republic was hemmed in by four armies. Here was being rehearsed in epitome the history of Rome for a thousand years, — her Pope, whom she rejected, calling in France, Austria, and Spain to crush her into submission. It was necessary that once again, and for the last time, the world should be convinced that the temporal power of the popes could be maintained by foreigners alone.

While Oudinot, who had without delay dispatched a

report of the combat of April 30 to Paris, was awaiting instructions, the Triumvirs did not omit to send special agents to both Paris and London to bespeak support. In France they hoped to arouse the sympathy of those French Republicans who perceived that, under the guise of Republicanism, the country was being bound hand and foot by the party of Reaction, behind which Louis Napoleon lay in ambush. Just as the French Revolution of 1830 had profited, not its originators, but the trickster Louis Philippe, so the Revolution of 1848 had slipped out of the control of its promoters, to serve the ambition of the Bonapartist trickster. The Constituent Assembly was on the point of dissolution, to be replaced by the Legislative Assembly. The Mountain, those Radicals who felt most keenly that they had been defrauded, were conspiring to bring back, by violence if necessary, the supremacy of genuine Republicanism. But besides them a large number of deputies were incensed when, on May 7, the ministers presented to the Assembly a report of Oudinot's baffled attack on Rome. Many who had voted money for the expedition, now turned in indignation upon the Cabinet and accused it of having cheated them. Some would even have impeached the Prince President for treason.[1]

The ministers defended themselves by declaring that Oudinot had been given no authority to march as an enemy against Rome; nevertheless, they persisted in representing the Roman Republic as a combination of outlaws from other parts of Italy and elsewhere, who not only did not embody the wishes of the citizens of the Papal States, but who actually prevented these from expressing their wishes. This assertion, frequently repeated at that time and for a long time afterward by French politicians, — even De Tocqueville repeated it, — was false;[2] as be-

[1] F. de Lesseps: *Recollections of Forty Years* (New York, 1888), 2.
[2] Mazzini's "Letter to De Tocqueville and Falloux" (reprinted in vol. v of his *Works*) disposes of this charge. As a masterpiece of invective, this letter has few superiors.

tween the Republic and the Papacy, three fourths of the
Papal inhabitants would choose the former. The British
might have declared in 1777 with equal speciousness that
the colony of Massachusetts was in the hands of outlaws
who did not represent the opinion of the "honest citizens,"
to wit, the Royalists. Jules Favre, in an impassioned
speech, repelled this charge. It was the French, he
said, not the Romans, who were foreigners at Rome.
He asked why a commission so vague that any enterprise
might be attempted had been given to Oudinot? He
indicted the ministers for having shed French and Italian blood in behalf of the Pope and of Absolutism.
"France," he concluded, "who sent her soldiers to America to combat English tyranny, was always, when guided
by men worthy of her, the champion of liberty and of
generous ideas. What have you made this France?
You have made it the policeman of Absolutism."[1] Under this indictment the ministers did not wince. On the
contrary, Odillon Barrot, the Premier, had no qualms of
conscience to prevent him from posing as a benefactor of
the Romans and as a jealous guardian of French honor.
He reiterated that it was absolutely necessary for France
"to put a weight in the scale in which the destiny of
Italy was vibrating; and to secure to the Romans the
conditions of a good government, a good liberty, — conditions which would have been changed by Reaction or by
foreign intervention." As if French intervention was
not foreign! He challenged any one to show proof that
the ministry had ordered Oudinot to attack the Republic;
a safe challenge, because he and his colleagues had taken
good care to trust no such order to writing. A committee of deputies, appointed to report on the situation,
after admitting that the Oudinot expedition had not fulfilled its original purpose, moved that the government be
invited "to take such measures as might be necessary to

[1] Farini, iv, 77.

enable the expedition to carry out the aim that had been assigned to it." This motion, which implied a want of confidence in the ministry, nevertheless passed by a vote of 388 to 240;[1] but the ministers did not resign; they knew, as the elections soon proved, that the majority of the country was unrepublican, and consequently on their side. With a show of repairing the mistakes thus far made they sent Ferdinand de Lesseps on a special mission to Rome.

De Lesseps is the only Frenchman officially connected with this affair who seems to have been honest; indeed, had he not been honest, or had he been more wary, he would never have accepted a task which he would have seen was unattainable. But when Drouyn de Lhuys and Louis Napoleon explained to him what he was to do, their plan seemed frank and feasible, and he pledged himself to accomplish it. In brief, he was to allay the ill-feeling which Oudinot's misjudged attack had aroused among the Romans, cause them to believe that France was their dearest friend, and persuade them to admit the French army into Rome; after which, the "honest citizens" would undoubtedly reorganize the government and effect a reconciliation with the Pope. While taking care to avoid wounding the susceptibilities of the Papal Court at Gaeta, he was also, if possible, to give no offense to the Roman Republicans. "You may remind them," said wily Louis Napoleon, "that I fought with them against the Temporal Power in 1831."[2] De Lesseps quitted Paris on May 10, and reaching the French camp five days later, he induced Oudinot to suspend hostilities whilst he negotiated with the Roman government. In his first interview with the Triumvirs, he found them desirous of preventing a rupture with the French. Mazzini with great address explained the situation to him. He showed how the Republic had established order in the land, and

[1] Bianchi, vi, 231.   [2] De Lesseps, 8.

how it truly represented the political aims of a vast majority of the inhabitants. The assertion that the Triumvirs imposed on the people a government which they would throw off if they could was, he said, false; there had just been municipal elections in the chief towns, and in every case the Republican candidates had been chosen; even those Romans who would prefer a constitutional monarchy to the Republic did not hesitate a moment to support the Republic against a restoration of the old Papal régime. "Remember," he said, "that a return to the past means neither more nor less than organized disorder, a renewal of the struggle of secret societies, the uprising of anarchy in the heart of Italy, the inoculation of vengeance into a people which is only desirous of forgetting, a brand of discord permanently implanted in the midst of Europe, the programme of the extreme parties supplanting the orderly Republican government of which we are now the organs."[1] De Lesseps, however, had strict instructions not to recognize the Triumvirate. He therefore cast about for an arrangement by which France, while peaceably securing control over the Roman State, might not destroy its independence. Accordingly, he proposed that the Triumvirs should resign and be replaced by a provisional government, appointed by the Assembly, until the country, in a general election, should signify what sort of administration should be permanently established and what guarantees should be given in favor of the Catholic religion and the Papacy.[2] To ask the Triumvirs to resign was fatuous. They existed by a right as incontestable as that by which Louis Napoleon himself was President of France, — they had been elected by forms which the majority of the people declared legal. Whether other men would have governed more wisely was not the question; if the wisest men alone are to hold office, then must the minority often rule the majority, for

[1] De Lesseps, 29. [2] Ibid, 30.

wise men are usually in the minority. Most of the historians, whether Italian or foreign, have blamed Mazzini for not accepting these terms which De Lesseps offered. They say that, instead of showing his devotion to Italy by an act of noble self-abnegation, he clutched power merely for the sake of power, and without regard for the misery which his stubbornness might entail on his countrymen. I cannot agree there. Let Mazzini's love of power be what it might, it is still possible to interpret his motives patriotically. He was actually the head of the Roman Republic; this no one denies. The deepest purpose of that Republic was to prevent the restoration of an Absolute government under the Pope. The French, who, uninvited, presumed to meddle in the affairs of the Romans, never guaranteed that the return of Pius should not involve the destruction of liberty; they never made this the condition on which they responded to his appeal for assistance; at the' utmost, they professed to believe that he would be too shrewd, if not too good-natured, to sweep away the constitutional privileges which he had granted and which had made him popular. For Mazzini, therefore, to have obliterated himself at the request, the very modest request, of the French, would have been equivalent to surrendering the Republic to the very doom which she sought to avert. It did not require wits as keen as his to discover that the French government was pursuing an underhand and disingenuous policy. What reason, then, had he to expect that, if he and his fellow "outlaws" resigned, the French would suddenly offer to the Roman State those pledges of independence which they had thus far artfully avoided giving? He had no right to shirk the responsibility which the Republic had conferred upon him; no right, by withdrawing, to leave her to the ruin which he, at least, saw impending over her.

De Lesseps, finding a reconciliation impossible on these terms, made the following proposal: The Romans shall demand the protection of France; they shall have the right to express themselves freely on the form of their government; they shall receive the French army into Rome, where the French and Roman troops shall unite to maintain order, and the Roman authorities shall act in accordance with their legal functions.[1] To this the Triumvirs replied that the Assembly did not understand why France insisted on occupying Rome. They had not invited French protection, because they felt quite able to protect themselves. Nevertheless, to show their friendliness towards the French Republic, they would vote to esteem the French troops as brothers, who were not, however, to enter the city unless especially requested to do so; provided the French Republic solemnly recognized the right of the Romans to settle their own affairs, and guaranteed to the Constituent Assembly power to conclude its work and to put into operation the Constitution it had framed.[2] This offer, made directly to Oudinot through the medium of Mr. Cass, the United States Minister, both Oudinot and De Lesseps rejected; the former being eager to cut short negotiations and avenge his recent defeat, the latter perceiving that to accept the Triumvirs' terms would be tantamount to recognizing the Republic. De Lesseps, however, still hoped to avert further bloodshed; moreover, having had good opportunity to inspect the armament of Rome, he prudently estimated that the French force was not yet strong enough to capture the city. So he offered a third series of proposals, — stipulating that the French army should enter Rome as a friend; should lodge in positions deemed most favorable for the defense of the city and most salubrious; should not meddle in the internal administration. If these offers were not accepted on or before May 30, the French would resume their liberty of action.[3] With diffi-

[1] De Lesseps, 38.   [2] Ibid, 40-41; Bianchi, vi, 234.
[3] Bianchi, vi, 234.

culty he prevailed on Oudinot to agree to postpone military operations until either the Romans had given an answer to this offer, or instructions had been telegraphed from Paris. Oudinot agreed, but the armistice did not restrain him from pushing forward his preparations, or from surprising the outposts on Monte Mario and occupying that position, as if there were no armistice in existence. Some lawless Frenchmen in Rome insulted one of the attachés to the French embassy, and De Lesseps believed that his own life was in danger. This led him to take a lurid view of things. Unable to move Mazzini, treated with a disrespect bordering on insult by Oudinot, wounded in his pride to see his mission failing, he nevertheless persisted to the end, out of his sympathy for the Romans. Against Mazzini personally, however, he seems to have been irritated to so high a degree that he denounced the obdurate Triumvir as "this modern Nero," "an enemy dangerous to society," a weaver of "dark and infernal plots," who, among other evidences of his wickedness, had had "frequent relations with English clergymen and Methodists!"[1] Even in the midst of the narration of these tragic events, we may pause to smile at the suggestion that a "modern Nero" should delight in the intercourse of Anglican parsons and Methodists! Hyperbole is sometimes a wonderful promoter of laughter.

But De Lesseps was, despite his comic outburst of passion, a loyal fellow, and when the Triumvirs replied to his third project, that they could only consent to permit the French troops to occupy positions outside the city, on condition that France would guarantee from foreign invasion the territory so occupied by them, he did not allow his personal hatred for Mazzini to hinder him from making one last effort for peace. In fact, he would have signed that counter-project, but Oudinot, in rage, refused to be a party to what he called an affront on French

[1] Perreus, 103.

honor, and actually proposed to reopen hostilities forthwith. De Lesseps declared that this would be contrary to the law of nations, since the truce had still several days to run. Oudinot cooled a little, and De Lesseps had time to draw up his fourth and final compromise, of which the following is an abstract: The French army shall be welcomed as an ally by the Romans; it shall be lodged in the city, but shall not interfere with internal affairs; the French Republic shall guarantee against foreign aggression the territory occupied by its troops; the present accord shall be ratified by the French Republic; not until fifteen days after the announcement that these terms have not been ratified shall they cease to operate.[1] This convention, presented to the Roman Assembly on May 29, was accepted by it that same evening. Oudinot, however, declared that he would not abide by terms in agreeing to which De Lesseps had, he asserted, overstepped his authority. The antagonism between the general and the envoy had become so bitter that, at one interview, De Lesseps had hardly restrained himself from drawing his sword; now he discovered that he had been the dupe of his government, which had been secretly abetting Oudinot's course. The long-expected dispatch came, bidding De Lesseps to return to Paris, as his mission was ended, and instructing Oudinot to lose no time in capturing Rome. So De Lesseps, who had acted in good faith throughout, went home to be reprimanded by the ministers who had lured him to undertake a negotiation which they did not wish should succeed. The three weeks consumed in this crafty intrigue had enabled them so to increase Oudinot's army that it was at once sufficiently strong to reduce Rome to subjection, and to deter the Austrians from interfering.

Whilst these negotiations were in progress, the Romans, secured by the armistice from aggression on the part of

[1] Bianchi, vi, 235; De Lesseps, 73.

the French, turned their attention to the Neapolitan army, which hovered among the Alban Hills. On the evening of May 16 the Roman troops marched out of the gate of St. John Lateran to force Bomba to fight. They were commanded by Joseph Roselli, an officer rather academic than experienced. His force, numbering about 12,000 men, was composed partly of regulars and partly of those corps or "legions" of volunteers that were to gain a picturesque renown in defending the Roman Republic. By far the most famous legion was that which Garibaldi led. This extraordinary man, of whom hitherto only brief mention has been made, had not yet completed his forty-second year. Born at Nice, July 4, 1807, he followed his father's calling as sea-captain until 1834, when, having been drawn into the conspiracies of Young Italy, he was forced to flee from Piedmont, where he was condemned to death in contumacy. Discerning no way in which he could promote the liberation of his native land, he crossed the Atlantic and plunged into the wild and variegated life of South America. For years he was lost to the knowledge of his countrymen, but gradually there came back to Europe reports of his daring exploits on the banks of the La Plata and the Parana. His wonderful courage, his romantic wooing, his hardships and his triumphs, sounded fabulous to the ears of commonplace Europe. Among the incessant brawls of Argentine and Uruguay, he was always on the side of the Republicans fighting against their would-be dictators, and when fortune turned against him he taught schoolboys their arithmetic, or herded cattle on the pampas. Going to Montevideo as a drover, he remained to direct the defense of that city during a long and memorable siege. And there it was that he heard of the election of Pius IX and of the new pope's amnesty, — news which impelled him to write to offer his services to Pius as the regenerator of Italy. No reply ever came to him, but early in

1848 he could no longer curb his desire to be at hand in the hour of Italy's redemption; accompanied by eighty-five "legionaries,"— fellow-exiles who had served under him in Uruguay,— he set sail for home. He reached Nice in June and hurried to Charles Albert's camp in the expectation of getting a commission. A strange meeting that, between the ex-tyrant and the ex-outlaw. But though the King was polite, he referred Garibaldi to the War Department, and the campaign was at its last stage before the impatient chieftain, irritated by official coolness and delays, gathered a corps of volunteers and began a guerrilla warfare along the lakes. After the Salasco armistice, he was soon forced to retire into Switzerland, whence he proceeded to the Papal States. Having been elected to the Roman Assembly, he went to Rome, and was the first to propose the immediate declaration of the Republic.

In person Garibaldi was of medium height, thickset and of great physical endurance, as became a man whose life had been passed in the saddle and among incessant hardships, although he was a frequent sufferer from rheumatism. His eyes were dark, his beard and hair were tawny. He wore the red blouse of the South American *guacho*, and a loosely-flowing white mantle. In character he was the most transparent of men, hiding neither his admiration nor his hatred, giving free play to his emotions, easily swayed on the surface, but cleaving immovably to his dominant purpose. Generous and humane, fond of applause, but fonder still of love, he inspired among men of the most various temperaments love that nothing could shake and devotion that fell little short of idolatry. In his simple but strong passions and frank egotism, he reminds us of the Homeric heroes, — of Achilles or of Diomed; in his romantic and chivalrous temper he recalls Roland or the Cid. Never was knight-errant more loyal to his vows to relieve distress and to battle against injustice. Freedom was his ideal, to be fought for in all lands and against any odds, but especially in Italy; she was the mistress of his endeavor, her freedom the embodiment of his ideal, and it is a proof of Garibaldi's good sense and unselfishness that he was always ready to subordinate his personal preference and to join any party, Royalist or Republican, which made her independence its aim. Writing about him, historians cannot refrain from exchanging the sober statements of history for the glowing rhapsodies of poetry; but, indeed, there is no need to seek aid of Pegasus. Garibaldi's life was epic; nothing commonplace could befall him; his deeds were irradiated by inner fires, and even trifles coming within the range of his personality took on the hue of romance. Posterity, looking back upon our age, which is accused of being materialist and commercial, will point to Garibaldi as evidence that the heart of nations can always be thrilled by a man who appeals by his example, not to their pocket nor their prejudice, but to their noblest instincts. Round this man, who while still alive enjoyed the worship and cast the spell of a legendary hero, flocked volunteers of all classes and ages, united by their common devotion to him. No condottiere of the Renaissance — neither Braccio nor Sforza nor Carmagnola had so complete control over his men as Garibaldi had over his Italian Legion. He promoted, or reduced to the ranks, and was equally beloved. His camp had the aspect of a Paraguayan bivouac: the soldiers, in strange garb, seated about the fires at which they roasted great cuts of beef or mutton; the horses allowed to wander untethered, to be captured by the lasso when needed; little baggage; little apparent discipline, yet real alertness and absolute obedience. Veterans toughened and bronzed by years of campaigning under the Southern Cross, youths fired by patriotism, poets, vagabonds, adventurers, from all parts of Italy and from most parts of

Europe, came to fight under Garibaldi's leadership; even young women, fascinated by the renown of this romantic chieftain, put on uniform, and begged to serve in his troop; even boys formed a company, and were proud to be allowed to follow his footsteps. He was not a great general, though he aspired to be one, but he was master in the art of guerrilla warfare; vigilant, untiring, fearless, he fought as the eagle pounces, or the tiger leaps. Devotion to Italy, abiding confidence in himself, courage and endurance, — these were the sentiments he inspired in all his followers.

On the second expedition against the Neapolitans, Garibaldi's Legion formed the vanguard, and on the morning of May 19 it fell in with the enemy's outposts near Velletri. Without waiting for reinforcements or for orders from the Commander-in-Chief, Roselli, who was several miles behind, Garibaldi decided to hold his ground, although it soon became evident that the Bourbon forces were in great strength, whilst his legion numbered only two thousand men. At the first assault, the Neapolitan cavalry broke through the Garibaldian line, but it was soon compelled to retreat, being showered upon by the red-shirted marksmen dispersed among the vineyards, and to take shelter under the walls of Velletri. Garibaldi then wished to make a flank movement upon a corps of Neapolitans commanded by Bomba himself on the other side of the town; but Roselli, who had now come up, was over-cautious, and restricted his operations until nightfall to an engagement with the enemy in front. The battle was inconclusive, but during the night Bomba withdrew his troops from Velletri, and retired by way of Terracina into his own dominion.[1] The fame of the Garibaldians spread terror among the superstitious Neapolitans, who regarded those strange warriors much as the Aztecs regarded Cortez's little band; believing

[1] Mariani, ii, 411-12; Guerzoni: *Garibaldi* (Florence, 1889), i, 285-91.

that they possessed some charm which made them invulnerable, to offset which many of the Neapolitans wore talismans and amulets furnished by their priests.[1] Garibaldi proposed that the Roman army should march after the retreating Bourbons, and believed that his presence would suffice to fire a general insurrection in Bomba's kingdom; but although the Triumvirs were not unfavorable to this scheme, the ever-prudent Roselli disapproved of it. Garibaldi did, indeed, make a raid southward, but before he had achieved his purpose he was recalled to Rome. The imminence of an attack by the French required the concentration at the capital of all the forces of the Republic.

Those forces numbered about 18,600 men, of whom 16,400 were citizens of the Papal States, 1,850 were natives of other parts of Italy, and the remainder were foreigners, — Poles, Frenchmen, Germans, and Americans.[2] The regular army numbered about 11,000, including the two battalions of Lombard sharpshooters under the gallant Manara; the irregulars were made up of bands of free lances, — divers in uniform, quality, and discipline. Most conspicuous among them were Garibaldi's legionaries, who competed with Manara's plumed sharpshooters for the first place in honor and popularity. Then there were a legion of 300 university students under Major Rosselli, and another of as many exiles under Arcioni; Medici had his legion of 300; Milbitz commanded 200 Poles; Gérard commanded the foreign legion of 120. Preparations for the defense had been pushed with vigor. The walls along the Janiculum, in which quarter the French attack was expected, had been strengthened. All the gates were barricaded. Whatever may have been the doubts of cool-headed Romans who watched these preparations for resistance, the sol-

[1] Guerzoni, i, 276.
[2] F. Torre: *Intervento Francese in Roma nel* 1849 (Turin, 1851), i, 250.

diers themselves were eager to fight; each troop being inspired by the enthusiasm of a leader, who, like the chieftain of a Scottish clan, stood in peculiar personal relations towards it. There was, perhaps, less general subordination than there should have been. A majority of the volunteers and probably of the regulars would have preferred Garibaldi as their commander-in-chief; Garibaldi himself had frequent disagreements with Roselli, and never hesitated to express his contempt for Mazzini's interference in military affairs. Roselli's supporters, on the other hand, would have had Garibaldi cashiered for insubordination in his recent hazardous exploit at Velletri, where he had exposed without instructions, not only his brigade but the entire corps to disaster. The truth is that Garibaldi, like Nelson, took risks which, had they been unsuccessful, would have merited punishment by court-martial; he could not be bound by the laws of military etiquette; his unique value as a condottiere depended upon his freedom to act without restraint. And this is true also, though in a smaller degree, of the captains of the other legions. Remembering this fact, we cannot judge the defenders of Rome by the same standard we should apply to an ordinary army, and we shall be surprised, not that there was discordance among the various elements, but that there was sufficient harmony to carry on a really effective resistance.

The French army had been augmented during De Lesseps's negotiations to the limit of 35,000 men. Oudinot, on June 1, announced his intention of renewing hostilities; Roselli, the Roman general, asked for a prolongation of the truce for another fortnight; Oudinot replied that he could not grant this request, as he had instructions from Paris to enter Rome as soon as he could, but that he would defer his attack on the town until the morning of Monday, June 4. Great, therefore, was the astonishment of the 400 Romans who were guarding the

Villa Pamfili when at three o'clock in the morning of June 3, they were awakened by the onset of the French. Oudinot, by this perfidy, literally stole a march on his adversaries. Striking them unprepared, he captured half of the detachment, and drove the rest back to the Vascello, a massive building just outside the gate of San Pancrazio and commanding the two roads which lead into the city by that gate. The noise of the conflict soon brought reinforcements to the hard-pressed Romans. Garibaldi hastened to the scene and directed for fourteen hours a defense which lacked nothing in heroism. To recover and hold the Villa Pamfili and the Corsini Casino of the Four Winds was, he knew, indispensable, as those buildings with their surrounding walls served as strong outworks for the protection of the Roman line. Four times during the day, therefore, he hurled his men at those positions; four times they recaptured the Casino; and four times they were driven back. The French, vastly superior in numbers but not in bravery, kept at evening the position they had treacherously seized at dawn. Many an intrepid Italian lost his life in that day's battle: Masina, nicknamed "the Italian Murat;" Enrico Dandolo, shot down treacherously by the French, who pretended that they wished to parley; Goffredo Mameli, the blond-haired young poet who, like the German Körner, wrote the war-songs of his people;[1] Daverio, Pollini, Melara, — these and many more disabused Oudinot of his notion that the Italians would not fight.

The French having by treachery captured the approaches to the San Pancrazio gate, as they had earlier seized Monte Mario, now laid formal siege to that part of Rome which lies beyond the Tiber. Day by day, they drew their lines of intrenchments nearer, gaining ground

[1] Mameli, mortally wounded on June 3, lingered in the hospital till July 6; see a sympathetic sketch of him in Countess Cesaresco's *Italian Characters*.

yard by yard, constantly having to repel the attempts of the Romans to drive them back. Oudinot poured an incessant shower of bombs into the city; and although he had instructions to spare the monuments, he could not prevent a stray shot now and then from falling among them. The dome of St. Peter's was struck several times; a shell injured one of Raphael's works in the Vatican, another crashed through the ceiling on which Guido Reni painted his Aurora. The Romans maintained the defense with admirable courage. Time after time they made sorties, but though they might temporarily win an advantage, the superiority of the French in numbers, discipline, and equipment prevailed in the end. For more than three weeks Medici held the Vascello, the ship-like edifice, against the storm of shot and frequent assaults. In the city the Triumvirs and the various committees worked unceasingly to furnish supplies to the troops, and to sustain the enthusiasm of the inhabitants. The Assembly sat in permanence. And yet no one could disguise from himself the fact that to a contest so unequal there could be but one conclusion. Hope of succor from the outside, there was none. The French Republic, whose vanity was staked to carry through this lawless enterprise, had unlimited means and could, if necessary, double or treble Oudinot's army. And if France desisted, Austria would advance. She had subdued Bologna after a gallant resistance, she had captured Ancona, her troops were in Umbria and the Marches. The Spanish contingent lay at Fiumicino, ready to take a hand in the Pope's restoration. Bomba, though scared away from Velletri, would return in stronger force at the first hopeful sign.

Nevertheless, Mazzini persisted in maintaining the defense. At first he kept up hopes by intimating that there was still a chance that England would interpose, — a delusive expectation. On May 23 Palmerston said to Marioni, the Roman envoy who appealed for British aid:

"Advise those who govern the Republic to treat at least with France, and quickly, with frankness and for possible conditions. . . . Accept the Pope with a large and real Constitution, with an unfettered press and every guarantee for liberty and future progress, with the express condition of the total and perpetual separation of the ecclesiastical and secular powers. Make one condition, *sine qua non*, that of the secularization of the government. It is my opinion that the French government, whatever may be its future ministry, will mediate on these terms, and make the Pope and his supporters accept them, even unwillingly. . . . For the present, content yourselves with what is possible: if you refuse, you will rue it, you will greatly rue it."[1] Rusconi, sent to London to urge Palmerston to act as mediator, got similar advice, and no more encouragement. "The English statesmen," he wrote, "do not look kindly upon a republic in the heart of Italy." Disappointed in this quarter, Mazzini still clung to the slender hope that the French Assembly would ratify the compact which De Lesseps, just previous to his departure, had drawn up; but the French Assembly had dissolved, and the French ministry, manipulated by Louis Napoleon, censured De Lesseps, and bade Oudinot make all speed to capture Rome. Nothing now could change the policy of France except a counter-revolution, and that Ledru-Rollin and the Mountain attempted on June 13, only to be quickly suppressed. Thenceforth, Mazzini could give the Romans no reasonable excuse for prolonging their struggle, and yet both he and they would not think of surrendering. Those critics who have disparaged his administration of the Roman Republic have yet to explain how it was that he persuaded the Romans to maintain a desperate defense for nearly thirty days. Confusion increased, there were many murmurers, many who were for abandoning the task; but he held the majority with him until the 30th of June.

[1] Farini. iv, 141.

By that time the Vascello had been demolished, the gate of San Pancrazio had been taken by the French, the Roman troops were at bay within the walls. When the Assembly met, Cernuschi declared that further resistance was impossible. Mazzini, pallid with excitement, replied that he saw three courses open to them: they might capitulate, which would be ignoble; they might imitate the Saragossans, and die resisting; or they might cut a path through the French lines, and retire with the Assembly and government into the provinces. There was silence, no man wishing to be the first to speak in favor of either of the latter alternatives. Then General Bartolucci announced that he had just received word from Garibaldi that the Trasteverine district could no longer be held. Garibaldi himself, summoned by a messenger, came blood-bespattered and dusty into the hall, and repeated what he had written to Bartolucci. The French occupied the heights and could at any moment drive the Romans across the Tiber; rather than undertake a defense of the old city, which could be defended at the longest for only a few days, he proposed that they should retreat to the mountains. The Assembly accordingly passed Cernuschi's motion, and empowered the Municipality to make terms with the French.[1] But Mazzini and his colleagues, unwilling to be parties to the surrender, resigned their office as Triumvirs, and were replaced by Saliceti, Mariani, and Calandrelli. The Municipality offered to capitulate on condition that though the French should occupy Rome, they should not meddle in its political affairs; but Oudinot, instead of listening to these proposals, exacted terms so severe that General Vaillant, the French general to whom the greatest credit belonged for conducting the siege, exclaimed, "What! shall the French grant less to Rome than the Austrians granted to Bologna or to Ancona?"[2] Oudinot, however, would not budge. When

[1] Farini, iv. 202.   [2] Perrens, 111.

his answer was delivered to the inhabitants, they were so infuriated that they were ready to fight till extermination; but the new Triumvirs united with the more prudent members of the Assembly to appease them and to stay further bloodshed. Nothing now remained to do but to await the entry of the conquering army. Mazzini and the more deeply compromised of the Republican leaders would not do that; Garibaldi and the foremost soldiers would not do that. The former departed under the protection of the foreign consuls; the latter, reviewing the troops in St. Peter's Place on July 1, said to them: "I offer you new battles, and new glory, at the cost of hardships and great perils; let him who has heart, let him who still has faith in the fortunes of Italy, follow me! We have tinged our finger in French blood, let us plunge our hand in Austrian blood!" Five thousand men pledged themselves to follow him, and on the next evening they marched out from the gate of St. John Lateran, and disappeared across the Campagna.[1] The story of their wanderings through the mountains, of their escape from French and Austrian pursuers, of their gradual dwindling in number, and of their final disbanding, belongs properly to the biography of Garibaldi, and may be read in an incomparable chapter of his "Memoirs." The end had come for the Roman Republic, and their escape in no wise affected her fate. The Assembly showed to the last a certain stately gravity worthy of the Eternal City; they celebrated the obsequies, and voted aid to the families, of the dead; they accorded the right of citizenship to every one who had defended the city; then, on July 3, having proclaimed on the Capitol the new Constitution, — as a man on his deathbed makes his will, — they remained calmly at their posts until the French army, which took possession of Rome on that morning, came and dispersed them.

[1] Hofstetter: *Giornale delle Cose di Roma nel* 1849 (Turin, 1851), 331-3.

Thus, unbefriended, succumbed the Roman Republic of 1849, which Europe had connived to treat as a conspiracy of bandits and foreigners, and which she could not fail to annihilate. But all her efforts only made the valor of the Republicans shine the brighter. That they had fought, and fought bravely, for seventy days withstanding the foremost military Power in Europe, unterrified by the menaces of Austria, Naples, and Spain, — that was a fact which neither Pius's imprecations nor Antonelli's guile, nor the Machiavellian slurs of Louis Napoleon could obscure. The world by a vital instinct cleaves to heroic deeds. It turns from the spectacle of Pius and his cardinals and the agents of European diplomacy looking down in sleek and cynical security from Gaeta, like some old emperor and his cronies upon a gladiatorial combat; it turns from them in pity if not in contempt, for there is nothing noble in their behavior; it turns from them to the gladiators, and finds, in the example of Manara dying at the breach, of Morosini and Dandolo and hundreds of others killed in the heat of battle, manifestations of heroism and devotion, — the two qualities which best fit men for life and for death.

CHAPTER VI.

VENICE ALONE.

WHEN the Pope's legates celebrated Oudinot's capture of the Holy City, and hailed him as Charlemain's peer, there remained in Italy, outside of Piedmont, only one spot untrampled by the forces of victorious Reaction. That spot was Venice, the last stay and refuge of Republican valor. During the winter her condition, although not yet desperate, had been hard. The Austrian lines invested her by land, leaving in her possession the islands of the lagune, and the little strip of shore on which she held the fortress of Marghera. By sea, there was only a partial blockade, so that she occasionally got provisions from blockade-runners, but this method was both precarious and expensive. The cold that winter was unusually severe; fuel gave out, and food was scarce. The Austrians had not included Venice in the terms of the Salasco armistice, so that she had to be prepared at any moment to repel an attack on her outposts. Yet in spite of all these hardships and dangers, she maintained her resolute attitude and tolerated no suggestion of compromise, no whisper of surrender.

The Triumvirs, Manin, Cavedalis, and Graziani, were incessant in their efforts to stimulate the fortitude of the citizens, to preserve order, to raise money, to complete the preparations for defense, and to distribute supplies as equally and economically as possible. Rarely has any city displayed greater harmony than was displayed by Venice in these trying times. On February 15 a new Assembly met, and having declared the dictatorship which

had been conferred on Manin and his colleagues at an
end, it gave them extraordinary powers to conduct the
defense. As time went on, however, and brought no
prospect, either of help from outside or of arranging a
satisfactory peace with Austria, a minority began to
murmur against the burdens heaped upon them, and they
proposed, by getting rid of Manin, to set up a government
which should pursue a different policy. But the
masses rose in anger at this scheme, and threatened to
invade the Assembly; nor could they be appeased until
Manin went down into the square of St. Mark's and said
to them, "If you love me, if you are Italians, disperse."[1]
Two days later, on March 7, the Assembly elected him
President of the Republic, and thenceforth he exercised
dictatorial power, with such firmness and justice that the
partisans of reaction, relatively few in number, were
silenced. Under his patriotic leadership, Venice presented
a united front to the world which hemmed her in.

Internal concord, resolution, courage, these were, indeed,
indispensable; but Manin knew that, though these
were the qualities without which no stable government
could be established, they could not of themselves bring
independence. Venice shared the misfortune common to
Italy, of being surrounded by a Europe which insisted
that living men must submit to conditions which men
long dead had, willingly or unwillingly, and under a
different social and political system, accepted. And
since the living could not make their rights respected
nor carry out their desires, unless they had force behind
them, Manin's chief endeavors had been from the first to
secure the protection of France and England. During
the months of weary and insincere mediation his agents
Tommaseo and Pasini had poured their appeals into the
foreign ministries at London and Paris. Lord Palmerston
offered them sympathy but no encouragement; he

[1] *Memoriale Veneto*, 163.

was too genuine an Englishman not to admire pluck, — and surely the spectacle of little Venice braving colossal Austria was plucky enough, — but he felt no sentimental impulse to interfere in behalf of the weaker combatant. The blotting out of a little republic was of small concern to him, compared with the preservation of peace and the reëstablishment of tranquillity, on which John Bull's commercial prosperity depended. While, therefore, he frequently praised the courage and orderliness of the Venetians, he warned them that their resistance would be fruitless, and that the sooner they came to an understanding with Austria, the better it would be. At the most, he used his influence to dissuade Austria from reopening war against Venice until the mediating Powers had concluded their work.

France, on the other hand, gave the Venetian envoys more hope. As long as Bastide was Foreign Minister, he expressed friendliness for their cause and left upon them the impression that, although he would not pledge himself, still he might be counted upon to support them in an extremity. But they could get no official recognition, and when, after the French elections in December, Bastide was superseded by Drouyn de Lhuys, they received even less verbal encouragement than before. Tommaseo went home, leaving Pasini, a far abler diplomat, to plead his country's cause. His zeal was combined with rare common-sense and tact, and if arguments or entreaties could have moved France and England to a generous deed, the independence of Venice would have been assured. He followed every twist and turn of eelish diplomacy, and always met it in the front. When England declared that she accepted the Treaty of Vienna as the basis of Europe's international policy, he asked how it was that England had permitted Austria to violate that treaty in destroying the freedom of Cracow. If England made an exception in favor of despotism in 1846, why

should she do less for liberty in 1849? The violation of
the treaty in behalf of Venice might in a measure offset
the cruelty done at Cracow. To the French minister,
bent on suppressing the Roman Republic, Pasini held up
Article V of the new Constitution, and he asked whether
France, plotting to restore an odious government at Rome
and willing to allow the Austrians to return to Venice,
would tolerate an attempt on the part of foreigners to
restore the Bourbons and their Henry V? By his consistency and scrupulous attention to legality, for which
European Cabinets professed the deepest reverence, he
showed how flimsy their reverence was. Pasini knew, of
course, that his appeal to consistency would have no
effect, but that if he omitted to make it, Diplomacy would
allege his omission as an excuse for its own injustice.
He touched the chord of self-interest, he tried to rouse
now the national pride and now the generosity of France
and England, and in all ways worked so loyally yet so
judiciously that he won the personal respect of the very
men who would not officially support him. His diplomatic correspondence, as a French historian remarked,[1]
deserves to be placed beside the *Relations* of the old-time
Venetian ambassadors, those pioneers in modern statecraft.

The upshot of all his activity was that by the middle
of March the Venetian government believed that the
Western Powers, especially France, would do more for
Venice than they cared formally to pledge. Manin had
been cautious in dealing with the Roman Republic, as
he did not wish to compromise Venice by meddling in an
affair which, he foresaw, would involve an international
dispute. He likewise held aloof from the Tuscan imbroglio after the Grand Duke's flight. Recognizing that
Piedmont must be the chief military agent in expelling
the Austrians, he gradually drew into friendlier relations

[1] Henri Martin. quoted by Errera. 188, note 3.

with Piedmont, and in this Gioberti met him half way. At length, on March 14, he received news that Charles Albert had broken the armistice. It behooved Venice, which had during the past four months remained on the defensive, to take the field, in order to divert the attention of the Austrians. Accordingly, General William Pepe, the commander-in-chief of the Venetian troops, planned an assault on Conche, a position on the Brenta, which was successfully captured on March 21. But the Austrians returned in greater force and retook Conche; then Pepe, anxious not to mark the beginning of his campaign by a defeat, sent reinforcements, who again drove out the enemy, and pursued him as far as Santa Margherita. Satisfied with this advantage, at best inconclusive, the Venetians retired within their lines. On March 22, the anniversary of the proclamation of the Republic, there was a great festival in Venice: the Cardinal Patriarch celebrated mass in St. Mark's and implored divine aid in behalf of the city, which, he said, was "the cradle and citadel of liberty, and had become the refuge of Italian hopes;" Manin reviewed the troops in the Piazza, and besought them neither to grow insolent through victory, nor to be cast down by defeat.[1] Five days later he received from Haynau, who commanded the Austrian army of investment, notice of the rout of Charles Albert at Novara, and a summons to surrender. Manin kept the news secret as long as possible; then, on April 2, when there was no longer any doubt of its exactness, he announced it to the Assembly. "What do you wish to do?" he asked the deputies. "We expect the government to make its proposition," some one replied. "Do you wish to resist?" asked Manin. "Yes," was the unanimous response. "At any cost?" "At any cost." "Will you give the government unlimited power to direct the resistance, and to repress, in case of need, even

---

[1] La Farina, iv, 521.

those who might attempt to prevent us from resisting?"
"We will," shouted the deputies to a man; and then they
voted to resist Austria at any cost, and to confer unlimited power on Manin.[1] The President left the hall and
told the multitudes in the Piazza the result of the Assembly's deliberation, and they enthusiastically approved.
A red flag, symbol that Venice would fight to the death,
was unfurled from the bell-tower of St. Mark's, and a
copy of the decree was sent, without comment, to Haynau.

Venice, having thrown down the gauntlet, prepared in
earnest to defend herself. She had about 16,000 infantry soldiers, besides 7,000 Civic Guards; 2,000 artillerymen, to serve 560 cannon; and 4,000 men in her navy.
As at Rome, there was great diversity of organization,
owing to the presence of bands or "legions" of volunteers, and to the lack of a first-rate commander; for,
though General Pepe was brave and willing, he was inexperienced in siege warfare, and both too old and too
opinionated to learn quickly. The engineer corps numbered only 250 men, — too few for the great work they
had to do. The troops had suffered throughout the winter for want of sufficient food and clothing and proper
quarters; many of the forts among which they were distributed lay in low, miasmatic places, so that at times
nearly half of the army was on the sick-list.[2] But in
spite of these grave defects, concord and patriotic zeal
pervaded all branches of the service, and hopes ran high.
The unique situation of Venice among her lagunes
seemed to justify the belief in her impregnability. At
only one point could she be approached from the mainland, — by the recently completed railway bridge, a magnificent viaduct thirty-six hundred metres in length,
starting from near Mestre and touching the westernmost

---

[1] Bonghi, 576.
[2] Le Masson: *Venise en 1848 et 1849* (Lugano, 1851), 129-34.

edge of the city. Seawards she was protected by three long, narrow sand-bars, running nearly north and south, the southernmost bar being separated from the shore only by the river Brenta. Along these bars many small forts and batteries had been planted, and the passage of the Brenta was defended by the fortifications of Brondolo. The lagunes, inclosed between the sand-bars and the sea, were unnavigable except for small boats, steered by men familiar with the sinuous and shallow channels. The shore itself, for a long distance inland, was a labyrinth of marshes, pools, and canals, — a haunt for creatures of web-foot or fin, but untenable for soldiers. If, therefore, Venice could defend the approaches by the railway bridge and at Brondolo, and if she could prevent a blockade by sea, she would be as impregnable as Gibraltar. Unfortunately, her fleet was relatively inferior to her army, not through downright neglect, but through the inexperience and incompetence of those who had charge of its construction, and through the general failure to realize early enough that communication by sea must be kept open or the city would starve. The approach to Venice by the railway bridge, on the contrary, was most carefully fortified. Half way from Mestre to the water's edge, the massive fort of Marghera commanded both the railway and the canal leading to Venice. The inner works formed an irregular pentagon, surrounded by a fosse; the outer works, likewise girdled by a fosse, had six bastions. Three lunettes, facing westward, facilitated a sortie in front; a ravelin on the easterly side guarded communications with the lagune.[1] To the north, about 500 metres away, was a smaller redoubt, protected by a basin, and called Fort Manin; to the south, beyond the railway, was Fort Rizzardi, both connecting with Marghera by a covered way. Just at the margin of the lagune, a third defense, the small fort of San Giuliano,

[1] La Farina, iv, 525.

protected Marghera on the rear. Throughout the winter the Venetians had endeavored to strengthen Marghera, the key to their city, and during the month of April, when the Austrian army of investment was getting ready to attack, they pushed on their works so efficiently that, despite certain defects, — most of the garrison, for instance, had to quarter in tents and wooden sheds, — they had completed a most formidable fortification.

The Austrians advanced slowly, being in no hurry to begin active operations against Venice, which they regarded as an easy prey, and preferring to finish their subjugation of Lombardy and to "restore order" in Tuscany and the Legations before they turned their attention to her. They reckoned, moreover, that every day's delay would reduce the provisions and wear out the courage of the Venetians, and so hasten their surrender. During April, therefore, both sides equipped themselves for the contest. Manin, meanwhile, renewed his diplomatic appeals to France and England. He knew that without help from the outside Venice could not long endure; therefore he tried all ways to persuade the Western Powers to intercede. He declared to them that Venice would accept any arrangement except that which aimed at handing her back to Austrian tyranny. The old proposition that she should be constituted a free port, or Hanseatic town, was revived; but both Palmerston and Drouyn de Lhuys shook their heads. He was willing to give her up either to France or England,[1] but again they remained impassive. Palmerston wrote that, as England would abide by the Treaty of Vienna, which assigned Venice to Austria, the Venetians had better make terms as speedily as possible with their legitimate sovereign.[2] Then Manin authorized Pasini to negotiate for the creation of a separate Lombardo-Venetian kingdom, under a Constitutional Government, as had been promised by the Austrian em-

[1] Errera, 177.   [2] Ibid, 180.

peror a year before. Pasini defended this proposal with all his might, showing how well a similar arrangement had worked in the case of Belgium, yet he could not move the French minister. "France will never help us with arms," he wrote on April 19; "she believes it impossible to obtain the absolute independence of Venice, nor is she disposed to attempt it; she sees no adjustment possible except one whereby Austria may save her vanity (*amor proprio*), to which she greatly holds." Nevertheless, he intimated that, if Venice persevered in her resistance, some event might come to pass in the unsettled condition of Europe that would dispose France to change her attitude.[1] The hope that out of the European confusion there might still issue salvation justified Manin, as it justified Mazzini, in prolonging a struggle which would otherwise have been a needless expenditure of money and men. Especially to the Hungarians, who had succeeded in beating the Austrian armies sent against them, did the Venetians look for military help. Kossuth wrote Manin to hold out, for the Hungarians intended to march to the Adriatic and attack the Austrian forces in Venetia. It was believed that the Republicans in Germany were about to rise again; Prussia and Austria were bickering, perhaps they might go to war; in France, too, a revolution might explode at any moment, and, after all, though France protested that she would not interfere, who could tell? If Venice surrendered now, she would forfeit whatever she had gained by her year of independence; she would also forfeit whatever advantage any of these contingencies might bring forth. Immediate submission would be no guarantee of better treatment from Austria, who meted out equal punishment to those who surrendered early and those who resisted up to the eleventh hour; indeed, if Austria discovered that Venice was no easy capture, she might of herself abate her exces-

[1] Bonghi, 586-7.

sive terms. Therefore, although Manin got no encouragement from the mediating Powers, he felt authorized to maintain the defense, and the Venetians unanimously approved of his determination.

By the first of May the Austrian army under Haynau, who had come red-handed from Brescia, numbered 30,000 men. A first line of trenches was begun at a distance of about 1,000 metres from Marghera, and on May 4 seven batteries, consisting of sixty pieces of artillery, opened fire on that fortress and on Fort Rizzardi. The Austrians expected but little resistance, for they had no higher opinion of the valor of the Venetians than Oudinot had had of Roman valor. Radetzky himself, accompanied by a bevy of archdukes, came out from Mestre, as on a pleasure party, to witness an easy victory. He knew, of course, that Venice would be hard to take if properly defended, but he did not imagine that the Venetians had either the pluck or the military skill to defend her. His pleasure party, however, miscarried. The garrison of Marghera, some 2,500 men, commanded by Colonel Ulloa, a young Neapolitan, returned the Austrian fire with unslackening vigor, and for several hours a tremendous cannonade lasted. The Venetians watched the contest from the roofs and towers of the city, or ventured in boats as near as they dared to the mainland. When night came and the firing ceased, the Austrians had suffered much damage to their ordnance; Ulloa, on the contrary, had had only three of his 120 guns injured, and only four men killed.[1] The jubilation of the soldiers and citizens was heightened the next day by the cessation of hostilities on the part of the Austrians. Radetzky, having recognized that the Venetians were both able and willing to resist, decided to parley. He sent to them an address in which he said: "To-day, I do not come as a warrior or as

[1] Le Masson, 166–7; La Farina, iv. 527; *Mem. Ven.*, 181–2. During the day the Austrians discharged 4,000 projectiles, and the Venetians 9,000.

a victorious general, — I wish to speak to you as a father. There has passed over you a year of troubles, of revolutionary and anarchical disturbances, and what are the consequences? The public treasury exhausted; private means lost; your flourishing city reduced to the last extreme, plunged into the abyss of misery. . . . You will be abandoned soon or late to the mercy of the victor! I have come from my headquarters at Milan to exhort you for the last time, — an olive-branch in one hand, if you listen to the voice of reason; the sword in the other, ready to inflict on you the scourge of war even to extermination if you persist in the path of rebellion, which would deprive you of every right to the clemency of your legitimate sovereign!" He then demanded the unconditional surrender of the city and lagunes, offering pardon to the soldiers and under-officers, and permission to any Venetian to depart unmolested. Not a word concerning a constitution! Not a reference to political rights! While awaiting a reply, he suspended the cannonade until eight o'clock on the following morning. Manin lost no time in returning an answer; merely referring Radetzky to the reply already given Haynau a month before, and adding that he had bespoken the good offices of England and France as mediators, but that he was ready to treat directly with the Austrian ministry for terms which the Venetians would ratify. He left it to the marshal to decide whether or not hostilities should be interrupted and needless bloodshed avoided, during the negotiations. Radetzky's rejoinder was evidently written with the hand that held, not the olive-branch but the sword. "His Majesty our Sovereign," he said, "having determined never to permit the intervention of foreign Powers between him and his rebellious subjects, any such hope of the Revolutionary Government of Venice is illusory, vain, and made only to deceive the poor inhabitants. From now onwards, therefore, any further correspondence ceases, and I deplore that Venice has to endure the fortunes of war."[1] On May 6 the Austrians resumed their cannonade.

To capture Marghera was henceforth the sole aim of the Austrian commander. Perceiving that his first parallel was too far away to enable his guns to demolish the fort, he ordered the excavation of a second parallel 500 metres nearer; but until the trenches were far advanced, his men had to work by night, because by day the batteries from Marghera swept the low plain. The garrison saw the earthworks grow in spite of all its efforts. Ulloa, intrepid, tireless, resourceful, left no means untried for impeding the enemy's work. He led a sortie, but the force at his disposal was too small to do more than drive in the Austrian skirmish line; he cut through a dike and flooded the fields in which the second parallel was drawn, and this proved a serious impediment, because, until the water could be got out and the dike repaired, the Austrian sappers stood in water up to their waists. Hundreds of them fell sick, many to die at Mestre, many more to be carried to the hospitals at Padua and Vicenza. But notwithstanding all hindrances, the trenches were dug, and on May 24 eleven new batteries belched shot and shell on the fort. All that day and the next Ulloa returned a vigorous fire; but at such short range nothing could withstand the Austrian bombardment. The casemates fell in, the bastions crumbled, the palisades connecting Marghera with the redoubts were battered down, the artillerists had to carry cannon-balls and sacks of powder on their shoulders; but neither Ulloa nor his men thought of abandoning the defense. And now their munitions ran low. On the morning of the 26th a barge laden with fresh supplies was sunk, and only with great difficulty could the shells be recovered from the shallow water. Nevertheless, Ulloa maintained so stubborn a

[1] Errera, 309-12.

resistance that the Austrians dared not venture to storm his works. Then the government at Venice, realizing that Marghera must soon succumb, ordered Ulloa to withdraw from it. Some of his men wept bitterly at being obliged to abandon a position they were still eager to defend. The evacuation was effected so quietly in the night of May 26–27 that on the following morning, when no guns thundered from Marghera, the Austrians were astonished. Cautiously advancing, they entered the fort, which they found in ruins, its guns spiked, its store of ammunition exhausted. The three weeks' defense had cost the Venetians above four hundred men in killed and wounded.[1]

Having been driven from their outer lines, the Venetians now prepared to defend the railway bridge. It would have been prudent to demolish that structure, but the government, unwilling to authorize its total destruction, consented to the blowing up of only nineteen arches. The bridge was divided into six sections by five broad *piazzali* or platforms, placed at equal distances along its course. Ulloa occupied the central platform and converted it into a miniature fort, covering its granite sides and front with two layers of sand-bags, and erecting a battery. His position was strengthened by the presence of mortar-boats on each side of the bridge, and by the small fort of San Secondo, which lay on a tiny island to the north of the bridge, and 500 metres towards the east.

Eight hundred feet of clear water, pierced here and there by the débris of the ruined arches, separated Fort Sant' Antonio, as the Venetians called the central *piazzale*, from the landward portion of the bridge, at the head of which the Austrians constructed three batteries. They had three more near by in Fort San Giuliano, and one each at Bottenigo and Campaltone, from which they could command the lagune as far as Venice itself. So

[1] La Farina, iv, 528–31; Le Masson, 169–75; *Mem. Ven.*, 182–4, 186–8.

persistent and effective were the Venetians in hindering
the completion of these works, that not before June 13
could the Austrians unmask their fire on Fort Sant' Antonio, whose guns they frequently silenced, but only for
a little while, for the defenders repaired damages by
night, and in the morning resumed the cannonade.
Week after week the Austrians expended their energy on
this point, but gained nothing. Finally, they planned a
surprise, which was carried out during the night of July
6-7. Sixty picked men crawled along the bridge, and
having swum or waded across the open space, they
climbed up the side of Fort Sant' Antonio and leapt from
its parapet upon the cannoneers. So sudden was their
dash that they captured the battery and held it for a few
moments, until Venetian reserves came up and literally
hurled them headlong into the water, where nearly all
were drowned. Failure so signal discouraged the Austrian general from repeating this attempt, but he let loose
burning boats in the hope of setting fire to the Venetian
flotilla, and, following the suggestion of an Englishman,
he fixed grenades and bombs to balloons which he expected would drift over the city; but the wind took them
elsewhere, and they did no harm.

Meanwhile, round Venice herself the coils of privation
were slowly tightening. She had no fear of being taken
by assault, but knowing the amount of her provisions,
she could compute how long they would last: so many
pounds of food, a hundred and twenty thousand mouths,
so many weeks, — an easy example in division. For she
could no longer expect to receive stores by sea. Early
in April the Austrian fleet patrolled her approaches, and
thenceforth but few boats succeeded in running the blockade. Actual famine there was not, because there was a
large supply of rye and grain which the government
would not allow to be sold at an exorbitant rate. Thus
the poorest inhabitant could depend upon a daily modi-

cum of bread, though all other eatables sold at famine prices. The blockade naturally cut off the exportation of those manufactures on which the commerce of the city chiefly throve, and this deprived many persons of employment; but some of them could earn a living by working for the State, at the arsenal, or in repairing fortifications, or in the ministerial departments. The Venetian fleet, which should have been ready first of all, was slowly fitted out. A large flotilla of barges, tow-boats, lighters, and a few small tugs was busy in the lagunes, transporting food and ammunition and troops, and this service also required many hands. Against the time when the supply of powder should be exhausted, powder-mills were started and men went from house to house, like the petremen of Tudor England, to collect nitre for them. Bullets and balls had to be moulded, and all the other accessories of war had to be provided. Corresponding to the dearth of food, was the dearth of funds. Where to find money to pay the current expenses of the government and the troops was an unceasing problem. In nothing did Manin and his colleagues display greater prudence and ability, in nothing was their honesty more conspicuous, than in their management of Venetian finances. Again and again they exacted heavy contributions, yet they always had regard to the day of reckoning, and their appeals were never denied. Venice required three million francs a month; her revenue from natural sources amounted to but 200,000 francs; the difference had to be raised by extraordinary means; and she tried them all, — forced loans, the issue of "patriotic currency," the increase of her internal tariff, the assessment of her richest citizens under a promise to repay principal and interest, the mortgaging of public buildings, the appropriation of unreclaimed articles in the Monte di Pietà. Regard for public morals had led Manin at the beginning of his administration to abolish the lottery; the exigencies of

the siege caused him to drop the tax on salt; the tobacco
monopoly was the last of any importance that remained.[1]
By the middle of May the paper money had depreciated
thirty per cent.; six weeks later, it had fallen sixty per
cent.[2] Early in the winter subsidies had been promised
from Italians elsewhere: Genoa subscribed a million
francs, the Piedmontese Parliament voted a monthly contribution of 600,000 francs, and the Roman Republic
one of 100,000 crowns; but of these only a fraction of
one month's stipend was paid by Piedmont. The Venetians themselves, besides subscribing to the forced loans
and bearing the weight of increased taxes, voluntarily
gave their plate, jewels, and other valuables to be converted into cash by the government. Official employees
renounced a considerable part of their not large salaries.
General Pepe presented to the State a portrait of Cæsar
Borgia attributed to Leonardo da Vinci. Yet in spite of
these attempts to replenish the treasury, Venice was con-
suming her wealth as surely as her provisions, with the
knowledge that neither could be replaced.

In May two sorties from Brondolo had given a little
fresh meat to the city; but the Austrians were more
watchful after that, and stripped the country in that direction of victuals. Nevertheless, the Venetians maintained their courage and their cheerfulness, although they
might well ask themselves, as their condition became
worse day by day, what chance there was that fortune
would turn in their favor. Nothing so fortified them as
their confidence in Manin. Opponents he had, of course,
critics who found fault with his administration, agitators
who would have stirred up discontent, self-seekers who
envied his unique popularity, backsliders and weaklings

---

[1] Details of Venetian finance are given by Errera, chap. x. Xavier Gnoinski, in his *Dix-Sept Mois de Lutte à Venise*, 1848-1849 (Paris, 1869), publishes the receipts and expenses, month by month, pp. 239-42.

[2] Bersezio. iv, 487.

who in secret longed even for Austrian despotism rather than the continuation of this grievous struggle; but nine tenths of the population trusted and revered him, and believed that he would not, without justifying reasons, call on them for new sacrifices. Whilst he superintended the defense, he was also unflagging in his efforts to secure from the Western Powers terms compatible with the existence of free Venice. To his surprise, he received on May 21 a letter addressed to "Lawyer Manin," from De Brück, Austrian Minister of Commerce, who asked on what terms an agreement could be made. This overture was all the more unexpected because Radetzky in his ultimatum had roughly announced that Austria would neither treat with rebels, nor allow foreign governments to interfere in their behalf. Could it be that the heroic defense of Marghera had convinced Austria that she had a tremendous task before her? Or had recent victories of the Hungarians put her Empire in jeopardy? Manin could not know, because news from Europe scarcely reached him, — it required nearly a month for him to receive an answer from Pasini in Paris, — but he inferred that Austria would not make overtures to him unless she were hard pressed. Accordingly he sent Calucci and Foscolo to confer with De Brück, who laid before them three plans: first, Lombardy and Venetia might be made a separate kingdom with Verona as capital under an Austrian lieutenant-general, with a senate and chamber of deputies, an extended suffrage, its foreign and military affairs to be regulated from Vienna; second, Venetia might be separated from Lombardy, but retain similar institutions, and Venice might remain the capital of Venetia; third, Venice might be constituted an Imperial city, under a municipal government, like Trieste.[1] All of these plans presupposed unconditional surrender. Manin did not immediately reject any of them, but again

[1] Perrens, 331-2; Bonghi, 641-2.

sent his envoys to request more definite explanations. De Brück thereupon declared that he had spoken unofficially, and that as his scheme had not yet been sanctioned by the Emperor, he could not even give a copy of it. The trick was plain enough; Austria hoped by vague promises to glide into Venice, and being once there, to reorganize the government to suit herself. The Assembly, by a vote of 105 to 13, approved Manin's decision to reject De Brück's wily overtures (June 30).[1] Nor could Valentino Pasini, who went from Paris to Vienna to confer with Prince Schwarzenberg, the Imperial Chancellor, get a more satisfactory answer. "Submit, and then we will discuss terms," was, in substance, the consistent demand Austria made to the Venetians. Doubting no longer her ability to starve them out, her only purpose in these specious negotiations was to save the expense of a few weeks' siege and to begin a little sooner her work of chastisement. Naturally, she had no idea of conceding to rebels rights which they lacked power to wrest from her.

Still ignorant of the events of the outside world, and still hoping that those events would beget a champion for her, Venice persevered in her doughty resistance. On June 13 the first cannon-balls that had ever fallen within her limits struck the houses along her western margin;[2] but as yet they did little damage. On June 16 the Assembly, in response to a general feeling that the military and naval management might be improved, appointed a commission, of which Ulloa, Sirtori, and Baldiserotto were the members, to push the defense with greater vigor; Pepe, at Manin's suggestion, presided over them. July came, but brought no change in the military situation of besiegers or besieged. The Austrians at the landward end of the bridge kept up an unremitting fire, to which the Venetians replied from Fort Sant' Antonio and the

[1] *Mem. Ven.*, 201-2. [2] *Ibid*, 195.

adjacent boats. Down at Brondolo the garrison wasted few shots, but watched against a surprise. In the city the people still bore their privations cheerfully. They complained at times of the poor bread, due to the baseness of certain dealers, who, even in such an emergency, sought to enrich themselves by using spoiled grain for their loaves. The inactivity of the fleet also caused complaint, although the government had latterly hurried on the completion of several vessels on the stocks, in order to make a naval demonstration. There were clamors that a general sortie should be undertaken by the land forces, but the government intimated that it would be madness to rush prematurely into an engagement with the Austrian army, superior in numbers and equipment. Twice the explosion of a powder magazine under suspicious circumstances created alarm and then indignation; but the suspicion that the crime had been committed by Austrian partisans could not be verified, and the excitement soon died away. The general order in the city was excellent, — crimes, whether against property or person, being less frequent than in the normal régime of peace. Even thefts, to which want and hunger might have been incentives, and the unusual conditions opened opportunities, were rare; the bakers themselves needed no extraordinary guard. So long as they could, the citizens buoyed up their courage with hope. Their clergy, who, be it said, were more in touch with the masses than were the clergy in other parts of Italy, cheered them by religious functions and by exhortations. As in the old days of the Republic, the citizens went in solemn procession to St. Mark's to implore the intercession of their patron saint. There were special prayers in all of the churches, special appeals to the Virgin. But Heaven sent no succor, and mankind seemed to have forgotten Venice, except Austria, pressing on to destroy her. News came successively of the Austrian occupation of Tuscany, of

the siege and capture of Bologna, of the surrender of
Ancona. But Hungary, they supposed, was independent
and victorious. Görgey, "who, after Napoleon," the Venetians would fain believe, was "the greatest general of
our century,"[1] had command of the Hungarian troops;
he would soon come over the mountains and give battle
to the last Austrian army in Venetia! The example of
Rome, gallantly repelling French invaders, made the Venetians emulously defiant. But alas, on July 10 there
drifted across the lagune bottles in which the Austrians
had put bulletins of the fall of Rome, and of the taking
of Raab by the Austrian and Russian armies. So Venice
was alone in Italy, and the Hungarians on whom she relied were being overwhelmed by the combined forces of
the Emperor and the Czar.

On the night of July 29 a new calamity befell the devoted city, — bombardment! The Austrian artillerists
discovered that by raising their pieces and by aiming at
an inclination of forty-five degrees, they could shoot quite
across the lagune. Their cannon-balls had a range of
5,200 metres, their grenades one of 3,800 metres, and as
the distance between their foremost batteries and the
town was only 3,200 metres, these projectiles penetrated
more than a mile and a fifth into the thickly settled western half of Venice.[2] To strike deeper terror, the bombardment was begun at dead of night, and for a while
there was, indeed, great consternation and confusion as
the dwellers in the threatened district, roused from sleep
and ignorant of the extent of the danger, hastily seized
whatever they held most precious and made their way
to a place of safety. When daylight returned, hundreds
of families had taken refuge in St. Mark's Place, along
the Riva degli Schiavoni, and under the porticoes of the
Ducal Palace; like suppliants they collected round the

[1] The anxious Venetians held this opinion of him ; *Mem. Ven.*, 202.
[2] Le Masson, 203 ; La Farina, iv, 540.

entrance to St. Mark's Church, and they soon gave to the Public Gardens, situated still farther eastward, the aspect of a gypsy encampment. The government ordered the evacuation of the imperiled quarters, which soon included three fourths of the area of the city, and had them patrolled by the Civic Guard. The bombardment proved less effective than the Austrians wished, for, by the time the balls struck the city their momentum was spent, and they rarely crashed through more than one story of a building. Many balls were heated for the purpose of starting a conflagration, but they were cooled in their passage through the air; and the Venetians were on the alert to put out any small fires they caused. Although more than 23,000 projectiles reached the city, only seven persons were killed and less than thirty were injured; one church was burned, many others were struck and slightly injured. Most of the palaces on the Grand Canal, the School of San Rocco, the Academy of Fine Arts, the Rialto bridge, the Fenice theatre, were within range of destruction.[1] But the bombardment, though it failed to wreak the havoc that the barbaric Austrians intended, kept the minds of the Venetians in constant suspense, and added new fatigues to their already worn-out bodies. Nevertheless, they preserved their cheerfulness. They had that sense of humor which enables men to bear the worst blows of Fate — a humor which is not levity, nor mocking persiflage. Thus an old beggar-woman, at whose feet a cannon-ball fell, exclaimed, "Just see! that good soul Radetzky sends me alms!" Which was literally true, because the government paid a franc for every ball brought to it.[2]

But now another scourge, more frightful than scarcity of food or Austrian cannonade, attacked Venice. The cholera appeared towards the end of July and found the

[1] Gnoinski gives a list of the principal buildings that were struck, p. 208.
[2] Errera, 341, note.

ill-fed Venetians an easy prey. By the beginning of August the pestilence had become epidemic. "And yet," writes Contarini in his diary on July 30, "amid miseries so great, woe to him who should talk of capitulation!"[1] The government took measures to care for the sick and to improve the sanitary arrangements; but it was powerless to stop the ravages of the disease. On one day (August 15) 402 cases and 270 deaths were reported to the Board of Health.[2] When the director of the hospitals appealed to the French naval commander, De Belvèze, to procure medicines, the latter refused. "That would be contrary to the law of nations," he replied, "since it is natural that the besieger seeks to do as much injury as possible to the besieged."[3] Hungry, bombarded, cholera-stricken, the condition of Venice was now truly terrible; and yet not so terrible as to drive her to surrender. Some citizens circulated a petition asking the government what justification it had in prolonging the agony of the city; but the masses, far from sympathizing with these petitioners, mobbed the residence of the Patriarch, who was one of them, and would have slain him had they found him at home. The hospitals were overcrowded; the boatmen who ferried the bodies of the dead over to the little island of burial could not keep pace with their task; in one week, from August 14 to August 20, 1,500 persons died. The food had been consumed to within a few days' rations; the munitions were almost exhausted; the artesian wells had been drained till they gave only a dirty fluid, which the poor drank as best they could, and the rich mixed with vinegar.[4]

Was there no chivalry in Europe, no generous and noble hearts, to be touched by the heroism of those Venetians? Not a statesman who would say to them, "You have deserved freedom, and you shall have it"? Could

[1] *Mem. Ven.*, 213.   [2] *Ibid*, 222.
[3] Bersezio, iv, 404.   [4] Gnoinski, 210.

not Venice, unique among cities, — Venice, which should
have been the world's especial ward, be set apart and
allowed to enjoy the liberty to which she had proved her
title? Ah, no! Generosity, chivalry, — there was not
one Cabinet in Europe capable of feeling either. Louis
Napoleon had shown his chivalry in bombarding Rome;
Lord Palmerston was bent on averting a general war in
which John Bull's commercial interests might be injured.
What, to them, who would not rescue the living, were
the incomparable treasures of art and the monuments of
the dead who had made Rome and Venice immortal?
They did not even protest against the bombardment of
either city, — a bombardment utterly wanton in the case
of Venice, because the Austrians knew well enough that
a few weeks would suffice to starve her into submission.
French men-of-war, English men-of-war, lay in Venice
beyond the range of missiles throughout the cannonade,
and their commanders watched, as at a play, the parabolic flight of bombs and the procession of corpse-laden
barges across the lagune. Not a protest from them!
"The law of nations" prohibited them from giving even
drugs to mitigate the last agony of fellow-beings in the
clutch of cholera. The day will come when that law
will be revised; the day has already come when we know
how to regard European diplomats who permitted Rome
and Venice to be in peril of destruction. The world
execrates the barbarians, — Alaric, Attila, Genseric:
wherein did Oudinot and Radetzky differ from them?

At no time during the siege was Manin's personality
more transcendent than during these last weeks of accumulated horrors, and on August 6 the Assembly, foreshadowing the end, delegated all responsibility to him.
There had been much talk of organizing a general sortie
in the hope of reprovisioning the city, but he had not
encouraged this scheme, which he believed to be infeasible owing to the enormous superiority of the besieging

army. A crowd collected in the Piazzetta under his window, and set up angry shouts. At length he appeared at the balcony. "What do you wish?" he asked sternly. "The people wishes to arm!" "You have no need to make this demand here," replied Manin; "for you know that the offices of enrolment are always open. If you will fight, enlist; and you will find a commander. I am weary of hearing you cry out thus; I must have deeds, not words." Then going down into the Piazza, he had a table brought, and sat down at it to register the names of volunteers. Only a score presented themselves.[1] At another time when demagogues had goaded the populace into turbulence by hints of treason, Manin said to them, "Venetians! is this conduct worthy of you? You are not the people of Venice; you are only an insignificant faction. I will never shape my measures to pamper the caprices of a mob. . . . I will always speak the truth to you, though you level muskets at my breast and point daggers at my heart. And now go home, all of you, — go home!"[2] And they went their way. On August 13 he held a last review of the Civic Guard in St. Mark's Place. "We have sown," he said to them; "good will bear fruit on good soil. Great disasters may arise, — they are perhaps imminent, — disasters amid which we shall have the great consolation of saying, 'They came through no guilt of ours.' If it be not in our power to ward off these disasters, it is nevertheless always in our power to preserve undefiled the honor of this city. I ask frankly of the Civic Guard, have you faith in my loyalty?" The Guardsmen and the vast throng of citizens with one voice shouted, "Yes." "This unconquerable love," Manin continued with great emotion, "saddens me, makes me feel still more poignantly how much this people suffers. On my mind, on my forces, physical, moral, and intellectual, you cannot rely; but on my affection, — great,

[1] Perrens, 340-1. [2] Cesaresco, 155.

passionate, undying, — I bid you to count always. And whatever happens, say, 'This man deceived himself,' but never say, 'This man deceived us.' I have never deceived any one; I have never spread illusions which I did not share; I have never said 'Hope' when I did not myself hope."[1]

At that moment Manin had no more hope. Four thousand of the troops lay in the hospitals. The supply of food, temporarily replenished by a sortie from Brondolo, was nearly gone; the water was a brackish ooze. The fleet had sailed out to break the blockade, but had returned unsuccessful, its crews, it was said, being stricken by cholera. On August 14 the news reached Manin that the Hungarian cause was lost; on the 20th he heard that Görgey had surrendered to the Russians. Manin made a last attempt to negotiate honorable terms with De Brück, but the Austrian minister replied that he would agree to nothing except immediate and absolute surrender. Manin, therefore, deputed the Municipal Government of Venice to draw up the formal capitulation; but to the end he exerted him to preserve the order and dignity of the city. A sedition having manifested itself in one of the regiments, he quelled it with his wonderful gift of speech. He was no orator of the schools, but if eloquence be measured by its power to sway multitudes at the most tragic crises, Manin's oratory must rank very high. Many a man, whose speeches in the senate or the rostrum are remembered, might have shrunk from going down to a howling mob, which discharged muskets at him, to put the brawlers to shame by his calm, fearless words. Manin did that. On August 24 he resigned his power to the Municipality, which had arranged with the Austrian generals Gorzkowsky and Hess the details of capitulation, which gave Venice, bound hand and foot, to the Emperor's pleasure. On the 22d the bombardment

[1] Errera, 374-6.

had ceased; on the 28th the victors entered the pest-ridden, starving, thirsting city, and two days later Radetzky came over from Verona to enjoy his triumph. But famine, thirst, and cholera had won the victory, not he.

The siege, reckoning from April 2, when the Assembly voted to resist at any cost, lasted 146 days; but the blockade by land began on June 18, 1848, when the Austrians first occupied Mestre. During the twenty-one weeks of actual siege, 900 Venetian troops were killed, and probably 7,000 or 8,000 were at different times on the sick-list. Of the Austrians, 1,200 were killed in engagements, 8,000 succumbed to fevers and cholera, and as many more were in the hospitals: 80,000 projectiles were fired from the Venetian batteries; from the Austrian, more than 120,000. During the seventeen months of her independence, Venice raised sixty million francs, exclusive of patriotic donations in plate and chattels. When Gorzkowsky came to examine the accounts of the defunct government he exclaimed, "I did not believe that such Republican dogs were such honest men."[1]

With the fate of Venice was quenched the last of the fires of liberty which the Revolution had kindled throughout Europe in 1848. Her people, whom the world had come to look down upon as degenerate, — mere trinket-makers and gondoliers, — had proved themselves second to none in heroism, superior to all in stability. At Venice, from first to last, we have had to record no excesses, no fickle changes, no slipping down of power from level to level till it sank in the mire of anarchy. She had her demagogues and her passions, but she would be the slave of neither; and in nothing did she show her character more worthily than in recognizing Manin and making him her leader. He repaid her trust by absolute fidelity. I can discover no public act of his to which you can impute

[1] Errera, 347.

any other motive than solicitude for her welfare. The common people loved him as a father, revered him as a patron saint; the upper classes, the soldiers, the politicians, whatever may have been the preferences of individuals or the ambition of cliques, felt that he was indispensable, and gave him wider and wider authority as danger increased. Yet he was, more than any other of the Italian leaders whom we have studied, a downright, practical man. His legal precision, his severe morals, were not the equipment, you might suppose, for a great popular leader at that time and among these people; but on the contrary, it was those characteristics, combined with absolute courage and patriotic unselfishness, which gave him supreme power over his countrymen. The little lawyer, with the large, careworn face and blue eyes, had redeemed Venice from her long shame of decadence and servitude. But Europe would not suffer his work to stand; Europe preferred that Austria rather than freedom should rule at Venice. At daybreak on August 28 a mournful throng of the common people collected before Manin's house in Piazza San Paterniano. "Here is our good father, poor dear fellow," they were heard to say. "He has endured so much for us. May God bless him!" They escorted him and his family to the shore, whence he embarked on the French ship *Pluton*, for he was among the forty prominent Venetians whom the Austrians condemned to banishment. At six o'clock the *Pluton* weighed anchor and passed through the winding channel of the lagune, out into the Adriatic. Long before the Austrian banners were hoisted that morning on the flagstaffs of St. Mark's, Venice, with her fair towers and glittering domes, had vanished forever from her Great Defender's sight.

Outwardly, the Revolutionary Movement had failed; in France it had resulted in a spurious Republic, soon to become a tinsel Empire; elsewhere, there was not even a make-believe success to hide, if but for a while, the failure. In Italy, except in Piedmont, Reaction had full play. Bomba filled his Neapolitan and Sicilian prisons with political victims, and demonstrated again that the Bourbon government was a negation of God. Pius IX, having loitered at Naples with his Paragon of Virtue until April, 1850, returned to Rome, to be henceforth now the puppet and now the accomplice of Cardinal Antonelli in every scheme for oppressing his subjects, and for resisting Liberal tendencies. He held his temporal sovereignty through the kindness of the Bonapartist charlatan in France; it was fated that he should lose it forever when that charlatan lost his Empire. In Tuscany, Leopold thanked Austria for permitting him to rule over a people the intelligent part of which despised him. In Modena, the Duke was but an Austrian deputy sheriff. Lombardy and Venetia were again the prey of the double-beaked eagle of Hapsburg. Only in Piedmont did Constitutionalism and liberty survive to become, under an honest king and a wise minister, the ark of Italy's redemption.

But though Reaction seemed thus to triumph, though splendid hopes had been dashed and achievements recently attainable seemed now far, far beyond reach, much had been gained. The Italians had learned much, — they had dared, they had suffered, and they had learned much. The fetters of despotism might be riveted upon them, they might pine again in prisons or wander in exile, but nothing could take from them the recollection that they had, by their own strength, won and enjoyed a fleeting freedom. They had become participators in the living drama of European history; they were no longer mere spectres, haunting a Land of the Dead, whom the living scorned. They had failed, and to the bitterness of failure was added the remorse that it had been deserved. Their mistakes lay patent to every one; but the cardinal mistake should be charged not to them, but to Fate. The Revolution into which they had been irresistibly drawn was premature; they had not yet acquired self-control; they had not yet had time to be moulded by the influences of the Constitutions they so rapidly secured; they did not know, they could know only from experience, the price that they must pay for their redemption. Fate seemed to blunder in calling them too soon to their great enterprise; but this was to be their ordeal, this the means by which they were to unmask chimeras and delusions, and to plant their feet on reality. Let us not say, then, that Destiny erred. It was teaching a nation as it teaches men individually, to become strong by conquering hardships and to become wise by taking counsel of experience. That babel of talk, those thousand schemes and extravagances, were all necessary to a people suddenly given its tongue and will after an age of repression. Let us not wonder that they could not in the twinkling of an eye create armies; they proved that they had courage, which is the stuff out of which, with discipline, armies are made. Let us not wonder that they did not establish a permanent government; that is a work of art requiring the longest training and undisturbed reflection, — the Italians had neither. They, and the whole continent of Europe, were in a current in which merely to keep afloat demanded all their powers. Finally, let us not wonder that Unity, which they had dreamt would be so easy, proved to be so hard. Against the forces which impelled them to unite, there warred the forces of the past which tore them asunder. Localism, individualism, were the inheritance of the Italians, embedded in their nature, artfully nurtured by their princes, stimulated by every tradition and every monument which reminded them of former glories. Only from experience could they learn what partial sacrifices they must make in order to attain a common union.

These things the Italians learned from their Revolution, — these and many more. It was like a great furnace which resolves objects into their elements. It dissipated forever illusions concerning the Papacy. Henceforth, no man could reasonably urge that the Pope might be the bond of concord among Liberal Italians. That pretty hope melted away in the hot flames of fact; Italian independence and the preservation of the temporal sovereignty of the Pope were incompatible, irreconcilable. The Revolution further left distinct the alternatives by which Italian Unity could be won: either by Constitutional Monarchy, or by Republicanism, never by a combination or alloy of both; and by revealing the inherent fallacy of Mazzinianism, — that reform could orginate in the ignorant and stolid masses, — it pointed to Constitutional Monarchy as the proper agent. It reiterated the fact, which none now questioned, that Austria was the great external adversary to Italian Independence. Internal adversaries, factional discords, perfidious princes, and the partisans of Absolutism, must be overcome before Austria could be expelled. Charles Albert's magnanimous phrase, "Italy will work out her own salvation," had been discredited. She saw now that foreign assistance, not merely foreign sympathy, must be gained. To be liberated from visions, from Neo-Guelfism on the one hand, and Mazzinianism on the other, to know exactly what she desired and how alone she could attain her ideal, this was the knowledge, sobering and bitter, but salutary, which the failures of 1848-9 brought to Italy.

If we cast our glance back over the period of which this book is the history, we shall see the transformation which one generation had wrought. Italy in 1814 was scarcely aroused to a national consciousness; in 1849 that consciousness was a dominant fact. Out of Carbonari plottings to mitigate the tyranny of local despots, out of the failures of 1820, '21 and '31, out of Mazzini's

Young Italy, and the preachings of Gioberti, had developed a strong and abiding desire not only for liberty, not only for independence, but also for unity, without which these could not endure. The idea of Nationality had sprung up in Italian hearts. The race which had given Christendom a religion, which had expressed itself in literature and in art and in science, and which had once led the world in commerce and industry, this race had at length set itself to win what it had hitherto lacked, — political freedom. Italy was to be no longer a geographical expression, but a nation. The men of 1814 only dimly apprehended this; their grandfathers did not dream of it. The descendants of a society which had amused itself by Arcadian inanities gave up their lives by thousands at Santa Lucia and Custoza and Volta; they defended Rome against the French, they defended Venice against the Austrians, for the sake of that ideal. They had come to love country more than ease or life; they were ashamed of their servitude; they felt national self-respect and the obligations of patriotism. They were, in brief, thrilled by a regenerating spirit, and they would attain, though the goal lay far ahead.

Having followed them up to this point, where the first phase of their regeneration is concluded, we leave them. They have proved their earnestness, their courage, their enthusiasm, they have discovered that these alone will not suffice. They must have a standard-bearer round whom they can devotedly flock; they must have a head to direct their ineffectual, because divided, enthusiasms. These they were soon to find in Victor Emanuel, the honest King, and in Cavour, the embodiment of Reason. In the achievement of these men you shall read the story of Italy's triumph. None nobler is recorded in the annals of Europe during the nineteenth century. You have seen dawn paint the clouds along the eastern horizon scarlet and orange, foreboding a beautiful day; but presently those clouds rise and curtain the east and turn a sombre face towards the earth, till disappointment takes the place of your glad expectancy. Such to the Italians was the outlook in 1849, after the auroral hopes of the preceding year. But not from its dawn can the day be predicted. What if, when the sun is risen, he burn away those clouds?

INDEX.

ABERCROMBY, Sir Ralph, British minister at Turin, ii, 96, 128, 157, 195, 214, 229, 230.
Abruzzi, i, 195, 203, 249, 250, 411, 440.
Aci. Prince d', i, 232.
Adda, river, ii, 214.
Adda, Lombard envoy, ii, 127.
Adelphi, secret society, i, 203.
Adige, river, ii, 145, 150, 163, 164, 197, 211.
Æschylus, i, 75.
Agogna, stream, ii, 323.
Aix-la-Chapelle, capital of Holy Roman Empire, i, 24; Congress of, 211.
Alaric, ii, 203, 406.
Albani, Cardinal, i, 357, 368; ii, 10.
Albany, Countess of. i, 95.
Aldobrandini, Prince, ii, 167.
Alessandria, i, 188-9, 268, 274, 276, 277, 290, 399; ii, 224, 239, 315, 320.
Alexander of Macedon, i, 18.
Alexander I, czar, i, 118, 126; quarrel with Metternich, 129; joins Holy Alliance, 132; 136; supports Piedmont against Austria, 188; receives Lombard delegation, 192; opposes Metternich, 240; wheedled by him, 245; disgust at Louis Philippe, 344.
Alexander III, pope, humbles Fred. Barbarossa, i, 34; ii, 174.
Alexander VI (Borgia), pope, i, 69.
Alfieri, Piedmontese premier, ii, 229, 265.
Alfieri, Victor, i, 79; sketch of life, 95; virility, *ib.*; works, 96, method, 97; 99, 110, 316.
Alfonso. king of Naples. i, 70.
Allegrini. murder of. ii, 7.
Allemandi. General, ii, 151.

Amalfi, i, 46.
Amat, Cardinal, i, 441.
American Hunters secret society, i, 203.
Amici, Monsignor, ii, 58.
Amnesty, decreed by Pius IX, ii, 18, 20.
Anacreon, i, 75.
Ancona, i, 240; garrisoned by Austria, 362; 365; occupied by French, 370; end of diplomatic wrangle over, 373; 374, 375, 442; ii, 168, 345, 381.
Andreoli, executed, i, 295.
Andryane, French Carbonaro, i, 300, 304, 308.
Anelli, Milanese consultor, ii, 218, 219.
Anfossi, Milanese insurgent, ii, 109, 116, 121.
Angelico, Fra, painter, i, 70.
Angennes, d', bishop of Vercelli, ii, 97.
Angoulême, Duke of, i, 310-11.
Aujou, Charles of, i, 72.
Annemasse, i, 400.
Antonelli, Cardinal, ii, 58, 167, 170, 173, 267, 268, 273, 350.
Antrodoco, i, 287.
Apice, leader of volunteers, ii, 237.
Apulia, i, 249.
Aquila, Count of, ii, 80.
Aquila, town of, i, 440.
Aquinas, Thomas, "the angelic doctor," i, 50, 315.
Aquitaine, i, 23.
Arago, Emanuel, French deputy, ii, 353.
Aragonese dynasty in Naples, i, 72.
Arcadians, i, 86-90.
Arcioni, leader of volunteers, ii, 237, 376.
Areso, Count, ii, 119, 129.

INDEX.

Aretino. Pietro, i, 73.
Arezzo, ii, 251.
Argentine, ii, 372.
Ariosto, i, 82.
Aristotle, i, 82, 85, 207, 208, 316.
Armato, Neapolitan general, i, 155.
Armellini, Roman deputy, ii, 289, 309, 342, 360.
Arnolfo, Florentine architect, i, 50.
Arrivabene, Count, i, 301.
Artichoke, Italy an, i, 255.
Arts, flourish during Renaissance, i, 66.
Ascoli, Duke of, i, 220.
Ascoli, town of, ii, 345.
Aspre, d'. Austrian general, ii, 163, 324, 340, 341.
Asti, Bishop of, i, 289.
Athens, Duke of, i, 72.
Attila, ii, 406.
Andinot, Roman deputy, ii, 291, 309, 355.
Auersperg, Austrian marshal, ii, 50.
Aurelius, Marcus, i, 75.
Ausonia, circumlocution for Italy, ii, 41.
Austerlitz, i, 125, 254, 310.
Austria, dominant in Italy, i, 91; by Vienna Congress acquires Venetia, etc., 119; the real enemy of local patriotism in Italy, 280; stronger after suppressing revolutions, 282; to garrison Piedmont, 290; first intervention in Papal States, 302; second intervention, 308; Eastern Question, 422; occupation of Ferrara, ii. 51; insurrection at Vienna and Metternich's downfall, 107; recovering from panic, 160; gaining time, 161; Hartig's mission fails, 162; rumors of schism, 168; flight of Emperor to Innspruck, 176, 192; extreme peril of Empire, 192; tries for an armistice, 193; treats directly with Lombards, 197; disingenuousness at Anglo-French mediation, 231-2; successful procrastination, 233; second insurrection, 244; Francis Joseph, emperor, 276; fast-and-loose policy, 302; replies to Piedmont's reasons for declaring war. 316; supremacy restored in Lombardy, 333; in Venice, 409. See also Metternich.
Avellino, i, 217, 218, 219.

Avignon, i, 69, 120.
Azeglio, Constance d', ii, 127.
Azeglio, Marquis d', i, 174.
Azeglio, Massimo d', biographical sketch, i, 448-9; political journey, 449; "Recent Events in Romagna," 448. 450; banished from Tuscany, 451; interview with Charles Albert, ib.; ii, 7, 18, 54, 76, 163; goes to the war, 134; 251, 265, 275, 356.
Azeglio, Robert d', ii, 94.

Bacchiglione, river, ii. 144.
Bagnasco, writes revolutionary placard at Palermo, ii, 78.
Baja, town of, i, 243.
Balbo, Cesare, Piedmontese. i, 82, 267, 431; his "Hopes of Italy," 437-8; comparison with Gioberti, 439; 447; ii, 54, 68, 93, 227, 265.
Balbo, Prospero, i, 263, 270.
Baldasseroni, Tuscan minister, ii, 50.
Baldiserotto, Venetian republican, ii, 401.
Balloons, used by Milanese during insurrection, ii, 115.
Balzac, H. de, i, 319.
Bandiera, Emilio and Attilio, expedition to Calabria, and death, i, 442-4.
Barberini, Prince. ii, 268.
Barclay and Perkins's brewers, ii, 333.
Barge, Count de, Charles Albert's incognito. ii, 327.
Bari, i, 214.
Barrot, Odillon, French deputy, ii, 353, 363.
Bartolucci, Roman general, ii, 381.
Basseville, Ugo, i, 99.
Bassi, Milanese podestà, ii, 220, 221.
Bastide, French foreign minister, ii, 231, 232, 241, 242, 244, 386.
Bautzen, battle of, i, 127.
Bava, Piedmontese general, ii, 145, 147, 148, 187, 200, 211, 220, 222.
Beauharnais. Eugène, i, 110, 118, 139, 140. 173, 256.
Beauregard de Costa, biographer of Charles Albert, ii, 299.
Bedini, Monsignor, ii, 288.
Beggars in Papal States, i, 162; ii, 34.
Belgiojoso, Milanese councilor, ii, 111.

INDEX. 419

Belgiojoso, Princess, ii, 138, 236.
Belgium, i, 346; ii, 302.
Belisarius, i, 44.
Bellard, French general, i, 345.
Bellarmine, i, 78.
Bellegarde, Austrian marshal, i, 140.
Bellini, Venetian painter, i, 70.
Bellotti, Milanese councilor, ii, 111.
Belvedere, Piedmontese general, ii, 318.
Belvèze, De, French naval officer, ii, 405.
Benedek, Austrian general, ii, 105.
Benedict, St., i, 435.
Benevento, Lombard settlement, i, 14; Papal possession, 120.
Bentinck, Lord, i, 119, 139, 182.
Benvenuti, Cardinal, i, 358, 359, 360.
Beuza, Mazzinian conspirator, i, 397.
Berchet, poet, i, 325.
Bergamo votes for fusion, ii, 189; 330.
Berlin, i, 123; ii, 205, 243.
Bernard, St., views on celibacy, i, 30.
Bernetti, Cardinal, i, 357, 364, 369, 371, 374, 415, 416; ii, 11, 13, 14.
Berri, Duke of, i, 238.
Bertani, Dr., ii, 117.
Bes, Piedmontese general, ii, 105, 144, 146, 318, 323, 324.
Bevilacqua, Papal politician, ii, 273.
Bianchi, Austrian general, i, 189.
Bini, Tuscan Mazzinian, i, 397.
Bixio, French minister at Turin, ii, 159.
Bixio, Nino, ii, 70.
Blücher, i, 112.
Boccaciampe, traitor, i, 443.
Boccaccio, i, 51, 171.
Bofondi, Papal secretary, ii, 88.
Bohemia, i, 69, 127, 128; ii, 192, 193, 232.
Bologna, i, 120, 212, 330, 353, 355, 359, 362, 397, 416; ii, 8, 47, 183, 247; repels Austrians, 256; 289, 363, 379, 384.
Bolza, Austrian minion, ii, 101, 123.
Bomba. See Ferdinand II of Naples.
Bonaparte, Caroline, wife of Murat, i, 124, 129.
Bonaparte, Charles, oldest son of Louis, i, 359, 360.
Bonaparte, Charles. See Canino.

Bonaparte, Eliza, queen of Etruria, i, 110.
Bonaparte, Joseph, king of Naples, i, 146.
Bonaparte, Louis Napoleon, a conspirator in Romagna, i, 359, 360; plans Roman expedition, ii, 351; instructions to De Lesseps, 366.
Bonner, i, 78.
Borelli, Neapolitan deputy, i, 242.
Borghese, Roman family, i, 73; Cardinal Scipio, i, 98; Prince Borghese, ii, 52, 93.
Borghetto, skirmish at, ii, 149.
Borodino, battle of, i, 254.
Borromeo, Count, ii, 104, 119, 236.
Borsieri, condemned, i, 304.
Bosco, town of, i, 408.
Bossuet, declared heretical, i, 286.
Botta, confessor of Victor Emanuel I, i, 177.
Botticelli, painter, i, 70.
Bourbons, possessions in Italy, i, 91; characteristics of, 143.
Bourges, i, 259.
Bozzelli, Neapolitan minister, ii, 85, 136, 137.
Brandenburg, i, 81.
Breindl, Austrian general, ii, 105.
Brennus, i, 356; ii, 293.
Brenta, river, ii, 144, 186, 390.
Brescia, joins Lombard league against Barbarossa, i, 48; arrests in, 299; ii, 105, 157, 189; revolt, 330-3.
Brigandage in Naples, i, 152-3, 286; in Papal States, 338.
Brignole, Piedmontese diplomat, i, 119, 270.
Brofferio Angelo, Piedmontese radical, ii, 202, 209, 227, 235, 274, 298.
Brondolo, Venetian outpost, ii, 390; sorties from, 399; 402, 408.
Brück, de, Austrian minister, ii, 400, 401, 408.
Brunelleschi, i, 70.
Brunetti, Angelo. See Ciceruacchio.
Brünn, capital of Moravia, i, 306.
Bruno, Giordano, i, 83.
Brussels, i, 331, 432; ii, 320, 303.
Bubna, Austrian general, i, 189, 276, 299, 300.
Bucatori, secret society, i, 203.
Buffalora, town of, ii, 222, 317, 318, 320, 322.
Bugeaud, French general, ii, 234.

420   INDEX.

Buonarotti, i, 66, 70, 73, 83 ; ii, 245.
Burke, Edmund, i, 109, 432 ; ii, 54.
Byron, Lord, i, 203, 325–6, 385.
Byzantium, seat of Eastern Empire, i, 13.

Cadiz, i, 215, 238, 310.
Cadorna, Piedmontese war minister, ii, 325, 326, 329.
Cæsar, Julius, i, 52 ; ii, 203.
Cagliari, i, 175.
Calabria, i, 203, 219, 411.
Calandrelli, Roman triumvir, ii, 381.
Calderari, the, i, 206, 336.
Calucci, Venetian envoy, ii, 400.
Calvin, i, 78, 315.
Camerata, member of Junta, ii, 270.
Camerino, i, 120.
Camoëns, i, 54.
Camorra at Naples, i, 340.
Camozzi, Piedmontese agent, ii, 305, 330.
Campana, Neapolitan general, i, 219.
Campanella, Mazzinian conspirator, i, 397.
Campanella, Neapolitan scholar, i, 85.
Campbell, consul at Milan, ii, 217.
Campbell, English commissary, i, 117.
Campello, Roman minister, ii, 262, 300.
Campo Formio, i, 100 ; ii, 210, 242.
Canino, Charles Bonaparte, Prince of, suggests Scientific Congress, i, 426 ; at Venice, ii, 92 ; in Roman parliament, 255 ; opposes motion favorable to Pius IX, 263 ; wishes to proclaim the Constituent, 256 ; 271, 274, 289 ; urges the Republic, 291.
Cannæ, i, 25.
Canning, George, i, 134 ; liberal policy, 327–8 ; ii, 56.
Canosa, Prince, director of police at Naples, i, 150 ; dismissed, 151 ; organizes secret society of Tinkers, 206 ; advice to the "kings of the earth," ib. ; 208 ; directs vengeance in Naples, 283 ; 336, 338 ; at Modena, 424.
Canossa, Hildebrand's triumph over Henry IV at, i, 33.
Cantoni, Prof., ii, 101.
Cantù, Cæsar, beset by police, i, 172 ; quoted 431.

Canute, i, 78.
Canuti, political writer, i, 453.
Capital punishment in Naples, i, 150 ; in Piedmont, 176.
Capitanata, the, i, 154, 155, 218.
Capo d' Istria, Russian statesman, i, 134, 240, 244, 247.
Capoquadri, Tuscan Liberal, ii, 336.
Cappellari, Cardinal. See Gregory XVI.
Capponi, Gino, i. 453 ; ii, 60 ; premier, 246 ; deals with Leghorn riot, 247–50 ; resigns, 251 ; 265, 314, 336, 337, 341, 356.
Capua, i, 25.
Caraffa, Neapolitan family, i, 73.
Caraman, French diplomat, i, 240.
Carbonari, i, 154, 161, 186 ; legendary origin, 195 ; rapid growth, ib. ; catechism, 196–7 ; organization, 197–8 ; initiation of apprentices, 199–200, of masters, 200 ; symbolism, 201 ; punishments, 202 ; rapid growth, 203 ; parallel with early Christians, 205 ; a state within the state, 206 ; lack of leader, 209 ; mutual distrust. ib. ; few results, 212 ; the Macerata affair, 212–13 ; papal bull against, 214, 293 ; triumphal procession, 222–3 ; control Naples, 225 ; moderation, 235, 238, 239 ; permanent session, 242 ; not discouraged, 249 ; enlist in army, 250, 280 ; in Piedmont, 257, 265 ; torture of, 284–5 ; excesses, 286 ; in Lombardy, 300, 330 ; Mazzini joins order, 387.
Cardinals, College of, ii, 11.
Carignano, Prince of. See Charles Albert.
Caroline, queen of Naples, i, 146, 182.
Carolingians, league of, with Roman bishops, i, 14.
Carpaccio, Venetian painter, i, 70.
Carrara, ii, 247.
Carrascosa, Neapolitan general, i, 218, 219, 220, 251.
Carrer, podestà of Venice, ii, 126.
Casacciello, last court buffoon, i, 159.
Casalanza, treaty of, i, 147 ; violated, 284.
Casale, i, 290 ; ii, 67, 327.
Casalnuova, ii, 318.
Casanova, Count, ii, 134.
Casati, Gabrio, i, 302–3 ; podestà of

INDEX. 421

Milan, ii, 102, 109, 110, 156, 189, 191, 197; forms ministry, 227, 230.
Cass, American minister at Rome, ii, 369.
Cassano, Prince of, i, 427.
Cassero, Prince of, i, 227.
Cassola, Brescian insurgent. ii, 331.
Castagnetto. Charles Albert's secretary. ii, 67, 188.
Castel di Guido, ii, 363.
Castelli, Piedmontese commissioner, ii, 237.
Castiglia, Gaetano, i, 298, 304.
Castlereagh, Lord, i, 134, 187, 188, 191, 239, 325, 327.
Castracane, Cardinal, ii, 268.
Castro S. Giovanni, ii, 318.
Catania, revolt at, i, 413; ii, 350.
Cateau Cambrésis, treaty of, i, 82.
Catholic revival, i, 430.
Cattaneo. Carlo, in Milanese insurrection, ii, 116, 118, 119, 120, 189, 264.
Cattolica, Prince of. i. 232.
Cava, La, town, ii, 317, 319, 320.
Cavaignac, French president, ii, 192, 229, 231, 234, 242, 271.
Cavedalis. Venetian triumvir, ii, 238, 384.
Cavour, Camillo di, political writings, i. 453; ii, 93; proposes to ask for Constitution, 95; favors war, 127; remark on Chrzanowski. 305; 330, 414.
Celibacy. sacerdotal, means of extending Roman hierarchy, i, 28; origin, 29; made obligatory. 30; source of hypocrisy and corruption, 31; Hildebrand sees its usefulness, 32.
Cellini, Benvenuto. i, 73.
Censorship, i, 317; ii. 41, 45, 93.
Centralization, i, 207.
Cerano, town of, ii. 318.
Cernuschi, Milanese insurgent, ii, 109. 116, 360, 381.
Cervantes. i, 54, 314.
Cesarotti, i, 101, 106.
Chambéry. persecution in, i, 399; 401.
Champollion. i, 111.
Changarnier, French general, ii. 234.
Charlemain. leader of Franks, i, 7; extent of his empire, ib.; fascinated by the spell of Rome, 16;

crowned emperor. 20; favors to the Church, 27, 45, 111, 115.
Charles, Archduke of Austria, i, 112.
Charles the Bald, i, 23.
Charles of Bourbon. king of Naples, i. 144.
Charles IV, king of Spain, i, 160.
Charles X, king of France, i, 328, 342, 345, 346.
Charles Albert, Prince of Carignano, king of Piedmont, early years, i, 258-9; Metternich's designs upon, 260; marriage, 261; life at Turin, ib.; popularity with Liberals, 262; sympathy for wounded students, 264; visited by conspirators. 265; his version, 266; draws back, 267; second interview, ib.; supports the King, 269; reluctantly accepts regency, 271; difficult position, 272; grants Constitution. 273; urged by Lombard conspirators. 274; resigns, 275; retires to Florence, 276; supposed connivance with Lombards, 300; succession to throne settled, 309-10; secret pledge, 310; Spanish Expedition, ib.; becomes king. 366; 376; letter from Mazzini, 396; orders Mazzini's arrest. 397; severity to rebels. 398-9; plan to assassinate, 403; inconsistencies at beginning of his reign, 418; prim court, 419; morbidness, ib.; piety, 420;" King See-Saw," ib.; encourages arts and charities, 422; hesitates between France and Austria, 422-3; "J'attans mon astre," 423; allows Balbo to remain unmolested, 439; distrust towards, 449; interview with M d'Azeglio, 451; popularity. 452; rejoices in Pius IX's election, ii. 38; believed to be the Sword of Italian Cause, 41; message to Pius. 52; Metternich's sneer, 55; conflicting actions. 65-6; supports Sonderbund, 66; startling letter to Castagnetto, 67; morbid hesitation, 93; objection to Constitution. 94; final deliberation, 96; interview with D'Angennes. 97; grants Constitution. 98; interview with Lombard envoys. 119; decides on war, 128; proclamation, 130; "It-

aly will work out her own salvation," 131; motives, *ib.*; a religious task, 132; enters Lombardy, 146; first military operation, 148-9; forces at end of April, 152; diplomatic complications with Rome, 154, with the Lombards, 155, with Venetians, 156-7, with England, 158, with France, 159-60; his devoutness, 162; at Pastrengo, 163; chagrin over Pius's defection, 175; loyalty to Venetia, 195; slowness of operations, 198; difficulties, 199; unjust suspicion, 200; anxiety at Parliament, 201; receives Venetian envoys, 209; defeat at Custoza, 211; rejects Radetzky's terms, 212; disastrous retreat, 213; motives for going to Milan, 214; decides to treat, 217; life threatened by Milanese mob, 218; awaits death, 220-1; rescue, 222; evacuates Milan, *ib.*; justification of his act, 223; despondency, 224; holds balance between Republicans and Retrogrades, 228; accepts terms of Anglo-French mediation, 230; desire of revenge, 234; leans toward war-party, 235; snubbed by Pius IX, 273; consents to Gioberti's plan, 295; accepts his resignation, 299; warlike speech, 301; declares war, 305; quits Turin, 315; at Novara, 318; crosses the Ticino, 319; news from Mortara, 322; battle of Novara, 323-5; despair, 325; abdication, 326; journey to Oporto, 326-8; death, 328; character, *ib.*

Charles Emanuel IV, of Piedmont, i, 175.

Charles Felix, king of Piedmont, heir to throne, i, 188, 259; advice concerning Charles Albert, 274; terms with rebels, 277; takes vengeance, 288-91; nicknamed "Charles Ferox," 289; snubbed by Bubna, 290; quits Modena, *ib.*; personal character, 291-2; remarks on Charles Albert, 309; reactionist rule, 336; 352, 378.

Charles Louis, of Lucca, i, 120, 337, 428; driven out, ii, 64; 72.

Charles Martel, Frankish leader, asked to defend Rome against Lombards, i, 14, 45, 72.

Charlotte Albertina, Charles Albert's mother, i, 258-9.

Chateaubriand, account of Italy in 1820, i, 329-31; 430; ii, 9.

Chaucer, i, 54.

Chiabrera, i, 93.

Chiese, river, ii, 143.

Childeric III, i, 14.

Chile, ii, 17.

Chiodo, Piedmontese premier, ii, 301.

Chioggia, ii, 126.

Cholera, great epidemic, i, 410; suspicion of poison, *ib.*; virulence in Sicily, 411; horrors, 412; at Venice during siege, ii, 405.

Christianity, a Hebrew product mingled with Roman formalism, i, 9; influence of Paul, 11; petrifies into literalism, 12; compact with Frankish emperors, 20; gradually adopted by barbarians, 47.

Christina, ex-queen of Sweden, i, 86.

Chrzanowski, Polish general, commands Piedmontese army, ii, 304, 317, 318, 319, 322, 323, 324, 325, 326, 331.

Church, general, i, 228.

Church and State, mediæval theory of, i, 21; summed up in Dante's epic, 51.

Ciacchi, Cardinal, ii, 50.

Cibrario, Piedmontese commissioner, ii, 237.

Cicero, i, 70.

Ciceruacchio, nickname of Angelo Brunetti, leader of Roman populace, ii, 43; infatuation for Pius IX, 44; and Prince Borghese, 52, 83; prevents riot, 87, 89; leads populace against Pius, 171; 259.

Cid, the, i, 40.

Cilento, the district of, ii, 82.

Cimella, cruelty of, i, 399.

Cipriani, Colonel, at Leghorn, ii, 240.

Cisalpine Republic, i, 101, 106, 110.

Cisterna, Prince della, i, 264.

Civitavecchia, French at, ii, 271; second expedition, 358, 362.

Classicists, i, 316, 385.

Clerici, Milanese insurgent, ii, 116.

Clubs, i, 194.

Cobden, Richard, ii, 93.

INDEX. 423

Cocle, Bomba's confessor, i, 408, 410; ii, 83.
Codogno, village of, ii, 214.
Collegno, i, 265, 267; ii, 227.
Colletta, historian of Naples, quoted, i, 148; sent to Sicily, 237, 250.
Colli, Piedmontese commissioner, ii, 237.
Colobiano, Piedmontese, ii, 67.
Columbus, i, 67.
Comacchio, i, 120, 179; ii, 51.
Combès, French captain, i, 370, 371, 373.
Commercial laws, in Naples, i, 150.
Como, town, ii, 105, 237.
Conche, skirmish at, ii, 388.
Concili, De, Neapolitan general, i, 217, 218, 223.
Conclave of 1823, i, 337; of 1830, 357; of 1846, assembles, ii, 8; Holy Ghost, 9; tricks, 10; intrigues, 11–13; Pius IX elected, 14.
Condottieri employed, i, 64.
Confalonieri, i, 191, 233, 207, 208; arrest, 290; description of tortures, 301; tried and condemned, 302–4; interview with Metternich, 314–5; at Spielberg, 308.
Confalonieri, Theresa, i, 300; journey to Vienna, 302–3.
Confessional violated, i, 158.
Congress, Agrarian, at Casale, ii, 67.
Congress, Scientific, i, 426; at Novara, ii, 41; at Venice, 72.
Consalvi, Cardinal, i, 120, 157, 185, 202, 337.
Conscription abolished in Naples, i, 149; in Papal States, 162.
Conspiracies, spring up after Restoration, i, 192; causes, 193; character of conspirators, 194; at Macerata, 212; discredited, 281; in Lombardy, 297; Chateaubriand on, 33); activity in 1830, 346–7; defects patent after 1830, 381; break out in Naples, 409; 412; Mazzinian, 441.
Constantine, i, 56, 214; ii, 293.
Constantinople, i, 19; taken by the Turks, 69.
Constituent, Italian, Montanelli's scheme, ii, 252; demanded at Rome, 267.
Conti, tortured, i, 295.
Contratti, Brescian insurgent, ii, 331.

Copernicus, i, 67.
Copyright league, i, 426.
Corboli Bussi, Papal diplomat, ii, 154.
Corfu, i, 365, 442, 443.
Corinne, i, 90.
Cornuda, ii, 183, 200.
Corsica, i, 352, 396.
Corsini, Prince, Roman senator, ii, 87, 89, 268, 270.
Corvinus, I, 69.
Cosmopolitan Committee, i, 346, 352, 354, 367.
Cosenza, town of, i, 412, 443, 446.
Cossato, Piedmontese general, ii, 325, 326, 329.
Costa, Charles Albert's equerry, i, 269, 274; ii, 162.
Cotrone, town, i, 443.
Count, origin of title, i, 41.
Counter-reformation, i, 78.
Cowper, i, 97.
Cracow, ii, 53, 387.
Cranmer, i, 78.
Cremona, i, 146, 148, 189; ii, 105, 213.
Crescimbeni, Arcadian, i, 86, 87, 88.
Croat rebellion, ii, 192.
Cromwell, i, 81, 222.
Cubières, French diplomatic agent, i, 371.
Curtatone, battle of, ii, 151, 187.
Customs Union, i, 426; ii, 58, 154.
Custoza, battle of, ii, 211–12, 213, 414.

Dabormida, Piedmontese general, ii, 229, 235.
Dall' Ongaro, republican priest, ii, 346.
Dalmatia, i, 119.
Dandolo, Doge, ii, 205.
Dandolo, Emilio, Milanese patriot, ii, 116.
Dandolo, Enrico, killed at Rome, ii, 378, 383.
Dante, i, 50; his unique position, 52; his "Divine Comedy," 53; his moral depth, 55; a political guide to his countrymen, 56; his dignity, 58; 59, 92, 99, 103, 107, 114; revived study of, 325; Mazzini's reference to, 385; comparison with Gioberti, 435; ii, 175.
Dardano, Neapolitan demagogue, ii, 178.

Dark age, i, 5.
Darwin, Charles, i, 383.
Daverio, killed at Rome, ii, 378.
David, i, 52.
Decisi, secret society, i, 203, 214.
Decretals, forged, i, 56.
Delcarretto, Neapolitan minister, i, 340, 408, 410, 413, 441; ii, 82, 83.
Della Porta, Milanese insurgent, ii, 116.
De Maistre, Joseph, quoted, i, 141; 430.
Demosthenes, i, 432.
Denon, i, 111.
Dickens, Charles, i, 319.
Divorce, abolished in Naples, i, 140; in Austrian provinces, 169; in Piedmont, 176.
Dolfin, Venetian envoy, ii, 209.
Döllinger, Dr., i, 430.
Donà, Venetian envoy, ii, 209.
Donatello, sculptor, i, 70.
Doria, Genoese envoy, ii, 68.
Dovizio, dramatist, i, 82.
Dragonetti, Neapolitan liberal, ii, 138.
Drama, i. 82.
Dresden, i, 123, 127, 128.
Drouyn de Lhuys, French minister, ii, 302, 366, 386, 391.
Ducat of Venice, i, 51.
Duchies, the, Parma and Modena, i, 263, 381; ii, 195, 223.
Duke, origin of title, i, 41.
Dupont de l'Eure, i, 346.
Durando, James, i, 453; ii, 151, 305, 318, 323, 324, 326.
Durando, John, commands Papal troops, ii, 134, 151, 166, 167, 168, 172, 186, 198, 200.
Dürer, painter, i, 71.
Durini, Milanese liberal, ii, 118.

Eastern Empire at Byzantium, i, 13; Irene, 19; almost complete separation from Western Empire, 23; destroyed, 69.
Eastern Question, in 1840, i, 422.
Ebro, river, i, 7.
Egypt, bishop of, ii, 310.
Elba, i, 117; ii, 286.
Elbe, i, 7.
Electric telegraph, ii, 243.
Eleusinian mysteries, i, 195.
Eliot, George, i, 319.

Elizabeth, Charles Albert's sister, i, 259.
Emanuel Philibert's epigram, i, 255.
Emerson, i, 383.
Emilia, i, 356, 377; ii, 247.
Empoli, tumults at, ii, 306.
Encyclical, of Nov. 9, 1846, ii, 39.
England, national growth, i, 68; Reform bill, 371. For diplomacy, see Abercromby, Canning, Castlereagh, Palmerston, Wellington.
Espiveut, French officer, ii, 358.
Este, House of, i, 74.
Esterhazy, Count, ii, 340, 350.
Esterhazy, Princess, ii, 107.
Etruria, kingdom of, i, 110.
Exiles, i, 331, 332.

Fabar, French officer, ii, 359, 360, 361.
Fabbri, Count, Papal premier, ii, 256, 257.
Fabrizi, conspirator, i, 440.
Faenza, revolt at, i, 355.
Falconieri, Cardinal, ii, 11, 12, 13.
Famine, i, 156.
Fanti, General, ii, 216.
Farini, Charles L., indites "Manifesto of Rimini," i, 447; quoted, ii, 34, 172.
Farioli, tortured, i, 295.
Farnese, Papal family, i, 73.
Favre, Jules, French deputy, ii, 353, 365.
Federation, Italian, i, 290.
Federatists, i, 256, 257, 265, 280, 348.
Feldsberg, ii, 107, 108.
Fenestrelle, Piedmontese prison, ii, 67.
Ferrara, i, 120, 161, 179, 185, 356; ii, 8; Austrian occupation, 50–1, 56, 67, 256.
Ferrari, commands Roman volunteers, ii, 134, 151.
Ferretti, Cardinal, Papal secretary, ii, 48, 49, 50, 52, 82, 88.
Ferretti, Mastai. See Pius IX.
Ferretti, Pietro, Neapolitan Liberal, ii, 138.
Feudalism, of Teutonic origin, i, 7; based on physical force, 8; weak in Italy, 47, 114; made ridiculous, 314; abolished in Sardinia, 422.
Ficquelmont, Austrian diplomat, sent to Milan, ii, 75; 101, 106;

INDEX. 425

succeeds Metternich, *ib.*; first negotiations for peace, 106–7.
Fieschi, Cardinal, ii, 12, 14.
Filicaja, i, 93.
Filopanti, Roman deputy, ii, 201.
Fiumicino, ii, 363, 379.
Fivizzano, town of, ii, 65.
Ferdinand I, of Two Sicilies (IV, of Naples). i, 120; restored, 142; promises, 147; reactionary measures, 148; debts, *ib.*; dispute with Pius VII over the *chinea*, 157; visits Rome, 159; personal character, 159–60; compact with Austria, 180; dealings with Sicily. 182; assumes title "King of the Two Sicilies," *ib.*; connives with Carbonari, 196; proclamation against Carbonari, 214; fright at rebellion. 218; grants Constitution, 220; permits military review, 222; takes oath, 225; attitude towards Sicilian rebellion. 234; opens Parliament, 235; invited to Laybach, 241; feigns honesty, 243; at Laybach, 246–7; Metternich's remark, *ib.*; messages to Naples, 249, 280; deputes Canosa to retaliate. 283; return to Naples, 287; last years. 288; death, 339.
Ferdinand I, emperor of Austria, i, 424; ii, 176, 177, 192, 244, 263, 276.
Ferdinand VII, king of Spain, i, 216, 310–11.
Ferdinand II, king of Two Sicilies, succeeds to throne, i, 358; first measures. 406; popular with Liberals, 407; true character revealed, 407–8; private life. 408–9; tool of Delcarretto and Cocle, 410; conduct during cholera, 411; odious reputation, 414; treatment of the Bandiera. 444; ii, 58; brutal rule, 73; irritation at Pius. 74; grants tardy reforms to Sicily. 80; consternation. 81; nicknamed "Bomba," 82; grants Constitution, 83; temporary popularity, *ib.*; pretense of patriotism, 136; consents to war, 137; patriotic proclamation, 138–40; Customs League. 154; fear his ruling instinct, 177; dispute with deputies, 179; exults at slaughter of Liberals, 181; Gladstone's description of, 182; joins Pius IX at Gaeta, 267; suppresses Liberals in Naples and rebels in Sicily, 348–9; eulogized by Pius IX, 357; sends troops against Romans, 363; retreats from Velletri. 375.
Ferdinand, duke of Genoa, ii, 120, 188, 221, 224, 318, 319, 323, 324, 326, 328, 349.
Ferdinand III, Grand Duke of Tuscany, i, 120; restoration, 141, 180, appearance, 164; resists Metternich's encroachments, 184, 244, 212, 310; death, 337.
Ferdinandea, political sect. i, 418.
Filangieri, Neapolitan general, ii, 83.
Florence, first florin coined, i, 51; glory waning, 60; artful tyranny, 65, 70; bastard Medici rule, 73; 287; Scientific Congress. 426; excitement over news from Milan, ii, 132; mob. 246; republic declared, 287; republican orgies, 306; threatened by Smith, 307.
Florin. first coined, i, 51.
Foggia, i, 155, 219.
Fontanelli, Modenese general. i, 354.
Forli, i, 120, 292, 356, 359, 446; ii, 7, 8, 52.
Foscolo, Ugo, birth and education, i, 106; exile and death, 107; estimate of, 108.
Foscolo, Venetian diplomatic agent, ii, 400.
Fossano, town of, i. 208.
Fossombroni, Tuscan minister, i, 163, 337, 424; ii, 59.
Fouché, i, 107.
Fra Diavolo, a brigand, i, 153.
France, dynastic expansion, i, 68; policy towards Austrian interference in Naples. 239; policy during Restoration, 328; treatment of Italy, 329; expected to take the initiative. 331; Revolution of July, 342; discontent of Republicans, 362; inconsistency. 363; outwitted by Austria, 375; tries to expel Mazzini, 397; Eastern Question, 422; Orleanist régime. 427; Revolution of February, ii, 90, 99; designs on Savoy. ii, 158; ministers pretend friendship to Italian war. 159; insurrection of May. 192; seeks compensation, 196; Piedmont asks aid. 229; mediates,

230-2; L. Napoleon president, 276; Roman expedition debated and voted, 352-4; revulsion of sentiment, 364; counter-revolution fails, 380.
Francis I, emperor of Austria, i, 102, 107, 117, 122, 125, 126, 132, 136, 188, 191, 240, 302, 307, 358, 406.
Francis Joseph, of Austria, ii, 276.
Francis I, king of Naples, appointed regent, i, 221; reviews parade, 222-3; 225, 227; message to Parliament, 242, 248, 251; becomes king, 339; despicable character, 349; 376.
Francis II, of Naples, ii, 75.
Francis IV, duke of Modena, restored, i, 141, 165; reactionary measures, *ib.*; attitude towards Metternich, 185; marries Piedmontese princess, 200; ambition, 203; punishes Liberals, 203-5; meddles in Parma, 205; surnamed the "Butcher," 206; proposition in regard to political prisoners, *ib.*; states causes of political discontent, 206-7; Chateaubriand on, 330; plan for transporting political prisoners, 333; connives with Liberals, 348; obscurity of compact, 349; possible motives, 350-1; dealings with Menotti, 352; duplicity, 353; captures Menotti and takes him to Mantua, 354-5; letter to Conclave, 357; 376, 424; ii, 55, 58; death, 65.
Francis, St., i, 435; ii, 328.
Francis V., of Modena, ii, 65, 72.
Frankfort-on-the-Main, ii, 192.
Franks, foremost German tribe, i, 7.
Franzini, Piedmontese general, ii, 147, 195.
Freddi, persecutor, ii, 40.
Frederick Barbarossa, does homage to Pope Alexander III, i, 34; attempts to subdue Lombard cities, 48; defeated at Legnano, 49.
Frederick II, of Prussia, i, 122.
Frederick II, of Sicily, i, 181.
Frederick of Urbino, i, 73.
Frederick William III, king of Prussia, i, 118, 132, 136, 188, 240.
French Revolution, significance of, i, 109; Metternich's view of, 120.

Frimont, General, i, 250, 251, 287, 360.
Frugoni, Arcadian, i, 88, 90.
Fulvizi, Nicholas, i, 354.

Gabrielli, Prince, ii, 88.
Gaeta, tumult suppressed, i, 412; Pius IX flies to, ii, 263; hotbed of intrigues, 272; 295, 297, 349, 350.
Gaetani, Prince, ii, 90.
Galateri, Piedmontese persecutor, i, 399.
Galdi, president of Neapolitan Parliament, i, 236.
Galilei, i, 83.
Gallenga, conspirator, plans to kill Charles Albert, i, 403.
Galletti, Roman politician, ii, 91, 261; premjer, 262; 266, 270; president of assembly, 292.
Galliate, ii, 318.
Gullicia, ii, 105.
Gallo, Count, conspirator, i, 212.
Gallo, Duke del, i, 248, 249.
Gallois, French captain, i, 370, 371, 373.
Gamallero, Charles Albert's courier, ii, 326.
Garda, Lake, ii, 144, 150.
Gardeneresses, secret society, i, 203.
Garelli, captain, executed, i, 288.
Garibaldi, Joseph, banished, i, 399; offers services to Pius IX, ii, 42; guerrilla fighting round Como, 237; 282; "long live the Republic," 289; popular hero, 309; repels Oudinot, 362; defeats Neapolitans at Palestrina, 363; early career in South America, 372; offers his services to Charles Albert, 373; personal appearance, *ib.*; romantic character, 374; fight at Velletri, 375; military rivalry, 377; defense of Villa Pamfili, 378; declares further defense futile, 381; retreat from Rome, 382.
Gas in Milan, i, 253.
Gattinara, Piedmontese persecutor, i, 399.
Gavazzi, Barnabite friar, ii, 88, 133, 248, 366.
Gaysrück, Cardinal, ii, 10, 11, 12, 13, 36.
Gazzoli, Cardinal, ii, 259.
Geneva, i, 400.
Genga, Annibale della. See Leo XII.

Genoa, early growth, i, 46; oligarchy, 64, 117; allotted to Piedmont, 119, 256; captured by revolutionists, 270, 289; Mazzinian propaganda, 397; persecutions, 399; celebrates centenary of Austrian expulsion, ii, 41; petitions for reforms. 68; Charles Albert's visit, 70; sullen symptoms, 95; 228, 235, 265; revolt, 330; 347.
Genseric, ii, 406.
Gentz, Austrian political tool, i, 244.
George IV, King of England, i, 134.
Gérard, leads Foreign Legion at Rome. ii, 376.
Germany, no nation, i, 68; Thirty Years' War, 81; agitation, 346; rumors of schism, ii, 168; revolution triumphs, 192; wanes, 244.
Ghiberti, sculptor, i, 70.
Ghilardi, leader of volunteers, ii, 250.
Giampietro, assassination of, i. 248.
Giffienga, Piedmontese general, i, 258, 267.
Gioberti, Vincent, banished, i, 399; book on "The Primacy," 432–5; comparison with Dante's "Monarchy," 435; his adroitness. 436; great popularity of his book, 437; comparison with Balbo, 439; 447; "Modern Jesuit," 453; ii, 18, 22, 36, 54, 55, 60, 66; overtures from Charles Albert. 235; ovation at Rome, 256; 265; leader of opposition, 274; forms Democratic Cabinet. 275; immense task, 276; would restore the national character of the struggle, 277; programme, 277–8; overtures to Pius, 279; views on Papacy, 280; negotiations with Roman Radicals, 281; with Tuscany, 281–2; determines on armed intervention. 294; dealings with Pius and Leopold. 295; defends his policy in Parliament. 297; resigns, 298; his character, 299–301; 356, 388, 414.
Giorgione, painter, i, 70.
Giotto, i, 50.
Giusti, Giuseppe, satirist and poet, ii. 60; compared with Lowell, 61; 64.
Gizzi, Cardinal, i, 446; candidate for pope, ii, 7, 8; supposed election, 15; Secretary of State, 22; 36, 37, 45; popularity wanes, 47; resignation, 48; opinion of Pius IX, ib.
Gladstone, on Bourbons. ii, 182.
Goethe, i, 317, 320; ii, 35.
Goito, first skirmish, ii, 148; battle, 186–7, 197, 211, 212. •
Goldoni, i, 83.
Goliardi, i, 50.
Görgey, Hungarian general, ii, 403, 408.
Goritz, Austrian province, ii. 144.
Gorzkowsky, Austrian general, ii, 408, 409.
Graham, English Postmaster-General, i, 442.
Grassellini, governor of Rome, ii, 49.
Gravina, Arcadian, i, 87, 88.
Gravina. Cardinal, i, 232, 233.
Graziani, Venetian triumvir, ii, 238, 384.
Greek Church, contrasted with Roman, i, 13.
Greeks, modern, struggle with Turks. i, 327.
Gregorians, Reactionist party, ii, 12; alarmed at Pius IX's Liberalism, 40; incite disorders, 48; alleged plot to abduct Pius, 49–50; 166.
Gregory III. first pope to call in foreign aid. i, 45, 72.
Gregory VII. See Hildebrand.
Gregory XVI (Maurizio Cappellari), elected, i. 357; appeals for aid, 358; weak rule. 367; submits to French occupation of Ancona, 373; relies on Austria, 378; incompetent rule, 415; bigotry, and arrogance. 417; concordat with Piedmont, 420; frowns on Scientific Congress. 426; employs military commission, 446; death anxiously awaited, 453; dies in solitude. ii, 2; obsequies, 8, 10.
Greppi. Milanese councilor. ii, 111.
Grimaldi, Piedmontese diplomat, i, 83.
Grimani, Venetian envoy, ii, 209.
Guarigli. brigand. i. 153.
Guerrazzi, F. D., Tuscan Radical, disciple of Mazzini. i, 397; in favor of violence. ii. 62; arrested, 86; on insurgent committee, at Leghorn, 248; curbs revolt, 250; appointed minister, 252; inter-

view with Leopold, 253; urges the Constituent, 283; duped, 286; triumvir, 287; virtual dictator, 306; military exploit, 307; rivalry with Montanelli, 333; chosen dictator, 334; intrigues, 335; stops tumult, 335-6; last grasp on power, 337; imprisoned, 338; character, 339-40.
Guerrieri, Lombard envoy, ii, 229.
Guizot, French premier, ii, 37, 47; turns to Metternich, 53; 90.

Habeas Corpus, i, 140, 284; ii, 32.
Hamilton, English Tory, i, 183.
Hamilton, Lady, i, 145.
Hamilton, Sir Charles, ii, 245.
Hamilton, Sir George, ii, 247.
Hannibal, i, 17, 25.
Hapsburg, House of, controls Empire, i, 68.
Harcourt, Duke d', ii, 263, 350, 361.
Hardenberg, Prussian premier, i, 123.
Hartig, Austrian diplomat, ii, 161, 162, 192, 195.
Haugwitz, Prussian minister, i, 123.
Haynau, Marshal, ii, 331, 332, 333, 388, 389, 393.
Henry IV, German emperor, submits to Hildebrand, i, 33.
Hermits, secret society, i, 203.
Hess, Austrian general, ii, 220, 408.
Hetairia, secret society, i, 204.
Hettinghausen, Major, ii, 117, 118.
Hildebrand, Pope Gregory VII, aims at universal theocracy, i, 33; ii, 6, 202.
Holbein, painter, i, 70.
Holy Alliance, made, i, 132; 328, 351.
Holy Ghost, the, supposed to preside at Conclaves, ii, 9.
Holy Roman Empire, established, i, 19; divided, 23; Emperor also German king, 24; contest with Papacy, 26; obstacle to national growth in Italy, 43; becomes appanage of House of Hapsburg, 68; extinguished by Napoleon, 110.
Homer, i, 53.
Hügel, loyal to Metternich, ii, 107, 108.
Hugo, Victor, i, 319.
Humanism, i, 60.

Hume, David, i, 313.
Hummelauer, Austrian envoy, ii, 193, 230.
Hungary, i, 69; revolution, ii, 193, 230, 232, 270.
Huns, i, 4, 9, 24, 82, 100.
Hunyadi, John, i, 69.
Hutten, Ulrich von, i, 54.

Iconoclastic controversy, i, 13.
Imbriani, Neapolitan Liberal, ii, 138.
Imola, i, 355; ii, 15, 17.
Individualism, how far salutary, i, 2; exaggeration during the Renaissance, 75.
Informers, paid, i, 284.
Innocent III, ii, 6.
Innspruck, ii, 176, 192.
Inquisition established, i, 78; 82, 114, 416; suppressed, ii, 310.
Intonti, Neapolitan minister, i, 340.
Invernizzi, Monsignor, i, 338-9.
Irene, Eastern Empress, i, 10.
Isonzo, river, ii, 144, 145, 186, 191.
Istria, i, 119.
Italian language used by Dante in his epic, i, 53; dispute over, 102.
Italy, nobility of her struggle for independence, i, 1, 2; tenacity of the past in, 3; never one nation, 4; barbarians invade, ib.; Holy Roman Empire established, 20; invasions by German kings, 25; three obstacles to national existence, 43; no royal dynasty, 46; home of the Renaissance, 61; dominance of great families, 64; decline, 72; prey to foreign invaders, ib.; Catholic reaction, 78; skepticism, 79; Spanish domination, 81, 82; Arcadian nonsense, 86-90; forebodings of change, 91; Austria supersedes Spain as dominant power, ib.; longing for freedom, 92; effect of French Revolution, 110; Napoleonic administration, 112; retrospect, 113; redistribution by Vienna Congress, 118; duped by false promises, 139; final dealings with Napoleon, 141; Metternich's attempt to Austrianize, 180-9; effects of Napoleonic upheaval, 190-1; conspiracies, 192; causes of discontent, 210; "Italy an artichoke," 255; causes of discontent stated

by Francis IV, 296; punishment of Lombard suspects, 297–310; conflict of Old and New, 312; force lacking, 313; Classicism vs. Romanticism, 316; John Bull's views on, 326–7; influence of exiles on Italy's condition, 334; hopes revive towards 1830, 341; confidence in French aid, 347; Menotti at Modena, 352–5; Gregory XVI elected, 357; memorandum of Powers, 363; Ancona affair, 370–5; result of revolution of 1831–2, 379; political quarantine, 381; Young Italy, 397; characteristics of third decade, 425; Scientific Congress, 426; symptoms of change, 451–2; rejoicings at Gregory's death, ii, 4; enthusiasm at Pius IX's decree of amnesty, 20; celebration of centenary of Austrian expulsion, 41; Metternich foresees danger, 53–6; influence of Pius's rule elsewhere, 59; feverish condition, at end of 1847, 75; Constitution at Naples, 85, at Florence, 87, at Rome, 91, at Turin, 98; insurrection at Milan, 109–122; Piedmont declares war, 129, Tuscany, 132; Roman volunteers, 134; Naples for war, 137; immense enthusiasm, 140; contradictions, 141; Radetzky retreats to Quadrilateral, 144; Charles Albert's plans, 148; skirmish at Goito, ib.; Lombard volunteers, 150; general enthusiasm, 151; roster of forces, 152; jealousies, 153; grumbling at slow campaign, 162; victory of Pastrengo, 163; defection of Pius, 170; influence on National Cause, 173–4; Bomba's wrangle with deputies, 179–80; bloody reaction at Naples, 181–2; Nugent's advance, 183; effects of Bomba's perfidy, 184; the turning point in the war, ib.; Tuscans defeated at Curtatone, 187; victory of Goito, 188; Peschiera surrenders, ib.; political discord, 189–90; plebiscites, 191; European situation in May, 1848, 192; second proposal from Austria, 193; Austrian advantage, 197; lethargy, 198; discord growing, 199; insinuations of treachery, 200; Venice votes for fusion, 209; military torpor, ib.; battle of Custoza, 211–12; retreat, 213–14; horrors at Milan, 218–22; Salasco armistice, 222–3; Anglo-French mediation, 230; Democratic gains in Piedmont, 234; triumvirate at Venice, 238; period of transition, 243–4; Radicalism gaining in Tuscany, 244; revolt at Leghorn, 248; Democratic ministry, 252; Rossi premier at Rome, 257; his assassination, 259; flight of Pius IX to Gaeta, 263; Peoples vs. Princes, 264; Pius IX draws Europe into his affairs, 271; Democratic régime in Piedmont, 275; Gioberti's diplomacy, 279–82; the Constituent in Tuscany, 283; Leopold's deceit and flight, 284–5; Roman assembly meets, 289; proclaims the republic, 292; Gioberti's downfall, 298; Salasco armistice broken, 305; political ferment in Tuscany, 308; exultation in Rome, 309; administration, 310; Mazzini in Rome, 312; Piedmontese plan of campaign, 317–18; battle of Novara, 323–5; Charles Albert abdicates, 326; end of Constitutional struggle, 330; Brescia revolts, 331–3; Guerrazzi's fall, 338; Leopold's restoration, 341; triumvirate at Rome, 342; conferences at Gaeta, 350; French expedition planned, 354; reaches Civitavecchia, 358; Oudinot's first attack repelled, 362; Neapolitan invasion, 363; siege of Rome, 378–83; fall of Roman Republic and entry of French, 384; Manin president of Venice, 385; Venice decrees resistance at any cost, 389; fall of Marghera, 396; bombardment, 403; cholera, 404–5; surrender, 408; criticism of the Italian revolution, 410–13; general retrospect, 413–14; outlook, 414–15.

" Italy an artichoke," i, 255.
" Italy a geographical expression," ii, 56.
" Italy, land of the dead," i, 318.
" Italy will work out her own salvation," ii, 131.

430   INDEX.

Jacobins, i, 194, 327, 330.
Janissaries, comparison with Roman clergy, i, 32.
Jankovich, Austrian officer, ii, 50.
Janson, Forbin de, French diplomat, ii, 350.
Jellacich, general, ii, 276.
Jena, i, 194.
Jerome, St., advocate of celibacy, i, 31.
Jesuits, i, 78, 82; suppressed, 91; control education in Naples, 158; in Papal States, 163; in Modena, 165; in Piedmont, 254; unpopular in Tuscany, 164, 208, 287, 291, 425; in Piedmont, 419, 420; Gioberti on, 434; at Pisa, 451; vilify Pius IX, ii, 74; Pius upholds them, 92, 134; in Genoa, 95; driven from Naples, 136, 226; under Roman Republic, 345.
Jesus Christ, utterances of, do not sanction a hierarchy, i, 10; Tutelar President of Arcadia, 86; Carbonaro, 108.
Jews, in Piedmont, i, 176; at Rome, 337; ii, 18.
Joan of Arc, ii, 131.
John of Bohemia, i, 72.
John V of Portugal, i, 87.
Jonson, Ben, i, 314.
Joseph II of Austria, anti-clerical reforms, i. 91.
Julius II, pope, i, 66; ii, 6, 174.
Justinian, i, 44.

Kant, philosopher of liberty, i, 314, 383.
Kaunitz, Austrian minister, i, 122.
Knox, John, i, 78.
Kossuth, Louis, letter to Manin, ii, 392.
Kutusoff, Russian general, i, 112.

La Bicocca, ii, 324, 325.
Labrador, Spanish diplomat, i, 119.
La Cecilia, Mazzinian, ii, 178, 180, 248.
Lacordaire, Père, i, 430.
Ladeschi, i, 297.
Ladislaus of Hungary, i, 72.
La Farina, on Roman Constitution, ii, 92; on suppression of Inquisition, 310.
Lafayette, i, 204, 343, 346, 352.

La Ferronays, French diplomat, i, 240.
Lafitte, French minister, i, 347.
La Marmora, Albert, sent to Venice, ii, 157.
La Marmora, Alexander, ii, 326.
La Marmora, Alfonso, ii, 212; rescues the King, 222; mission to Paris, 234; to intervene in Tuscany, 294, 297, 298; 318; at Genoa, 330.
Lamartine, French president, i, 318, 430; ii, 159, 161.
La Masa, Sicilian Liberal, ii, 78, 79.
Lambruschini, Cardinal, appointed Secretary of State, i, 416; leader of Reactionists, ii, 5; first tilt with Micara, 6; leads on first ballot, 11; tide turns, 12; defeated, 14; 16, 18.
Lamennais, i, 430; ii, 55.
Lamoricière, French general, ii, 353, 354.
Lanari, Lieut., executed, i, 288.
Lanza, Dr., at Casale, ii, 67.
Las Cabezas de San Juan, village of, i, 215.
Lascarena, Piedmontese minister, i, 427.
La Sforzesca, ii, 321.
Latimer, i, 78.
Latin language, i, 54; enforced use, 338; ii, 32.
Latour, Austrian minister, ii, 276.
Laugier, Tuscan general, ii, 187, 200, 207.
Laybach, i, 242; Congress, 243-8, 270.
Lazise, town, ii, 230.
Lazzari, Piedmontese general, ii, 217.
Leblanc, French colonel, ii, 359, 360.
Ledru-Rollin, French republican, ii, 380.
Legations, the, reassigned to pope, i, 120; 216, 263, 338, 350, 352, 377, 418, 441, 446.
Leghorn, i, 203, 307; disturbances, ii, 62; revolt, 248; provisional government, 248-9; Cipriani expelled, 249; Guerrazzi, 250; Moutanelli, 251; taken by Austrians, 341.
Legnago, ii, 144, 197, 209, 230.
Legnano, battle of, i, 48.
Leipzig, i, 128, 194.

INDEX. 431

Leo X. pope. i. 66, 74. 204.
Leo XII. election. i. 337; first measures. *ib.;* 357, 378; ii, 17, 310.
Leonidas. i. 252.
Leopardi, James, wretchedness. i. 321; genius, 322; pessimism, 323; patriotic odes, 324.
Leopold I, Grand Duke of Tuscany, restricts power of church, i, 91; coronation as emperor. 122.
Leopold II, of Tuscany, mild rule, i. 337; government. 425; retrogrades. 451; lectured by Metternich. ii, 54; concessions, 63; annexes Lucca, 65; grants constitution, 87; consents to war, 132; customs league, 154; conflicting interests, 245; difficulties. 246; Austrian menace, 247; anxiety over Leghorn riot. 248; consents to Democratic ministry. 253; interview with Guerrazzi. *ib.;* excited by Montanelli. 282; coquettes with the project of the Constituent. 283; at Siena, 284; flight. 285; secret understanding with Austria. 286; letter to Charles Albert. 296; paltering, *ib.;* embarks for Gaeta. 297; intrigues for restoration, 334; demonstration in his favor. 337; relations with Tuscan moderates, 339; correspondence with Esterhazy, 340; return. 341.
Lesseps, Ferdinand de. sent to Rome. ii, 366; first interview with Mazzini, *ib.;* first terms, 367; second offer. 369; dislike of Mazzini, 370; third and fourth projects. 370-1; quarrel with Oudinot, 371; recalled. *ib.*
Liberty, the modern watchword, i, 314.
Liechtenstein, Prince. ii. 106.
Ligne. Prince de, epigram by, i. 117.
Liguori, Alfonso de', canonized, i, 159.
Liris. river, i, 7, 250.
Lisio, Moffa di, i, 265, 268.
Litta, Milanese Liberal, ii, 118, 218, 219. 236.
Locke. John, i. 313.
Lodi. ii. 143, 216.
Lollards. i, 69.
Lombards harass the popes, i, 14, 44.

Lombardy, Austrian rule after restoration. 167 *et seq.;* apparent prosperity, 169; unconquerable aversion to Austria, 170; ubiquitous police, 171; army, 172; delegation to Paris in 1814, 191; plots in, 254; conspirators exhort Charles Albert, 274, 297; arrests, 297; milder policy, 336; cholera, 410; 424; Austrian army increased, ii. 56; petty persecution, 70; bloodshed, 71; Nazzari's demand. *ib.;* violence. 94; sevenheaded government, 101; antitobacco agitation, *ib.;* viceregal proclamation, 102; passive rebellion and increased oppression. 103-4; more troops. 105; general insurrection, 121; Charles Albert's proclamation, 130; Piedmontese army crosses frontier, 145; overconfidence, 146; volunteers in Lower Tyrol. 150; Republicans hostile to Charles Albert. 156; discord over fusion, 189; plebiscite to be held. *ib.;* votes for fusion, 191; refuses to treat with Austria, 197; reinvaded by Radetzky, 214; evacuated by Charles Albert. 222; severity of Austrian reoccupation, 236; Camozzi's mission, 306; Brescia's struggle, 330-3; Austrian régime restored, 333.
London, exiles in, i, 331.
Lothair, i. 24.
Lottery, ii, 34; abolished at Venice, 398.
Louis XI. ii. 301.
Louis XIII. ii, 209.
Louis XIV, i, 81.
Louis XV. i, 314.
Louis XVI. i. 194.
Louis XVIII, i, 246, 310, 328, 345.
Louis Philippe, i. 204; becomes king, 342-3; conduct towards Liberals and autocrats. 343; adroitness, 345; 353; advice at Naples, 358, 406; allusion to Italian affairs, 364; doctrine of the *juste milieu*, 380; 427: ii, 37; breaks with England, 53; downfall, 90, 99, 263.
Louis the German, i. 24.
Louise, queen of Prussia, i, 122.

Lowell, J. R., compared with Giusti, ii, 61.
Loyola, Ignatius, i, 78, 407.
Lucca, i, 120, 167, 426; ii, 55, 64, 251, 337.
Ludolf, Austrian diplomat, ii, 82, 350.
Ludovisi, Prince, i, 120.
Lunigiana, the, ii, 65, 247.
Lupatelli, executed, i, 444.
Luther, i, 69, 71, 204.
Lützen, battle of, i, 127.
Lützow, Austrian diplomat, ii, 11, 37.
Lyons, i, 400.

Maccabæus, Judas, on Rome, i, 17.
Macerata, conspiracy at, i, 212.
Machiavelli, i, 73, 82, 92; ii, 86, 270.
Madrid, i, 210.
Maestri, Dr., ii, 216.
Magenta, ii, 222, 319.
Maghella, a Carbonaro, i, 195.
Mahometans, conquer Constantinople, i, 69.
Maison, Marshal, French ambassador, i, 372.
Maistre, Joseph de, quoted, i, 256.
Majo, General de, Lieut.-Governor of Sicily, ii, 80.
Malamocco, ii, 126.
Malta, i, 440.
Mameli, Goffredo, soldier-poet, ii, 300, 378.
Maniani, Terenzio, Papal premier, ii, 173; tries to revive league, 210; patriotic policy, 254; resigns, 256; minister of Foreign Affairs, 262; 265, 266, 270; final withdrawal, 271; protest against French interference, 272; opposes declaration of republic, 290, 291; 309, 356.
Manara, Lucian, leader of volunteers, ii, 116, 121, 359, 383.
Manhès, French general in Naples, i, 153.
Manin, Daniel, demands legal rights, ii, 73; leads insurrection, 124; proclaims republic, 125; military preparations, 150; 202; report to National Assembly, 205; speech, 208; declines to continue in office, 209; governs alone, 237; triumvir, *ib.*; overtures to France and England, 239, and Piedmont, 240;

elected president, 385; negotiations with Italian neighbors, 387; to aid Piedmont, 388; authorized to resist at any cost, 389; proposals to Western Powers, 391; rejects Radetzky's demand, 394; financial measures, 398; negotiations with De Brück, 400–1; fortitude amid distress, 406; addresses mob, 407; his eloquence, 408; resigns, *ib.*; his character, 409–10; departure, 410.
Manners in Italy, i, 51.
Mannucci, mayor of Civitavecchia, ii, 358.
Mantua, given to Austria, i, 119, 263, 299; ii, 105, 143, 144, 148, 149, 150, 186, 187, 188, 197, 209, 210, 211, 230.
Manzoni, i, 253; a Romanticist, 316, 317; literary rank, 319; religion, *ib.*; great personality, *ib.*; plays and poems, 320; "The Betrothed," *ib.*; 324, 411, 431, 449.
Maranesi, tortured, i, 295.
Marat, ii, 251.
Maratta, Faustina, i, 87.
Marches, the, given back to the pope, i, 120, 216.
Maremme, the, i, 425; ii, 285.
Marengo, i, 100, 125, 310.
Margarita, Solaro della, Piedmontese minister, i, 421, 452; ii, 38, 68, 69.
Marghera, Venetian outpost, ii. 126, 390; attack, 393; abandoned, 395.
Maria Louisa, Empress of French, settled at Parma, i, 120; marriage, 125; rule at Parma, 167; 302, 355, 367; ii, 64, 72.
Maria Louisa, Spanish Infanta, gets Lucca, i, 120, 337.
Mariani, Roman triumvir, ii, 381.
Maria Theresa, Duchess of Modena, i, 261, 271, 273, 309, 310.
Maria Theresa, Empress, i, 122.
Maria Theresa, queen of Piedmont, i, 177, 261, 271, 352.
Maria Theresa, of Tuscany, wife of Charles Albert, i, 261; ii, 315.
Marini, poet, i, 89.
Marinovich, murder of, ii, 125.
Marioni, Roman envoy, ii, 379.
Mariotti, Giovanni, i, 294.
Maroncelli, i, 297, 308.

INDEX.   433

Marquis, origin of title, i, 41.
Marriage, civil, prohibited, i, 149.
Marseilles, i, 331, 352, 396.
Martial, i, 75, 79.
Martini, Count, ii, 119, 120, 128, 129.
Martini, diplomatic agent, ii. 279.
Masi, Canino's secretary, ii, 290.
Masina, killed in defense of Rome, ii, 378.
Massa, i, 119; ii, 247, 307.
Massimo, Cardinal, i. 446.
Mastai, Cardinal. See Pius IX.
Mauri, Milanese insurgent, ii, 118.
Maxentius, Roman emperor, i, 214.
Mayer, Henry, Mazzinian, i, 397.
Mazzini, Joseph, the Great Conspirator, i, 382; distinguish between his ideals and deeds. 383; early years, 384; views on Romanticism, 385–6; joins Carbonari, 387; disgust with mummery, 388; arrested and imprisoned at Savona, *ib.*; formulates his doctrines, 389–92; plans Young Italy, 393; released and banished, 396; at Marseilles, *ib.*; addresses Charles Albert, *ib.*; founds Young Italy, *ib.*; to be expelled from France, 398; plans rising in Piedmont, *ib.*; Savoy expedition, 400–1; becomes head of European conspirators, 401; settles in London, 402; terror of autocrats, *ib.*; the counterpart of Metternich, 403; too far from centre of operations, 404; 427; plans fresh revolt, 440; plot of 1844, 441–2; the Bandiera brothers, 442–4; replies to accusers, 444; hatred of Moderates, 445; ii, 41, 54; doctrines popular in the South, 73; confers with French ministers, 159; agitates Milan, 188; rejoices in Charles Albert's defeat, 264; at Florence, 306; speech at Rome, 312–13; inconsistency, 314; favors aiding Piedmont, *ib.*; elected triumvir, 342; his personality, 342–3; prepares to defend Rome, 344–5; his Easter pageant, 346; remark on Genoese revolt, 347; suspects Oudinot's purpose, 359–60; first interview with Lesseps, 366; rejects first terms, 367; justification. 368; counter-proposal, 369; other terms offered, 370–1; persists in defending Rome, 380–1; refuses to surrender, 381; departs from Rome, 382; 413.
Mazzoni, Tuscan triumvir, ii, 287.
Medici, leader of legion at Rome, ii, 376, 379.
Medici, Lorenzo de', the Magnificent, i, 66, 73.
Medici, Lorenzo de', grandson of preceding, i. 93.
Medici, de', Neapolitan minister, i, 157.
Melara, leader of volunteers, ii, 359, 378.
Melenchini, ii, 249.
Meloncelli, Arcadian, i, 89.
Melville, Lord, i, 183.
Memling, German painter, i, 71.
Memorandum of 1831, i, 363; disregarded, 415; 447; ii, 38.
Menichini, Carbonaro, priest, i, 217, 223.
Menotti, Ciro, i, 352; suspects Duke, 353; hastens revolt, 354; captured, *ib.*; taken to Mantua, 355; executed, 366; 381.
Mercenaries, i, 64.
Mercier, French agent, ii, 318.
Mercogliano, i, 217.
Messina, decrees issued at, i, 147; rebels, 227; 442; Liberals attempt to capture, ii, 73.
Mestre, Venetian outpost, ii, 126, 204, 390, 395.
Metternich, Prince Clement, at Vienna Congress, i, 117; measures at Napoleon's escape, 118; divider of spoils in Italy, 119; 120; view of Old Régime, 121; his birth and education, 122; first diplomatic service, 123; ambassador at Paris, 124; Austrian premier, 125; intrigues in 1812–13, 126; interview with Napoleon at Dresden, 127 *et seq.*; intrigues during invasion of France, 129; quarrel with Czar, *ib.*; his political creed, 130; mistaken view of French Revolution, 131; opinion of Holy Alliance, 133; criticism of rivals, 134; his policy, 135; his talents, 136; manners, 137; controls Ferdinand IV, 157; attitude towards Duke of Modena, 165; rule in Lombardy and Venetia, 167; provides dissi-

pations, 170; principle of legitimacy, 179; attempts to Austrianize Italy, 180 *et seq.;* compact with Naples, 180; abets tyranny in Sicily, 183; intrigues in Tuscany, 183-4, in Parma, 184, in Modena, 185, in Rome, *ib.;* checked in Piedmont, 186-9; view of secret societies, 204; watching Carbonari, 210; visits Italy, 211; angered by revolution of 1820, 238; interferes in Naples, 239; at Troppau, 241; at Laybach, 244; note to Gentz, *ib.;* persuades the Czar, 245; opinion of Ferdinand I, 246; frightens Piedmontese government, 257; designs on Charles Albert, 260; quenches revolutions, 278; Italians learn that he must be reckoned with, 280; favors a central police-station for political offenders, 296; 302; interview with Confalonieri, 304; 308; intrigues against Charles Albert's succession, 309-10; 325, 327; watches exiles, 333; 335; milder policy, 336; conduct towards Louis Philippe, 344; determines on intervention, 360; alarms Louis Philippe, 361; second intervention, 368; sarcastic treatment of French cabinet over Ancona affair, 372; indispensable to Papacy, 378; contrast with Mazzini, 403; contempt for Papal rule, 416; secures Lambruschini's appointment, *ib.;* resents Papal interference at home, 418; spies employed, 427; self-complacency, 428; tries to coerce Piedmont, 452; interference at Conclaves, ii, 10; attitude towards Pius IX, 36; advises against amnesty, 37; complicity in Gregorian plot, 50; the Ferrara affair, 51; wheedles Guizot, 52-3; foresees calamity, 53; denounces Liberals, 54; tries to scare Pius, *ib.;* sneers at Charles Albert, 55; "Italy a geographical expression," 56; meddles in Lucca, 65; desperate efforts, 75; Cassandra warnings, 100; sneers at Italians, 101; compact with Parma and Modena, 106; downfall, 107; flight, 107-8; final exit, 108; succeeded by Ficquelmont, 161; 263.

Metternich, Princess Melanie, ii, 107, 108.
Mezzacapa, Roman officer, ii, 315.
Mezzanacorte, ii, 321.
Mezzofanti, Cardinal, ii, 91.
Micara, Cardinal, ii, 5-6; candidate for pope, 7, 8, 9, 12, 13, 16.
Michael Angelo. See Buonarotti.
Michelet, i, 62.
Middle Age, condition of men in, i, 35; bequests to modern world, 38.
Milan, kings of Italy crowned there, i, 24; destroyed by Barbarossa, 48; 70, 107; given to Austria, 119, 204, 258, 263, 275; coercion, 298; arrest of Confalonieri, 299; "devoured by Austrians," 330; surface gayety, 336; cholera, 411; bloodshed, ii, 71, 94; riot over "no smoking," 101; stricter police measures, 103; passive rebellion, 104; martial law declared, 105; news of Vienna revolution, 109; rising, *ib.;* Casa Vidiserti, 110; Broletto captured, 112; description of city, 112-13; barricades, 114; quaint arms, *ib.;* Casati removes to Casa Taverna, 115; contest in inner city, 117; no surrender, 118; question as to the future, 119-20; last fighting, 121; Milan free, 122; Austrian atrocities, 122-3; losses, 123; Republicans against Royalists, 145; Provisional Government appeals to France, 160; agitation over fusion, 188; Mazzini, *ib.;* Gioberti, 189; Schnitzermeaay's mission, 196; excitement at news of Charles Albert's defeat, 214; preparations for defense, 215; Committee of Public Defense, *ib.;* Austrian attack, 216; mob attacks Charles Albert in Casa Greppi, 218-21; his escape, 222; exodus of citizens at Radetzky's entry, *ib.*
Milbitz, leader of Polish legion, ii, 376.
Minghetti, Marco, Bolognese, founds the *Felsineo,* ii, 45; minister, 91; tries to counteract Pius's allocution, 172; on the violence at Milan, 223; 255, 260, 261, 265, 309, 356.
Minto, Lord, ii, 75, 137.
Mirabeau, i, 109.

Misley, Modenese conspirator, i, 352.
Missi, or imperial inspectors, i, 7.
Mithras, i, 195.
Modena, Duchess of, wife of Francis IV. See Maria Theresa.
Modena, reactionist government in, i, 105; schemes, 185, 203; atrocities, 294; plots, 347; Menotti, 352; renewed cruelties, 366; 424; Austrian garrison, ii, 72, 120; votes for fusion, 191.
Molière, dramatist, i, 52.
Molière, general, ii, 271.
Molise, i, 219.
Monarchical government, theory of, i, 39.
Moughini, Ravennese deputy, ii, 291.
Montaigne, i, 54.
Montanara, ii, 151; Tuscan defeat, 187.
Montanari, ii, 45, 260.
Montanelli, Tuscan patriot, ii, 61–2; shrewd tactics, 63; appointed governor of Leghorn, 251; premier, 252; conflict with Gioberti, 281; flatters Leopold, 282; seems to prosper, 283; bedside interview, 284; discovers Leopold's flight, 285; returns to Florence, 287; elected a triumvir, ib.; defends Florence against Smith, 307; goes to frontier, 308; will not compete with Guerrazzi, 333.
Mt. Cenis, i, 187, 443.
Montecchi, Roman politician, ii, 309.
Montechiaro, ii, 143, 145, 148.
Monteforte, i, 219, 220, 221.
Montevideo, ii, 42, 372.
Monti, Vincenzo, birth, i, 98; life in Rome, 99; decries French Revolution, ib.; turns Republican, 100; lauds Napoleon, 101; truckles to Austria, 102; pedantic disputes, 103; character, ib.; rank as poet, 105; compared with Young, 106; 171, 320.
Montléart, M. de, Charles Albert's step-father, i, 259.
Monza, ii, 121.
Monzambano, ii, 149.
Morals, low ebb at Renaissance. i, 73; of Neapolitan clergy, 158; at Rome under Gregory XVI, ii, 34.
Morandi, governor of Rome, ii, 49.

Moranti, tortured, i, 294.
Moreau, i, 107.
Morelli, leads revolt, i, 217, 218, 222.
Morichini, Monsignor, ii, 176.
Moro, Domenico, joins Bandiera expedition, i, 442.
Moroni, Gaetano, barber, and favorite of Gregory XVI, i, 415, 416; ii, 2.
Morosini, doge, ii, 205.
Morosini, volunteer killed at Rome, ii, 383.
Mortara, ii, 318, 319, 320, 321, 322.
Murat, Achille, i, 361, 367.
Murat, King of Naples, i, 110, 119, 129, 139, 140, 141; defeat, 142, 146, 157; execution, 159; dealings with Carbonari, 195, 222.
Muscovy, i, 60, 81.
Music, i. 82.
Muzio, Monsignor, ii, 17.
Muzzarelli, Monsignor, ii, 260, 262, 309.

Naples, city of, Scientific Congress at, i, 426; arrests, ii, 74; revolution of May, 15, 181.
Naples, kingdom of, becomes Parthenopean Republic, i, 110; Ferdinand IV restored, 120, 141; reforms under Charles of Bourbon, 144–5; reaction, 145; finances, 148; jealousy in army, ib.; administration of justice, 149; lawless character of the people, 151–2; exemption of criminals, 152; brigands, 153; the Vardarelli, 154–6; distress, 156; Austrian army evacuates, ib.; Concordat with pope, 157; Carbonari in, 203; revolt at Nola, 217; Constitution granted, 220; new ministry, 221; grand demonstration, 222–3; Ferdinand I takes oath, 225; Parliament meets, 235; first deliberation, 236; consents to king's departure, 242; Austria to interfere, 247; apprehension, and disorders, 248; king's perfidy discovered, 249; preparations for war, 250; defeat by Austrians, ib.; Parliament adjourns, 251; revolution crushed, 252; seditious aspect of revolution, 282; punishment of revolutionists, 283–8;

Canosa head chastiser, 283; recrudescence of tyranny, 287; public debt, 288; Chateaubriand's account, 330; depraved rule of Francis I, 340; hopes of Liberals, 350; Ferdinand II succeeds, 358; his early reign, 406–8; corrupt government, 408; cruel repression, 409; cholera epidemic, 410–12; arrest of Liberals, 441; Bandiera expedition, 442–4; vigilance of government, 445; tyranny unabated, ii, 38; outbreaks, 73; Sicilian revolution, 78–81; Liberals triumph, 82; Constitution granted, 83; its character, 85, rapid changes, 135; Bomba dissembles, 136; war with Sicily, 137; National War declared, *ib.*; new ministry, 138; Bomba's proclamation, 138–40; his perfidy, 176; noisy wrangles, 177; pandemonium, 178; deputies assemble, 179; riot, 180; Liberals suppressed, 181; Gladstone's condemnation, 182; Liberals suppressed, 348; Sicily reconquered, 349.

Napoleon I, i, 18, 100, 101, 102, 106, 107; uses the revolution for his own ends, 110; becomes emperor, *ib.*; downfall, *ib.*; genius, 112; 115; escape from Elba, 117, 122; first acquaintance with Metternich, 123; marriage with Maria Louisa, 125; defeat in Russia, 126; interview with Metternich at Dresden, 127 *et seq.*; 136; return from Elba, 141; 190, 207, 238, 240, 259, 310, 404; ii, 109, 147, 149.

Napoleon II, i. 360.
Napoleon, Louis. See Bonaparte.
Napoletano, Neapolitan general, i, 223.
Narbonne, French diplomat, i, 126.
Narses, i, 44.
Naselli, Lieut.-Governor of Sicily, i. 227, 228, 231, 232.
Nationality, spirit of, i, 130.
Nazzari, Lombard delegate, ii. 71.
Neipperg, favorite of Maria Louisa, i, 167.
Nelson, Horatio, i, 112, 146; ii, 377.
Neo-Guelfs, description of, i, 431; Gioberti's " Primacy " their creed, 432; 436, 437; ii, 35, 60, 414.

Nero, i, 90.
Nesselrode, Russian statesman, i, 244.
Neto, river, i, 443.
Neustria, i, 23.
Newman, Cardinal, i, 430.
Newspapers, *Conciliatore*, i, 253, 299, 325; Turin *Gazette*, i, 289; *Antologia*, i, 325, 425; *Voce della Verità*, i, 424; *Diario di Roma*, ii, 45, 50; *Bilancia, Contemporaneo*, at Rome, ii, 45; *Felsineo* and *Italiano*, at Bologna, ii, 45; *Amica Veritas, Sentinella del Campidoglio*, clandestine journals, ii, 45; in Tuscany, ii, 62; *Risorgimento*, ii, 93, 127; *Official Gazette*, Rome, ii, 167, 170.
Niagara, ii, 76.
Niccolini, G. B., i, 316, 317, 318; ii, 60.
Niccolò, the Pisan sculptor, i, 50.
Nice, i. 271; ii, 159, 327, 372.
Nicholas III, pope, i, 56.
Nicholas V, pope, ardent Humanist, i, 64, 70.
Nicholas, Czar, allied with Austria, i, 426; beset by Papal beggars, ii, 34.
Niebuhr, quoted, ii, 35.
Nizzoli, Antonio, tortured, i, 294.
Nola, i, 217, 219, 409.
Nominalists, i, 433.
Non-intervention proclaimed, i, 347.
" Northern Powers," i, 329.
Novara, joins league against Barbarossa, i, 48, 274, 275; skirmish at, 277–8; Scientific Congress, ii, 41; 318, 322; description, 323; battle, 323–5.
Novarese, Upper, Austrian schemes against, i, 187, 189, 257.
Novendiale, the, ii, 3, 8.
Nugent, manifesto at Ravenna, i, 139; at Modena, 140; commander-in-chief at Naples, 148, 218; brings reinforcements to Radetzky, ii, 183; effects junction, 186; 191, 203, 331.
Nunziante, Neapolitan general, i, 219.

Odoacer, i, 19, 44.
O'Donell, Count, ii, 106, 109, 110.
O'Faris, Neapolitan general, i, 231.
Oglio, river, ii, 212.

INDEX. 437

Old Régime, its character in 1815, i, 143 *et seq.*
Oleggio, town of, ii, 317, 318.
Olengo, ii. 323, 324.
Olivieri, Piedmontese commissioner, ii, 216.
Oporto, ii, 327, 328.
Oppizzoni, Cardinal, ii, 14.
Oppizzoni, Monsignor, ii, 103.
Oppressed, not Conquered, secret society, i, 203.
Origen. advocate of celibacy, i, 31.
Orsini. Felice, ii, 345.
Osimo, town of, ii, 8.
Osone, river, ii, 151.
Otranto, i, 214.
Otto, French diplomatic agent, i, 126.
Otto I, German Emperor, i, 45.
Oudinot, French general, ii, 354, 355, 356, 358, 359, 360, 361, 362, 363, 364, 366, 369, 370, 371, 377, 384, 406.
Ovid, i, 75.

Pachta, Austrian agent, ii, 101, 123.
Padua, i, 203, 426; ii, 105, 202, 395.
Painting, decline of, i, 74, 79.
Paleario, free-thinker. i, 84.
Paleocapa. Venetian Liberal, speech in favor of fusion, ii, 206.
Palermo, excitement in, i, 227; riot, 228; rebels capture the city, 231-2; atrocities. 232-3; surrender, 234, 237; tumult, 409; cholera, 412; revolution, ii, 77-81; 348, 349.
Palestrina, battle at, ii, 363.
Palestrina, musician, i, 83.
Palffy, governor at Venice, ii, 124, 125.
Pallavicini. i, 298, 304.
Pallotta, Cardinal, i, 338.
Palma, Monsignor, ii. 262.
Palmanova, blockaded, ii, 183.
Palmerston, Lord, annoys Metternich. ii. 53; check to Austria's scheme, 56; attitude towards Italian war. 157-8; tries to prevent European war, 160; hears Ficquelmont's first proposal, 161; Hummelauer's proposals, 163; urges Italians to accept. 194; proposes mediation. 229; sounds Austria, 230-1; advises her to make peace, 232-3; overtures from Manin, 239; reply to Pasini, 241-2; unshaken amid general confusion, 244; negotiations with Austria, 302; pacific advice unheeded, 303; opinion of Haynau, 333; on Roman Republic, 356; advice to Romans, 380; will not help Venice, 386; reply to Manin, 391; 406.
Panizzi, Anthony. i, 295.
Pannonia, i, 7.
Pantaleoni, Dr., ii, 268.
Pantelleria. galleys at, i, 150, 286.
Pantelleria. Prince of, ii, 79.
Papacy. origin, i, 12; contest with Empire, 26; growth, 27; enemy of Italian nationality, 43; denounced by Dante, 56; saved by Reformation, 77; nepotism, 79; dependent on foreign protection, 417; Gioberti's scheme for restoring influence, 433; incompatible with Italian independence, ii, 174; abolition decreed, 292.
Papal States, Pius VII. restored, i, 160; administrative scheme, 161; finances, 162; many criminals and beggars, *ib.;* incompetent judiciary, 163; Metternich's schemes, 185, 253; Chateaubriand's account of, 330; misery in, 337; plots, 347; revolution of 1831 breaks out. 355; election of Gregory XVI. 357; panic, 358; memorandum from Great Powers, 363; disturbances, 367; Austrian and French intrigues, 369; French occupy Ancona. 370; Papal protest, 371; conditions grow worse, 375; corruption and incompetence. 415-16; Papacy must have foreign support. 417; disorders, 446; rejoicing at Gregory's death, ii, 4; election of Pius IX, 14; amnesty, 18-20; rottenness of Papal Government. 28; nepotism, *ib.;* pious oligarchy. 29; irresponsibility of officials. 30; finances, *ib.;* dishonesty, *ib.;* taxes. 31; trade, *ib.;* smuggling, *ib.;* judiciary system, 32; police, 33; education. *ib.;* morals, 34; beggars, *ib.;* encyclical. 39; paradoxes, 40; reforms delayed, 42; new press law, 45; newspapers, *ib.;* Consulta prom-

ised, 46; Council of ministers, ib.; vigilance committee, 47; Civic Guard granted, 48; excitement over attempted abduction of Pius, 49; patriotic demonstrations, 52; list and functions of Consulta, 58; agitation, 87; new ministry, 90; constitution, 91; preparations for war, 133-4; troops in the field, 151; reaction, 166; ministers try to persuade Pius, 167; conflicting instructions, 168; allocution of April 29, 170; ministers resign, ib.; Mamiani forms ministry, 173; his patriotic policy, 254; parliament meets, 255; Austrian invasion, 256; Rossi premier, 257; his assassination, 259; Galletti ministry, 262; deputies vote against Pope, 263; flight of Pius, ib.; uncertainty at Rome, 266; Papal brief, 267; Junta at Rome, 270; new ministry, 271; Europe meddles in restoration of Pope, 272; Radical and Reactionist plots, 288; clerical impositions, 289; Constituent meets, ib.; debate, 290-92; republic voted and proclaimed, 292; radical administration, 309; Inquisition suppressed, 310; diplomacy, 311; Mazzini's arrival, 312; war fervor, 314; triumvirate elected, 342; Mazzini's measures, 344-6; Papal intrigues, 349-50; Louis Napoleon's scheme, 351-2; Oudinot lands at Civitavecchia, 358; his messengers at Rome, 359; repel force with force, ib.; martial preparations, 360; Oudinot driven back, 362; Neapolitan invasion, 363; Austrians and Spaniards approaching, ib.; armistice with French, 366; second campaign against Bomba, 372; fight at Velletri, 375; strength of Romans, 376; siege of Rome begun, 378; Mazzini's diplomacy, 380-1; defense abandoned, 381; French in Rome, 382; Pius's return, 411.

Paraguay, i, 434.
Parana, river, ii, 372.
Pareto, Piedmontese minister, ii, 129, 154, 190, 194, 227.
Parini, forerunner of native poets, i, 97; likened to Cowper, ib.

Paris, i, 230; resort of exiles, 331; ii, 205.
Parma ruled by Farnese, i, 73; assigned to Maria Louisa, 119; restoration in, 167; Austrian influence, 184; Duke of Modena meddles, 295; rebellion at, 355; lenient restoration, 367; Austrians predominant, ii, 72; occupied by Austria, 130; votes for fusion, 191; 318.
Partesotti, Metternich's spy, i, 442.
Parthenopean Republic, i, 110.
Pascal, i, 432.
Pasini, Valentino, Venetian Liberal, negotiations with France, 240; letter to Palmerston, 241; reply, 242; renews appeals, 385-7, 391-2; at Vienna, 401.
Pasolini, ii, 26, 90; 172, 260, 273, 309.
Pasquier, French foreign secretary, i, 245.
Passalacqua, Piedmontese general, ii, 145, 325.
Pastrengo, battle of, ii, 163, 165, 185.
Paternò, Prince of, i, 234.
Paul, St., influence of, on Christianity, i, 12; compared with Dante, 58.
Paulovich, confessor at Spielberg, i, 308.
Pavia, i, 106, 107; ii, 105, 146; ii, 320.
Peasantry, unresponsive to political agitation, i, 280.
Pellico, Silvio, i, 253, 297, 308, 316, 317, 319, 431.
Penne, outbreak at, i, 412.
Pepe, Florestan, sent to subdue Sicily, i, 234.
Pepe, William, i, 217, 218; joins revolutionists, 219, 220; triumphal progress, 221-2; interview with king, 223-4; 224, 235; defeat near Rieti, 250; tries to make a last stand, 251; flight, 252, 270; proposed descent on Sicily, 352, 367; commands Neapolitan army, ii, 138; disingenuous orders, 178; refuses to obey, and goes to Venice, 183; plans assault on Conche, 388; too old, 389, 399, 401.
Pepin the Short, i, 14, 45.
Perfetti, Arcadian, i, 89.
Peri, musician, i, 83.

Pericles, i, 52.
Périer. Casimir, French premier. "non-intervention," i, 361; lame explanatious, 364; perplexity, 369; decides on military intervention, *ib.;* snubbed by Metternich, 372; meekness. 373; holds Ancona, *ib.;* suspected collusion with Rome, 374–5.
Perrone, chevalier, i, 264.
Perrone, general, ii, 229, 274, 318, 323, 324, 325.
Peschiera, ii, 143, 148, 149, 150, 163, 186; surrender, 188; 211, 230.
Petitti, economical writings, i, 453.
Petrarch, i, 51, 54, 92, 322.
Pharos, or Straits of Messina, i, 237.
Piacenza, in league against Barbarossa. i. 48; Farnese tyrants, 73; occupied by Austria, ii, 129; votes for fusion, 191; 214, 217, 318.
Piagine, village of, i. 152.
Pians. adherents of Pius IX, ii, 40.
Piave, river. ii, 144, 183, 191.
Piazzone. Milanese agent. ii, 172.
Piccolomini, Cardinal, ii, 12.
Pichat, journalist. ii. 45.
Pico della Mirandola, i, 66.
Piedmont, frontiers established by Congress of Vienna, i, 119; restoration of Victor Emanuel I, 174; petty tyranny, *ib.;* so-called reforms, 176; lack of civic life. 177; peculiar position of, 187; Metternich tries to get control. *ib.;* peculiar situation of plotters, 254; dynastic ambition, 255; discussion as to new capital, 256; fooled at Troppau, 257; new ministry, *ib.;* preparations of plotters, 262; student riot, 263; arrests, 264; revolution breaks out. 268; Victor Emanuel abdicates. 270-1; Charles Albert regent, 272; grants Constitution, 273; Charles Albert resigns. *ib.;* revolution suppressed, 277–8; had aspect of a sedition, 282; chastisement begun. 288; mock pardon decreed. 290; Chateaubriand's account of. 329; reaction under Charles Felix, 336; Charles Albert's succession. 366; abortive uprising, 398; severe punishment, 399; Savoy expedition, 400–1; conflicting opinions at Charles Albert's accession, 418; Concordat with Rome. 420; reforms, 422; wine and salt controversy, 452; ii, 38, 66; enthusiasm for Pius and Gioberti. 66; Solaro and Villamarina dismissed, 68; reforms, 69; inpatience. 93; Constitution granted, 98; excitement over Milanese insurrection, 127; war declared, 129; motives alleged. 129–30; condition of army, 147; first Parliament, 189; discussion of fusion. 190; Lombardy unites with, 191; Parliamentary discord, 201; Venetian delegates. 202; Venice for fusion, 209; party virulence, 226; Balbo ministry resigns, 227; news of disaster, *ib.;* conflict between Radicals and Aristocrats, 228; negotiations for French aid, 229; internal discontent, 234; truculence of the clubs, 274; Democratic Cabinet led by Gioberti, 275: his programme, 277-8; isolated by Republics at Florence and Rome. 293; opposition to Gioberti's plan. 297; his resignation, 298; Parliament meets, 301; resources for second campaign, 303–4; Chrzanowski to command, 304; war declared. 305; enthusiasm revives, 315; official reason for war. 316; Austria's reply, *ib.;* opening of the campaign, 319; Radetzky's advantage, 320; his victory at Mortara. 321; battle of Novara. 323–5; Charles Albert's abdication, 326; Victor Emanuel II makes terms with Radetzky, 329.
Pinelli, Piedmontese general, ii, 229.
Piombino, principality of, i, 120.
Pisa, flourishes early, i, 46, 65; 425. 426. 451; ii, 250, 251.
Pistoja, ii, 335.
Pius II, pope, Humanist, i, 70.
Pius VI, pope. i, 99, 110.
Pius VII. restored to Rome. i, 141, 160; dispute over *chinea,* 157; assertion of rights. 161; restores Jesuits. *ib.;* relations with Metternich, 185; death expected, 212; bull against secret societies. 214, 293; 244, 286; death, 337, 378.

Pius VIII, i, 357; ii, 4.
Pius IX, Giovanni Maria Mastai Ferretti, candidate for pope, ii, 11; Micara's advice, 12; election, 14; announcement, 15; his previous history, 16-17; supposed Liberalism, 18; unostentation, *ib.*; decree of amnesty, 18-20; immense popularity, 21; mutual deception of Pius and Romans, 22; his real motives, 24; his intellect, 25; religious opinions, *ib*; political views, 26; how far patriotic, *ib.*; inadequate to his task, 27; Metternich's tutelage, 30-7; vibrates between French and Austrian counsel, 37; Retrograde encyclical, 39; popularity, 41; dilatoriness, 42; Ciceruacchio's devotion, 44; first reforms, 45-6; asked for Civic Guard, 47; grants it, 48; Gizzi's opinion of, *ib.*; alleged plot to abduct, 49-50; resists Austrian encroachment at Ferrara, 50-1; indecision, 88; memorable address, 89; on French revolution, 90; embarrassment over war, 133-4; blesses volunteers, 134; negotiations for Customs League, 154; intolerable position, 165; disavows Durando's manifesto, 167; afraid of schism, 168; allocution of April 29, 170; remark to ministers, 171; Liberals wish him to visit Milan, 172; apparent insincerity, 173; letter to Emperor, 175; hampers Mamiani, 254; quarrels with ministers, 255; interview after Rossi's murder, 260-2; summons Democratic ministry, 262; flies from Rome, 263; message to ministers, 266; ruled by Bomba and Antonelli, 267; refuses to receive Liberals, 268-9; cunning policy, 269; snubs Piedmont, 273; monitory against Constituent, *ib.*; rejects Gioberti's overtures, 279-80; frightens Leopold II, 285; renews appeals for armed help, 349; allocution of April 20, 356; eulogy of Bomba, 357; restoration, 411.
Pizzo, Murat shot at, i, 159.
Plague, i, 156.
Plata, river, i, 215; ii, 372.

Plato, i, 75.
Plautus, i, 82.
Plutarch, i, 106.
Poerio, Charles, Neapolitan Liberal, ii, 84, 136.
Poerio, Joseph, Neapolitan deputy, i, 249, 251.
Poetry, decadence, i, 79.
Poland, i, 346, 370.
Politian, i, 66.
Pollini, killed at Rome, ii, 378.
Pompei, excavations at, i, 159.
Ponsonby, British diplomat, ii, 193.
Pontremoli, town of, ii, 86.
Ponza islands, i, 150, 286.
Ponzoni, unjustly accused, i, 294.
Porro, Count, i, 253, 297.
Porto Ferrajo, ii, 86.
Portugal, i, 238, 370.
Potenziani, Roman deputy, ii, 263.
Prierio, Marquis di, i, 264.
Principato Citra, i, 218.
Propaganda, Congregation of, i, 161.
Prussia, i, 81, 239, 344, 372, 426; ii, 53.

Quadrilateral, the, ii, 144, 148.

Raab, taken by Austrians, ii, 403.
Rabelais, i, 71.
Racconigi, Charles Albert's country-seat, ii, 67.
Radetzky, Marshal, ii, 50, 75, 101, 103; threatens Milanese, 104; 106, 110; demands instant submission, 111; takes Broletto, 112; abandons inner Milan, 117; cannot bring insurgents to terms, 118; second offer rejected, 119; critical situation, 121; abandons Milan, 122, 128; his cruelty, 123; retreats to Montechiaro, 143; plan of campaign, 145; retires to Quadrilateral, 148; intercepts Lombard volunteers, 150; forces at end of April, 152; secure position, 161; protects the Adige, 162; attempts to relieve Peschiera, 186; defeats Tuscans at Curtatone, 187; beaten at Goito and retreats, 188; improved condition, 197; takes Vicenza, *ib.*; ready to take offensive, 210; victory at Custoza, 211; offer of peace, 212; larger demands, 214; consents to

truce, 217; receives second embassy, 220; enters Milan, 222; harshness to reconquered provinces, 236–7; stands firm amid flux, 244; denies responsibility for Welden, 256; secret letter to Leopold, 286; 297; crosses the Ticino, 319; first advantage, 320; victory at Mortara, 322; at Novara, 323–5; terms with Piedmont, 329; note to Leopold, 340; expects capture of Marghera, 393; letter to Venetians, 394; entry into Venice, 400.

Ragona, Palermitan insurgent, ii, 78.

Railways, ii, 36, 243.

Ramorino, Jerome, soldier of fortune, commands Mazzini's expedition into Savoy, i, 400; commands division at La Cava, ii, 317; surprised by Radetzky, 321–2; charge of treason, 321, note.

Raphael, i, 71.

Rapp, Austrian general, i, 173.

Ravenna, i, 120, 203, 213, 356, 441, 446; ii, 8.

Raynier, Viceroy of Lombardy and Venetia, i, 174; ii, 101, 103, 106, 109.

Realists, i, 434.

Rebizzo, Piedmontese envoy, ii, 157.

Recanati, town of, i, 322.

Recchi, Roman Liberal, ii, 91, 172.

Reformation, i, 76; mixture of politics and religion, 77; saved Papacy from destruction, *ib.*

Reggio, in Calabria, ii, 73.

Reggio, in Emilia, i, 165, 204.

Reiset, De, French consul at Milan, ii, 217, 230.

Renaissance, message of, i, 61; immense influence, 62; introduces new standards, 63; not a religious movement, 64; apparent failure in Italy, 67; effects, 69; 114.

Renzi, Peter, i, 447, 448, 450.

Republics, mediæval, develop rapidly, 44; relations with Emperors and Popes, 45; internecine feuds, 49; energy spent, 50.

Restelli, Milanese politician, ii, 216, 218.

Retribution on revolutionists, in Naples, i, 283–8, in Papal States, 365–6.

Revel, Thaon di, governor of Turin, i, 264, 288.

Revel, son of preceding, ii, 227, 229, 230.

Rhine, ii, 54.

Ribotti, conspirator, i, 440.

Ricasoli, Bettino, Tuscan Liberal, ii, 60, 132, 251, 265, 336, 341.

Ricci, Papal politician, ii, 273.

Ricci, Piedmontese envoy, ii, 220.

Ricciardi, conspirator, i, 453.

Richelieu, i, 299.

Ridolfi, Marquis, Tuscan Liberal, ii, 60, 64; premier, 86; 132, 245; resigns, 246.

Riego, Raphael, i, 215.

Rienzi, i, 4, 92; ii, 290.

Rieti, battle near, i, 250.

Rimini, i, 213, 365; "manifesto of," 447; 448.

Ringhetti, Rossi's secretary, ii, 259.

Rivarola, Cardinal, i, 338, 368.

Rivoli, captured by Piedmontese, ii, 197; Austrian attack, 211.

Roberti, G., Livornese radical, ii, 248.

Roberti, Monsignor, ii, 268.

Rollin, Ledru, French deputy, ii, 353.

Romagna, i, 203; disturbances, 338; distrust of Menotti, 353; Périer on, 364; disturbances, 367; troubles in, 447–8.

Roman Church, organization, i, 12; reverence for symbols, 14; crushes Arianism, 15; highest expression in Dante, 55; schism, 69; fails to foster morals, 75; dogmatic reaction, 78; persecutes free thought, 83; allies itself with despotism, 138.

Roman Empire, completes conquest of Italy, i, 4; division, 13, 113.

Romanticists, i, 316, 385.

Rome, significance of the word, i, 16; Judas Maccabæus on, 17; influence still potent through Roman Church, 22; cholera, 410; temporary government after Gregory XVI's death, ii, 4; ovation to Pius IX, 22–3; adroitness of masses, 24; pomp and squalor, 35; excitement over Gregorian plot, 49–50; municipality created, 57; agitations, 87; war fever, 133; tumults, 171; disorders after Rossi's assassination, 259; inef-

fective junta, 270; Constituent,
289; republic, 292; Mazzini's
speech, 312; triumvirate, 342;
Good Friday and Easter theatri-
calities, 346-7; approach of Oudinot repelled, 362; Monte Mario
captured by deceit, 370; number
and character of forces, 376-7;
Oudinot's second treachery, 378;
formal siege begun, 378-9; injury
to monuments, 379; defense abandoned, 381; departure of defenders, and obsequies of the Republic,
382; nobility of the defense, 383;
Oudinot's entry, 384.
Romentino, ii, 318.
Romeo, Neapolitan Liberal, ii, 174.
Ronca, brigand, i, 152.
Rosa, Martinez de la, ii, 263, 350.
Roselli, Joseph, Roman general, ii, 372, 375, 376, 377.
Rosicrucians, i, 195.
Rosmini, i, 431; ii, 262.
Rossaroll, Neapolitan plotter, i, 409.
Rosselli, leader of volunteers, ii, 376.
Rossi, Pellegrino, French ambassa-
dor, addresses Conclave, ii, 9;
influence over Pius IX, 37, 38;
quoted, 47, 89; declines premier-
ship, 255; accepts, 257; charac-
ter and policy, 257-8; assassina-
tion, 259; 356.
Rossi, Piedmontese general, ii, 217.
Rothschilds, bankers, ii, 36.
Rousseau, J. J., i, 90, 91, 315.
Roverbella, Charles Albert's head-
quarters, ii, 195, 209, 211.
Rovigo, i, 213; ii, 202.
Rubiera, horrors perpetrated at, i, 291-4.
Rudini, Sicilian Liberal, ii, 79.
Ruffini, James and John, Mazzini's
disciples, i, 397; James kills him-
self, 399.
Ruffo, Cardinal, i, 146, 150.
Ruggiero, Neapolitan minister, ii, 178.
Rusconi, vice-president of Roman
Chamber, ii, 261, 380.
Russia, beginnings of, i, 69; intrigues
in Italy, 211; favors Austrian in-
tervention, 360; ready to fight,
372; withdraws minister from Tu-
rin, ii, 157.
Ruviano, Prince di, ii, 268.

Sacchetti, Marquis, ii, 266.
Saffi, A., Roman triumvir, ii, 309, 342.
St. Cloud, i, 343.
Sainte-Aulaire, French diplomat, sent to Rome, i, 362; 363, 369.
St. Gotthard, ii, 106.
St. John, Knights of, i, 195.
St. Just, French Terrorist, ii, 251.
St. Marc, French adventurer, ii, 296.
St. Petersburg, i, 123.
Salasco, Charles Albert's chief of
staff, ii, 147, 220; signs armistice, 223.
Salerno, medical school, i, 46; 217, 219; arrests in province, 441; re-
volt, ii, 82.
Salerno, Prince of, i, 225.
Saliceti, Neapolitan minister, ii, 309, 381.
Salic law, in Piedmont, i, 259, 260, 273, 293.
Salionze, on the Mincio, ii, 211.
Saluzzo, i, 270.
Salvagnoli, Tuscan Liberal, ii, 251.
Salvotti, i, 298, 300, 301, 302, 304.
San Donato, Radetzky's headquar-
ters, ii, 220.
Sanfedists, political sect, i, 335, 338, 350, 366; ii, 256.
S. Giovanni in Fiore, village, i, 443.
San Marzano, Charles di, i, 265, 267, 268.
San Marzano, Piedmontese minister, i, 270.
San Michele, Colonel, i, 267.
Sanseverino, Cardinal, i, 292.
Santa Lucia, battle of, ii, 185, 414.
Santa Margherita, village, ii, 388.
Santangelo, Neapolitan minister, i, 408.
Santarosa, Santorre, i, 265, 266, 267, 268, 272, 276, 277, 278, 289; ii, 328.
Santo Stefano, Tuscan village, ii, 286, 295, 296, 297.
Saracens, i, 9.
Sardinia, i, 175, 254; feudalism abol-
ished, 422.
Sarpi, historian, i, 85.
Sarzana, town of, ii, 298, 318.
Sauget, General de, sent to Sicily, ii, 80.
Savages, secret society, i, 203.
Savona, fortress of, i, 388, 391.
Savonarola, i, 69.

INDEX. 443

Savoy, i, 119, 367; Mazzini's expedition against, 400-1; French designs upon, ii, 158, 196.
Savoy, House of. See Piedmont.
Scandinavians, i, 24.
Schamyl, ii, 68.
Schiller, criticism of De Staël, i, 97; 317.
Schnitzermeraay, Austrian envoy, ii, 196.
Schoelcher, French deputy, ii, 354.
Schwarzenberg, Prince Charles, i, 112, 118.
Schwarzenberg, Prince Felix, ii, 302, 401.
Science in Italy, i, 83.
Scinà, naturalist, i, 412.
Scipio, i, 25.
Scott, Sir Walter, i, 319.
Sebastiani, Marshal, i, 347. 364.
Sects, political. See Carbonari. Calderari, Conspiracies, Sanfedists, etc.
Sedlintzky, Austrian minister, i, 172.
Sercognani, insurgent leader, ii, 17.
Sereni, Roman minister, ii, 262.
Serfs. i, 6.
Sermide, town of. ii. 256.
Serristori, Tuscan Liberal, ii, 60, 64, 336, 340.
Sesini, Modenese, i, 294, 295.
Sessa. i, 216.
Settembrini, Neapolitan Liberal, ii, 73.
Settimo, Ruggiero, Sicilian patriot, ii, 79, 349.
Severoli, Cardinal, ii, 10.
Seymour, English diplomatic agent, i. 427.
Shakespeare, i, 52, 58, 96, 99, 316, 349; ii, 225.
Sicily, i, 120; unique historical position of, 180-1; during Napoleonic upheaval, 182; hatred of Neapolitans, 226; rebellion. 227; insurgents uppermost, 231-2; atrocities, 233; rebellion subdued, 234; Colletta sent. 237; new measures, 287; Count of Syracuse sent as governor, 406; cholera. 411-12; revolt, 413; Delcarretto's vengeance, 413-14; revolution of 1848 begins, ib, 77; Palermo free, 81; Bourbon atrocities. ib.; war with Naples, 136; gives no aid to National War, 141; subdued, 349.
Siena, i, 65, 425; ii, 284, 285.

Silvati, leads revolt, i, 217, 222.
Simone, Catherine di, i, 340, 406.
Simplon Pass, i, 187.
Sinigaglia, birthplace of Pius IX, ii, 16.
Sirtori, Venetian patriot, ii, 402.
Sixtus V, ii, 27.
Slaves, i, 24.
Sleepers, secret society, i, 203.
Slums, i, 228.
Smith, Englishman, leads attack on Florence, ii, 307.
Smucker, Metternich's agent, i, 428.
Smugglers, i, 185, 330; ii, 31.
Soglia, Cardinal, ii. 8, 11, 12, 13.
Solaro. See Margarita.
Solaroli, Piedmontese general, ii, 318.
Solfatara, i, 204.
Sommacampagna, ii, 185, 211, 213.
Sonderbund, the Swiss, ii, 66.
Sonnaz, Piedmontese general, ii, 147, 163, 211, 212.
Sons of Mars, secret society, i, 203.
Sophocles, i, 75, 96, 349.
Sottocorni, heroic deed of, ii, 121.
South American republics, i, 327.
Spain, dominates Italy, i, 81; cruelty of, 82; revolutions in, 215; French expedition, 309-10; interference in behalf of Pius IX, ii, 363.
Spaty, Diamante, i, 106.
Spaur, Austrian governor of Lombardy, ii, 71, 101, 106, 109, 263.
Spaur, Countess, ii, 263.
Spedalotto, prætor of Palermo, ii, 79, 80.
Spezzia, i, 240.
Spielberg, Austrian prison, i, 306, 307, 308, 335, 424.
Spies, on the judges in Naples, i, 149; in Austrian provinces, 171, 286; watch exiles. 333.
Spilla Nera, secret society, i, 203.
Spinola, Cardinal, i, 441.
Spoleto. i, 14; ii, 17.
Stackelberg, Austrian general, i, 189.
Stadion, Austrian minister. i, 125.
Statella, Neapolitan general, ii, 183.
Stein, Prussian statesman. i, 194.
Stephen III. pope. i, 20.
Sterbini, Roman demagogue. ii. 261, 262, 265, 271, 288, 289, 291.
Stewart, Lord, English diplomat, i, 240.

Strassoldo, Austrian general, ii, 216.
Sturbinetti, Roman minister, ii, 90, 259, 260, 261.
Superga, i, 272; ii, 328.
Sweden, i, 81.
Swiss mercenaries, i, 64; 416.
Syracuse, Count of, sent to govern Sicily, i, 406.
Syracuse, town of, cholera, i, 412; revolt, 413.

Taaffe, Count, ii, 107.
Tacitus, i, 75, 106.
Taddei, president of Tuscan chamber, ii, 327.
Tagliamento, river, ii, 144.
Talleyrand, i, 119, 343.
Tanfano, Colonel, i, 412, 440.
Tartini, sent to govern Leghorn, ii, 250.
Tasso, i, 74, 79, 95, 105.
Telegraph, electric, ii, 243.
Terdoppio, stream, ii, 323.
Terence, i, 82.
Terracina, i, 157; ii, 268, 375.
Terra di Lavoro, i, 210.
Terzaghi, Milanese insurgent, ii, 116.
Teutons, i, 4; compared to English in India, 47.
Thackeray, i, 319.
Theiss, river, i, 7.
Theobald, St., i, 108.
Theocracy, Hildebrand's scheme, i, 32.
Theocritus, i, 181.
Theodoric, i, 44.
Thermopylæ, i, 252.
Thucydides, i, 411.
Thugut, Austrian minister, i, 125.
Tinkers, rivals to Carbonari, i, 206, 336.
Tintoret, Venetian painter, i, 74.
Titian, i, 71, 73.
Tocqueville, de, ii, 364.
Tommaseo, N., Venetian patriot, i, 431; leader in insurrection at Venice, ii, 124; speech against fusion, 206; mission to Paris, 239, 385; return to Venice, 386.
Tommasi, Neapolitan minister of finance, i, 148.
Torre, General della, i, 275, 277, 280.
Torrelli, i, 304.
Torres, military adventurer, ii, 250.

Torresani, director of police at Milan, i, 172; ii, 101, 102, 110, 123.
Torrigiani, Tuscan Liberal, ii, 336.
Tortona, i, 290.
Tortures, in Naples, i, 284-5; in Modena, 294; by Austrians, 301; in Piedmont, 399.
Tosti, Papal treasurer, ii, 30.
Toulon, i, 370; ii, 354.
Tradition, power of, in Italy, i, 4, 113.
Trapani, i, 228.
Trecate, ii, 318, 319.
Trent, council of, i, 78, 81, 83, 85.
Treviglio, town of, ii, 146.
Treviso, ii, 202.
Trieste, ii, 193.
Trigona, Cardinal, i, 412.
Trocadero, i, 310.
Troppau, conference at, i, 240-2.
Troya, Neapolitan Liberal, ii, 138, 179.
Tugendbund, i, 194.
Turin, student riot, i, 263; 277, 278, 289; ovation to Charles Albert, ii, 69; petition to king, 96; Feast of the Statute, 98; lack of volunteers, 228; impending violence, 235.
Tuscany, Austrian province, i, 91, 119; restoration of Grand Duke, 163; mild government, 164; Metternich's wiles, 183-4; Leopold II succeeds, 337; 350, 352, 425; the Renzi affair, 447-8; Retrograde policy, 451; ii, 38; the Liberal party, 60-1; Radicals, 61-2; demonstrations and disorder, 62; concessions, 63; patriotic fervor, 64; annexation of Lucca, 65; agitation, 86; Constitution, 87; war fever, 132; troops in the field, 151; Radicalism gaining, 244; Leopold's divided interests, 245; Legislative Assembly meets, 245-6; interrupted by mob, 246; Capponi ministry, ib.; alarm at Livornese revolt, 249; Montanelli forms cabinet, 252; parliament meets, 283; Leopold goes to Siena, 284; flight, 285; provisional government, 286; patriotic orgies, 306; Laugier and Smith, 307; political ferment, 308; who shall be dictator? 333; Guerrazzi chosen, 334; triangular intrigue,

334–5; tumult in Florence, 335;
Guerrazzi's last chance, 336–7;
his fall, 338; Moderates make
overtures to Leopold, 339; appeal
to Piedmont, 340.
Two Sicilies, i. 182. See also under
Naples and Sicily.
Tyranny follows civic feuds in mediæval republics, i, 50.
Tyrol, ii, 145, 150.

Udine, ii, 183.
Ulloa, defender of Marghera, ii, 393, 395, 396, 401.
Unitarians, political sect, i, 348, 392.
Unshirted, the, secret society, i, 203.
Uruguay. ii, 312.
Ururi, village of, i, 155.

Vaglica, Joachim, i, 231, 233.
Vaillant, French general, ii, 381.
Valerio, Piedmontese envoy, ii, 306, 308, 314, 342.
Valese, Count, i, 270.
Valesia, Piedmontese foreign secretary, i, 257.
Valtellina, ii, 237.
Van Eyck, painter, i, 71.
Vannicelli, Cardinal, ii, 14.
Vannini, free thinker, i, 84.
Vardarelli, Neapolitan brigands, i, 154–6.
Varese, Lake of, ii, 237.
Velletri, fight at, ii, 375.
Venaissin, the, i, 120.
Venetia, assigned to Austria, i, 119;
Austrian rule in, 167; tribunals,
ib.; taxes, tariff, currency, 168;
education, religion, 169; ubiquitous police, 171; quiet on surface,
297; arrests, ib.; milder policy,
336; little change, 424; Austrian army increased, ii, 56; revolutionary symptoms, 72–3; Austrian
army increased, 105; insurrection,
124; Republic, 125; Austrians
expelled, 126; Charles Albert's
proclamation, 130; war preparations, 156; Nugent's march, 183;
Austria's offer, 194; evacuated by
Charles Albert. 223; Pasini's negotiations, 240; Manin president,
385; Austrians at Mestre, 393;
Marghera lost, 396; bombardment of Venice, 401; surrender,
408. See also Manin, Pasini, Tommaseo, Venice.
Venice, early growth, i, 46; ducat,
51; oligarchy not democracy, 64;
republic extinguished, 110; shipbuilding declines, 169; 256, 299;
Scientific Congress, ii, 72; revolution breaks out, 124; Republic
declared, 125; rejoicing, 126; appeal to France, 160; Pepe arrives,
183; need of fusion with Piedmont, 203; Austrian line of investment, ib.; National Assembly meets, 204; Manin's report,
205; Tommaseo's speech, 206;
Paleocapa's reply, 207; fusion
with Piedmont voted, 209; Piedmontese Commissioners take formal possession, 237; triumvirate
appointed, 238; help asked of
France and England, 239; beginning of hardship in the city, 240;
Pasini's diplomacy, 240–3; no
hope, 243; attack to be resumed,
303; new Assembly, 384; elects
Manin president, 385; harmony
of Venetians, ib.; skirmish, 388;
resist at any cost, 389; troops
and defenses, 389–91; outlook at
end of April, 1849, 392; first attack on Marghera, 393; Marghera abandoned, 396; defense of
railway bridge, ib.; surprise, 397;
scarcity of food, 397–8; fleet,
398; finances, ib.; money promised by other Italians, 399; Austrian negotiations, 400–1; first
bombs in the city, 401; good order in spite of hardships, 402;
active bombardment, 403; damage done, 404; famine and cholera, 404–5; indifference of Europe, 406; news of Hungarian
collapse, 408; prepares to surrender. ib.; Austrian entry, 409;
statistics of siege, ib.
Venuti, Palermitan insurgent, ii, 78.
Vercelli, i, 268, 276; ii, 323, 326.
Verden, Saxons massacred at, by
Charlemain, i, 8.
Verona, leagued against Barbarossa,
i, 48, 263; congress of, 297, 308;
ii, 143; fortress, 144, 149, 150,
163, 164, 185, 186, 187, 197, 209,
210, 211, 230.
Vespolate, ii, 318, 323.

Viale, Monsignor, ii, 52.
Vicenza, desires immediate fusion with Piedmont, ii, 157; threatened by Nugent, 183; 186; capitulates, 197; 198, 200, 202, 396.
Victor Emanuel I, king of Piedmont, i, 119; return from exile, 141, 174; belief in absolutism, 175; reforms, 176; bigotry, 177; resists Metternich's schemes, 187–9, 255; anti-Liberal, 256; tries to calm revolt, 208; perplexity, 269; decides to abdicate, 270; departure, 272.
Victor Emanuel II, Duke of Savoy, i, 310; ii, 97, 129, 147, 185, 318, 323, 326, 329, 330, 414.
Vienna, congress of, i, 116; treaty signed, 118; its provisions concerning Italy, 119 *et seq.*; 260; treaty of, ii, 51, 64; revolution, 106; Metternich ousted, 107; precarious times, 197; 243; second insurrection, 244.
Vigevano, ii, 318, 321, 322.
Villafranca, Prince of, i, 227.
Villafranca, town, ii, 148, 211, 212, 230.
Villamarina, Piedmontese minister, i, 421; ii, 68, 297.
Vinci, Leonardo da, i, 71, 83; ii, 245, 399.
Virgil, i, 53.
Vistula, river, ii, 53.
Vochieri, executed, i, 309.
Volta, town, ii, 149, 187, 211, 212, 414.
Voltaire, i, 90, 313.
Volterra, ii, 16.
Volunteers, exaggerated reliance in, ii, 199.

Wagram, battle of, i, 125.
Waldenses, i, 176.

Ward, Tom, ex-jockey, premier at Lucca, ii, 64.
Washington, George, quoted, i, 376.
Waterloo, i, 118, 192, 239, 404; ii, 12, 147, 212.
Welden, Austrian general, ii, 197, 247, 256.
Wellington, Duke of, i, 112, 260, 310; ii, 212.
Wessenberg, Austrian minister, ii, 176, 196, 231, 232.
"Western Powers," i, 320.
White Pilgrims, secret society, i, 203.
William I, Emperor of Germany, i, 120; ii, 263.
Winspeare, Neapolitan general, ii, 363.
Wittgenstein, i, 112.
Wohlgemuth, Austrian general, ii, 148.

Xenophon, i, 106.
Xerxes, i, 252.

Young, English poet, compared with Monti, i, 106.
Young Italy, planned by Mazzini, i, 393; principles, *ib.*; methods of activity, 394; watchwords, 395; initiation and oath, 395–6; founded at Marseilles, 396; expansion in Italy, 397; 404, 410, 440; ii, 414.

Zichy, Count, ii, 125.
Zucchi, General, banished from Modena, i, 354; returns, 359; 381; commands Lombard National Guard, ii, 216; to reorganize Papal army, 257; intrigues in Pius's behalf, 288; 363.
Zucchini, Bolognese Senator, ii, 270.
Zuppetta, Neapolitan deputy, ii, 180.

www.ingramcontent.com/pod-product-compliance
Lightning Source LLC
Chambersburg PA
CBHW022135300426
44115CB00006B/201